The
Dow Jones-Irwin
Banker's Guide
to
Online Databases

The
Dow Jones-Irwin
Banker's Guide
to
Online Databases

J. Thomas Monk
Kenneth M. Landis
Susan S. Monk

Richard D. Irwin, Inc.

Homewood, Illinois 60430

We recognize that certain terms in this book are trademarks,
and we have made every effort to print these throughout
the text with the capitalization and punctuation used
by the holder of the trademark.

©Richard D. Irwin, Inc., 1988

Dow Jones-Irwin is a trademark of Dow Jones & Company, Inc.

This publication is designed to provide accurate and
authoritative information in regard to the subject matter
covered. It is sold with the understanding that the
publisher is not engaged in rendering legal, accounting, or
other professional service. If legal advice or other expert
assistance is required, the services of a competent
professional person should be sought.

*From a Declaration of Principles jointly adopted by a Committee
of the American Bar Association and a Committee of Publishers.*

Project editor: Joan A. Hopkins
Production manager: Stephen K. Emry
Compositor: Publication Services
Typeface: 11/13 Melior
Printer: The Maple-Vail Book Manufacturing Group

Library of Congress Catalog Card No. 87–73533

Library of Congress Cataloging-in-Publication Data

Monk, J. Thomas.
    The Dow Jones-Irwin banker's guide to online
databases.

    Includes indexes.
    1. Business—Data bases.   2. Finance—Data bases.
I. Landis, Kenneth M.   II. Monk, Susan S.   III. Title.
HF5548.2.M596   1988   025′.0633   87-73533
ISBN 0-87094-749-4

Printed in the United States of America

1 2 3 4 5 6 7 8 9 0 MP 5 4 3 2 1 0 9 8

Table of Contents

Foreword

We started this book naively underestimating the volume of information that we would accumulate and the amount of time it would take to bring some sense to all of it. Fortunately we had a great deal of help in bringing it all together. In these few paragraphs we would like to thank some of the people who provided that assistance.

Dick Staron of Dow Jones-Irwin and Marvin Weinberger and Steve Fogel of Telebase Systems helped us to collect our thoughts, narrow our focus and attempted to get us on some kind of schedule. Marian Sheeran, also from Telebase Systems, was invaluable for her initial editing and suggestions as was Caron Brodsky for her skills as an information broker.

Two MBA students at Washington University in St. Louis, Missouri, Larry VandenBusch and Dave Kaplan, assisted in compiling all the data from the database providers. They spent many hours on the phone inquiring, clarifying, and sometimes even begging for information. They spent more hours at a word processor on rough drafts for the company and product snapshots.

The editors and production people at Publication Services have suffered through several months with us editing and re-editing the matrices and the snapshots, and we appreciate their forbearance.

Finally we would like to thank our families who were drafted into helping us with this huge effort. Constance Landis initially volunteered to help with the mailing of the questionnaires to the database providers, but her involvement soon escalated to all kinds of behind-the-scenes help ranging from hundreds of hours on the telephone tracking down questionnaires to keeping track of the incoming data. Even Tom and Susan's teenage son, Justin, was drafted to stuff envelopes and alphabetize companies and zip codes.

Preface

As with most great technologic advances of this century, the requirement and the money for basic and applied research stemmed from America's need to expand its influence. Be it the aerosol can, which was developed by the Army Corps of Engineers to reduce the risk of contracting malaria in the Canal Zone, or the semiconductor, our government was there.

The drive to conquer space and reach the moon demanded that we also conquer the problem of managing the information needed to get there. The National Aeronautics and Space Administration's (NASA) need to manage huge amounts of technical information drove the development of what is today the DIALOG system. From this beginning, the information industry has grown to over 3300 public databases under the management of 500 different companies.

While a trust officer's need to measure the performance of assets in a portfolio is by no means as large and as complex a problem as going to the moon, there are a number of similarities, specifically in the decision-making process. In both instances, the moon-shot planner and the trust officer have to develop their objectives, evaluate alternative plans, gather the necessary information, and then perform their analysis.

The change in the amount of information about business has been exponential. This growth has compounded the problems incurred in finding it in the form and quality required for analysis and decision making. Once an individual embarks on the search, he or she finds ahead a perpetual odyssey through the information frontier—a constant search for data on which to base a decision. It is this unexplored, vast area that we chart in this book.

Not thirty years ago, our economy, as well as the rest of the world, was fueled by paper. Today the world runs on electronic pulses. In the 1950's, funds transfers from one bank to the next took three or four pieces of paper passing through three or four people's hands. Today, the process involves a few pieces of electronic information passing directly from one computer to the next.

An even clearer distinction is that in the manual system each transaction represented a discrete piece of data. To summarize the total number of transactions between two institutions for management reports or to analyze their characteristics took an army of sleeve-gartered, visored accountants. In the electronic environment, the transactions are in such a form that they can be quickly transformed into management or control information with the aid of the computer.

The reason is simple—the power of the computer supplanted our need for the army of accountants and compressed the time it took them to do their work from weeks to less than a second. Now think of this power in terms of librarians. The computer power employed by the online information industry today far exceeds the available manpower on the planet. In essence, we have developed an entirely new class of citizen—not in the Orwellian sense, but in the Darwinian sense—superbly adapted to its environment and tasks. It is this new citizen that has transformed our world from one based on paper to one based on electrons—for in its environment, paper is an inhibitor to growth and progress, and we have clearly decided that this new species will flourish. With its growth, we grow.

In our day-to-day lives, in this information ecosystem, we have adapted in a kind of symbiosis. Today workers interact freely with technology, and in some industries, especially banking, they prefer a terminal to a file folder and disk storage to a vault. In many cases, businesses that banks are in today would be impossible without the electronic delivery systems on which they are built. Transactions, no matter whether they are requests for status on an account or research into a company's credit worthiness, are submitted and processed and the results usually returned in less than a minute. These systems have become the storytellers of our age.

Selecting an online information source has unfortunately never been as easy as selecting a storyteller. The industry has long had its own vernacular, a peculiar way of communicating with people, and a number of features and functions that made it hard to compare one with the other. Our intent in this book is to make finding these companies easy and comparing them to their competition possible.

In Chapter One, we discuss the pros and cons of gathering and analyzing information electronically versus using paper—why and when you should go online, what the risks and rewards are, and how you can bring additional value to the process.

In the second chapter, we introduce the basic vocabulary of the information industry to provide a common understanding of the industry vernacular. Building on this foundation, we then examine the relationship among producers, providers, and gateways, as well as the basic structure of the industry.

Chapter Three explains the methodology we used as a framework for organizing the industry. We developed two matrices that delineate producers by the target market they serve and the general subject areas they cover with their products. A third matrix focuses on individual products and subjects addressed.

The type of information required to solve this problem will determine which of the matrices is appropriate for you to use. These will, in turn, lead you to the appropriate Company and Product Snapshots in Chapter Four. A Company Snapshot is a discussion of the demographics of each producer covered in the matrices and an overview of that product set of online databases and value-added products and services.

Unlike the traditional industry directories, more than a short synopsis of each online database has been compiled. The Product Snapshots go into some detail about the contents of the database and how it is accessed. The value of having this degree of detail is that it allows you, the online user, to evaluate competitive products head-to-head, long before you go online. The result can be a substantial savings of time, money, and frustration.

Whether you are a novice or an expert, the matrices and snapshots are the reason that this guide will be invaluable to you. Each provides a different view, or perspective, of the industry. Every time you need to find a source of online information, these tools will provide the way to get it quickly and cheaply.

Chapter Five discusses telecommunications alternatives and what to look for in communications software. In addition, third party software packages that make using online services easier or provide additional analysis capabilities are covered. These complementary software packages are often cost-effective additions to your analytical tool box.

Finally, a series of Appendixes have been compiled, which provide quick indexes to Providers, Gateways, and Communications Software.

According to David P. Norton, former Harvard professor and president of Nolan, Norton & Co., committing to and using electronic information requires a "leap of faith," one not much different than that taken by the alchemists who first refined lead and changed the world, or by the first man in space, who was catapulted with untried and unproven technology. "The right stuff" may have a little to do with it, but we believe, more likely, that the pioneers of the information age will not be the visionaries, but instead the professionals who understand what the online industry can mean to the fulfillment of their career objectives.

The
Dow Jones-Irwin
Banker's Guide
to
Online Databases

CHAPTER ONE

Why Electronic: Pros and Cons of Online Information

Why electronic? Why should you go through the effort of learning how to find and retrieve information electronically, and why should you incur the expense? After all, you learned how to read in grade school, and for the hourly charge of many online services, you could buy an autographed first edition novel. The reasons are straightforward: Time is money; only in electronic form can raw data be exhaustively manipulated to become useful, on-demand information; and in many cases there is at least as much, if not more, information available online than off. Stated bluntly, you can't afford not to go electronic unless you want to be eclipsed by your peers.

THE PROS OF ONLINE INFORMATION

In today's business environment, time is a precious commodity. If you trade financial instruments, such as equities, options, or futures, a few seconds can mean the difference between profit and loss. If you are a corporate manager, a few hours can mean the difference when you are trying to complete a project or best your competition. In either case, professionals are paid to analyze information, not to search and retrieve it. The mechanics of finding information are a necessary evil. Once the information is found, the value of an online service is that electronic information can

1

be exhaustively manipulated at a considerably lower cost in both time and money than paper-based data can.

An online service is the fastest way to do both. Starting from ground zero, you can work your way through a succession of services to find exactly what you need. In the case of textual material, you first tap into a bibliographic service to identify sources of information, then into either an abstract service to get a summation of the reference or a full-text service to retrieve the information online. In some cases all of the information you need may be on one service. If it's financial or econometric information you are after, a simple search of any one of the many online services that provide this information will yield results; the question then becomes which one to use.

The sheer availability of information and the velocity at which it can be retrieved can be both wonderful and frightening. Suddenly, entirely new avenues of thought can be opened with the press of a few keys. It doesn't take long to realize how much information there is and how little of it can be mastered.

Nevertheless, you still cannot ignore the inexorable change in the ways that we manage information. Two thousand years ago a database was a piece of papyrus, which at best may have contained a hundred pieces of information. Today, in the time it would take us to read that same amount of information, we can search, retrieve, and even perform analysis on millions of pieces of information. The impact of this power can be staggering. As we noted in the preface, the printed word has remained fundamentally unchanged in the way that it has been created and distributed since Gutenberg's Bible. It is only in the last 10 years or so that we have seen the electronization of both the written word and numbers.

For example, we were asked to identify acquisition candidates for a Fortune 200 corporation that manufactured a rather esoteric product. Only privately held companies having patents with remaining lives of at least 10 years were to be included. Using a combination of online services, we were able to complete the work in less than two hours. A previous similar request handled manually had taken over 80 labor-hours.

The available computer power on the planet today is easily sufficient to do as much "knowledge work" in one hour as all the human labor on the planet could do in one year. With that kind of power being harnessed to fuel commerce, it is not surprising that we have applied the same technology to decision making.

Speed is king. We want to find ways to do things faster, better, and at less expense. There is no question that managing information electronically is just such a way. No one would dispute that the New York Stock Exchange could not possibly trade 120 or 130 million shares a day without computer systems, yet management may question why $300 was spent searching an online service for information on a competitor.

It is clear that the benefits of managing information electronically have not been sold well, either by the industry or by the people who use it. Cost/benefit, risk/reward, or investment/return: No matter how you analyze it, managing information online is the best way. Why? Because when you spend the time to justify online information, you find that the hidden costs of managing information manually are staggering. Consider staff cost for research, time in transit doing research, photocopying time and cost, the cost to transform the information into a usable form, and so on. The key distinction between manual and electronic management of information is that in the manual environment, the costs are either fixed, as in staff, or variable but not identifiable, as in photocopies or typing time.

In an electronic environment we readily see the cost—if a service is $100 an hour and we use it for two hours, then we have spent $200, and that $200 is clearly attributable to a given task or project. It is not often that people get over the shock of the hourly cost of a service to look beyond and see what they are getting for that money. For example, at $150 an hour an econometric service may provide raw data that took thousands of hours to collate and analyze. For one hour of charges you could conceivably get information that took three years to create. When was the last time you found a skilled employee who would work for $50 a year?

In the retail banking business, understanding demographics is the key to success. Define your market, find it, and then saturate it. Where is the majority of all demographic information found? Online, such as in the DORIS and ACORN databases. Census material, sales statistics, buying patterns, and a plethora of other consumer information are all online so that the information can be easily distributed and manipulated.

For commercial lending, knowing the latest on a major borrower or its industry can easily mean the difference between a profitable and an unprofitable loan. Where can this information be found? Perfect examples are databases such as INVESTEXT or Predicasts' Forecasts. For publicly held corporations, the latest SEC filings can be quickly scanned using SEC Online. Various news services and newsletters that cover industries ranging from the button business to farm implements can also be found online. Why trudge through reams of paper when you can zero in on the relevant information?

Additionally, of course, there are the U.S. and world economies. Next to the stock market, this is probably the most widely covered online topic. You can quickly get the latest government statistics, economic forecasts from the economists themselves, or an analysis of a foreign economy. Don't forget that you can also get up-to-the-minute time series that provide economic profiles from companies such as Data Resources, Inc. (DRI).

What has been the net effect of the online industry on banking? More information is available faster for making a decision, and this has affected the manner in which the decisions themselves are made. The manner in which we manage an enterprise or shape a decision has been changed by this online environment. The markets have adjusted their expectations because information is instantaneous. The time to research and make decisions has been compressed, in many cases, from weeks to hours. Thus, decisions are made faster, and the business moves faster.

Compared to paper, electronic information is easy to store, index, retrieve, and massage. The inherent flexibility of data in this format means that new information can be created quickly. For example, by searching through and amalgamating three econometric databases for foreign currency exchange rate forecasts we are able to create a consensus opinion. News headlines can be coupled to financial statements and stock price movements to give the reader an unparalleled view of corporate performance in light of external developments. The permutations are endless.

Consider for a moment that by just combining information from disparate sources, even with no editing, we create a view that was probably not economically possible before. The online systems themselves act as our editor, culling only the information we desire. From this perspective, it becomes clear that the cost of online information includes both the information retrieved and the "hidden" analytic and editorial services that are a natural part of this environment.

THE CONS OF ONLINE INFORMATION

So far, we have described a world where the sun never sets and it never rains. Well, as always, a little rain must fall. There are problems with online information. They are not insurmountable, but they must be understood and addressed.

The foremost is learning how to "speak" to the various online services. Unlike the automotive industry, where the way to start, drive, and stop a car has been standardized, the online industry requires you to learn almost as many "languages" as there are services. Every large provider (a provider is a company that retails information such as DIALOG and CompuServe) has its own way of doing things. If you want to retrieve information from two sources, the odds are high that you will need to learn two different ways of doing things, for three sources three different ways, and so on. On average, we believe that the avid online user needs to master at least four different online languages to get the information desired.

By no means are these languages easy to learn. They are complex combinations of expressions that come from disciplines such as Boolean algebra, library science, and computer science. The result is a syntax, or set of grammatical rules, that rivals the *London Times* crossword puzzle in complexity and subtlety. Recognizing this inefficiency in the industry, a number of companies have created *gateways*, which translate simple English expressions into the complex set of queries needed to use an online system. A good example of this type of product is Western Union's InFact.

As information becomes more accessible, there is a propensity to use more and more of it—the stereotypical information overload. Gauging when to stop searching when there is a diminishing marginal return can be learned only through experience. One gains a feel for what is available and how much information is needed. In this industry, as in any other, experience counts.

Costs must be taken into account. Retrieving data is only part of the cost. Many online systems provide value-added processing such as statistical analysis, programming languages, and so on.

While these value-added services can be extremely important in the final analysis, they do have a cost—a cost that may be prohibitive.

Value-added services are often the online industry's equivalent of chrome and a leather interior. For a casual or occasional user, their cost is appropriate. But for a volume user, the costs, even with price breaks, are usually far in excess of the cost of bringing the tools in-house in the form of off-the-shelf software packages such as spreadsheets, financial planning languages, database management systems, and statistical packages. With the continuing improvement in price/performance in computer hardware, it is not unlikely that 80–90 percent of the day-to-day analysis of data can be done on a personal computer, with the remaining percentage processed on a minicomputer or a mainframe.

WHEN TO GO ELECTRONIC

Identifying when to bring your processing in-house, versus doing it with your online vendor, is a simple cost/benefit analysis. Compare the costs you are incurring today versus the cost of providing the necessary software and hardware infrastructure internally. To facilitate the cost/benefit analysis, Chapter 5 indexes some of the more popular software packages for analyzing data.

We would be remiss if we didn't provide some rules of thumb for when you should go online for your information. Electronic information is most cost effective and beneficial if:

The information is priceless—the cost of not having it far outweighs any reasonable cost for obtaining it. Priceless information could be an analysis of a federal or state regulation that will have repercussions on a given industry's profitability, including your own, or information from arcane sources that indicates that a new, highly profitable product is in the offing. Priceless information also includes what your competitors are doing and an analysis of how well they are doing it.

The information is numeric—and can be manipulated later by a computer. Rather than spend valuable time collecting the information manually and going through the cumbersome and error-prone intermediate step of having to key it, collect what you need from online sources and place it in a computer file for immediate use. The information is then available for whatever later manipulation is needed.

The body of knowledge or discipline is broad—but you want only a small, specialized slice. Manually sifting through references or abstracts is not only time-consuming, but small and important references can easily be missed. With the proper search strategy, information that was previously buried can be easily found.

The availability of the information is limited—geographically or otherwise. If you live and work in a small town, online information services give you the same access to information that you would have in the big city. If travel or other similar considerations are an issue, consider online resources first.

If you use online information and keep it in its native electronic form, you can continue to take advantage of the inherent power of electronic versus paper-based information. The computer revolution is only possible if the information is in a form that can be mastered by the computer. Online services provide that form.

CHAPTER TWO

The Ways and Means of the Information Industry

The transformation of the American economic base from agriculture to information has taken less than a hundred years. Since the wide-spread use of computer technology in business began in the 1960s, information about how businesses operate has come to be viewed as a valued strategic and tactical planning tool. Computer technology provides a powerful and cost-effective tool for the acquisition and analysis of business information concerning markets, products, and services.

Today, access to information is an essential component of a decision maker's toolkit. Information reduces the uncertainty surrounding any decision, thus producing a higher likelihood of success. Success, in today's economy, means knowing the market, competitors, products, players, and their impact on you.

The key element in this scenario is time. In today's global economy, time—or the passage of it—makes or breaks you. Time makes information valuable. Today, your competitive edge evaporates with each tick of the clock.

In order to gain that competitive edge, it's mandatory to know something about the industry. In the information business, as in many others, there is no one set of definitions that everyone uses and understands. In fact, because this industry is still in its infancy, many of the participants have freely used marketing hype to carve out a niche. We decided that spending a short time understanding the industry vocabulary and players would be a good investment of time and effort.

BASIC INDUSTRY VOCABULARY

Each company that plays a key role in this industry may use terms such as *database*, *bibliographic*, *abstract*, and *full text*. However, we have found that there are no universal definitions on which all of them agree. For our purposes, we define the terms in the following manner:

Database

A database is a collection of information. An online database has been stored on a computer and replaces file drawers and index cards. A database can be in either text or numeric format, basic or summarized, or a combination of both. In this reference, we use the term to indicate all products and services that can be accessed online.

Bibliographic

If a database is bibliographic, it contains references to other works by title, subject, or author, and provides information such as number of pages, illustrations and graphs included, and publication source and date.

Abstract

Bibliographic databases can also use abstracts, which provide a brief overview of a more comprehensive work.

Full Text

Full-text databases are just that; they contain the unedited versions of textual material, such as research reports or journal articles.

Numeric

Many of the databases covered by the Matrix Methodology are numeric. Stock quotes, annual reports, and SEC filings are available for further analysis.

THE INDUSTRY PLAYERS

Before examining the methodology in depth in the next chapter, a few additions to your basic vocabulary have to be made. It is important to know the difference between *producers, providers, information brokers*, and a recent entry in this industry, *gateways*.

Producers

Producers are the heavy manufacturers of the information industry. At year-end 1986, more than 3300 online databases were publicly accessible. Producers gather raw material, process it into intermediate and final products, and package it for the customer. Producers may provide access to their databases through their own computer and communications system. However, most producers are very small specialty companies and do not have the financial resources necessary to operate the systems required to service their customers. Database providers fill this role.

Providers

Providers, also known as vendors, perform the role of the distributor in this industry by means of wholesale acquisition, warehousing, and retail delivery of the producers' products. By capitalizing on economies of scale, these companies provide access to specialized products that individual producers could deliver only at high unit costs. Additionally, whereas the names of the big providers such as DIALOG, Dow Jones, The SOURCE, and BRS are well known, most producers are relatively small with specialized products. Thus, market visibility for small producers is an added attraction offered by the major database providers.

Providers are continually changing their product mix in reaction to the needs of the market. Therefore, we did not specifically include them in the Company Snapshots because much of the information would be immediately dated. As a quick reference, Appendix A contains the names, addresses, and telephone numbers of the major providers. Current products, services, and costs can be obtained directly from each company.

Information Brokers

Information brokers are usually very small companies that execute the mission of an Information Center in the Fortune 500. They will accept questions from you and, for a charge, produce a report using whatever resources to which they have access. There is certainly a place for these small companies in the industry, but many will fail before the right formula is found for success.

Gateways

As discussed in Chapter One, the online information industry requires you to learn almost as many languages as there are services. Every large provider has its own way of doing things. In order to retrieve information from different providers, you will be required to learn different ways of doing things for each one.

Because of this inefficiency in the industry, a number of services have been created that act as gateways to the various providers. These services, such as EasyNet, are designed to acquire access to the large providers and their databases. They often provide software that translates your search expression into the complex set of queries needed to successfully access the information you are looking for. The gateway system can automatically choose a provider, initiate the telephone connection, submit the required identifications and passwords, and transmit your query. Gateways usually charge only for successful searches.

There were more than 230 gateway connections in service in early 1987. Appendix B is another quick index to the major gateway services. As with the major providers, gateways are continually changing their service and connections in reaction to the needs of the market. Current offerings can be obtained directly from the companies.

Table 2.1 demonstrates the complexity of the information industry of the 1980s. As can be seen, the entities between the raw industry data and the information consumer are varied. Their relationships can be as simple as a one-to-one or as complex as a many-to-many. The methodology in Chapter 3 was designed to reduce the complexity by providing a road map through the maze.

TABLE 2.1

How It All Fits Together—The Information Industry of the 1980s

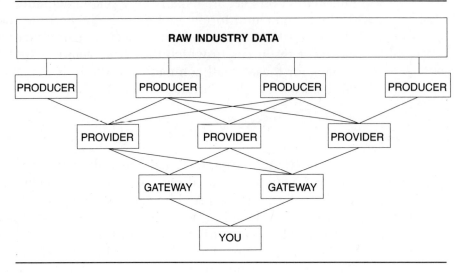

CHAPTER THREE

The Methodology and Matrices

What usually happens when information is required to develop a new product or service, support a move into new markets, or enhance a current offering? You may begin a search by asking questions of your associates, scanning professional publications, or calling a few vendors you know. In time, you will narrow down the possible companies that offer the information you want, call the companies, compile and analyze the results, and finally reach a decision.

After finding ourselves in this position more than once, we decided we needed a structured approach when looking for new information sources or just seeing what had changed in our own portfolio of information tools. Our Matrix Methodology approach was developed to provide the framework to get the answers. The methodology is the vehicle that separates the market into manageable pieces. In addition, just because business today is so volatile, the value of using this selection methodology is clearly not in using it one time and forgetting about it: The value of the methodology is that it provides a quick way to locate key information and make it accessible each time a strategic decision has to be made in the face of a rapidly changing market.

The Matrix Methodology is nothing more than a structured approach to help you make a decision. The methodology classifies the information marketplace from the perspective of the Producers and the Product. These views take the form of matrices: Producers By Target Markets, Producers By Subject, and Product By Subject Coverage. Each of these matrices contain varying levels of specific detail on the horizontal axis. The Producer matrices identify which of the producers market to you, as well as the general subjects they cover. The Product by Subject Coverage Matrix goes into detail about the contents of the online databases.

While the matrices are used to determine the producers and products that appear to manufacture or distribute the information you need, the Company and Product Snapshots provide the detail you need for comparative analysis. The Snapshots provide company financial data, products and services, markets, access methods, and contacts. These in-depth reviews provide quantitative as well as qualitative material for the decision maker.

THE PRODUCER MATRICES

The Producer Matrices help you determine which producers have identified you as a target market as well as what general subjects their products cover. We've found that you can use the Product Matrix first, but the producer may not have thought of your needs when packaging the product. You might view it in this manner: If a producer knows your industry well enough to specifically identify it as a target market, it has probably tailored its product delivery systems to closely fit your requirements.

The Producers By Target Markets Matrix

We've segmented the banking and financial services industry into several general classifications. When structured by target market, it is relatively simple to determine which producers have identified you as a target of opportunity and have tailored their products to satisfy your needs. A quick glance vertically will highlight the producers for you to use as entry points on the next matrix.

The Producers By Target Markets Matrix segments the universe of products and companies into "to whom do they market." You may be surprised to find that certain companies market to specific groups. The value of this type of searching is that vendors with specific target markets know the ins and outs of that market. When they speak the vernacular of your profession, they will be able to understand and respond quickly.

	Commercial banks	Credit unions	Fortune 1000 corporations	Government agencies	Investment banks	Law firms	Mortgage banks	Real estate firms	Specialized librarians	Thrift institutions
ADP, Inc. Data Services	•		•		•		•		•	•
American Banker	•	•		•	•		•		•	•
American Institute of Certified Public Accountants	•	•	•	•	•	•	•	•	•	•
Bank Marketing Association	•	•			•	•	•	•		•
Bridge Data Company	•				•		•			

The Producers By Subject Coverage Matrix

The Producers By Subject Coverage Matrix illustrates the relationship of each producer with the general subject matter it deals with. As previously indicated, most producers are specialists. When you have identified those producers that market to you, you would use

	Company information/statistics	Demographic information/statistics	Econometric data	Industry information/statistics	Real-time/Historic market quotations	News services	Newsletters	Research reports/evaluations	Trading/Brokerage services
ADP, Inc. Data Services	•		•	•	•	•			
American Banker				•		•			
American Institute of Certified Public Accountants	•			•					
Bank Marketing Association				•			•	•	
Bridge Data Company					•	•			

this matrix to determine if they cover the subjects you want to know more about. After applying these criteria, you should have eliminated all but three to five of them for further evaluation.

The Producers By Subject Coverage Matrix narrows your search. Even though a company markets to you, it may not offer the general or specific information you are interested in. Using this matrix will further eliminate companies on which you need not spend any more time.

The Products By Subject Coverage Matrix

This matrix associates producers and their individual products with the subjects their products cover. It is the most detailed, but using the producer matrices to eliminate companies that don't market to you or that cover subjects of no interest to you should produce a manageable list of potential products. If you are interested in a product that offers company information in general and performance forecasts in particular, this is where you would find the information.

	Annual reports	Company background	Forecasts	Insider trading	Lines of business	Market activity	Monthly reports	Officers/Directors	Quarterly reports	SEC filings	Stockholder information	Consumer preference	Income and housing	Industry specific	Local	Monetary aggregates	International	National	Regional
Bancall II	•								•										
(ADP, Inc. Data Services)																			
Bancorp	•								•										
(ADP, Inc. Data Services)																			
Bank Holding Companies	•																		
(Chase Econometrics)																			

Using the Matrix Methodology

In order to answer this question, the Matrices were used to select producers that had identified commercial banks as a target market. A quick scan of the Producer by Target Market Matrix produced several candidates that could be used as entry points into the Producer by Subject Matrix.

The Producer by Subject Matrix narrowed the field to a manageable size. In this instance, you wanted to know which producers covered "Company Information/Statistics," "Industry Information," "News Services," and "Research Reports." This process of elimination resulted in the following list:

Bunker Ramo Corporation
Dow Jones News/Retrieval
ADP, Inc Data Services
Predicasts
Standard & Poor's Corporation

A review of the Company Snapshots produced some important information. In addition to company demographics, the Snapshots contained a concise overview of each database including subject, type of database, and other services. If a particular database or product looked as if it provided the information required, the Product Snapshot was consulted to gain more detailed information.

In less than an hour, it was discovered that many of the databases were online and available through DIALOG. Rather than approaching each producer individually, DIALOG appeared to be the best all-around choice in terms of coverage, ease of use, support, updating, responsiveness, flexibility, and longevity. If you were starting from scratch, DIALOG would have to be contacted for specific features, products, and costs. However, since you found that you already had an account, you initiated your search.

Needless to say, some vendors provide better, more comprehensive information concerning particular subjects. If this type of information is required, they can be accessed as needed. However, most search work is accomplished using a core group of 20 general files, adding industry specific databases where appropriate.

The Products By Subject Coverage Matrix indicates those databases (or products) that have been developed with specific features. For example, if you needed to know how to get information concerning certain companies traded OTC, your first inclination would be to call a broker. This may work once or twice, but this source usually dries up rather quickly. If you used the matrix, you would find that only a few products had been listed as capable of offering research reporting.

When you compare the results of your analysis using the Target Market and Subject matrices, the comparison will indicate those products or databases that contain the subject matter you want, and those producers that regard you as an important component of their market.

COMPANY AND PRODUCT SNAPSHOTS

The last, and most detailed, component of the methodology are the Snapshots. The Company and Product Snapshots are detailed examinations of core features such as subjects covered, providers, and access rules. The details are presented in such a way that they can be transferred to a worksheet to facilitate comparison with other companies and products.

Company Snapshots

The Company Snapshot (pp. 89–251) is a detailed view of a producer. A demographics section provides the company mailing, telex, and E-Mail address and its telephone number. The "At-A-Glance" feature is a cross-reference back to the Target Market and Subject matrices. In the Description section you will be able to gain a flavor of the corporate structure, ownership, size, and date established in a few concise paragraphs.

The Database section briefly describes all of the online databases the company produces that are pertinent to the subject of this book. In addition, all applicable third party databases the company markets are described. This section can be used to construct a list of products that you want to know more about by referring to the Product Snapshots, which are in-depth reviews of each database.

The Value-Added Products and Services section lists additional products and services the company sells to facilitate product or market differentiation. There are seven different categories used to classify the products and services: Customer Support, Documentation, System Features/Software Packages, Online Communication, Reference Services, SDI (Selective Dissemination of Information) Services, and Document Formatting and Delivery.

Customer Support covers "people to people" interaction such as training, help desk functions, account representative services, and conferences.

The Documentation category includes a list and description of online and hardcopy aids such as user manuals, newsletters, brochures, dictionaries, and thesauri. If online search criteria such as ticker symbols and SIC codes are used, they will also be identified in this category.

Online Communication encompasses network-based services offered by the company such as bulletin boards, electronic mail (E-mail), or online conferencing.

If a company provides "on request" research, these services will be found in the Research Services category. Many producers provide numeric or textual data tailored to specific individual needs.

The SDI Services category lists and describes the services provided for selective dissemination of information. These services periodically retrieve information from selected database sources based on a predetermined profile of customer needs.

The last category, Document Formatting and Delivery, provides details concerning company services that provide customers with special order hardcopy reports or the results of searches.

The absence of a specific value-added product or service does not necessarily mean that the service or product is not available. It means that the information about a particular product or service was not made available to us. The reader should contact the company directly to receive the current status or full description of the products or services of interest.

Product Snapshots

Product Snapshots (pp. 255–532) are in-depth reviews of individual database products. The Snapshot focuses on the personality of the product. Each one includes a detailed discussion of the subjects covered and the beginning and ending dates of the coverage.

Included in the discussion is information on how the p sold and distributed, and what user support services a able for it. An important feature of each Snapshot is a re possible applications for the data.

The Product Snapshots are not designed to stand alon should be used in conjunction with Company Snapshots th out your analysis. Everything you need to know before mak decision to go online, starting with what information is re and ending with knowing where to get it, is contained i Snapshots. These reviews become your road map through the of the information industry.

These in-depth reports provide further quantitative and q tative facts for your decision-making process. Construct your matrix, listing the attributes such as subject, availability, acc and available software that are important to you. This evaluat should clearly indicate the producer or product that meets yc needs. Your next step should be to telephone the company to up demonstrations.

USING THE METHODOLOGY TO OBTAIN THE INFORMATION YOU NEED**

Last Monday morning, the following memo was on your desk:

> The CEO and the Policy Committee are looking for new cities for expansion. One of the locations mentioned was New Orleans. Please gather as much demographic and economic data on the New Orleans area as you can to determine market growth and profitability for banking or financial services. In conjunction with this search, identify all Fortune 500 corporations that are in the area, and review their industries' characteristics and each company's financial strength.

** The online search was provided by Readisearch, an information brokerage firm specializing in corporate information and market research. The president of the company, Caren Brodsky, has worked in various research and financial planning and analysis positions at InfoSource, the Federal Reserve Bank of Philadelphia, ARA Services, and Telebase Systems (EasyNet). Major Readisearch clients include Citicorp Homeowners, Scott Paper, Dun & Bradstreet, ICI, and Bank Street College of Education.

The Products By Subject Coverage Matrix indicates those databases (or products) that have been developed with specific features. For example, if you needed to know how to get information concerning certain companies traded OTC, your first inclination would be to call a broker. This may work once or twice, but this source usually dries up rather quickly. If you used the matrix, you would find that only a few products had been listed as capable of offering research reporting.

When you compare the results of your analysis using the Target Market and Subject matrices, the comparison will indicate those products or databases that contain the subject matter you want, and those producers that regard you as an important component of their market.

COMPANY AND PRODUCT SNAPSHOTS

The last, and most detailed, component of the methodology are the Snapshots. The Company and Product Snapshots are detailed examinations of core features such as subjects covered, providers, and access rules. The details are presented in such a way that they can be transferred to a worksheet to facilitate comparison with other companies and products.

Company Snapshots

The Company Snapshot (pp. 89–251) is a detailed view of a producer. A demographics section provides the company mailing, telex, and E-Mail address and its telephone number. The "At-A-Glance" feature is a cross-reference back to the Target Market and Subject matrices. In the Description section you will be able to gain a flavor of the corporate structure, ownership, size, and date established in a few concise paragraphs.

The Database section briefly describes all of the online databases the company produces that are pertinent to the subject of this book. In addition, all applicable third party databases the company markets are described. This section can be used to construct a list of products that you want to know more about by referring to the Product Snapshots, which are in-depth reviews of each database.

The Value-Added Products and Services section lists additional products and services the company sells to facilitate product or market differentiation. There are seven different categories used to classify the products and services: Customer Support, Documentation, System Features/Software Packages, Online Communication, Reference Services, SDI (Selective Dissemination of Information) Services, and Document Formatting and Delivery.

Customer Support covers "people to people" interaction such as training, help desk functions, account representative services, and conferences.

The Documentation category includes a list and description of online and hardcopy aids such as user manuals, newsletters, brochures, dictionaries, and thesauri. If online search criteria such as ticker symbols and SIC codes are used, they will also be identified in this category.

Online Communication encompasses network-based services offered by the company such as bulletin boards, electronic mail (E-mail), or online conferencing.

If a company provides "on request" research, these services will be found in the Research Services category. Many producers provide numeric or textual data tailored to specific individual needs.

The SDI Services category lists and describes the services provided for selective dissemination of information. These services periodically retrieve information from selected database sources based on a predetermined profile of customer needs.

The last category, Document Formatting and Delivery, provides details concerning company services that provide customers with special order hardcopy reports or the results of searches.

The absence of a specific value-added product or service does not necessarily mean that the service or product is not available. It means that the information about a particular product or service was not made available to us. The reader should contact the company directly to receive the current status or full description of the products or services of interest.

Product Snapshots

Product Snapshots (pp. 255–532) are in-depth reviews of individual database products. The Snapshot focuses on the personality of the product. Each one includes a detailed discussion of the subjects covered and the beginning and ending dates of the coverage.

Included in the discussion is information on how the product is sold and distributed, and what user support services are available for it. An important feature of each Snapshot is a review of possible applications for the data.

The Product Snapshots are not designed to stand alone. They should be used in conjunction with Company Snapshots throughout your analysis. Everything you need to know before making the decision to go online, starting with what information is required and ending with knowing where to get it, is contained in the Snapshots. These reviews become your road map through the maze of the information industry.

These in-depth reports provide further quantitative and qualitative facts for your decision-making process. Construct your own matrix, listing the attributes such as subject, availability, access, and available software that are important to you. This evaluation should clearly indicate the producer or product that meets your needs. Your next step should be to telephone the company to set up demonstrations.

USING THE METHODOLOGY TO OBTAIN THE INFORMATION YOU NEED **

Last Monday morning, the following memo was on your desk:

> The CEO and the Policy Committee are looking for new cities for expansion. One of the locations mentioned was New Orleans. Please gather as much demographic and economic data on the New Orleans area as you can to determine market growth and profitability for banking or financial services. In conjunction with this search, identify all Fortune 500 corporations that are in the area, and review their industries' characteristics and each company's financial strength.

** The online search was provided by Readisearch, an information brokerage firm specializing in corporate information and market research. The president of the company, Caren Brodsky, has worked in various research and financial planning and analysis positions at InfoSource, the Federal Reserve Bank of Philadelphia, ARA Services, and Telebase Systems (EasyNet). Major Readisearch clients include Citicorp Homeowners, Scott Paper, Dun & Bradstreet, ICI, and Bank Street College of Education.

Using the Matrix Methodology

In order to answer this question, the Matrices were used to select producers that had identified commercial banks as a target market. A quick scan of the Producer by Target Market Matrix produced several candidates that could be used as entry points into the Producer by Subject Matrix.

The Producer by Subject Matrix narrowed the field to a manageable size. In this instance, you wanted to know which producers covered "Company Information/Statistics," "Industry Information," "News Services," and "Research Reports." This process of elimination resulted in the following list:

  Bunker Ramo Corporation
  Dow Jones News/Retrieval
  ADP, Inc Data Services
  Predicasts
  Standard & Poor's Corporation

A review of the Company Snapshots produced some important information. In addition to company demographics, the Snapshots contained a concise overview of each database including subject, type of database, and other services. If a particular database or product looked as if it provided the information required, the Product Snapshot was consulted to gain more detailed information.

In less than an hour, it was discovered that many of the databases were online and available through DIALOG. Rather than approaching each producer individually, DIALOG appeared to be the best all-around choice in terms of coverage, ease of use, support, updating, responsiveness, flexibility, and longevity. If you were starting from scratch, DIALOG would have to be contacted for specific features, products, and costs. However, since you found that you already had an account, you initiated your search.

Needless to say, some vendors provide better, more comprehensive information concerning particular subjects. If this type of information is required, they can be accessed as needed. However, most search work is accomplished using a core group of 20 general files, adding industry specific databases where appropriate.

Some Rules of the Road Before Getting Started

Most online bibliographic databases provide fact-packed abstracts, not complete articles. It is worthwhile to examine the full text for that small group of really promising abstracts culled from several hundred. Photographs, graphs, maps, and advertisements are only available by reading the original article, although abstracts mention their presence.

Abridgement is not a concern with nonbibliographic databases and wire services. Directory, financial, and demographic files are usually full text, i.e., company names and addresses, comparative years of earnings statements, stock prices, entire time series, census data, and news flashes.

The main advantage of using one basic provider is having to learn only one command language. For example, the command to search two words together (INTERSTATE BANK), with the second word truncated to pick up variable word endings (BANK, BANKs, BANKing, BANKer), is expressed on different systems as: INTERSTATE(1W)BANK?; INTERSTATE ADJ BANK$; and INTERSTATE WITHIN 2 BANK/. The print commands to print the first five items are even more dissimilar: TYPE 1/5/1–5; ..PRINT ALL/DOC = 1–5; PRINT 1,1–5. Familiarity with the command language of one vendor for the majority of searches will result in greater productivity.

It is clear that the distinctive syntax of more than one command language may be a big problem for an occasional user. If the use of online resources appears to be increasing, this may be the best time to build the business case to hire an information broker or experienced information professional to do the searching. Alternatively, the occasional user can access a database through a gateway such as EasyNet or InFact.

Finding the Fortune 500

Let's consider the second part of the search request first. There are several methods for identifying the Fortune 500 companies located in New Orleans. The quickest way is to scan the hardcopy issue of Fortune, if you happen to have it lying around. Another way is to search the Disclosure database using the city, New Orleans, as the search term, and the Fortune Number as a range 1–500. The search and display commands for Disclosure on DIALOG are:

```
BEGIN 100
SELECT CY=NEW ORLEANS AND FO=0001:0500
156 CY=NEW ORLEANS
480 FO=0001:0500

S1 2 CY=NEW ORLEANS AND FO=0001:0500

TYPE 1/5/1-2
```

The example shown is a native language search. The first line says to exit the default database and enter database 100, Disclosure. The second line says to select the city of New Orleans and any *Fortune*-ranked company located therein. CY= indicates the city prefixed field, New Orleans is a bound phrase, FO= indicates the Fortune number field, 0001:0500 means Fortune numbers ranging form 1 to 500, and the AND is a Boolean operator for intersection of the two sets of New Orleans as city and Fortune numbers 1–500.

The S1 section in the middle is a message from DIALOG that indicates that two entries in the database satisfied the search criteria. The TYPE command instructs DIALOG to type the set of two companies in full format.

Getting the Details About the Fortune 500

Disclosure is "one-stop shopping" for annual and quarterly report excerpts and SEC information. Disclosure lists the company name and address, lines of business, Fortune number, five years of income statements, balance sheets and financial ratios, quarterly financials, executives' names, subsidiaries, SEC filings, and much more. The area searched can be strictly New Orleans. It can be broadened to search the telephone area code (504) or the state (Louisiana). The search can also be narrowed by selecting the zip code. After Disclosure has expediently identified the top companies in the target city, a profile for each of the two Fortune 500 companies can be retrieved.

The Fortune 500 criterion for companies narrowed the number of companies significantly, from 27 down to 2; Louisiana Land & Exploration Company, ranked 348, and Freeport McMoran Inc., ranked 406. Other databases can be searched to gather other business information. For example, to get a list of companies operating in certain SIC codes in New Orleans, regardless of Fortune ranking or the absence thereof, Dun & Bradstreet's Market Identifiers, Standard & Poor's Register—U.S. Corporate, or the Trinet databases could be accessed.

More About the Business Climate

To answer the first part of the search request concerning demographic and economic data on New Orleans, it is important to search industry-specific databases as well as general business ones. Databases that focus on an industry often provide a wealth of minor news stories and detail, and they can pick up obscure sources. Some worthwhile industry or special interest databases are American Banker, Bond Buyer, and McGraw-Hill Business Backgrounder.

Local and Regional News

Data Courier's Business Dateline and ABI/INFORM, Predicasts' PROMT and Predicasts' Business & Industry News, Standard & Poor's News Online, Moody's Corporate News (US and International), and Dow Jones form the basis of any news search. Business Dateline is especially good for its full-text coverage of regional business publications.

The Predicasts databases, PROMT and Business & Industry News, also have very good regional coverage, such as New Orleans CityBusiness. Predicasts' Business & Industry News is the most recent week's worth of abstracts. The abstracts are moved to the other Predicasts databases after one week.

The search by the city name, New Orleans, back for two years, may produce an overwhelming number of entries. When this happens, the search criteria should be narrowed by adding the terms economy or economics or industry or market. The search statement in DIALOG is:

SEARCH NEW(W) ORLEANS AND (ECONOM? OR INDUSTR?)

The ? represents a wild letter match, also known as truncation. Different database vendors use different symbols to accomplish the same purpose—$, *, ?, # are common. Econom? picks up economy and economic; industr? picks up industry, industrial, and industries.

A subject classification code may also be used if one exists. Business Dateline has the following classification codes, which can be combined with New Orleans. The Predicasts databases and ABI/Inform also have similar category or event codes.

CC = 1100 (ECONOMICS)
CC = 1110 (ECONOMIC CONDITIONS & FORECASTS)
CC = 1120 (ECONOMIC POLICY & PLANNING)
CC = 1130 (ECONOMIC THEORY)

SEARCH NEW(W)ORLEANS AND CC = 11?

Abstracts covering the following topics relating to New Orleans were produced using the above search:

a general economic overview of the city
the effects of state spending cuts
the oil and gas slump
banking
job decline leading to falling housing prices
the planned Republican Party's 1988 convention
analysis of the 1984 Louisiana World Exposition
travel and tourism
hotel industry
restaurant industry
trade with Latin America
ports and terminals
coal and steel
the Regional Transit Authority's renovation plans
the economic impact of the aquarium
employee buyout of Rexnord Instrument Products
Tidewater's restructuring of its debt
McDermott International
advertising industry
numerous abstracts about local businesses, business figures,
   and politics

The gold mine articles, all dated the current year, included:

"Economy, loan losses cause rough year for banks, S&Ls" from *New Orleans CityBusiness*, retrieved through Predicasts' PROMT.

"Louisiana Bank to Expand into Florida Market" from *American Banker*, retrieved through Predicasts' PROMT.

"Hibernia takes over Lafayette Bank" from *New Orleans Times-Picayune*, retrieved through Predicasts' PROMT.

"Plus and Cirrus Enter New Orleans" from *American Banker*, retrieved through American Banker database.

"Louisiana's New Banking Commissioner is Learning on the Job" from *American Banker*, retrieved through American Banker database.

"Four Louisiana Thrifts swam while neighbors sank: some top performers tell how they managed it despite shaky economy" from *American Banker*, retrieved through American Banker database.

This exercise should take about an hour or two online, simultaneously searching, printing, and reading, and then downloading at intervals. A good practice is to look for patterns and repeating stories. Initially, there should be the need to print citations and abstracts for the first two or three general news databases (usually PROMT and Business Dateline) and the short newswire databases (e.g., Dow Jones with its full text of stories within the past 90 days). After the first pass, when it's time to be more critical, only print the title and descriptors. Read the headings as they appear and jot down the heading numbers for abstract retrieval after all the headings are reviewed.

Looking for Industry Investment Reports

A lot of information can be gleaned from relevant industry reports. Mead Data Central's Company and Industry Reports (COIND) is a good source database for investment reports. An online search reveals brokerage house reports covering New Orleans Public Service, Louisiana Power & Light, Bank of New Orleans & Trust Company, and the New Orleans Banking Industry. The INVESTEXT database provides the full text of brokerage house reports.

Going Offline to Complete the Picture

Certain organizations collect economic and demographic data on cities, counties, and states. A round of telephone calls to the local Chamber of Commerce, appropriate city, county, and state government offices, the district Federal Reserve Bank, a major local bank, a major local university, and the Department of the Census will result in an avalanche of printed reports, statistics, and brochures. A telephone call to the main industry association, in this case the American Banking Association, should provide additional insight into the feasibility of the project. The New Orleans Chamber of Commerce material included valuable material covering the major industries (oil and gas, port and port-related industries, and tourism) and employers with over 2,500 employees (Winn-Dixie Supermarkets, Martin Marietta, Tulane University, and Shell Oil). The Chamber also sent their most recent reports on key economic sectors, economic growth indicators, cost of living comparisons, business mix, industrial investments, construction activity, regional taxes, tourism industry, and retail market growth.

The context of this research request is the profitability potential for retail banking in New Orleans. There are essential hardcopy sources to consult—Polk's and Rand-McNally to identify the banks in a city; Sheshunoff and the FDIC data book for financial information; and the Federal Reserve research publications, especially the Atlanta Fed's Southeastern Economic Indicators and the Business Reviews.

Making Sense of It All

The next stage of the project involves a synthesis of this mass of data, not merely a reordering of the databases' output. An executive summary should be written organizing the most important abstracts into related sections and subsections. Additional quantitative analysis may be performed, but this requirement usually surfaces after the report has been issued and read by several people.

The research project has probably produced a stack of computer paper 3–4 inches high, 100–200 abstracts, a few excellent full-text articles, pages of government statistics, and handwritten notes. Because most of the material has been downloaded from a database computer, it is easy to organize the downloaded file and other sources into discrete topics, using word processing software. The report is easy to clean up on the computer by eliminating duplicate abstracts and line noise. Graphics, maps, and tables can be added to make the information easier to understand. Table 3.1: 1975–1986 Population Growth and Table 3.2: Number of Employ-

TABLE 3.1 _____

1975–1986 Population Growth, New Orleans

Year	Population	% Chg	# Chg
1975	1,217,100		
1976	1,240,000	1.9%	22,900
1977	1,255,200	1.2%	15,200
1978	1,270,200	1.2%	15,000
1979	1,285,600	1.2%	15,400
1980	1,303,500	1.4%	17,900
1981	1,333,000	2.3%	29,500
1982	1,348,800	1.2%	15,800
1983	1,367,600	1.4%	18,800
1984	1,373,800	0.5%	6,200
1985	1,377,868	0.3%	4,068
1986	1,385,611	0.6%	7,743

Source: Bureau of the Census and Louisiana Tech University

TABLE 3.2 _____

Total Number of Employees by Parish, 1984

Parish	Number of Employees	% of Total
Orleans	222,160	48.4%
Jefferson	165,368	36.0%
St. Bernard	11,176	2.4%
St. Tammany	22,683	4.9%
St. Charles	12,058	2.6%
St. James	5,341	1.2%
St. John	8,511	1.9%
Plaquemines	12,174	2.6%
Total	459,471	100.0%

Source: County Business Patterns, 1984

ees by Parish, 1984 were both created by downloading numeric information into a simple LOTUS 1-2-3 spreadsheet. All results of the online search and other requested offline sources (government reports, Chamber of Commerce documents, etc.) should be included in the report as background material.

Producers by Target Markets

This Matrix is the result of information industry research performed during 1986 and 1987. Thousands of labor-hours have gone into this reference work, hours that usually cannot be devoted during the course of an individual search.

The Methodology, explained earlier in Chapter 3, discusses how the Matrices are to be used to reach a decision faster and maximize the effect of your efforts.

The "Target Market" classifications assigned are a result of our own research or were obtained directly from the Producers. From time to time, product or company ownership, as well as product descriptions, may change as the industry matures. *Inclusion in this chapter does not constitute an endorsement by either the authors or the publisher.*

PRODUCERS BY TARGET MARKETS MATRIX

	Commercial banks	Credit unions	Fortune 1000 corporations	Government agencies	Investment banks	Law firms	Mortgage banks	Real estate firms	Specialized librarians	Thrift institutions
ADP, Inc. Data Services	●		●		●		●		●	●
American Banker	●	●		●	●		●		●	●
American Institute of Certified Public Accountants	●	●	●	●	●	●	●	●	●	●
Bank Marketing Association	●	●			●	●	●	●		●
Bridge Data Company	●				●		●			
Bunker Ramo Corporation	●		●		●		●			●
The Bureau of National Affairs, Inc.	●	●	●	●	●	●	●	●	●	●
Business Research Corporation	●		●	●	●	●		●	●	
CACI Inc.–Federal	●	●	●	●	●			●	●	●
Chase Econometrics	●		●	●	●				●	●
Claremont Economics Institute	●		●		●				●	
Commodity Information Services Company	●				●		●			●
Commodity Systems Inc.	●		●		●				●	
The Conference Board, Inc.	●	●	●	●	●		●	●	●	●
Data Courier Inc.	●		●		●				●	
Data Resources, Inc.	●	●	●	●	●		●	●	●	●
DATATEK Corporation	●	●	●	●	●	●	●	●	●	●

	Commercial banks	Credit unions	Fortune 1000 corporations	Government agencies	Investment banks	Law firms	Mortgage banks	Real estate firms	Specialized librarians	Thrift institutions
Disclosure	•		•	•	•	•			•	
Donnelley Marketing	•	•	•					•	•	•
Dow Jones News/Retrieval	•	•	•	•	•	•	•	•	•	•
Duff and Phelps, Inc.	•		•		•				•	•
Dun's Marketing Services	•		•	•	•				•	
Evans Econometrics, Inc.	•	•	•	•	•				•	•
Financial Post Information Service	•				•					
Gregg Corporation	•		•		•					•
The H.W. Wilson Company	•	•	•	•	•	•	•	•	•	•
I.P. Sharp Associates Limited	•	•	•	•	•	•	•	•	•	•
Info Globe	•		•	•	•	•			•	
Information Access Company	•	•	•	•	•	•	•	•	•	•
Interactive Data Corporation	•		•		•		•		•	•
Journal of Economic Literature	•		•	•	•				•	•
Kenny Information Systems	•				•					
Knight-Ridder Financial Information	•	•	•		•			•	•	•
McGraw-Hill, Inc.	•		•	•	•				•	

PRODUCERS BY TARGET MARKETS MATRIX

	Commercial banks	Credit unions	Fortune 1000 corporations	Government agencies	Investment banks	Law firms	Mortgage banks	Real estate firms	Specialized librarians	Thrift institutions
Mead Data Central, Inc.	•	•	•	•	•	•	•	•	•	•
MLR Publishing Company	•		•		•	•			•	
Money Market Services, Inc.	•		•		•		•			•
Moody's Investors Service, Inc.	•	•	•	•	•	•	•		•	•
Multinational Computer Models Inc.	•		•		•					
National Register Publishing Co.	•				•	•			•	
Predicasts Inc.	•	•	•	•	•	•	•	•	•	•
Quotron Systems, Inc.	•				•					•
SAGE DATA, Inc.	•		•	•	•				•	
SEC Online, Inc.	•		•		•	•			•	
Standard & Poor's Corporation	•		•	•	•	•			•	•
Technical Data Corporation	•	•	•	•	•		•	•		•
Trinet, Inc.	•		•		•			•	•	
Wharton Econometric Forecasting Associates	•	•	•	•	•				•	•

32

Producers by Subject Coverage

This Matrix is the result of information industry research performed during 1986 and 1987. Thousands of person-hours have gone into this reference work; Hours which usually cannot be devoted during the course of an individual search.

The Methodology, explained earlier in Chapter 3, discusses how the Matrices are to be used to reach a decision faster and maximize the effect of your efforts.

The "Subject Coverage" classifications assigned are a result of our own research or were obtained directly from the Producers. From time-to-time, product or company ownership, as well as product descriptions, may change as the industry matures. *Inclusion in this chapter does not constitute an endorsement by either the authors or the publisher.*

PRODUCERS BY SUBJECT COVERAGE MATRIX

	Company information/statistics	Demographic information/statistics	Econometric data	Industry information/statistics	Real-time/Historic market quotations	News services	Newsletters	Research reports/evaluations	Trading/Brokerage services
ADP, Inc. Data Services	•		•	•	•	•			
American Banker				•		•			
American Institute of Certified Public Accountants	•			•					
Bank Marketing Association				•			•	•	
Bridge Data Company					•	•			
Bunker Ramo Corporation	•			•	•	•		•	
The Bureau of National Affairs, Inc.				•		•			
Business Research Corporation	•			•				•	
CACI Inc.–Federal		•							
Chase Econometrics	•	•	•	•	•				
Claremont Economics Institute			•						
Commodity Information Services Company					•				
Commodity Systems Inc.					•				
The Conference Board, Inc.		•	•	•			•		
Data Courier Inc.						•		•	
Data Resources, Inc.	•		•	•	•				
DATATEK Corporation						•			

	Company information/statistics	Demographic information/statistics	Econometric data	Industry information/statistics	Real-time/Historic market quotations	News services	Newsletters	Research reports/evaluations	Trading/Brokerage services
Disclosure	•								
Donnelley Marketing		•							
Dow Jones News/Retrieval	•		•	•	•	•		•	
Duff and Phelps, Inc.								•	
Dun's Marketing Services	•								
Evans Economics, Inc.			•						
Financial Post Information Service	•				•				
Gregg Corporation					•				
The H.W. Wilson Company	•	•	•	•					
I.P. Sharp Associates Limited	•		•		•			•	
Info Globe	•			•	•	•			
Information Access Company	•	•	•	•		•		•	
Interactive Data Corporation	•		•		•				
Journal of Economic Literature			•						
Kenny Information Systems					•				
Knight-Ridder Financial Information					•	•		•	
McGraw-Hill, Inc.	•			•	•				

	Company information/statistics	Demographic information/statistics	Econometric data	Industry information/statistics	Real-time/Historic market quotations	News services	Newsletters	Research reports/evaluations	Trading/Brokerage services
Mead Data Central, Inc.	●			●		●			
MLR Publishing Company	●			●					
Money Market Services, Inc.					●				
Moody's Investors Service, Inc.	●					●			
Multinational Computer Models Inc.			●		●	●			
National Register Publishing Co.	●								
Predicasts Inc.	●	●	●	●		●			
Quotron Systems, Inc.					●				
SAGE DATA, Inc.			●	●					
SEC Online, Inc.	●								
Standard & Poor's Corporation	●			●	●	●			
Technical Data Corporation			●		●	●	●	●	
Trinet, Inc.	●								
Wharton Econometric Forecasting Associates		●	●		●	●			

Products by Subject Coverage

This Matrix is the result of information industry research performed during 1986 and 1987. Thousands of person-hours have gone into this reference work; Hours which usually cannot be devoted during the course of an individual search.

The Methodology, explained earlier in Chapter 3, discusses how the Matrices are to be used to reach a decision faster and maximize the effect of your efforts.

The "Subject" classifications assigned are a result of our own research or were obtained directly from the Producers. From time-to-time, product or company ownership, as well as product descriptions, may change as the industry matures. *Inclusion in this chapter does not constitute an endorsement by either the authors or the publisher.*

PRODUCTS BY SUBJECT COVERAGE MATRIX

	Annual reports	Company background	Forecasts	Insider trading	Lines of business	Market activity	Monthly reports	Officers/Directors	Quarterly reports	SEC filings	Stockholder information	Consumer preference	Income and housing	Industry specific	Local	Monetary aggregates	International	National	Regional
		Company information/statistics										Demographic information/statistics				Econometric data			
ABI/INFORM																			
(Data Courier Inc.)																			
Accountants																			
(American Institute of Certified Public Accountants)																			
ACORN												•	•						
(CACI Inc.–Federal)																			
Agricultural Commodities																			
(I.P. Sharp Assoc. Ltd.)																			
American Banker																			
(American Banker)																			
American Banker News Service																			
(American Banker)																			
Annual Reports Abstract (ARA)	•																		
(Predicasts Inc.)																			
Annual Survey of Manufactures																			
(Chase Econometrics)																			

Business intelligence	Emerging technologies	Industry leadership changes	Industry overviews	Legal actions and issues	Market news and forecasts	Product developments	Spot prices	Bonds, notes and bills	Futures	Currencies	Money rates	Mortgage backed securities	Options	Stocks, mutual funds, warrants, and rights	Municipals	Local	National	Regional	International	Newsletter	Company	Industry	Products	Fixed income	Capital markets	Trading/Brokerage services
																•	•	•	•							
			•																							
							•		•																	
•	•	•	•	•	•	•																				
																	•									
		•																								

PRODUCTS BY SUBJECT COVERAGE MATRIX

	Company information/ statistics											Demographic information/ statistics				Econometric data			
	Annual reports	Company background	Forecasts	Insider trading	Lines of business	Market activity	Monthly reports	Officers/Directors	Quarterly reports	SEC filings	Stockholder information	Consumer preference	Income and housing	Industry specific	Local	Monetary aggregates	International	National	Regional
Bancall II	•								•										
(ADP, Inc. Data Services)																			
Bancorp	•								•										
(ADP, Inc. Data Services)																			
Bank Holding Companies	•																		
(Chase Econometrics)																			
Bank of Canada Weekly Financial Statistics																•		•	
(I.P. Sharp Assoc. Ltd.)																			
Blue List Bond Ticker																			
(Standard & Poor's Corp.)																			
BNA Executive Day																			
(The Bureau of National Affairs, Inc.)																			
The Bond Buyer																			
(American Banker)																			
BondData																•			
(Technical Data Corp.)																			

	Industry information/statistics							Real-time/Historic market quotations									News services					Research reports/evaluations					
	Business intelligence	Emerging technologies	Industry leadership changes	Industry overviews	Legal actions and issues	Market news and forecasts	Product developments	Spot prices	Bonds, notes and bills	Futures	Currencies	Money rates	Mortgage backed securities	Options	Stocks, mutual funds, warrants, and rights	Municipals	Local	National	Regional	International	Newsletter	Company	Industry	Products	Fixed income	Capital markets	Trading/Brokerage services
									●						●											
																	●									
																	●	●								
							●	●			●															

PRODUCTS BY SUBJECT COVERAGE MATRIX

	Company information/ statistics											Demographic information/ statistics			Econometric data				
	Annual reports	Company background	Forecasts	Insider trading	Lines of business	Market activity	Monthly reports	Officers/Directors	Quarterly reports	SEC filings	Stockholder information	Consumer preference	Income and housing	Industry specific	Local	Monetary aggregates	International	National	Regional
Branch Deposit															●				
(Chase Econometrics)																			
Bridge Information System																			
(Bridge Data Co.)																			
Brokerage Information Data Base																			
(Bunker Ramo Corp.)																			
Business & Industry News																			
(Predicasts Inc.)																			
Business Conditions Digest																		●	
(Chase Econometrics)																			
Business Dateline																			
(Data Courier Inc.)																			
Business Periodicals Index																			
(The H.W. Wilson Co.)																			
Business Software Database																			
(Data Courier Inc.)																			

Business intelligence	Emerging technologies	Industry leadership changes	Industry overviews	Legal actions and issues	Market news and forecasts	Product developments	Spot prices	Bonds, notes and bills	Futures	Currencies	Money rates	Mortgage backed securities	Options	Stocks, mutual funds, warrants, and rights	Municipals	Local	National	Regional	International	Newsletter	Company	Industry	Products	Fixed income	Capital markets	Trading/Brokerage services
								•	•				•	•												•
								•	•	•	•			•	•											
																	•									
																		•								
																	•		•							
																							•			

	Company information/ statistics											Demographic information/ statistics		Econometric data					
	Annual reports	Company background	Forecasts	Insider trading	Lines of business	Market activity	Monthly reports	Officers/Directors	Quarterly reports	SEC filings	Stockholder information	Consumer preference	Income and housing	Industry specific	Local	Monetary aggregates	International	National	Regional
Canadian Bonds																			
(I.P. Sharp Assoc. Ltd.)																			
Canadian Chartered Banks, Annual Financial Statements	●								●					●					
(I.P. Sharp Assoc. Ltd.)																			
Canadian Chartered Banks, Monthly Statements							●							●					
(I.P. Sharp Assoc. Ltd.)																			
Canadian Chartered Banks, Quarterly Income Statements									●					●					
(I.P. Sharp Assoc. Ltd.)																			
Canadian Dept. of Insurance	●													●					
(I.P. Sharp Assoc. Ltd.)																			
The Canadian Financial Database	●																		
(Info Globe)																			
Canadian Options																			
(I.P. Sharp Assoc. Ltd.)																			
CISCO																			
(Commodity Information Services Co.)																			

Business intelligence	Emerging technologies	Industry leadership changes	Industry overviews	Legal actions and issues	Market news and forecasts	Product developments	Spot prices	Bonds, notes and bills	Futures	Currencies	Money rates	Mortgage backed securities	Options	Stocks, mutual funds, warrants, and rights	Municipals	Local	National	Regional	International	Newsletter	Company	Industry	Products	Fixed income	Capital markets	Trading/Brokerage services
								●																		
													●													
							●	●	●		●		●													

PRODUCTS BY SUBJECT COVERAGE MATRIX

	Company information/statistics											Demographic information/statistics		Econometric data					
	Annual reports	Company background	Forecasts	Insider trading	Lines of business	Market activity	Monthly reports	Officers/Directors	Quarterly reports	SEC filings	Stockholder information	Consumer preference	Income and housing	Industry specific	Local	Monetary aggregates	International	National	Regional
Claremont Economics Institute														•			•	•	
(Claremont Economics Institute)																			
Commodities																			
(I.P. Sharp Assoc. Ltd.)																			
Commodity Options																			
(I.P. Sharp Assoc. Ltd.)																			
COMPUSTAT	•								•										
(Standard & Poor's Corp.)																			
COMPUSTAT II	•								•										
(Standard & Poor's Corp.)																			
Computer Database																			
(Information Access Company)																			
Conference Board																		•	
(Chase Econometrics)																			
The Conference Board Data Base												•	•	•	•	•		•	•
(The Conference Board, Inc.)																			

46

Industry information/statistics							Real-time/Historic market quotations									News services					Research reports/evaluations					
Business intelligence	Emerging technologies	Industry leadership changes	Industry overviews	Legal actions and issues	Market news and forecasts	Product developments	Spot prices	Bonds, notes and bills	Futures	Currencies	Money rates	Mortgage backed securities	Options	Stocks, mutual funds, warrants, and rights	Municipals	Local	National	Regional	International	Newsletter	Company	Industry	Products	Fixed income	Capital markets	Trading/Brokerage services
									•																	
													•													
					•																					
																	•		•							
																				•						

PRODUCTS BY SUBJECT COVERAGE MATRIX

	Company information/statistics											Demographic information/statistics				Econometric data			
	Annual reports	Company background	Forecasts	Insider trading	Lines of business	Market activity	Monthly reports	Officers/Directors	Quarterly reports	SEC filings	Stockholder information	Consumer preference	Income and housing	Industry specific	Local	Monetary aggregates	International	National	Regional
Consumer Price Index Database (Chase Econometrics)																		•	
Consumer Price Index Database (SAGE DATA, Inc.)																		•	
Consumer Spending Forecast (Chase Econometrics)												•	•					•	
Corporate Affiliations (National Register Publishing Co.)		•																	
Corporate Descriptions Online (Standard & Poor's Corp.)	•	•																	
Corporate Profiles (Moody's Investors Service)	•	•	•		•	•	•	•	•	•	•								
CPI (Wharton Econometric Forecasting Assoc.)													•					•	
CROPMOD (Wharton Econometric Forecasting Assoc.)																		•	

		Industry information/ statistics							Real-time/ Historic market quotations									News services					Research reports/ evaluations					
Business intelligence	Emerging technologies	Industry leadership changes	Industry overviews	Legal actions and issues	Market news and forecasts	Product developments	Spot prices	Bonds, notes and bills	Futures	Currencies	Money rates	Mortgage backed securities	Options	Stocks, mutual funds, warrants, and rights	Municipals	Local	National	Regional	International	Newsletter	Company	Industry	Products	Fixed income	Capital markets	Trading/Brokerage services
																					•					
				•																						

PRODUCTS BY SUBJECT COVERAGE MATRIX

| | Company information/statistics | | | | | | | | | | | Demographic information/statistics | | | Econometric data | | | |
	Annual reports	Company background	Forecasts	Insider trading	Lines of business	Market activity	Monthly reports	Officers/Directors	Quarterly reports	SEC filings	Stockholder information	Consumer preference	Income and housing	Industry specific	Local	Monetary aggregates	International	National	Regional
Daily Currency Exchange Rates																			
(I.P. Sharp Assoc. Ltd.)																			
Daily Report for Executives																			
(The Bureau of National Affairs, Inc.)																			
Daily Washington Advance																			
(The Bureau of National Affairs, Inc.)																			
DataTimes–Associated Press																			
(DATATEK Corp.)																			
DataTimes–Southwest Newswire																			
(DATATEK Corp.)																			
Disclosure Online	•									•									
(Disclosure Inc.)																			
Disclosure/Spectrum Ownership										•	•								
(Disclosure, Inc.)																			
DORIS												•	•						
(CACI Inc.–Federal)																			

Business intelligence	Emerging technologies	Industry leadership changes	Industry overviews	Legal actions and issues	Market news and forecasts	Product developments	Spot prices	Bonds, notes and bills	Futures	Currencies	Money rates	Mortgage backed securities	Options	Stocks, mutual funds, warrants, and rights	Municipals	Local	National	Regional	International	Newsletter	Company	Industry	Products	Fixed income	Capital markets	Trading/Brokerage services
										•																
				•	•												•									
			•	•	•																					
																•	•	•	•							
																•	•	•								

Column group headers: Industry information/statistics · Real-time/Historic market quotations · News services · Research reports/evaluations

PRODUCTS BY SUBJECT COVERAGE MATRIX

	Company information/ statistics											Demographic information/ statistics			Econometric data				
	Annual reports	Company background	Forecasts	Insider trading	Lines of business	Market activity	Monthly reports	Officers/Directors	Quarterly reports	SEC filings	Stockholder information	Consumer preference	Income and housing	Industry specific	Local	Monetary aggregates	International	National	Regional
Dow Jones Current Quotes																			
(Dow Jones News/Retrieval)																			
Dow Jones Futures Quotes																			
(Dow Jones News/Retrieval)																			
Dow Jones Historical Quotes																			
(Dow Jones News/Retrieval)																			
Dow Jones News																			
(Dow Jones News/Retrieval)																			
Dow Jones Text-Search Services																			
(Dow Jones News/Retrieval)																			
DQI^2												●	●						
(Donnelley Marketing)																			
DRI Bank Analysis System	●																		
(Data Resources, Inc.)																			
DRI Commodities																			
(Data Resources, Inc.)																			

Industry information/statistics							Real-time/Historic market quotations									News services					Research reports/evaluations					
Business intelligence	Emerging technologies	Industry leadership changes	Industry overviews	Legal actions and issues	Market news and forecasts	Product developments	Spot prices	Bonds, notes and bills	Futures	Currencies	Money rates	Mortgage backed securities	Options	Stocks, mutual funds, warrants, and rights	Municipals	Local	National	Regional	International	Newsletter	Company	Industry	Products	Fixed income	Capital markets	Trading/Brokerage services
								•					•	•												
									•																	
														•												
																	•		•							
																	•									
							•		•																	

3

53

PRODUCTS BY SUBJECT COVERAGE MATRIX

	Annual reports	Company background	Forecasts	Insider trading	Lines of business	Company information/statistics — Market activity	Monthly reports	Officers/Directors	Quarterly reports	SEC filings	Stockholder information	Demographic information/statistics — Consumer preference	Income and housing	Industry specific	Local	Econometric data — Monetary aggregates	International	National	Regional
DRI Financial and Credit Statistics	•								•										
(Data Resources, Inc.)																			
DRI Securities																			
(Data Resources, Inc.)																			
Duff and Phelps Equity Ideas																	•		
(Duff and Phelps, Inc.)																			
Duff and Phelps Fixed Income																			
(Duff and Phelps, Inc.)																			
Dun's Financial Records	•	•			•				•										
(Dun's Marketing Services)																			
Dun's Market Identifiers	•	•			•				•										
(Dun's Marketing Services)																			
Economic Literature Index														•		•	•	•	
(Journal of Economic Literature)																			
EIAPRICE														•				•	
(Wharton Econometric Forecasting Assoc.)																			

Industry information/statistics							Real-time/Historic market quotations									News services					Research reports/evaluations						
Business intelligence	Emerging technologies	Industry leadership changes	Industry overviews	Legal actions and issues	Market news and forecasts	Product developments	Spot prices	Bonds, notes and bills	Futures	Currencies	Money rates	Mortgage backed securities	Options	Stocks, mutual funds, warrants, and rights	Municipals	Local	National	Regional	International	Newsletter	Company	Industry	Products	Fixed income	Capital markets	Trading/Brokerage services
									•	•	•															
								•					•	•												
																		•							
																							•		

PRODUCTS BY SUBJECT COVERAGE MATRIX

	Company information/statistics											Demographic information/statistics				Econometric data			
	Annual reports	Company background	Forecasts	Insider trading	Lines of business	Market activity	Monthly reports	Officers/Directors	Quarterly reports	SEC filings	Stockholder information	Consumer preference	Income and housing	Industry specific	Local	Monetary aggregates	International	National	Regional
Electronic Company Filing Index										•									
(Disclosure, Inc.)																			
Employment and Earnings Database																		•	
(SAGE DATA, Inc.)																			
Evans Economics Full Service Database																•		•	
(Evans Economics, Inc.)																			
Evans Economics Macro Core Database																•		•	
(Evans Economics, Inc.)																			
EXCHANGE	•								•	•									
(Mead Data Central, Inc.)																			
F&S Index																			
(Predicasts Inc.)																			
Fastock II																			
(ADP, Inc. Data Services)																			
FDIC	•						•								•			•	
(Chase Econometrics)																			

	Industry information/statistics							Real-time/Historic market quotations									News services					Research reports/evaluations					
	Business intelligence	Emerging technologies	Industry leadership changes	Industry overviews	Legal actions and issues	Market news and forecasts	Product developments	Spot prices	Bonds, notes and bills	Futures	Currencies	Money rates	Mortgage backed securities	Options	Stocks, mutual funds, warrants, and rights	Municipals	Local	National	Regional	International	Newsletter	Company	Industry	Products	Fixed income	Capital markets	Trading/Brokerage services
																						●	●				
																	●		●							
								●						●	●	●											

PRODUCTS BY SUBJECT COVERAGE MATRIX

	Annual reports	Company information/statistics										Demographic information/statistics		Econometric data					
	Annual reports	Company background	Forecasts	Insider trading	Lines of business	Market activity	Monthly reports	Officers/Directors	Quarterly reports	SEC filings	Stockholder information	Consumer preference	Income and housing	Industry specific	Local	Monetary aggregates	International	National	Regional
Federal Reserve Board Weekly Statistics														●		●			
(I.P. Sharp Assoc. Ltd.)																			
Financial														●				●	
(Chase Econometrics)																			
Financial Forecast																		●	
(Chase Econometrics)																			
Financial Post Bond Database																			
(Financial Post Information Service)																			
Financial Post Canadian Corporate Data	●								●										
(Financial Post Information Service)																			
Financial Post Securities																			
(Financial Post Information Service)																			
FINIS																			
(Bank Marketing Assoc.)																			
Finsbury Data Services	●																		
(Information Access Co.)																			

Business intelligence	Emerging technologies	Industry leadership changes	Industry overviews	Legal actions and issues	Market news and forecasts	Product developments	Spot prices	Bonds, notes and bills	Futures	Currencies	Money rates	Mortgage backed securities	Options	Stocks, mutual funds, warrants, and rights	Municipals	Local	National	Regional	International	Newsletter	Company	Industry	Products	Fixed income	Capital markets	Trading/Brokerage services
								•																		
													•	•												
																	•		•							
																•	•	•	•							

PRODUCTS BY SUBJECT COVERAGE MATRIX

	Annual reports	Company background	Forecasts	Insider trading	Lines of business	Market activity	Monthly reports	Officers/Directors	Quarterly reports	SEC filings	Stockholder information	Consumer preference	Income and housing	Industry specific	Local	Monetary aggregates	International	National	Regional
					Company information/statistics							Demographic information/statistics			Econometric data				
Flow of Funds (Chase Econometrics)																		●	
Forecasts (Predicasts Inc.)														●	●	●	●	●	
Foreign Exchange (Chase Econometrics)																			
Foreign Exchange Forecast (Chase Econometrics)																			
FSLIC (Chase Econometrics)	●								●									●	
FundamentalData (Technical Data Corp.)														●		●		●	
Futures Price Quotation Service (Bridge Data Co.)																			
The Globe and Mail Online (Info Globe)																			

Business intelligence	Emerging technologies	Industry leadership changes	Industry overviews	Legal actions and issues	Market news and forecasts	Product developments	Spot prices	Bonds, notes and bills	Futures	Currencies	Money rates	Mortgage backed securities	Options	Stocks, mutual funds, warrants, and rights	Municipals	Local	National	Regional	International	Newsletter	Company	Industry	Products	Fixed income	Capital markets	Trading/Brokerage services
										•																
										•	•															
																	•		•	•						
							•						•				•									
																•	•	•	•							

PRODUCTS BY SUBJECT COVERAGE MATRIX

	Company information/statistics											Demographic information/statistics		Econometric data					
	Annual reports	Company background	Forecasts	Insider trading	Lines of business	Market activity	Monthly reports	Officers/Directors	Quarterly reports	SEC filings	Stockholder information	Consumer preference	Income and housing	Industry specific	Local	Monetary aggregates	International	National	Regional
Historical Dow Jones Averages																			
(Dow Jones News/Retrieval)																			
IDCPRICE	●																	●	
(International Data Corp.)																			
IMF International Financial Statistics																	●		
(Wharton Econometric Forecasting Assoc.)																			
Industrial Financial	●	●																	
(Standard & Poor's Corp.)																			
Industry Data Sources																			
(Information Access Co.)																			
Industry 480														●					
(Chase Econometrics)																			
Insider Trading Data Base				●															
(ADP, Inc. Data Services)																			
INSIGHT					●	●			●		●								
(Info Globe)																			

	Industry information/statistics							Real-time/Historic market quotations									News services					Research reports/evaluations					
Business intelligence	Emerging technologies	Industry leadership changes	Industry overviews	Legal actions and issues	Market news and forecasts	Product developments	Spot prices	Bonds, notes and bills	Futures	Currencies	Money rates	Mortgage backed securities	Options	Stocks, mutual funds, warrants, and rights	Municipals	Local	National	Regional	International	Newsletter	Company	Industry	Products	Fixed income	Capital markets	Trading/Brokerage services
														•												
							•	•	•	•	•		•	•	•											
		•												•												
																	•		•							
•	•	•	•	•	•	•																				

PRODUCTS BY SUBJECT COVERAGE MATRIX

	Annual reports	Company background	Forecasts	Insider trading	Lines of business	Market activity	Monthly reports	Officers/Directors	Quarterly reports	SEC filings	Stockholder information	Consumer preference	Income and housing	Industry specific	Local	Monetary aggregates	International	National	Regional
International Corporate News																			
(Moody's Investors Service)																			
International Dun's Market Identifiers	•	•	•		•				•										
(Dun's Marketing Services)																			
INVESTEXT																			
(Business Research Corp.)																			
Legal Resource Index																			
(Information Access Co.)																			
Long-Term Interindustry Forecast														•				•	
(Chase Econometrics)																			
LTMOD																		•	
(Wharton Econometric) (Forecasting Assoc.)																			
M&A Database					•	•													
(MLR Publishing Co.)																			
McGraw-Hill Business Backgrounder																			
(McGraw-Hill, Inc.)																			

Column groups: "Company information/statistics", "Demographic information/statistics", "Econometric data"

	Industry information/ statistics							Real-time/ Historic market quotations									News services					Research reports/ evaluations					
	Business intelligence	Emerging technologies	Industry leadership changes	Industry overviews	Legal actions and issues	Market news and forecasts	Product developments	Spot prices	Bonds, notes and bills	Futures	Currencies	Money rates	Mortgage backed securities	Options	Stocks, mutual funds, warrants, and rights	Municipals	Local	National	Regional	International	Newsletter	Company	Industry	Products	Fixed income	Capital markets	Trading/Brokerage services
																		•		•							
																						•	•				
			•																								
	•																										
																	•										

PRODUCTS BY SUBJECT COVERAGE MATRIX

	Company information/statistics											Demographic information/statistics		Econometric data					
	Annual reports/Fin. info	Company background	Forecasts	Insider trading	Lines of business	Market activity	Monthly reports	Officers/Directors	Quarterly reports	SEC filings	Stockholder information	Consumer preference	Income and housing	Industry specific	Local	Monetary aggregates	International	National	Regional
MACROECONOMIC														•	•	•		•	•
(Data Resources, Inc.)																			
Magazine ASAP																			
(Information Access Co.)																			
Magazine Index																			
(Information Access Co.)																			
Management Contents																			
(Information Access Co.)																			
Marketing and Advertising Reference Service (MARS)												•	•						
(Predicasts Inc.)																			
Marketscan																			
(Info Globe)																			
MARSTAT																			
(Commodity Systems Inc.)																			
MATREX																	•		
(Multinational Computer Models, Inc.)																			

Business intelligence	Emerging technologies	Industry leadership changes	Industry overviews	Legal actions and issues	Market news and forecasts	Product developments	Spot prices	Bonds, notes and bills	Futures	Currencies	Money rates	Mortgage backed securities	Options	Stocks, mutual funds, warrants, and rights	Municipals	Local	National	Regional	International	Newsletter	Company	Industry	Products	Fixed income	Capital markets	Trading/Brokerage services
																	•									
																	•									
																	•									
•	•				•	•																				
														•												
									•				•	•												
								•		•									•							

PRODUCTS BY SUBJECT COVERAGE MATRIX

	Annual reports	Company background	Forecasts	Insider trading	Lines of business	Market activity	Monthly reports	Officers/Directors	Quarterly reports	SEC filings	Stockholder information	Consumer preference	Income and housing	Industry specific	Local	Monetary aggregates	International	National	Regional
					Company information/statistics							Demographic information/statistics				Econometric data			
Metals Week																			
(Chase Econometrics)																			
Million Dollar Directory	•	•	•		•				•										
(Dun's Marketing Services)																			
MMS Currency Market Analysis																			
(Money Market Services, Inc.)																			
MMS Fundamental Analysis																			
(Money Market Services, Inc.)																			
MMS Technical Research																			
(Money Market Services, Inc.)																			
MoneyCenter																			
(Knight-Ridder Financial Information)																			
MoneyData																			
(Technical Data Corp.)																			
Money Market Price Quotation Service																			
(Bridge Data Co.)																			

	Industry information/statistics							Real-time/Historic market quotations									News services				Research reports/evaluations					
Business intelligence	Emerging technologies	Industry leadership changes	Industry overviews	Legal actions and issues	Market news and forecasts	Product developments	Spot prices	Bonds, notes and bills	Futures	Currencies	Money rates	Mortgage backed securities	Options	Stocks, mutual funds, warrants, and rights	Municipals	Local	National	Regional	International	Newsletter	Company	Industry	Products	Fixed income	Capital markets	Trading/Brokerage services
							•			•																
										•																
											•															
							•	•	•			•	•													
							•	•	•	•	•		•	•			•	•	•			•		•		
							•			•										•		•				
								•		•							•									

PRODUCTS BY SUBJECT COVERAGE MATRIX

	Annual reports	Company background	Forecasts	Insider trading	Lines of business	Market activity	Monthly reports	Officers/Directors	Quarterly reports	SEC filings	Stockholder information	Consumer preference	Income and housing	Industry specific	Local	Monetary aggregates	International	National	Regional
Company information/statistics												**Demographic information/statistics**				**Econometric data**			
Money Market Rates																			
(I.P. Sharp Assoc. Ltd.)																			
Munibase																			
(Kenny Information Systems)																			
NAARS	●																		
(American Institute of Certified Public Accountants)																			
National Newspaper Index																			
(Information Access Co.)																			
New Product Announcements (NPA)																			
(Predicasts Inc.)																			
NEWSEARCH																			
(Information Access Co.)																			
News Online																			
(Standard & Poor's Corp.)																			
News Perspectives																			
(Wharton Econometric Forecasting Assoc.)																			

Industry information/statistics							Real-time/Historic market quotations									News services					Research reports/evaluations					
Business intelligence	Emerging technologies	Industry leadership changes	Industry overviews	Legal actions and issues	Market news and forecasts	Product developments	Spot prices	Bonds, notes and bills	Futures	Currencies	Money rates	Mortgage backed securities	Options	Stocks, mutual funds, warrants, and rights	Municipals	Local	National	Regional	International	Newsletter	Company	Industry	Products	Fixed income	Capital markets	Trading/Brokerage services
											•															
															•										•	
				•																						
																•	•	•								
					•	•																				
																•	•	•								
																	•									
																	•		•							

PRODUCTS BY SUBJECT COVERAGE MATRIX

	Annual reports	Company background	Forecasts	Insider trading	Lines of business	Market activity	Monthly reports	Officers/Directors	Quarterly reports	SEC filings	Stockholder information	Consumer preference	Income and housing	Industry specific	Local	Monetary aggregates	International	National	Regional
News Release System (Wharton Econometric Forecasting Assoc.)																			
NEXIS (Mead Data Central, Inc.)																			
North American Stock Market (I.P. Sharp Assoc. Ltd.)																			
PC Bridge (Bridge Data Co.)																			
PETROL (Wharton Econometric Forecasting Assoc.)													●				●	●	
Population Database (SAGE DATA, Inc.)																		●	
Producer Price Index Database (SAGE DATA, Inc.)																		●	
Producer Price Index by Commodity (Chase Econometrics)																		●	

	Industry information/statistics							Real-time/Historic market quotations									News services					Research reports/evaluations					
Business intelligence	Emerging technologies	Industry leadership changes	Industry overviews	Legal actions and issues	Market news and forecasts	Product developments	Spot prices	Bonds, notes and bills	Futures	Currencies	Money rates	Mortgage backed securities	Options	Stocks, mutual funds, warrants, and rights	Municipals	Local	National	Regional	International	Newsletter	Company	Industry	Products	Fixed income	Capital markets	Trading/Brokerage services
																	•									
																•	•	•	•							
														•												
									•				•	•												

PRODUCTS BY SUBJECT COVERAGE MATRIX

	Annual reports	Company background	Forecasts	Insider trading	Lines of business	Market activity	Monthly reports	Officers/Directors	Quarterly reports	SEC filings	Stockholder information	Consumer preference	Income and housing	Industry specific	Local	Monetary aggregates	International	National	Regional
					Company information/ statistics							*Demographic information/ statistics*				*Econometric data*			
PROMT																			
(Predicasts Inc.)																			
QTRMOD																		•	
(Wharton Econometric Forecasting Assoc.)																			
QUOTDIAL																			
(Quotron Systems, Inc.)																			
Real-Time Quotes																			
(Dow Jones News/Retrieval)																			
REGIONAL and COUNTY Database															•				•
(Data Resources, Inc.)																			
Regional Financial Forecast																			•
(Chase Econometrics)																			
Regional Industry Forecast														•					•
(Chase Econometrics)																			
Regional Macro Forecast																			•
(Chase Econometrics)																			

Business intelligence	Emerging technologies	Industry leadership changes	Industry overviews	Legal actions and issues	Market news and forecasts	Product developments	Spot prices	Bonds, notes and bills	Futures	Currencies	Money rates	Mortgage backed securities	Options	Stocks, mutual funds, warrants, and rights	Municipals	Local	National	Regional	International	Newsletter	Company	Industry	Products	Fixed income	Capital markets	Trading/Brokerage services
																	•									
								•	•				•	•												
													•	•												

PRODUCTS BY SUBJECT COVERAGE MATRIX

| | Company information/statistics | | | | | | | | | | | Demographic information/statistics | | | Econometric data | | | |
	Annual reports	Company background	Forecasts	Insider trading	Lines of business	Market activity	Monthly reports	Officers/Directors	Quarterly reports	SEC filings	Stockholder information	Consumer preference	Income and housing	Industry specific	Local	Monetary aggregates	International	National	Regional
Register-Biographical								•											
(Standard & Poor's Corp.)																			
Register-Corporate		•			•			•											
(Standard & Poor's Corp.)																			
Report on Business Corporate Database	•								•										
(Info Globe)																			
Savings and Loan	•								•										
(ADP, Inc. Data Services)																			
SEC Online	•									•	•								
(SEC Online, Inc.)																			
Securities Regulation and Law Report																			
(The Bureau of National Affairs, Inc.)																			
SMSA Macro																			•
(Chase Econometrics)																			
State and SMSA Financial																			•
(Chase Econometrics)																			

	Industry information/statistics							Real-time/Historic market quotations									News services					Research reports/evaluations					
	Business intelligence	Emerging technologies	Industry leadership changes	Industry overviews	Legal actions and issues	Market news and forecasts	Product developments	Spot prices	Bonds, notes and bills	Futures	Currencies	Money rates	Mortgage backed securities	Options	Stocks, mutual funds, warrants, and rights	Municipals	Local	National	Regional	International	Newsletter	Company	Industry	Products	Fixed income	Capital markets	Trading/Brokerage services
			•																								

3

PRODUCTS BY SUBJECT COVERAGE MATRIX

	Annual reports	Company background	Forecasts	Insider trading	Lines of business	Market activity	Monthly reports	Officers/Directors	Quarterly reports	SEC filings	Stockholder information	Consumer preference	Income and housing	Industry specific	Local	Monetary aggregates	International	National	Regional
					Company information/statistics							Demographic information/statistics				Econometric data			
State Macro																			•
(Chase Econometrics)																			
SUPERSITE												•	•						
(CACI Inc.–Federal)																			
Time Series												•	•	•		•	•	•	
(Predicasts Inc.)																			
Toronto Stock Exchange Intra-Day Information for Stocks and Indices																			
(I.P. Sharp Assoc. Ltd.)																			
Toronto Stock Exchange Real-Time Information for Stocks and Indices																			
(I.P. Sharp Assoc. Ltd.)																			
Toronto Stock Exchange 300 Index and Stock Statistics																			
(I.P. Sharp Assoc. Ltd.)																			
Trade & Industry ASAP																			
(Information Access Co.)																			
Trade & Industry Index																			
(Information Access Co.)																			

Business intelligence	Emerging technologies	Industry leadership changes	Industry information/statistics				Real-time/Historic market quotations									News services					Research reports/evaluations					
			Industry overviews	Legal actions and issues	Market news and forecasts	Product developments	Spot prices	Bonds, notes and bills	Futures	Currencies	Money rates	Mortgage backed securities	Options	Stocks, mutual funds, warrants, and rights	Municipals	Local	National	Regional	International	Newsletter	Company	Industry	Products	Fixed income	Capital markets	Trading/Brokerage services
														•												
														•												
														•												
																	•									
																	•									

PRODUCTS BY SUBJECT COVERAGE MATRIX

	Annual reports	Company background	Forecasts	Insider trading	Lines of business	Market activity	Monthly reports	Officers/Directors	Quarterly reports	SEC filings	Stockholder information	Consumer preference	Income and housing	Industry specific	Local	Monetary aggregates	International	National	Regional
		Company information/statistics										Demographic information/statistics			Econometric data				
Tradeline Securities Database																			
(Gregg Corp.)																			
TRADSTAT																			
(SAGE DATA, Inc)																			
Trinet Company Database		●			●	●		●											
(Trinet, Inc.)																			
Trinet Establishment Database		●																	
(Trinet, Inc.)																			
UKFT																			
(Wharton Econometric Forecasting Assoc.)																			
U.S. Corporate News																			
(Moody's Investors Service)																			
U.S. Cost Planning Forecast																		●	
(Chase Econometrics)																			
U.S. Econ	●								●										
(ADP, Inc. Data Services)																			
U.S. Economic Database																		●	
(SAGE DATA, Inc.)																			

	Industry information/statistics							Real-time/Historic market quotations									News services					Research reports/evaluations					
Business intelligence	Emerging technologies	Industry leadership changes	Industry overviews	Legal actions and issues	Market news and forecasts	Product developments	Spot prices	Bonds, notes and bills	Futures	Currencies	Money rates	Mortgage backed securities	Options	Stocks, mutual funds, warrants, and rights	Municipals	Local	National	Regional	International	Newsletter	Company	Industry	Products	Fixed income	Capital markets	Trading/Brokerage services
---	---	---	---	---	---	---	---	---	---	---	---	---	---	---	---	---	---	---	---	---	---	---	---	---	---	---
								•					•	•												
					•																					
							•			•	•			•												
																	•									
		•			•																					

PRODUCTS BY SUBJECT COVERAGE MATRIX

	Annual reports	Company background	Forecasts	Insider trading	Lines of business	Market activity	Monthly reports	Officers/Directors	Quarterly reports	SEC filings	Stockholder information	Consumer preference	Income and housing	Industry specific	Local	Monetary aggregates	International	National	Regional
				Company information/statistics								Demographic information/statistics					Econometric data		
U.S. Macroeconomic																		●	
(Chase Econometrics)																			
U.S. Macroeconomic Forecast																		●	
(Chase Econometrics)																			
United States Bonds																			
(I.P. Sharp Assoc. Ltd.)																			
United States Options																			
(I.P. Sharp Assoc. Ltd.)																			
United States Stock Market																			
(I.P. Sharp Assoc. Ltd.)																			
The Wall Street Journal Highlights Online																			
(Dow Jones News/Retrieval)																			
Washington Financial Reports																			
(The Bureau of National Affairs, Inc.)																			
The Weekly Economic Update																			
(Dow Jones News/Retrieval)																			

Industry information/statistics							Real-time/Historic market quotations									News services					Research reports/evaluations					
Business intelligence	Emerging technologies	Industry leadership changes	Industry overviews	Legal actions and issues	Market news and forecasts	Product developments	Spot prices	Bonds, notes and bills	Futures	Currencies	Money rates	Mortgage backed securities	Options	Stocks, mutual funds, warrants, and rights	Municipals	Local	National	Regional	International	Newsletter	Company	Industry	Products	Fixed income	Capital markets	Trading/Brokerage services
								●																		
													●													
														●												
																	●	●	●							
		●	●																							
																	●									

PRODUCTS BY SUBJECT COVERAGE MATRIX

	Company information/statistics											Demographic information/statistics				Econometric data			
	Annual reports	Company background	Forecasts	Insider trading	Lines of business	Market activity	Monthly reports	Officers/Directors	Quarterly reports	SEC filings	Stockholder information	Consumer preference	Income and housing	Industry specific	Local	Monetary aggregates	International	National	Regional
WEFA																•		•	
(Wharton Econometric Forecasting Assoc.)																			
WEFAAG																		•	•
(Wharton Econometric Forecasting Assoc.)																			
WEFAHF																•		•	•
(Wharton Econometric Forecasting Assoc.)																			
WEXBASE																	•		
(Wharton Econometric Forecasting Assoc.)																			
WLDREI																	•		
(Wharton Econometric Forecasting Assoc.)																			

	Business intelligence	Emerging technologies	Industry leadership changes	Industry overviews	Legal actions and issues	Market news and forecasts	Product developments	Spot prices	Bonds, notes and bills	Futures	Currencies	Money rates	Mortgage backed securities	Options	Stocks, mutual funds, warrants, and rights	Municipals	Local	National	Regional	International	Newsletter	Company	Industry	Products	Fixed income	Capital markets	Trading/Brokerage services
							•																				

Column group labels: Industry information/statistics; Real-time/Historic market quotations; News services; Research reports/evaluations

CHAPTER FOUR

Company and Product Snapshots

COMPANY SNAPSHOTS

These Snapshots are the result of information industry research performed during 1986 and 1987. Thousands of labor-hours have gone into this reference work—hours that usually cannot be spent during the course of an individual search. From an initial list of 350 producers, detailed questionnaires were sent to over 300 companies. Our information specialists analyzed the producer replies, their marketing literature, and technical specifications, and condensed this immense amount of information into Snapshots.

The Methodology, explained earlier in Chapter 3, discusses how the Snapshots are to be used in conjunction with the Matrices. Using the Methodology gets you to a decision point faster and maximizes the effects of your results for your company.

The material contained in the Company Snapshots was obtained directly from the companies as well as from reliable industry sources. From time to time, product or company ownership, as well as product descriptions, may change as the industry matures. **Inclusion in this chapter does not constitute an endorsement by either the authors or the publisher.** We have provided a listing at the end of the Company Snapshots Index of those companies that chose not to answer our questionnaire or provide material for our review.

COMPANY SNAPSHOTS INDEX

Nonresponding Company Name

Global Financial Information, Inc.
Gnostic Concepts, Inc.
Goldman Sachs
GTE Telenet
High Tech Publishing Company
Huntington National Bank
Impact 1040
INFO-MART
Information Intelligence, Inc.
Information Resources
International Marine Banking Co.,
  Ltd.
Isys Corporation
James LymBurner & Sons
KEYCOM Electronic Publishing
Market Information, Inc.
Maryland Center for Public
  Broadcasting
Max Ule & Co., Inc.
National Planning Association
Network Concepts
News-a-tron Corporation

The Newsletter Association
Phillips Publishing, Inc.
Real Estate Information Network,
  Inc.
Reuters, Ltd.
Simmons Market Research Bureau
Specialized Media On-Line
Stewart Data Services
Stock Search, Inc.
Strategic Information
Target, Inc.
Townsend-Greespan & Co., Inc.
TRW Information Services Division
U.S. Census Bureau
U.S. Dept. of Labor
U.S. Dept of Commerce
Value Line, Inc.
Wall Street Transcript
Walsh, Greenwood Information
  Systems, Inc.
Warner Computer Systems, Inc.
Zacks Investment Research, Inc.

ADP, INC. DATA SERVICES

175 Jackson Plaza
Ann Arbor, MI 48106
Telephone: (313) 769-6800
E-Mail: none
Telex: none

COMPANY AT-A-GLANCE

Target Market(s):

Commercial banks
Fortune 1000 corporations
Investment banks
Mortgage banks
Specialized librarians
Thrift institutions

Subject Coverage:

Company information/
statistics
Econometric data
Industry information/
statistics
Real-time/Historic market
quotations
News services

DESCRIPTION

ADP Data Services is a division of Automatic Data Processing, Inc. Founded in 1949, Automatic Data Processing today serves more than 125,000 clients in North America, South America, and Europe through its specialized computing services and its international public data network.

ADP Data Services offers specialized computing and advanced applications programs in planning, business and investment analysis, treasury management, and project management. Its international teleprocessing network links major centers of business and commerce to its three advanced computer centers.

ADP does not charge subscription fees for any of its databases. Rather, pricing is transaction-based, with fixed-price packages available for frequent users. Each database is accessible on a 24-hour basis via ADP Data Services' own network.

DATABASES

Proprietary

Bancall II.   Derived from Federal Reserve Call Reports, Bancall II contains geographical and financial information on FDIC commercial banks, including five years of historical data.

Bancorp.   Derived from Federal Reserve Call Reports, Bancorp contains information on over 2,000 U.S. bank holding companies, including consolidated and parent company financials. It also contains geographic information, stock market data, and predefined analytic ratios.

Fastock II.   Fastock II is a comprehensive online source of historical securities information. Beginning with 1971, it provides daily coverage of 92,000 issues, including common and preferred stocks, warrants and rights, convertible and municipal bonds, corporate debt issues, mutual and money market funds, options, convertible preferreds, and United States Government or agency debt issues and unit trusts. Fastock II also contains 244 market indicators. In addition to ADP's network, users may access Fastock II through the Infomaster gateway.

Insider Trading Data Base.   An online source of corporate insider trading information, Insider Trading Data Base contains the latest data on securities trades made by officers, directors, or owners of 10 percent or more of a publicly held company's stock, as filed with the SEC.

Savings and Loan.   Derived from reports to the Federal Home Loan Bank Board, Savings and Loan contains information dating back to 1977 on federally chartered savings and loan institutions.

U.S. ECON.   U.S. ECON provides consolidated balance sheet information for banks designated by the Federal Reserve Board as "weekly reporting member banks." Updated each week, these consolidated summary Call Reports are compiled by the FRB and made available to U.S. ECON users within hours of their release.

Third Party

COMPUSTAT II. The COMPUSTAT II database contains quarterly and annual financial data, including balance sheets, income statements, statements of change in financial position, operating statistics, and market items, on over 20,000 companies. Compustat II's data are compiled by Standard & Poor's COMPUSTAT Service.

DISCLOSURE II. DISCLOSURE II, which is produced by Disclosure Partners, contains financial and narrative data on public companies extracted from annual and periodic reports filed with the SEC. It includes company names, addresses, phone numbers, officers and directors, subsidiaries, ownership information, management discussions, balance sheets, income statements, and five-year summaries. ADP adds related stock market information and 20 preformatted reports.

ECONALYST. ECONALYST is an online economic forecasting service offered in conjunction with Townsend-Greenspan & Co. Inc.

M&A Database. M&A Database contains over 18,000 transactions on deals since January 1977 for both public and private companies. It contains information on investments abroad and all completed, pending, and unsuccessful tender offer mergers, acquisitions, buyouts, and divestitures valued at $1 million or more that have occurred since January 1979.

PROMT. A vast collection of information on industry and market trends, PROMT is a leading supplier of current news on over 100,000 public and private companies, including banks and related financial institutions. Compiled by Predicasts, Inc., PROMT contents span the past four years and provide concise summaries of almost 400,000 articles from over 1,500 periodicals.

VALUE-ADDED PRODUCTS AND SERVICES

Customer Support

Through a local ADP representative, users receive complete training, documentation, custom development, and ongoing support.

Users can also call ADP's Data Hotline for help with special needs or to obtain current information on data updates, additions, or revisions. Customer assistance is available from 8 A.M. to 5 P.M. (EST), Monday through Friday. Also, Infomaster's SOS service is available 24 hours a day for those users who connect to Fastock II via gateway access.

Documentation

The *ADP Information Edge* is a bimonthly client newsletter designed to help ADP database users become more informed and productive. Additional documentation is available according to customer needs through ADP representatives. Users may also take advantage of online help available on ADP databases.

System Features/Software Packages

TSAM II is ADP's powerful time series analysis and modeling language. It allows users to combine data from the ADP databases with advanced tools for forecasting, reporting, and graphing interest rates and loan demand.

DATAPATH is a data-access system enabling users to quickly and easily download information from ADP's central systems to their PCs. It then makes it easy for users to integrate this data with Lotus Development Corporation's 1-2-3 spreadsheet, graphics, and data management programs.

ADP's SCREEN feature allows users to easily access the information they need based on a set of specified criteria. This program provides standard mathematical functions as well as flexible formats so users can quickly analyze financial performance, growth rate, sales volume, and other data. SCREEN also allows users to construct their own ratios. Precalculated ratios are available as well. To facilitate reporting, ADP has preformatted more than 10 reports for those data items users most frequently choose to examine. These include:

Company Profile
Description of Business and Segment Information
Annual Balance Sheet
Annual Income Statement
Quarterly Income Statement

Five-Year Financial Summary
SEC Filings and Exhibits
Director and Officer Information
Ownership Information and Company Subsidiaries
Stock Market Information
Auditor Information, Comments, and Corporate Events
Management Discussion

Online Communication

ADP provides users with general interest bulletin boards.

Research Services

If ADP does not already have online the publicly held data subset a client needs, it will obtain the necessary information and install it on the system for a fee. Additionally, ADP customer support includes a search service to provide special reports for users.

4

AMERICAN BANKER

1 State Street Plaza
New York, NY 10004
Telephone: (212) 943-4846
Telex: 129233

COMPANY AT-A-GLANCE

Target Market(s):

Commercial banks
Credit unions
Government agencies
Investment banks
Mortgage banks
Specialized librarians
Thrift institutions

Subject Coverage:

Industry information/
  statistics
News services

DESCRIPTION

The American Banker is a subsidiary of the International Thomson Organisation, Inc., a publisher and information producer based in the United States. The parent company, International Thomson Organisation Limited, is a leader internationally in the publishing and electronic information industries, with strong additional interests in leisure travel and natural resources.

The American subsidiary is divided into four groups: International Thomson Professional Publishing, International Thomson Business Press, International Thomson Publishing, and International Financial Networks, or InFiNet. The American Banker is a member of the InFiNet group, as is a companion company, The Bond Buyer.

The American Banker has three online databases: The Bond Buyer, American Banker, and American Banker News Service. These databases are marketed via direct mail, space advertising, conferences, and personal presentations. The major subscribers to all three databases are banks and related service companies.

Subscribers access the databases through private networks. Access to The Bond Buyer and the American Banker is provided either through DIALOG or NEXIS (Mead Data Central). User access to American Banker News Service is via BRS or NewsNet. The subscribers of all databases are billed on a monthly basis.

DATABASES

Proprietary

American Banker.   The American Banker, which also spans the time from 1981 to the present, contains the complete text of the daily financial services newspaper of the same name. It provides users with banking industry information updated within 24 hours of publication of the newspaper.

Industry coverage focuses on federal and state banking regulations and legislation, plus all phases of domestic banking, including commercial, investment, and trust banking; mortgage lending; thrift institutions; and credit card operations.

American Banker News Service.   Launched in 1983, the American Banker News Service is a daily news provider for the financial industry. It contains key stories from the preceding five days' activity in the financial services industry, available by 6 A.M. (EST) each news day. Both full text and highlights of major stories from *American Banker* are provided, as well as executive personnel changes and a calendar of events.

The Bond Buyer.   The Bond Buyer, which spans the time from 1981 to the present, provides the complete text, with the exception of stories credited to other news services, of the printed daily newspaper of the same name. It contains municipal bond information updated within 24 hours of the publication of the newspaper.

The Bond Buyer contains the most complete record available of actual borrowing by municipal authorities. Detailed articles address such topics as federal laws and regulations affecting tax-exempt financing, IRS rulings, Treasury Department borrowings, and the general economy. Every aspect of the municipal bond market, including data on planned bond issues and information on the results of bond sales, is covered.

VALUE-ADDED PRODUCTS AND SERVICES

Customer Support

Customer service is provided for all three databases Monday through Friday, from 9 A.M. to 5 P.M. (EST). Additional support is available according to the customer service schedules of individual vendors. User training is provided through exhibits at conferences and training workshops in large cities.

Documentation

Both the American Banker and The Bond Buyer have hard copy counterparts for which annual subscriptions may be arranged. Online retrieval instructions and examples are available, at varying levels of detail, from the various vendors that supply each database. ONLINE COMMUNICATION users accessing The Bond Buyer or the American Banker via DIALOG may take advantage of DIALOG's electronic mail service, DIALMAIL, at an additional cost.

Online Communication

Users accessing The Bond Buyer or the American Banker via DIALOG may take advantage of DIALOG's electronic mail service, DIALMAIL, at an additional cost.

**AMERICAN INSTITUTE
OF CERTIFIED PUBLIC
ACCOUNTANTS**

1211 Avenue of the Americas
New York, NY 10036-8775
Telephone: (212) 575-6326
  (213) 453-6194 (Local)
  (800) 352-6689 (California)
  (800) 421-7229 (National)
Telecopier: (212) 575-3846
Telex: 70-3396

COMPANY AT-A-GLANCE

Target Market(s):

Commercial banks
Credit unions
Fortune 1000 corporations
Government agencies
Investment banks
Law firms
Mortgage banks
Real estate firms
Specialized librarians
Thrift institutions

Subject Coverage:

Company information/
  statistics
Industry information/
  statistics

DESCRIPTION

The American Institute of Certified Public Accountants (AICPA) is a nonprofit organization founded in 1887 as a professional association of accountants. Its goals include establishing auditing and reporting standards, influencing accounting standards, developing and monitoring the national uniform CPA examination, researching issues pertinent to the accounting profession, and educating its members.

AICPA members number approximately 230,000. From these ranks, committees are created that study accounting, auditing, federal taxation, computer services, and other topics of interest to the general membership.

DATABASES

Proprietary

Accountants Data Base.   Accountants is a bibliographic database providing access to worldwide English-language literature on accounting, auditing, data processing, financial management, investments and securities, management and taxation, and special businesses and industries. This database corresponds to the hard-copy *Accountants' Index.* Accountants is available through Orbit Information Technologies (formerly SDC) and Infomaster.

NAARS.   Codeveloped with Mead Data Central, the National Auto-mated Accounting Research System, or NAARS, currently includes detailed financial information contained in over 8,000 published annual reports to shareholders. It also includes the vast body of offi-cial accounting and auditing literature that has a bearing on current financial reporting practices.

VALUE-ADDED PRODUCTS AND SERVICES

Customer Support

Accountants search assistance is available via the Orbit Hotline ((800) 421-7229) from 8 A.M. to 6:30 P.M. (EST), Monday through Friday. Infomaster provides both online textual help and 24-hour online human assistance.

Documentation (*see also* Research Services)

The AICPA publishes an extensive line of guides and indexes, thereby providing the practitioner with guidelines, standards, and auditing and reporting information on all aspects of business activity.

Of direct pertinence to online searching in the Accoun-tants database is the *Accountants' Index,* the printed counterpart to the online database. *Accountants' Index* facilitates retrieval of accounting and related business materials by telling where, and when, accounting and related topics have been addressed in print.

It is published annually and supplemented quarterly. An addi-tional reference source, *Accountants' Index Master List of Subject Headings,* provides a complete alphabetical list of subject terms used in preparing the *Accountants' Index.* This master list is of value to accounting firms, corporations, government agencies, and universities—virtually anywhere the online index is being utilized. A discount on the *Accountants' Index Master List of Sub-ject Headings* is available to AICPA members.

The Orbit *Accountants User Manual* is available from Orbit Information Technologies for a fee. This manual contains an overview of the database sample records, a description of record categories, sample searches, and a directory of journal and book publishers for items included in the database.

Research Services

Many AICPA publications consist of study and monitoring of accounting and related fields. For example, *New Guides for the Professional Accountant* examines some of the major challenges facing the accountant.

The *Industry Audit and Accounting Guides* provide background information as well as guidelines for auditing and reporting on specific industries. Discounts on these guides are offered to AICPA members.

Other printed material available from the AICPA includes *Digest of State Accountancy Laws and State Board Regulations, Compliance with Federal Election Campaign Requirements: A Guide for Candidates,* and a host of *AICPA Audit and Accounting Guides.* All AICPA members receive a discount on the guidebooks.

Document Formatting and Delivery

AICPA members and special libraries' staff may borrow items listed in the Accountants' database from the AICPA Library. A photocopy service is available via Infomaster.

4

**BANK MARKETING
    ASSOCIATION**
309 West Washington
Chicago, IL 60606
Telephone: (312) 782-1442
    (800) 433-9013
E-Mail: 9102212897 BKMRKTGAS
    CGO
Alanet: BMA.FINIS

COMPANY AT-A-GLANCE

Target Market(s):

Commercial banks
Credit unions
Investment banks
Law firms
Mortgage banks
Real estate firms
Thrift institutions

Subject Coverage:

Industry information/
    statistics
Newsletters
Research reports/
    evaluations

DESCRIPTION

The Bank Marketing Association (BMA) is a not-for-profit affiliate of the American Bankers Association. It is dedicated to providing marketing education, information, and services to the financial services industry.

The BMA has a staff of 65 full-time employees serving the bank marketing areas of advertising, public relations, community banks, research and planning, electronic banking, and others.

DATABASES

Proprietary

FINIS (Financial Industry Information Service). A product of the Information Center of the Bank Marketing Association, FINIS contains more than 35,000 entries providing information on the financial services industry. Every month more than 1,000 articles, books, case studies, and sample brochures are identified, summarized, and made available online in the form of bibliographic citations and abstracts. FINIS is available through DIALOG and Mead Data Central.

VALUE-ADDED PRODUCTS AND SERVICES

Customer Support

In addition to its headquarters in Chicago, the BMA has 21 active local and regional chapters across the United States. These organizations assist marketers in tailoring programs to their specific locales.

FINIS provides toll-free customer assistance ((800) 433-9013) through which customers may receive search assistance. Assistance is also available from individual vendors.

A schedule of FINIS training seminars is available upon request. Training may also be arranged for individual financial institutions and other organizations. The BMA hosts conferences, seminars, and workshops on a variety of financial services marketing topics. It also makes available a number of audiovisual training programs on a wide range of topics that are equally suitable for use alone or for incorporation into in-house presentations. Audiocassette programs provide edited presentations of BMA workshops and seminars.

BMA hosts an annual convention each fall. This three-day program features up to seventy different workshops, round-table discussions, and general sessions featuring leading practitioners in the financial services marketing field.

Finally, the BMA conducts six professional schools for both seasoned practitioners and inexperienced marketers. These courses focus on the growth and enhancement of individual marketing and management skills.

Documentation (*see also* Research Services)

A number of search aids are available for FINIS users. The *Thesaurus of Financial Services Marketing Terms* is a controlled vocabulary that allows precise searching of FINIS. The *FINIS Users Manual* is an instructional guide to searching FINIS. A quarterly *FINIS Newsletter* provides users with searching hints, announcements, and exhibit schedules.

BMA also publishes the following specialized newsletters:

Community Bank Marketing—for banks with less than $250 million in assets;

Resource—for trust and financial service marketing professionals;

Information Center Newsletter—for members interested in materials available from the Bank Information Center;

Marketing Update—a monthly, members-only publication that provides timely analysis of "hot topics" of interest to financial marketers.

Additional BMA documentation includes an annual *Membership Directory,* which includes a "Service Member" section that describes the services of outside suppliers.

Online Communication

Two electronic mail services, DIALMAIL and ITT DIALCOM, allow subscribers to send correspondence to BMA staff 24 hours a day.

Research Services

BMA publishes a wide range of documents that study the financial services marketing industry as a whole. BMA's monthly magazine, *Bank Marketing,* monitors trends, provides insights into the latest service innovations, and outlines successful marketing programs through practitioner- and consultant-authored articles.

Another publication, *Action Gram,* informs marketers of changes in legislation and regulations that affect financial services marketing. Regularly published monographs give marketers an in-depth look at current issues.

Comprehensive research services and database searching are available from BMA's Information Center. One of the services BMA offers its clients is, in fact, the use of its Information Center. The Center is located at BMA's headquarters in Chicago and is staffed by business information specialists. They provide:

Research services using the association's resource collection and database.

Database services using a subscription base of nearly 200 external online databases, in addition to direct access to FINIS.

Three-week loan periods for the latest financial marketing books, reports, and thesis, plus interlibrary loan service.

If an organization is an American Banking Association dues-paying member, individuals within that organization may become BMA members for $150 each per year. They would then receive all BMA benefits. Otherwise, there is an hourly research fee. All Information Center users are charged nominal fees to cover costs of photocopying, customized online searching, bibliographies, and shipping. Deposit accounts may be opened with the Center.

Document Formatting and Delivery

Full-text articles may be ordered by telephone, mail, or electronic mail. Rush service is available for both research services and document delivery requests.

4

BRIDGE DATA COMPANY
10050 Manchester Road
St. Louis, MO 63112
Telephone: (314) 821-5660
E-Mail: none
Telex: none

COMPANY AT-A-GLANCE

Target Market(s):

Commercial banks
Investment banks
Mortgage banks

Subject Coverage:

Real-time/Historic market
  quotations
News services

DESCRIPTION

Bridge Data Company is a publicly held company founded in 1974. Bridge is a vendor of real-time, last sale, and quote information on all listed and unlisted stocks, options, futures, and bonds. Bridge also provides technical analysis capabilities on most securities by way of a historic price and volume database in which information is stored for up to 10 years. This real-time and historic data are available in a variety of display formats.

Bridge also supplies extensive real-time and historic information on the market as a whole. Market information is stored in the form of indicators and indexes, thus enabling Bridge users to gauge the performance of the market or specific market segments.

DATABASES

Proprietary

Bridge Information System.   The Bridge Information System supplies information on over 30,000 listed and OTC stocks, financial futures, commodities, foreign securities, and all listed options to individual investors, stockbrokers, and traders.

Futures Price Quotation Service.   Continuous access to the Futures Price database is available via dedicated phone lines and/or satellite connection to Bridge Market Data's central processing system in St. Louis. This database is updated continuously to reflect commodity exchange activity, including the American Gold Coin Exchange, Chicago Board of Trade, Commodity Exchange Center, and New York Futures Exchange. Features include quotations, inquiries, graphics, and news.

Money Market Price Quotation Service. This is an information service providing prices and yields on domestic and international money market instruments and fixed-income securities, spot and forward foreign exchange quotations, and financial futures prices. The information is continuously updated throughout the trading day. A financial news wire is also offered as part of the service.

PC Bridge. Developed jointly by Bridge Data Company and PC Quote, Inc., PC Bridge delivers real-time and historical market data via satellite and land lines to customers with IBM PC/ATs. Users may access an automatic-updating market watch of 100 securities, plus the Bridge Information System for charts, technical data, and other historical and real-time information. PC Bridge, designed for multiterminal installations, was developed with the information needs of the trader in mind.

Third Party

Dow Jones News/Retrieval. This service provides access to displays of current financial news, as well as news on related topics and news recall for up to three months. Special authorization and payment of fees to Dow Jones are required before this service can be accessed.

VALUE-ADDED PRODUCTS AND SERVICES

Customer Support

Customer support is available 24 hours a day, seven days a week. Bridge also provides user training sessions.

Documentation

The Look-Up provides an online list of company names, parameter codes and headings, explanations of relevant terms, and general information.

Documentation for every display, be it the Price-Volume Chart or the Market Summary, is similarly organized, though unique sectors are added as needed. Further documentation is available in the form of user manuals and newsletters.

System Features/Software Packages

The Bridge Speech System enables customers using a tone-dial telephone to obtain real-time prices and quotes on any of over 30,000 securities on the Bridge Information System. Requests must be keyed into a telephone keypad. A computer-generated voice responds with the requested information. Users may also obtain information on their own portfolio of stocks.

Bridge Market Watch enables users, at one time and on one screen, to monitor trades as they occur on up to 60 stocks, options, futures, bonds, and indexes.

SUPERTICKER allows clients, through special network interface hardware, to receive instantaneous market quotations from all the major markets. Price quotes received via SUPERTICKER may be retransmitted to third parties under license from Bridge Market Data. Exchange approval is also required.

In order to make it easier for users to enter lengthy, frequently used requests, Bridge created the Canned Command program. This facility allows users to abbreviate, or "can," their requests.

Bridge Interface Language (BIN) permits direct customer access to Bridge databases and data downloading to customer-operated computers. This special capability was designed for experienced programmers.

Finally, the Bridge Terminal Emulation diskette is available to customers with IBM PC and PC-compatible, and Apple II series computers.

Online Communication

Bridge's electronic mail service enables users to communicate instantaneously with people throughout the United States, Australia, the United Kingdom, and anywhere else there is a Bridge hardwired customer. Bridge also features general interest bulletin boards for user-to-user communication.

BUNKER RAMO CORPORATION
35 Nutmeg Drive
Trumbull, CT 06609
Telephone: (203) 386-2700
  (203) 386-2000
  (609) 235-7300
Telex: none

COMPANY AT-A-GLANCE

Target Market(s):

  Commercial banks
  Fortune 1000 corporations
  Investment banks
  Mortgage banks
  Thrift institutions

Subject Coverage:

  Company information/
   statistics
  Industry information/
   statistics
  Real-time/Historic market
   quotations
  News services
  Research reports/
   evaluations

DESCRIPTION

Bunker Ramo, recently acquired by ADP Financial Services, has specialized in the design and operation of information systems and communications networks for the financial community since 1928. Bunker Ramo's nationwide Market Decision System (MDS) network supplies service to over 30,000 brokerage professionals. The information and communications services provided by MDS are delivered to the MDS-7 family of office products over high-speed communications lines. The MDS network provides a comprehensive set of quotation, news, database, and communication services to MDS-7 users.

DATABASES

Proprietary

Brokerage Information Data Base.   Bunker Ramo's Brokerage Information Data Base is billed as one of the world's largest summaries of financial market data available to the investment community. It contains trading information on stocks, warrants, rights, bonds, notes, bills, commodities, futures, options, gold and silver, and indexes. The database covers all U.S. stock, bond, options, and commodities exchanges, all Canadian stock and options exchanges, as well as several European exchanges. This securities database, currently containing over 40,000 financial instruments, is continually updated and expanded.

Third Party

ARGUS Research.   ARGUS Research provides a continuously updated database on approximately 450 leading listed and over-the-counter corporations. It contains a variety of investment advisory information prepared by the security analysts of Argus Research Corporation of New York. In addition to a two-page commentary on all companies covered by ARGUS, the database provides lists of buy recommendations, economic forecasts, industry commentary, daily hot pages, and other information of particular interest to investors.

Dow Jones News/Recall.   Dow Jones News/Recall contains news items covering approximately 6,000 listed and over-the-counter companies.   Headlines and news items are maintained for up to three months in the News/Recall database. In addition, the database includes items that the Dow Jones editors consider appropriate from the daily publication of *The Wall Street Journal* as well as from *Barron's.*

Moody's Electronic Fact Sheet.   Moody's Electronic Fact Sheet provides historical financial and business information, recent developments, and the future outlook on more than 4,000 companies listed on the NYSE, AMEX, NASDAQ, and regional stock exchanges.   For each company listed, Moody provides information on interim earnings, interim dividends, recent developments, future prospects, annual earnings and dividend data, business information, corporate bond information, and company news reports.

S&P MarketScope.   The online database, S&P MarketScope, is prepared by Standard & Poor's Corporation. The database provides authoritative financial information, analysis, and investment guidance for the business, financial, and marketing communities, as well as for individual investors.

S&P MarketScope user services include: Text Page, providing descriptions of operations of over 4,600 companies; Statistical Page, providing current and historical data on over 4,600 companies; Market Commentary; MarketMovers, providing rationale for volatile stock issues of the day; Stock(s) in the News; Today's Interest Rates; Investment Ideas; Technical Selections; Industry Group Action; Earnings per share Forecasts; EconomyWatch; Economic Calendar/Forecast; MoneyWatch; and Stock Index Futures.

VALUE-ADDED PRODUCTS AND SERVICES

Customer Support

Bunker Ramo provides system support to help subcribers with technical requests. Special services are defined according to the stated customer requirements and problems.

Bunker Ramo's Operations Control System tracks the up-to-the-minute status of every user problem. The Operations Control System works through a dispatcher who insures that the most appropriate engineer is assigned to handle a given assignment.

Documentation

With the touch of a single key, users can get on-screen assistance in the form of system instructions and tutorials. Once the "Help" screen is displayed, a single keystroke returns users to the point from which they sought assistance. Bunker Ramo and its third party database suppliers also provide printed manuals to assist users in data retrieval.

System Features/Software Packages

The MDS product family display format includes features ranging from comprehensive quote displays and stock watches to montages/class displays, market data, time and sales, and historical information. In addition, access to a portfolio management system is available.

The MDS system network provides current data on stocks, bonds, options, mutual funds, commodities, index futures, and currencies, as well as news on corporations, industries, and the government. In addition, access to several third party research and advisory databases is provided to supplement in-house research information.

SuperNet, Bunker Ramo's brokerage information communications network, provides a range of services, from data transfer to access to its IBM PC-based brokerage automation system, Top-Broker. This shared network supports interactive communication with multiple host computers. Subscribers can access TopBroker, a portfolio management system providing complete broker support that can help registered representatives become more responsive to their clients. TopBroker performs functions such as automated broker book, automated pricing, portfolio valuation, and account or security inquiries. The major functions of TopBroker include client tracking, inquiries, portfolio reporting, and financial modeling. These functions can be customized to fit the needs of a particular broker.

Another Bunker Ramo system feature is the capability for stock exchange and news wire ticker services to be displayed on user's terminals. The ticker service is processed for display at the user's location by the MDS office controller, according to the user's needs.

THE BUREAU OF NATIONAL AFFAIRS, INC.

1231 25th Street NW
Washington, DC 20037
Telephone: (800) 862-4636
E-Mail: none
Telex: none

COMPANY AT-A-GLANCE

Target Market(s):

Commercial banks
Credit unions
Fortune 1000 corporations
Government agencies
Investment banks
Law firms
Mortgage banks
Real estate firms
Specialized librarians
Thrift institutions

Subject Coverage:

Industry information/
 statistics
News services

DESCRIPTION

The Bureau of National Affairs, Inc., begun in 1929, strives to meet the information needs of professionals in the legal, labor, business and economic, environmental safety, and tax fields. It has national and international networks of correspondents gathering information and wiring it to the BNA offices in Washington, D.C. where it is organized and analyzed and printed in hard copy and online.

BNA Online is the electronic publishing division of the Bureau of National Affairs, Inc. Its online information products have been designed with two purposes in mind—research and current notification.

Its notification products provide electronic versions of BNA's print publications such as the *Daily Report for Executives* or the *Daily Tax Report.* In other cases, they provide summaries of congressional actions, IRS Private Letter Rulings, and the SEC *News Digest.* Its research products allow the user access to information on patents, labor law, energy, chemical regulations, international trade, and more.

The Bureau of National Affairs' databases are available through five online systems. These five are: LEXIS/NEXIS of Mead Data Central, ITT DIALCOM, DIALOG, Human Resource Information Network (HRIN), and Pergamon-InfoLine.

DATABASES

Proprietary

AdvanceLine. This is the electronic information service of the Bureau of National Affairs and is available through ITT-Dialcom. AdvanceLine is a collection of seven of BNA's databases providing notification of legal, legislative, and regulatory developments in the areas of business, finance, taxation, labor, and securities. These databases are Daily Washington Advance, Daily Tax Advance, Private Letter Rulings, Daily Congressional and Presidential Calendar, Daily Labor Advance, Daily SEC Advance, and Securities Law Advance.

BNE Executive Day. BNA Executive Day is an electronic news magazine containing information on governmental, economic, and financial developments; tax breaks and liabilities; labor relations; and USDA; nontax monetary issues; health care; management concerns; and women's issues. The BNA Executive Day database covers topics involving the economy, business, taxes, labor, management, women, and agriculture. The database is updated every day, and users can obtain up to a week's coverage online.

Daily Report for Executives. Daily Report for Executives covers judicial, regulatory, and legislative activity in areas that affect business. These areas include taxation and accounting, securities regulation, export and import regulations, energy development and regulation, product liability, federal grants and contracts, environmental controls, international finance, farm legislation, and the federal budget. The database also includes statistical and economic data such as information on employment, prices, construction, and other economic indicators. The database is updated on a daily basis.

Daily Washington Advance. The Daily Washington Advance covers judicial, regulatory, and legislative activity in areas that affect business. These areas include import and export regulation, international finance, energy development and regulation, product liability, federal grants and contracts, farm legislation, environmental controls, and the federal budget. The database also contains economic data on employment, prices, industrial production, construction, and other economic indicators.

Securities Regulation and Law Report. The Securities Regulation and Law Report provides information on securities and commodities activity from January 1982 to present day. The database contains information on both the state and federal levels. It includes information on the SEC, securities regulation, the stock market, commodities regulations, and securities.

Washington Financial Reports. Washington Financial Reports contains information on and analysis of financial institutions, regulatory policy, litigation, banking legislation, and investment. Agencies reported on include the Federal Reserve Board, the Federal Deposit Insurance Corporation, the Comptroller of the Currency, the Federal Home Loan Bank Board, the National Credit Union Administration, and the Federal Savings and Loan Corporation.

VALUE-ADDED PRODUCTS AND SERVICES

Customer Support

User training is provided through workshops at conventions and training sessions in major cities as well as through the database vendors.

The Bureau of National Affairs offers BNA Online Help Desk for assistance and information on any BNA database. This hotline is available from 8 A.M. to 5:30 P.M. (EST), Monday through Friday. The numbers of the hotline are: (800) 862-4636 and (202) 452-4132 in Washington, D.C. Online help is provided through the vendors of each database.

Documentation

The Bureau of National Affairs offers search guides, user manuals, and quick reference guides to assist users of the databases.

BNA Online publishes a newsletter every other month. Special editions of the newsletter are printed to notify users of upcoming conventions and workshops.

Research Services

BNA Plus services include a research team for such customized services as analysis of issues and trends, collecting and summarizing data, profiling collective bargaining agreements and labor/management reports, tracking issues, and locating and delivering documents.

Document Formatting and Delivery (*see* Research Services)

**BUSINESS RESEARCH
CORPORATION**

12 Farnsworth Street
Boston, MA 02210
Telephone: (617) 350-4044
 (800) 662-7878
E-Mail: none
Telex: 466199

DESCRIPTION

Business Research Corporation (BRC), recently acquired by International Thomson (Toronto), was founded in 1976. The primary function of the firm is to produce and market its Investext database. The Boston-based firm has also designed and produced the Harvard Business Review Database, the Industry Data Sources Database, and the Arthur D. Little Decision Resource Database.

DATABASE

Proprietary

INVESTEXT. INVESTEXT is a full-text database containing company and industry research reports produced by leading domestic investment banking firms (Wall Street and regional) as well as by financial research organizations in major industrial countries worldwide. Updates are loaded on a weekly basis. INVESTEXT is accessible via DIALOG, NewsNet, BRS, The Source, Data-Star, Dow-Jones News Retrieval, and Business Research Corporation's private network. Volume/usage discounts are available.

VALUE-ADDED PRODUCTS AND SERVICES

Customer Support

Business Research Corporation offers day-long training seminars to teach users how to answer even the most challenging queries by uncovering online otherwise elusive company, industry, and product data. A detailed workbook and two hour-long online search sessions are included in the fee. Users who have attended training sessions are welcome to attend sessions again, free of charge. Seminars are scheduled regularly for cities throughout the nation. Additionally, a toll-free number ((800) 662-7878) is available for ongoing customer support.

Documentation

A comprehensive user manual is available from BRC. It provides detailed, easy-to-follow search suggestions and strategies aimed at specific user applications, plus instructions on how to communicate using a variety of terminals and modems. Additionally, the manual is designed to serve as a dictionary and search thesaurus. Its appendixes provide INVESTEXT's subject- and product-controlled vocabularies and a listing of the 7,000+ companies, with their respective ticker symbols, and the 50+ industry groups covered in the database.

A loose-leaf guide to INVESTEXT is available to users who access via DIALOG. Complete access and search instructions are provided, including full descriptions of all search fields, ticker symbols, subject descriptors, and a product thesaurus of over 1,000 terms.

INVESTEXT Quicksearch is available free upon request. It is a basic start-up guide to using INVESTEXT in menu-driven format. *Quicksearch* contains valuable tips and step-by-step instructions on some of the most common search functions (finding company information, retrieving full reports, and so on). It is a helpful aide to effective use of INVESTEXT.

INVESTEXT NEWS is a newsletter available to all INVESTEXT users. It covers such topics as new brokerage firms added to the database, recent enhancements, and any information on the database that is considered important to the INVESTEXT user.

Finally, *New Research Reports,* a biweekly listing of selected new company and industry research reports recently added to INVESTEXT, is available to users. These reports provide detailed financial and market analyses of both domestic and foreign companies and over 50 industry groups. The reports are designed to help the INVESTEXT user keep track of more than 150,000 pages of investment banking research prepared by professional analysts each year.

System Features/Software Packages

BRC offers downloading capability.

INVESTEXT/Plus is a new version of BRC's own search software designed for the novice user. It offers menu-based searching along with full-text searching on a limited basis.

Online Communication

BRC offers electronic mail service.

Selective Dissemination of Information (SDI) Services

A weekly alert titled *Competitive Tracking Service* is available to users. It advises subscribers of new analysts' reports available on specific companies and industries they have chosen to follow. The alert includes report titles and numbers, publication dates, and report length. Subscribers may track up to 10 companies and 2 industries.

Another BRC service, *INVESTEXT Monitor*, provides the user with the same investment banking research data found in the INVESTEXT database, but with the added feature that subscribers receive only those reports that cover the companies and industries they have chosen to follow.

Document Formatting and Delivery

Offline photocopies are available via BRC and a number of the vendors through which INVESTEXT is available.

CACI INC.–FEDERAL
1815 North Fort Meyer Drive
Arlington, VA 22209
Telephone: (703) 841-4760
 (Virginia)
 (800) 292-2224 ext.
 ONLINE
Telex: 814429

COMPANY AT-A-GLANCE

Target Market(s):

Commercial banks
Credit unions
Fortune 1000 corporations
Government agencies
Investment banks
Real estate firms
Specialized librarians
Thrift institutions

Subject Coverage:

Demographic information/
 statistics

DESCRIPTION

CACI Inc., a publicly held company traded OTC under the symbol CACI, has been a registered clearinghouse for census data services since 1972. CACI has the world's largest up-to-date databases of demographic and buying power facts and forecasts.

To maintain the currency of these databases, CACI has established a Board of Demographers, comprised of full-time staff demographers who formulate CACI's Update Methodology (updating current estimates and five-year projections of the composition of all areas of the United States) and oversee its implementation.

CACI updates its databases every year using census tracts (66,000) and/or demographic models of population and composition changes. CACI pioneered the development of a sales potential system that measures consumer spending power for any area, of any size or shape, anywhere in the United States. To develop and update this system, CACI gathers data on consumption patterns, purchasing power, and changes in consumer behavior. Key sources of data are the *Consumer Expenditure Survey,* the *Survey of Consumer Credit,* the *Commerce Department Monthly Retail Sales Reports,* FDIC, FSLIC, and other published market research studies.

Subscribers access the databases through several national time-sharing networks: Compuserve Incorporated, Comshare Incorporated, and Chase Econometrics. Any terminal or PC with a modem (300 baud or 1200 baud) can be used to access any of the three databases. All three databases are available 24 hours a day, seven days a week.

CACI's databases can be linked with a number of other databases and surveys to make them even more powerful. These include Accountline, a financial services usage survey; On-Line Research, a database of all property owners and mortgage holders in California; Strategic Locations Planning, which provides Atlas mapping; Mediamark Research, Inc., a media and product consumption survey; Geographic Data Technology, a provider of digitized computer mapping; Scarborough Syndicated Research Associates, a provider of media audience profiling; National Business Lists, a provider of lists of U.S. businesses; NFO Research, a marketing survey; Values and Lifestyles Program, a Values and Lifestyles Analysis; Communications Data Services, a provider of subscription lists; Market Facts, a network of custom and panel surveys; and several mailing list databases including Metromail, Urban Data Processing, American Info Network, and Direct Marketing Group, Incorporated.

DATABASES

Proprietary

ACORN. ACORN (A Classification Of Residential Neighborhoods) was first published in 1978. Its purpose is to provide socioeconomic and demographic housing information that can be used in market research and customer targeting. The demographic information in ACORN is based on data from the 1980 Census of Population and Housing.

DORIS. The Demographic Online Retrieval Information System gives access to CACI's Instant Demographics database of demographic and buying power facts and forecasts. DORIS allows the retrieval and manipulation of any of over 16 million data items on demographics, market segmentation, market research, and financial services potential. Users can create their own customized reports, select their own demographic variables for market research, and obtain lists of areas with specific characteristics.

SUPERSITE. First published in 1973, SUPERSITE contains over a million records of information on demographics, market research, market segmentation, and financial services potential. The database provides updates and forecasts that include historical, current, and projected data for site of interest.

VALUE-ADDED PRODUCTS AND SERVICES

Customer Support

Through the SITELINE call-in service, users can call a toll-free 800 number and request reports for areas of any size throughout the country. Orders are mailed within 24 hours and can be sent via Federal Express or Zap Mail. Report charges vary between $55 and $185; the average report cost is $85.

System support is provided by the time-sharing companies and their representatives. Questions can be directed to CACI at (800) 292-2224 from 8 A.M. to 6 P.M. (EST), Monday through Friday. CACI also provides training to its customers.

Documentation

The *Sourcebook* is a compilation of the most frequently requested statistics listed for all zip codes in the United States. The current cost of the annually issued *Sourcebook* is $295; it is also available on magnetic tape for $3,200.

Diskettes contain the most frequently requested statistics for all zip codes or all census tracts in a state, SMA, or ADI. The diskettes are available for all states, including Washington, D.C., all SMSA's, and all ADI's. There are separate diskettes for basic demographic information, employment, housing, health care, and forecasts. The first diskette costs $395; additional diskettes cost $195. All three databases provide the user with "Help" files to assist with questions or problems.

CACI provides users with ongoing mailings describing new formats, company services, and new information being added to the databases.

Research Services

Customized Services and consulting are available on a per request basis. CACI will tailor its data to exactly fit the needs of any user. Customized services include reports, profiles of customers, site evaluation models, and market research databases. Information about these customized services is attained by contacting CACI directly toll-free at (800) 292-2224 (extension: ONLINE and Custom Data Services).

Users can call CACI to find out the exact longitude and latitude of a particular street intersection. The charge for this service is $10 per street intersection.

(*See also* reference to *Sourcebook;* diskettes under Documentation heading.)

4

CHASE ECONOMETRICS

150 Monument Road
Bala Cynwyd, PA 19004
Telephone: (215) 667-6000
E-Mail: none
Telex: 831609

COMPANY AT-A-GLANCE

Target Market(s):

Commercial banks
Fortune 1000 corporations
Government agencies
Investment banks
Specialized librarians
Thrift institutions

Subject Coverage:

Company information/
    statistics
Demographic information/
    statistics
Econometric data
Industry information/
    statistics
Real-time/Historic market
    quotations

DESCRIPTION

Chase Econometrics, previously owned by the Chase Manhattan Bank, was recently acquired by WEF Associates AG, the Swiss parent company of Wharton Econometric Forecasting Associates. Presently, in addition to its world headquarters in Bala Cynwyd, Pennsylvania, Chase Econometrics has offices in fifteen U.S. cities, one Canadian city, five European cities, and two Far Eastern cities.

Chase Econometrics provides the largest selection of online economic and financial databases commercially available. In addition, Chase Econometrics provides demographic databases and associated support products for all databases. Data coverage spans the current century via historical, current, and forecast databases.

DATABASES

Proprietary

Annual Survey of Manufactures. The Annual Survey of Manufactures database contains Historical Census of Manufactures' data and the Annual Survey of Manufactures' data. Data are available out to the four-digit level of the Standard Industrial Classification (SIC) code. The database contains 5,650 time series and company data and is updated annually.

Bank Holding Companies. The Bank Holding Companies database contains balance sheet and income statement data for bank holding companies and their consolidated subsidiaries. The database information is taken from bank filings with the Federal Reserve System. The database information is either semiannual or annual data.

Branch Deposit. The Branch Deposit database contains deposit information for 85,000 branches of commercial savings banks, mutual savings banks, savings and loan associations, and federal savings banks. Information includes geographic detail at the state, SMSA, county, and zip code levels. Data are obtained from the branch office reports filed with the Federal Deposit Insurance Corporation and the Federal Savings and Loan Insurance Corporation. The database is updated on an annual basis.

Business Conditions Digest. The Business Conditions Digest database provides historical coverage of economic time series contained in the *Business Conditions Digest,* including series developed by the Bureau of Economic Analysis. Subscription to the U.S. Macroeconomic database includes access to the Business Conditions Digest database. Data are updated on a monthly basis.

Conference Board. The Conference Board database provides coverage of economic data that is monitored by the Conference Board. Database information includes the Conference Board's economic forecasts, as well as consumer and business survey results. The database contains 1,000 time series of data in 10-day, monthly, bimonthly, quarterly, semiannual, and annual form.

Consumer Price Index. The Consumer Price Index database provides monthly historical consumer price indexes for the entire United States, 28 urban metropolitan areas, regional areas, and population-size class regions provided by the Bureau of Labor Statistics. The database's 10,000 time series are updated on a monthly basis.

Consumer Spending Forecast. The Consumer Spending Forecast database provides detailed forecasts of U.S. personal consumption expenditures, retail sales, and consumer credit. Selected data from the U.S. Macroeconomic database are also included in the Consumer Spending Forecast database. Short-term forecasts are updated monthly and extend 12 months into the future. Long-term forecasts are updated semiannually and extend 10 years into the future.

FDIC. The FDIC database contains balance sheet and income statement information for commercial banks. Data are derived from the Reports of Condition and Income filed by banks with the Federal Reserve Board, Federal Deposit Insurance Corporation, and the Comptroller of the Currency. The database is updated twice quarterly using preliminary and final data releases.

Financial. The Financial database provides historical key financial indicators for the U.S. market from the Federal Reserve Board and other relevant sources. The database contains 3,500 series of weekly, monthly, quarterly, and annual data.

Financial Forecast. The Financial Forecast database provides forecasts of key financial market indicators for the U.S. economy. The database also includes historical data beginning in 1950. Forecasts are updated on a monthly basis and extend at least 24 months into the future.

Flow of Funds. The Flow of Funds database provides 3,500 quarterly series, historical flow of funds data, and Federal Reserve Board accounting system data. The database provides information on the effects the nonfinancial economy has on the financial markets, while simultaneously identifying the influence that the financial sector has on demand for goods and services, sources and amounts of savings and investment, and income structures. The database is updated each quarter, approximately six weeks after the end of the quarter.

Foreign Exchange. The Foreign Exchange database contains historical data for foreign exchange rates vis-á-vis the U.S. dollar for 200 countries. The database contains 1,300 series of weekly and monthly data. The database is updated on a weekly basis.

Foreign Exchange Forecast. The Foreign Exchange Forecast data base provides foreign exchange and interest rate forecasts for more than 30 currencies. The database also includes macroeconomic forecasts for industrialized countries and provides historical data beginning from 1960. Monthly and quarterly forecasts are updated on the first business day of every month.

FSLIC. The FSLIC database contains balance sheet and income statement information from quarterly financial reports filed by savings and loan associations and federal savings banks with the Federal Savings and Loan Insurance Corporation and the Federal Home Loan Bank Board. The database is updated on a quarterly basis.

Industry 480. The Industry 480 database provides complete long-term forecasts for 480 U.S. industries. Information includes industry output, sales to all other industries, sales to final demand, and SIC-based production prices. In addition, profit and loss statement forecasts are provided for 50 manufacturing and service industries. The database can be accessed on a time-sharing basis on Chase Econometrics' mainframe computer or by downloading data to a personal computer.

Long-Term Interindustry Forecast. The Long-term Interindustry Forecast database provides detailed forecasts for more than 400 industries. Forecasts include industry production, sales to major markets, investment, employment, value-added, profits, and other income. Forecasts are updated semi-annually and extend 10 years into the future.

Metals Week. The Metals Week database provides historical data for all metal prices quoted by *Metals Week*, as well as for currency exchange rates. The database's 500 series are daily, weekly, monthly, and annual in nature. Metals Week is updated on a weekly basis.

Producer Price Index by Commodity. The Producer Price Index by Commodity database provides monthly historical producer price indexes for nearly 3,200 commodities listed by commodity and by stage of processing. Database information is obtained from the Bureau of Labor Statistics. The database is updated monthly.

Regional Financial Forecast. The Regional Financial Forecast database provides detailed forecasts of financial activity for all 50 states, the District of Columbia, and 263 Standard Metropolitan Statistical Areas. The short-term forecast is updated quarterly and extends 10 quarters into the future. The long-term forecast is updated semi-annually and extends 10 years into the future.

Regional Industry Forecast. The Regional Industry Forecast database provides detailed industrial employment forecasts for all 50 states and the District of Columbia by two- and three-digit SIC codes. The short-term forecast is updated quarterly and extends 12 quarters into the future. The long-term forecast is updated semi-annually and extends 10 years into the future.

Regional Macro Forecast. The Regional Macro Forecast database provides detailed macroeconomic forecasts for all 50 states, the District of Columbia, and 276 Standard Metropolitan Statistical Areas. The short-term forecast is updated quarterly and extends 10 quarters into the future. The long-term forecast is updated semi-annually and extends 10 years into the future.

SMSA Macro. The SMSA Macro database provides historical macroeconomic information for more than 350 Standard Metropolitan Statistical Areas (SMSA's) and Standard Consolidated Statistical Areas (SCSA's). The database contains 39,000 monthly, quarterly, and annual series. Database information is updated according to the frequency of the source update.

State Macro.   The State Macro database provides historical macro-economic detail for 50 states, 9 census divisions, the total United States, and the District of Columbia, and selected detail for Puerto Rico, the Virgin Islands, BEA regions, and census regions. The database's 47,000 series are monthly, quarterly, and annual in nature. The database is updated according to the frequency of the source update.

State and SMSA Financial.   The State and SMSA Financial database contains statistics from the FDIC and FSLIC income and condition reports covering four major types of financial institutions: commercial banks, mutual savings banks, savings and loan associations, and federal savings banks. Data are available for all 50 states, the District of Columbia, and more than 300 Standard Metropolitan Statistical Areas. The database is updated on both a quarterly and annual basis.

U.S. Cost Planning Forecast.   The U.S. Cost Planning Forecast database provides forecasts of growth rates for more than 300 industrial commodities and wage rates for more than 30 industries. Price forecasts cover all sectors of the U.S. economy. The short-term forecast is updated monthly and extends eight quarters into the future. The long-term forecast is updated quarterly and extends 10 years into the future.

U.S. Macroeconomic.   The U.S. Macroeconomic database provides 13,200 time series of short-term and long-term analysis and forecasts of the U.S. economy. The database provides detailed forecasts on over 700 national income and product accounts, price, financial, and industry variables. Specific sector analysis includes the areas of consumer demand, housing, industrial production, foreign trade, the public sector, the monetary sector, energy, commodity prices, corporate profits, and agriculture. Data provided are of a weekly, monthly, quarterly, semiannual, and annual form.

U.S. Macroeconomic Forecast.   The U.S. Macroeconomic Forecast database provides detailed forecasts for the U.S. economy. Special emphasis is placed on national expenditures, income, and production. The short-term forecast is updated within five days of release of the most recent National Income and Product Accounts data. These short-term forecasts extend 9 to 13 quarters into the future. The long-term forecast is updated monthly and extends 10 years into the future.

Third Party

DORIS.   DORIS is a third party database developed in conjunction with CACI Inc. The database contains historical and forecasted demographic data for counties, zip codes, and census tracts based on information from the Census of Population and Housing. Current-year estimates and five-year forecasts, as developed by CACI Inc., are updated on an annual basis.

SUPERSITE.   SUPERSITE is a third party database developed in conjunction with CACI Incorporated. The database provides historical and forecasted demographic data for any area, of any size or shape, in the United States. The database information is based on the Census of Population and Housing. Current-year estimates and five-year projections for population, households, and income distribution are updated annually by CACI Incorporated.

VALUE-ADDED PRODUCTS AND SERVICES

Customer Support

Chase Econometrics provides continuous consulting services to all clients. User help and instructions are available via contacting either the Chase Econometrics' world headquarters in Philadelphia or any local office. In addition to Chase's headquarters, offices are located in 24 cities throughout North America, Europe, and the Far East. Subscribers may call the world headquarters at (215) 667-6000 for more information and the location of the nearest office.

Documentation

The *Data Reference Guide* is a single volume containing information on Chase Econometrics' products and services. Included is information pertaining to:

Chase Econometrics' approach to database services.

DIMENSIONS—Chase Econometrics' information access system.

XPLORE—Chase Econometrics' electronic data search and retrieval facility.

Data Locators—Matrices providing a cross-reference of general data categories and geographic coverage for each historical database.

A profile of each Chase Econometrics database.

An index of databases by type of data.

A database documentation catalogue.

DATA LINE is Chase Econometrics' database newsletter. It is issued on a quarterly basis and is distributed to all Chase Econometrics clients.

4

CLAREMONT ECONOMICS INSTITUTE

250 West First Street
Suite 220
Claremont, CA 91711
Telephone: (714) 625-1441
E-Mail: none
Telex: 298608

COMPANY AT-A-GLANCE

Target Market(s):

Commercial banks
Fortune 1000 corporations
Investment banks
Specialized librarians

Subject Coverage:

Econometric data

DESCRIPTION

Claremont Economics Institute (CEI) is a privately held company providing financial and strategic operating advice to the chief executive officers, chief financial officers, and boards of nearly 150 manufacturing and financial corporations in the United States and abroad. CEI provides its clients with concise conclusions on the direction of the U.S. economy and the economies of 10 other countries. CEI also provides recommendations on appropriate financial and operating strategies to best position its clients for future shifts and to protect them from high-probability risks.

The company markets its basic service through the use of a very small sale force. Most of the growth in its client base in recent years has been through referrals from satisfied customers and from publicity it receives from articles appearing in publications such as *The Wall Street Journal, Barron's,* and *Fortune.*

DATABASES

Proprietary

Claremont Economics Institute.   The Claremont Economics Institute database includes the text of the two most recent issues of each publication of the Claremont Economics Institute. The data are derived from proprietary models and may contain both text and data in tabular form.

VALUE-ADDED PRODUCTS AND SERVICES

Customer Support

Services include several on-site visits a year, three conferences in seven cities each year, and unlimited telephone consultation.

Documentation (*see* Research Services)

System Features/Software Packages

United States only, United States and Currencies, and Full Global packages are available on a yearly basis. Asset allocation and other custom projects are available on a bid basis.

Online Communication

CEI's plans for the future include consideration of other forms of electronic mail distribution services.

Research Services

Main Street Journal provides news updates, forecasts, commentary, letters, and investment recommendations. It is directed to the small businessperson and individual investor.

Currency Manager is a monthly publication of CEI's Global Economic Intelligence Service, which develops integrated international asset/liability management strategies for its corporate clients. The forecasts used in these strategies are based upon economic and political intelligence from a network of international associates and the output of CEI's international and U.S. forecasting models.

Special Analyses are letters of topical interest distributed as events occur.

CEI Bulletin is a brief weekly update on currencies and interest rates.

News Updates are letters of topical interest distributed as events occur.

Money Market Letter is a weekly analysis of the Fed and interest rates.

**COMMODITY INFORMATION
SERVICES COMPANY**

327 South LaSalle
Suite 800
Chicago, IL 60604
Telephone: (312) 922-3661
E-Mail: none
Telex: none

COMPANY AT-A-GLANCE

Target Market(s):

Commercial banks
Investment banks
Mortgage banks
Thrift institutions

Subject Coverage:

Real-time/Historic market
quotations

DESCRIPTION

Commodity Information Services Company (CISCO) is a privately held company located in Chicago. It provides database, personal computer, and custom services to stockbrokers, investment analysts, portfolio managers, and personal investors.

In addition to the CISCO database, which covers futures in great detail, the company also provides sophisticated financial analysis on futures, as well as historical records dating back to 1970. Historical data are available online, on diskette or magnetic tape, or in hard copy.

DATABASES

Proprietary

CISCO. The CISCO database is comprised of a variety of sub-databases associated with futures including standard futures, cash T-bonds and T-bills, GNMA's, and the underlying cash on many futures, options, continuations, interest rates, and indexes. CISCO data take the form of either raw trading statistics (prices, volumes, open interest) or tables of information that are preprocessed to some degree. Access to the database is available via an ASCII terminal or a personal computer with a 300 or 1200 baud modem.

VALUE-ADDED PRODUCTS AND SERVICES

Customer Support

CISCO provides user discounts for nonprofit organizations that subscribe to its service. Special evening rates are also available.

Documentation

CISCO provides a number of system support publications to users, for a fee. These include:

The CISCO Database Users Manual
EXPRESS: Page Retrieval and Futures Options
Municipal Bonds Services
Financial Futures
Trading Systems, Volume I
FUTURESOFT Users Manual
Interactive Accounting
Margin/Equity Accounting
The CISCO Bond Strategist
Technical Currency Hedging
CISCO Subroutines
FORTRAN Programming Manual
VOS Operations Guide
CISCO Reviews

System Features/Software Packages

Library programs, which include data list, spread, analytical calculations, economics, plotting, financial futures, and trading programs are available.

Data storage can be purchased by full-access subscribers.

Options analysis software is available for the Black-Scholes model, EQUIVALUS, volatility studies, and price behavior statistics. FUTURESOFT is also available to provide market analysis for the IBM PC. The FUTURESOFT package includes trading programs, database collection, and management tools, and the ability to produce high-resolution computer graphics.

Brokers Support consists of electronic mail pages covering margin accounting, cycles, consensus indexes, interest rate projections, trading models, options, settlements, and relative strength indexes.

Cycle Analysis provides daily calculations of long-term and short-term cycles.

CISCO Express is a page-oriented system composed of five groups that provide:

A thumbnail sketch of all front month futures
The CBOT Liquidity Data Bank
Options valuation tables
A detailed analysis of every future
The CBOT Market Profile

Research Services

Through the Commodity Management Service, CISCO provides individual management of accounts since 1973; CTA/CTO support through leased trading models; buying and writing of options strategies; and institutional, bank and corporate hedge consulting services.

Futures Flash are daily research reports on futures cycles, relative strength, interest rate projections, and trading models.

CISCO's CONTINUA aids in the research of trading models. CONTINUA allows for testing of two consecutive years of data. CISCO's custom features include:

Interest rate forecasting and risk management hedging strategies, via CISCO's Bond Strategist.
Currency forecasting and risk management hedging strategies, via CISCO's Forex Advisor.
Municipal bond beta analysis, provided through the Bond Buyer 40 and customer holdings.
Contract programming, which allows for numerous trading programs and models to run under the control of the user.
Custom charts, including bar, spread, RSI, oscillator, stochastic, consensus index, and volume and open interest.

Selective Dissemination of Information (SDI) Services

Personalized information reports, which include trading systems, analyses, and data tailored to each user's needs, are available.

Document Formatting and Delivery

CISCO data are available online, on diskette, in printed hard copy form, and on magnetic tape.

4

COMMODITY SYSTEMS INC.
200 W. Palmetto Park Road
Suite 200
Boca Raton, FL 33432
Telephone: (305) 392-8663
  (800) 327-0175
E-Mail: none
Telex: 522107

COMPANY AT-A-GLANCE

Target Market(s):

Commercial banks
Fortune 1000 corporations
Investment banks
Specialized librarians

Subject Coverage:

Real-time/Historic market
  quotations

DESCRIPTION

Commodity Systems was founded by Bob Pelletier in 1970 to manage commodity accounts and to provide trading advice. As the company grew, however, it migrated toward providing commodity information rather than trading advice. The decision was made to concentrate on database products and to deliver them quickly and inexpensively.

Commodity Systems now provides a multitude of financial data products that support the interests of commodity traders, stock traders, and economic and financial analysts. The company works exclusively out of its headquarters in Boca Raton, Florida.

CSI has a staff of over 50 full-time employees in its various functional areas and supports over 3,000 customers. The information provided in its MARSTAT database is gathered by its Database Department, which has approximately 20 employees, including 3 database specialists.

DATABASES

Proprietary

MARSTAT. The Market Statistics database, or MARSTAT, includes data on futures, financial instruments, individual line market comparisons, stocks, options, and financial indicators. Data going back to the 1940s are available on options, cash prices, every futures contract traded, and about 800 stocks. Information for the database is gathered from all major U.S. and foreign exchanges. The Database Department checks the information obtained from these sources against various secondary sources (printed publications, annual books from the exchanges, prices furnished from the exchanges by wire) before entering it into the database.

MARSTAT is updated daily and presented in numeric format. It is accessible through Tymnet, Uninet, or Telenet. Users may also access the system by dialing direct.

VALUE-ADDED PRODUCTS AND SERVICES

Customer Support

Assistance is available to users from 7 A.M. to midnight weekdays, and 9 A.M. to 5 P.M. (EST) on Saturday.

Documentation

The *QUICKTRIEVE User's Manual* provides directions for logging on to the system and storing, printing, and deleting files. Examples and illustrations of typical searches are also provided.

A monthly newsletter is sent to users along with their invoice. Featured in the newsletter are new database developments, additions and deletions to MARSTAT, and any changes in network access numbers.

System Features/Software Packages

A program known as QUICKSTUDY is available for graphic analysis, manipulation, and combination of MARSTAT data. Users can choose from moving averages calculations and relative strength indexes, among other studies, in order to evaluate market behavior.

Another CSI software package, QUICKPLOT, graphically displays time series held in the user's private data bank for immediate review and analysis.

QUICKMONEY is a program that looks for extreme market conditions between pairs of related commodities. It is used as an intermarket straddle tool. The system is designed to make relatively safe trades where a high-priced commodity is sold short against the simultaneous purchase of a low-priced commodity. Related commodities on a historical basis are identified through an indexing method, thereby minimizing risk.

4

CSI's QUICKMARKET ANALYZER program features a bar chart of daily market activity and a point and figure chart current through the last day. It is anticipated that this package will be expanded to accommodate additional studies and to incorporate moving averages. It is a longer term market analysis system that provides the user with a methodology for trading with or against the market trend.

QUICKTRIEVE is a package designed to interact with MARSTAT. It captures intraday, daily, and historical data for each user's portfolio.

Finally, QUICKACCOUNT WATCH provides commodity traders with an ongoing assessment of the dollar net change in their accounts since the previous day's close. Users can use the package to determine their account value within a few minutes of calling time throughout the trading day.

THE CONFERENCE BOARD, INC.
Info Services Department
845 Third Avenue
New York, NY 10022
Telephone: (212) 759-0900
Telex: RCA International
  Telex 237282 and 234465

COMPANY AT-A-GLANCE

Target Market(s):

Commercial banks
Credit unions
Fortune 1000 corporations
Government agencies
Investment banks
Mortgage banks
Real estate firms
Specialized librarians
Thrift institutions

Subject Coverage:

Demographic information/
  statistics
Econometric data
Industry information/
  statistics
Newsletters

DESCRIPTION

The Conference Board, founded in 1916, is a worldwide network of leaders in the public and private sectors who exchange information on management, economic, and public policy issues. The board not only encourages this sharing but supports it with independent data and analyses.

The Conference Board and its affiliate, The Conference Board of Canada, employ over 350 people at offices in New York, Washington, Ottawa, and Brussels. Most of the financial support comes from multinational business concerns.

DATABASES

Proprietary

The Conference Board Data Base (CBDB).   The Conference Board Data Base contains monthly, quarterly, and annual data on 1,013 time series extending back to 1951. Focus is on sectors of the macroeconomy, with secondary attention to regional and industrial indicators. Current, historical, and forecasted time series data are included. In addition, economic projections; attitude surveys; consumer, financial, and capital investment; and other proprietary, macroeconomic data are provided. Weekly economic forecasts from The Conference Board's chief economist are also featured.

With the exception of two textual files, information is presented in statistical form. Because The Conference Board produces its own data, the information contained in CBDB provides subscribers with a unique economic perspective.

VALUE-ADDED PRODUCTS AND SERVICES

Customer Support

The Conference Board answers user questions about CBDB contents via its telephone hotline ((212) 759-0900), which is available Monday through Friday, 9 A.M. to 5 P.M. (EST). All software support is provided by individual time-sharing vendors. Questions regarding access may be directed to the vendors, who also provide telephone support.

Documentation

All subscribers to CBDB receive a directory of The Conference Board data series and newsletters covered in the database. Updates are mailed to all subscribers whenever the content of the database is changed.

The Conference Board descriptive files include:

The Sommers Letter provides users with a concise view of financial, industrial, and policy issues and how they affect the economy. The newsletter content is provided weekly by Albert T. Sommers, The Conference Board's chief economist.

Monthly Comment provides users with explanations of changes in CBDB data and their relation to the economy.

Assumptions provides users with background information on the type of input used to develop The Conference Board Forecast.

Document Formatting and Delivery

All data in The Conference Board Data Base are published in printed publications available only to The Conference Board Associates.

DATA COURIER INC.
620 South Fifth Street
Louisville, KY 40202-2297
Telephone: (800) 626-2823
 (United States)
 (800) 626-0307 (Canada)
 (502) 582-4111 (Kentucky)
Telex: 204235

COMPANY AT-A-GLANCE

Target Market(s):

Commercial banks
Fortune 1000 corporations
Investment banks
Specialized librarians

Subject Coverage:

News services
Research reports/
 evaluations

DESCRIPTION

Data Courier Incorporated was, until recently, a privately held subsidiary of Courier-Journal and Louisville Times Company of Louisville, Kentucky. In the fall of 1986 Bell & Howell Company bought it, with intentions of making it an operating unit of their subsidiary, University Microfilms, Inc.

Data Courier specializes in the collection, development, production, marketing, and electronic distribution of business and management information. Its staff which consists of approximately 60 full-time employees and a host of free-lance information abstractors, provides online services for security analysts, marketing managers, financial managers, business executives, data processing professionals, venture capitalists, researchers, purchasing managers, computer hardware and software executives, government agencies, and universities. A wide range of services are provided to assist and support clients in gathering information from Data Courier databases.

User costs for accessing the databases vary depending on the database used. Potential customers should contact Data Courier for up-to-date database charges.

DATABASES

Proprietary

ABI/INFORM. ABI/INFORM is a business and management informations system database produced by Data Courier. It contains over 300,000 business articles from over 660 business and management publications worldwide. Articles are presented in 200-word summaries, which are indexed and cross-referenced for easy access. Access to the database is available through several online vendors, including BRS, BRS/After Dark, BRS Brkthru, Data-Star, DIALOG, ESA-Quest, ETSI, ITT Dialcom, Knowledge Index, Mead Data Central, Orbit, and Vu/Text.

Business Dateline. Data Courier introduced its Business Dateline database in the fall of 1986. It contains approximately 15,000 full-text articles from more than 100 regional U.S. and Canadian business publications. Access is available via DIALOG, Dow Jones News/Retrieval, and Vu/Text.

Business Software Database. Business Software Database describes computer software packages having business applications for use on micro- and mini-computers. The database contains approximately 6,600 records of software company and manufacturer literature. Access to the database is provided by BRS, BRS/After Dark, BRS/Brkthru, Data-Star, DIALOG, and ESA-quest.

VALUE-ADDED PRODUCTS AND SERVICES

Customer Support

Data Courier provides search assistance from 9 A.M. to 5 P.M. (EST), Monday through Friday, via toll-free telephone number (800) 626-2823. User inquiries may also be sent 24 hours a day, seven days a week by Telex 204235.

User training seminars are provided, free of charge, in major cities across the United States. In addition, the company sponsors joint training sessions with Predicasts and Disclosure.

4

Documentation

Two free database newsletters, *LOG/ON* and *NET NET*, are provided to subscribers. These newsletters discuss online applications, new products, training seminars, business topics, and database search tips.

SEARCH ACT is Data Courier's guide to its Advertised Computer Technologies databases. This reference manual identifies companies, products, and services in the computer industry. Similarly, *SEARCH INFORM* is a users' guide to ABI/INFORM. It contains company and organization names, geographic terms, searching instructions, and a full explanation of the editorial policies employed in developing and maintaining ABI/INFORM.

In addition to offering the basic support services of all its other databases, Data Courier also provides database journals, a classified codes list, and brochures designed to assist users in retrieving information from ABI/INFORM.

Research Services

Custom research services are offered for all Data Courier databases. With Data Courier's customer service department filling the role of information broker, custom searches are executed on the ABI/INFORM database for an hourly charge plus connect time and hit charges.

Document Formatting and Delivery

Data Courier's Article Delivery Department provides users with photocopies of advertisements and articles listed in the database. Articles can be ordered online, by telephone, telex, mail, or facsimile transmission. Orders placed by 2 P.M. (EST), Monday through Friday, are shipped by the following workday. Rush service is available at additional cost.

DATA RESOURCES, INC.

24 Harwell Avenue
Lexington, MA 02173
Telephone: (617) 863-5100
 (202) 663-7600
 (212) 208-1217
E-Mail: none
Telex: none

COMPANY AT-A-GLANCE

Target Market(s):

Commercial banks
Credit unions
Fortune 1000 corporations
Government agencies
Investment banks
Mortgage banks
Real estate firms
Specialized librarians
Thrift institutions

Subject Coverage:

Company information/
 statistics
Econometric data
Industry information/
 statistics
Real-time/Historic market
 quotations

DESCRIPTION

Data Resources Incorporated (DRI) is a division of FEICO, a McGraw-Hill Financial and Economic Information Company. DRI is the largest provider of information products and analytic services for professionals in the financial marketplace. Its financial information network has been created through a three-way link-up between DRI, Standard & Poor's Corporation, and Monchik Weber.

In addition to its corporate headquarters in Lexington, Massachusetts, and financial headquarters in New York City, Data Resources has regional offices in Philadelphia, Atlanta, Chicago, Los Angeles, New York, Detroit, Houston, Pittsburgh, Washington D.C., San Francisco, and Stamford, Connecticut. DRI also has international offices in Toronto, Brussels, Frankfurt, Milan, Paris, and London.

DRI products and services include international financial and economic analyses, with complete international coverage; regional and industrial perspectives for investment and marketing strate-

4

gies; proprietary data for trading and money management; and custom research and consulting services.

Full DRI services include published reports and economic analyses by DRI and industry experts; published news and commentary on the financial marketplace; access to forecasting models and related databases; client conferences; reports on economic and industry activity; consultation services via telephone access to DRI professionals; personal computer capabilities; and operational support on using DRI's data, system, and computer software.

DRI's databases are available either as stand-alone products or as part of a DRI database system. Database access is either via time-sharing on a mainframe computer or by downloading on a personal computer. DRI data are also available on magnetic tape, diskettes, or in published reports. The price of the data varies depending on the nature of the data and the frequency of use. DRI's proprietary software can be used on personal computers, microcomputers, or mainframe systems to facilitate analysis, create reports, and produce graphics.

DATABASES

Proprietary

Data Resources Incorporated assembles and manipulates data from various sources to provide users with the following databases:

DRI Bank Analysis System.   DRI Bank Analysis System (DRI-BAS) is a composite database containing detailed balance sheet and income statement data on holding companies, commercial banks, and thrift institutions, as well as deposit information on the individual branch level. The major sources of data for the DRI Bank Analysis System are the Board of Governors of the Federal Reserve System, Federal Deposit Insurance Corporation, and Federal Home Loan Bank Board.

DRI Commodities.   DRI Commodities database contains historical and current price and trading activity data on commodity futures, spot commodities, and options traded on the U.S., Canadian, and London markets. The major sources of data for the database are

Market Data Systems Incorporated, the *Journal of Commerce*, U.S. Department of Agriculture, the *London Times*, and all relevant exchanges.

DRI Financial and Credit Statistics. DRI Financial and Credit Statistics (DRIFACS) database contains high-frequency financial data including money market rates, foreign exchange data, commercial banking assets and liabilities, thrift institution activity, cash options and stock indexes, and financial futures. Data coverage is both domestic and international on a daily, weekday, weekly, and monthly basis. The major sources of data for the database are the Bank of America, Barclay's Bank International, Board of Governors of the Federal Reserve System, Chicago Board of Options Exchange, Federal Home Loan Bank Board, Moody's Investor Service Incorporated, U.S. Department of the Treasury, and Telerate Systems Incorporated.

DRI Securities. DRI Securities (DRISEC) database contains daily price, volume, and fundamental information on over 45,000 security issues including debt, equity, government agency issues, and options traded on the New York, American, over-the-counter, regional, and Canadian exchanges. In addition, the database contains information on over 200 industry and market indexes. Price histories are available on all New York and American stock exchange equity issues dating back to 1968 and for over-the-counter stocks and mutual funds dating back to 1972. The database's major sources of data are Merrill Lynch historical prices and yields and Telstat Systems Incorporated.

MACROECONOMIC Databases. The MACROECONOMIC database contains measures of financial, economic, and demographic activity in the United States. The major sources of data for the database include the Board of Governors of the Federal Reserve System, Federal Home Loan Bank Board, and all major United States Government departments and agencies.

REGIONAL and COUNTY Databases. The REGIONAL and COUNTY Databases monitor indicators of demographic and economic activity in U.S. census regions, Federal Reserve districts, states, metropolitan areas, and counties. The major sources of data for the database include the U.S. Department of Commerce, Bureau of Economic Analysis, Bureau of the Census, National Planning Data Corporation, Federal Home Loan Bank Board, and major U.S. departments and agencies.

Third Party

Banktrak. Banktrak contains data on sales, lead bank, employment, location, and Standard Industrial Classification (SIC) code for publicly and privately held companies and wholly owned subsidiaries. The major source of data for the database is Standard & Poor's annual survey data for approximately 45,500 companies. This data is validated through secondary research on company annual reports, 10-K reports, and IRS data and then standardized by company name, state, and zip code.

Compustat Financial Information. Compustat Financial Information contains annual and quarterly financial statement information on publicly traded industrial firms, utilities, and banks. Detailed business segment, Standard Industrial Classification code, industry, and company-specific data such as price, dividends, and earnings data are also available. The database's major source of data is Standard & Poor's Compustat Services Incorporated, a division of McGraw Hill's Financial & Economic Information Company (FEICO).

Institutional Brokers Estimate System. Institutional Brokers Estimate System contains research analysts' earnings estimates for over 3,000 major corporations whose stocks are traded on U.S. stock exchanges. Analysts' estimates include earnings per share for the current quarter, one- and two-year forecasted earnings, five-year earnings growth, and projected price-earnings ratios. The major source of data for the database is Lynch, Jones, & Ryan Institutional Brokers Estimate System.

Merrill Lynch Bond Pricing. Merrill Lynch Bond Pricing database contains closing prices for over 35,000 corporate bonds, private placements, floating rate notes, zero coupon bonds, equipment trusts, Treasury issues, and government agency securities. The database also provides historical daily prices on these financial instruments for the previous 12 years. Merrill Lynch Capital Markets provides the data for the Merrill Lynch Bond Pricing database.

Securities Industry Association. Securities Industry Association (SRI) database contains information on capital market indicators and data on the financial condition and performance for securities firms. Only members of the Security Industry Association have access to the information contained in the database. The major sources of information for the database include the Security Industry Association and the New York Stock Exchange.

Standard & Poor's Industry Financial. The Standard and Poor's Industry Financial database contains selected income statement and balance sheet data, as well as Standard & Poor's stock price indexes for over 100 Standard & Poor's composites. The Standard & Poor's corporation is the supplier of data for the Standard & Poor's Industry Financial database.

TRINET. The TRINET Database contains detailed company information on approximately 500,000 businesses with 20 or more employees. Major sources of data for the database include company annual reports, the U.S. Department of Commerce, Bureau of the Census, and telephone verification of reported data. Local information sources include state, industrial, and trade association directories and registers; clipping services; press releases; and data swaps with other information collection agencies.

Zacks Earnings Estimates. Zacks Earnings Estimates database contains consensus earnings projections for over 2,700 publicly held corporations. Zacks Investment Research Incorporated surveys over 1,200 analysts at 65 brokerage firms in compiling current and historical earnings projections on a fiscal year basis, five-year earnings per share growth rates, and earnings estimates for the current and previous quarters. Standard & Poor's Compustat Service is the major provider of data for the Zacks Earnings Estimates database.

VALUE-ADDED PRODUCTS AND SERVICES

Customer Support

DRI provides toll-free customer assistance via an 800 number during regular business hours. Database assistance is also available 24 hours a day, seven days a week at the Washington and Lexington offices. Other user aids include user manuals, seminars, and online "help" service.

DRI provides user training and on-site support services. Training sessions include coverage of the use of the DRI system, data retrieval, software applications, and DRI proprietary programming language.

Documentation

DRI provides weekly, monthly, and quarterly reviews of economic, financial, and industrial trends; weekly and monthly newsletters; and detailed commentary on U.S. money and credit, via Telerate or the DRI system.

System Features/Software Packages

DRI's proprietary software can be used on PC's, micro-, or mainframe systems to analyze data, create reports, and produce graphics. Packages include:

Banktrak: Summarizes competitive information for publicly and privately held companies and their wholly owned subsidiaries.

EPS: Provides clients with an interactive analytic and reporting system.

Examine: Tabulates the most recent fundamental data, price, or dividend data over any time period for a company name, stock CUSIP number, or ticker symbol.

FuturesMonitors: Examines rates of return resulting from various spreads between futures contracts.

FuturesPlot: Displays graphically comprehensive price and volume information on all futures contracts.

Keyissues: Analyzes daily stock, bond, and option information for over 45,000 issues. Simulation Models: DRI provides computer-based forecasting systems on all national, regional, and industrial markets.

Research Services

DRI provides consulting expertise for special projects involving portfolio analysis, investment selection, equity and fixed-income research, and lending and credit.

Document Formatting and Delivery

Database data are available on diskettes and magnetic tape.

4

DATATEK CORPORATION
818 N.W. 63rd
Oklahoma City, OK 73116
Telephone: (405) 843-7323
  (800) 642-2525
E-Mail: none
Telex: none

COMPANY AT-A-GLANCE

Target Market(s):

Commercial banks
Credit unions
Fortune 1000 corporations
Government agencies
Investment banks
Law firms
Mortgage banks
Real estate firms
Specialized librarians
Thrift institutions

Subject Coverage:

News services

DESCRIPTION

DATATEK Corporation was founded in 1979 and acquired by the Oklahoma Publishing Company in 1983. Its mission is to provide online support and marketing services for the electronic library database of *The Daily Oklahoman* and *Times*.

DATATEK has six marketing and support offices nationwide. The corporate office is located in Oklahoma City, with branch offices in Seattle, San Francisco, Dallas, Houston, and Baton Rouge. DATATEK's primary data center, located in Oklahoma City, houses three Digital Equipment Corporation VAX 785 superminicomputers. These systems are clustered and provide complete redundancy.

DATABASES

Proprietary

DataTimes–Associated Press: The DataTimes–Associated Press database contains national and international stories produced by AP writers in full-text form. Coverage includes not only business news, but also sports, entertainment, and features. Daily updates add 400 stories to the database. The database is available through

SATPAC, Uninet, Tymnet, EasyLink, and DATATEK's own network.

DataTimes–Southwest Newswire. The permanent database of the Southwest Newswire provides companies and news sources with historical, full-text, unedited research material. It contains press releases from newspapers, news bureaus, radio and television, financial institutions, companies, public relations groups, and government agencies. Daily updates add 400 stories to the database. The database is available through Uninet, Tymnet, EasyLink, and DATATEK's own network.

DATATEK provides online access to many newspapers throughout the country. All newspaper databases are updated daily and available in full-text, as well as abbreviated form. The following newspapers are available online but will not be treated in detail.

The Washington Post
LegisTrak
The Arkansas Gazette
The San Francisco Chronicle
Baton Rouge Morning Advocate & State-Times
The Daily Oklahoman and *Oklahoma City Times*
The Journal Record
The Dallas Morning News
The Daily Texan
The Houston Chronicle
The Seattle Times
The Chicago Sun-Times

VALUE-ADDED PRODUCTS AND SERVICES

Customer Support

DataTimes, DATATEK's online database service, provides numerous customer support services including comprehensive user's guides, free on-site training or free online time for instruction for users not within reach of a DATATEK office, and an 800 hotline.

The branch offices provide a base from which customer support staffers offer one-on-one on-site training to DataTimes customers.

A user hotline (800) 642-2525 is available to assist subscribers. The hotline hours are from 8 A.M. to 7 P.M. (CST).

Research Services

DATATEK's staff will provide user searches. The cost is $1.58 per minute with a minimum charge of $10.

Documentation

DATATEK provides quarterly newsletters, user's manuals, and database updates to all subscribers. Charges for these products are included in the subscription fee. Additional user's manuals may be purchased for $10.50.

An online thesaurus is available for some databases that Data-Times accesses.

System Features/Software Packages

DataTimes uses the BASIS search and retrieval software for database maintenance, access, and search capabilities. BASIS allows users to search any word or combination of words, since virtually every word is indexed by this software.

SportsTrak is a computer program that allows a newspaper to collect sports-related statistics. SportsTrak can be purchased to run on Digital Equipment Corporation's VAX line of computers. Or, DATATEK, acting as a service bureau, can provide the publication with SportTrak statistics.

In conjunction with Digital Equipment Corporation, DATATEK will provide disk production service to assist in transferring data onto compact disks. A single compact disk has storage capacity equal to 200,000 typed pages, the equivalent of 1,600 floppy disks, or approximately three years of daily newspaper production.

Along with Infomart, DataTimes has announced the formation of a U.S./Canadian gateway giving subscribers to each company access to the other's service. The Canadian newspaper databases from Infomart will add to the international information provided to DataTimes customers.

Document Formatting and Delivery

DATATEK provides document delivery in its initial fee. Additional copies may be acquired for $35.

Research Services

DATATEK provides database management and computerized library services for several newspaper publishers. DATATEK provides design, programming, communications, database management, updating, and 24-hour support.

4

DISCLOSURE

5161 River Road
Bethesda, MD 20816
Telephone: (301) 951-1300
  (800) 638-8076
E-Mail: none
Telex: none

COMPANY AT-A-GLANCE

Target Market(s):

Commercial banks
Fortune 1000 corporations
Government agencies
Investment banks
Law firms
Specialized librarians

Subject Coverage:

Company information/
  statistics

DESCRIPTION

Disclosure is a privately held company that, since 1968, has provided access to reports filed with the Securities and Exchange Commission. Information is entered into the Disclosure databases daily from thousands of 10-Ks, annual reports, proxies, and other documents. These databases are accessible through a number of vendors, including BRS, Compuserve, and DIALOG, and through several communication networks, including Tymnet, Telenet, Uninet, and individual vendor networks, such as Dialnet.

In addition to its database services, Disclosure converts to microfiche more than 110,000 documents filed each year by 11,000 publicly owned companies whose stock is traded on the New York and American Stock Exchanges, NASDAQ, and over-the-counter. These documents—more than a million spanning 1966 to the present—are organized so as to allow users a means of quickly and easily selecting the latest corporate and financial information as it is needed.

DATABASES

Proprietary

Disclosure Online. This database contains detailed résumé, financial, and management information for American and non-American public companies. Data are extracted from the original reports received by the Securities and Exchange Commission (10-K, 10-Q, 8-K, 10-C, 13-F, 13-D, 13-G, etc.) and updated as new reports are filed. Disclosure also provides corporate information gathered from other sources to give users more rounded profiles of the 100,000 companies it covers.

Disclosure Corporate Profiles contain information extracted from 10-K's, 10-Q's, 8-K's, proxies, and new issue registration statements. They are updated as reports are received from the Securities and Exchange Commission. Included are all New York and American Stock Exchange companies and NASDAQ and other OTC companies. Profiles include descriptions of business; current outstanding shares; number of shareholders; number of employees; auditors' two-year annual balance sheet; three-year annual income statement; quarterly income statements; five-year summary (sales, net income, and earnings per share); names, ages, and remuneration of officers and directors; pension plans; other corporate events; and full-text management discussion.

Disclosure/Spectrum Ownership Database. This database provides detailed and summary stock ownership information for over 5,000 publicly held companies. Produced by Computer Directions Advisors, Inc., this information is derived from reports filed by the stockholders with the Securities and Exchange Commission on an annual, quarterly, and as-required basis. Each company record contains tables listing name; most recent shares traded; and total number of shares held by institutions, 5 percent owners, and corporate insiders.

Electronic Company Filing Index. With this index and a personal computer, users can discover which SEC documents have just been filed by any of more than 30,000 registrants. In addition, an up-to-the-minute corporate profile is generated for each of the 10,000 public companies whose securities are traded on the American

Stock Exchange, New York Stock Exchange, NASDAQ, or over-the-counter.

VALUE-ADDED PRODUCTS AND SERVICES

Customer Support

Customer support services are available directly from Disclosure between 9 A.M. and 5 P.M. (EST), Monday through Friday. Additional assistance may be obtained through the customer services provided by the vendor in use. Training is available through both Disclosure and the various vendors.

Documentation

Each vendor providing access to the Disclosure databases also supplies users with the guides and manuals necessary for effectively searching on its system. Database structure and search methods vary from one vendor to the next.

System Features/Software Packages

A software package, microDISCLOSURE, provides access to the Disclosure online database through a personal computer and provides the capability to search in clear, everyday English. In effect, this package acts as a translator between users and the complex command language normally required to search the database on a vendor's host computer.

The microDISCLOSURE software package consists of a program disk (the translator), a database disk (allows users to save retrieved financial information for future use), a reports & analysis disk (allows users to manipulate the data), and a manual of easy-to-follow instructions. This package is compatible with the IBM PC, XT, and AT.

Online Communication

Electronic mail availability varies for each of the vendors through which Disclosure is available.

Research Services

Disclosure's SEC Research Service will obtain specific information that is often not readily available. This service can save users time and money, as Disclosure specialists can quickly and inexpensively retrieve the information required.

Selective Dissemination of Information (SDI) Services

Disclosure's Watch Service automatically forwards reports to users as they are filed with the SEC. Users may request all reports or specific filings (10-K, 10-Q, and/or 8-K) for one or more companies. There is no charge for "watching," only for the documents delivered.

Disclosure's Subscription Service automatically forwards selected reports to users shortly after they are filed. If required, users may subscribe to all or specific reports for a wide range of public companies.

Annual reports are available for more than 2,500 foreign companies. Users may elect to receive reports from specific countries, industries, or companies. With a subscription, users will receive the current annual reports of all companies they have chosen. Any updates to these reports will be sent automatically as they are received.

Document Formatting and Delivery

Disclosure supports an on-demand service designed for attorneys, corporate executives, bankers—anyone requiring immediate information about public companies—as well as Disclosure subscribers seeking to supplement their regular files.

Upon calling Disclosure, users are informed as to which reports are on file for the company in which they are interested. They then specify the reports they need, and Disclosure sends them via overnight mail. Deposit account services are available for frequent users of this service.

COMPACT DISCLOSURE is comprised of one compact disk that holds all information currently in the Disclosure database. For one flat annual fee that includes cumulative quarterly updates, this disk turns a user's PC, XT, or AT into a powerful database containing complete profiles for over 10,150 public companies; 157 annual financial variables; 43 quarterly financial elements; five-year summaries for operating income, sales, and earnings per share; names, titles, ages, and salaries of officers and directors; full text of the president's letter from the annual report; the complete text of management discussion; a list of subsidiaries; abstracts of extraordinary events; ownership information; and a list of documents filed with the SEC.

The Compact Disk Reader may be chosen as part of a user's subscription. The price is included in the regular subscription price. After two years, users own the reader. If users do not wish to have the reader included, its price is subtracted from the regular subscription price. Required hardware includes an IBM PC (with at least 256K memory), or an IBM XT or AT, plus a printer.

The Disclosure database may also be leased in whole or part on magnetic tape. Weekly, monthly, and quarterly updating is available. Finally, print or microfiche copy of complete filings from 1966 to the present may be obtained, either on demand or automatically by subscription.

DONNELLEY MARKETING
P.O. Box 10250
1515 Summer
 Street
Stamford, CT 06904
Telephone: (203) 956-5400
E-Mail: none
Telex: none

DESCRIPTION

Donnelley Marketing is a subsidiary of the Dun & Bradstreet Corporation, a publicly owned company with assets of more than $2 billion. Donnelley has been in existence since 1922. With more than 3,000 employees, Donnelley is the largest integrated direct marketing system available to business in the United States. Donnelley Marketing has branch offices located in Stamford, Connecticut; Oak Brook, Illinois; and Fullerton, California.

Other services, in addition to its database, include: customized and cooperative mailing programs, seven facilities located across the United States to dispatch these mailings, research specialists who analyze customer files and make recommendations on market segmentation and promotion strategies, and a staff for implementing direct marketing solutions for the customer.

DATABASES

DQI^2.   DQI^2 is a demographic database that records and redefines the U.S. population. These demographics are derived from U.S. census and proprietary list data. The database covers more than 90 percent of U.S. households. The master file is compiled from telephone and automobile registration data. Accuracy is checked by matching data against as many as 24 outside lists.

VALUE-ADDED PRODUCTS AND SERVICES

Customer Support

Donnelley account executives are professional direct marketing consultants backed by a team of experts. These account executives act as a user's staff, implementing direct marketing solutions to achieve desired objectives.

System Features/Software Packages

Donnelley Marketing software can be used in conjunction with customer profiles to analyze customer lists and generate new prospect lists.

Research Services

Donnelley research specialists will recommend market segmentation and promotion strategy based on analysis of a user's current customer file.

Selective Dissemination of Information (SDI) Services

Donnelley's research team can create market databases to fit specific user needs. Donnelley can also maintain and operate these databases.

DOW JONES NEWS/RETRIEVAL

Dow Jones & Co., Inc.
P.O. Box 300
Princeton, NJ 08543-0330
Telephone: (800) 257-5114
 (609) 452-1511
E-Mail: none
Telex: none

COMPANY AT-A-GLANCE

Target Market(s):

Commercial banks
Credit unions
Fortune 1000 corporations
Government agencies
Investment banks
Law firms
Mortgage banks
Real estate firms
Specialized librarians
Thrift institutions

Subject Coverage:

Company information/
 statistics
Econometric data
Industry information/
 statistics
Real-time/Historic market
 quotations
News services
Research reports/
 evaluations

DESCRIPTION

Dow Jones News/Retrieval, a subsidiary of Dow Jones & Company, Inc., is an online electronic information service that provides business news and financial information, as well as current and historical stock quotes and general information services. The primary goal of the company is to provide the most timely, comprehensive, and accurate business and financial information to both businesses and private investors.

The service began commercial operation in 1974 by offering Dow Jones business and financial news to stockbrokers over dedicated phone lines. Most of this news came from the Dow Jones News Service and was inserted in the database within 90 seconds after appearing on the news wire.

In 1978 and 1979, its target market was widened to include companies outside the brokerage industry and personal computer owners accessing the system over dial-up phone lines. Current quotations on stocks and other financial instruments and historical stock quotes were added.

By the beginning of 1986 more than 180 administrative, editorial, technical, and marketing employees were working on News/Retrieval. The current service is organized into four broad areas—business and economic news, financial and investment services, quotes and market averages, and general news and information.

DATABASES

Proprietary

Dow Jones Current Quotes. The Dow Jones Current Quotes database provides current stock quote information on companies listed on the New York, American, Midwest, and Pacific Stock Exchanges, and NASDAQ over-the-counter market, as well as composite quotes. Stock quotes are available from the floor of the exchanges with a minimum 15-minute delay during market hours. Current quotes are updated on a continuous basis during trading hours.

Dow Jones Futures Quotes. The Dow Jones Futures Quotes database provides commodities quotes from the major North American exchanges. Delayed price data are given for more than 80 commodities. Information includes daily open, high, low, last, and settlement prices; lifetime high and low prices; and volume and open interest.

Dow Jones Historical Quotes. The Dow Jones Historical Quotes database provides daily high, low, and closing stock prices, as well as the trading volume for common and preferred stocks, dating back one year. Quotes are available for companies listed on the New York, American, Midwest, and Pacific Stock Exchanges, and NASDAQ over-the-counter companies.

Dow Jones News. This provides news from *The Wall Street Journal, Barron's*, and the Dow Jones News Service (the Broadtape). News stories in the database are from 90 seconds to 90 days old.

The database provides in-depth coverage of companies, industries, the stock market, and the general economy.

Dow Jones Text-Search Services.   This provides full text of all stories that appeared or were scheduled to appear in *The Wall Street Journal* from January 1984 to present day. The database also provides selected articles from *Barron's*, Dow Jones News Service, and *The Wall Street Journal* from June 1979 to present.

Historical Dow Jones Averages.   The Historical Dow Jones Averages database provides daily summaries of the transportation, industrial, utility, and 65 stock composite indexes. The Dow Jones industrial stock average, comprised of 30 industrial stocks, is commonly used as an indicator of changes in the general level of stock prices. The Historical Dow Jones Averages database contains high, low, and closing prices, as well as volume information for the previous trading year.

Real Time Quotes.   This database provides no-delay price quote information for stocks that are traded on the New York, American, Pacific, and Midwest stock exchanges. The database service features a news alert that identifies companies on which current-day news has run on the Dow Jones News Service.

The Wall Street Journal Highlights Online.   The Wall Street Journal Highlights Online database gives headlines and summaries of major news stories in *The Wall Street Journal*. Headlines and summaries include front-page news, front- and back-page features, market pages, editorial columns, and commentaries.

The Weekly Economic Update.   It provides a review of the week's top economic events and statistics. The database is compiled by the News/Retrieval editorial staff from the resources obtained from *The Wall Street Journal*, *Barron's*, and the Dow Jones News Service.

Third Party

Corporate Earnings Estimator.   The Corporate Earnings Estimator database is compiled by Zacks Investment Research Incorporated.

It provides consensus forecasts of earnings per share of 3,000 companies. The forecasts for the next two fiscal years are based on estimates provided by more than 1,000 research analysts at more than 60 major brokerage firms.

Disclosure II.   The Disclosure II database contains extensive business and financial information on approximately 9,400 companies. The data in Disclosure II are compiled from updated filings with the Securities and Exchange Commission. The information includes corporate profiles; balance sheets; income statements; line-of-business data; five-year summary of revenues; income and earnings per share; names of corporate officers, directors, and subsidiaries; management discussions; and a full two-year list of documents filed with the SEC.

The Economic and Foreign Exchange Survey.   The Economic and Foreign Exchange Survey database is provided by Money Market Services, Incorporated. The database offers a consensus of analyses and forecasts by leading economists. Analysis includes money supply data, unemployment, federal funds rates, consumer price indexes, and retail sales data. The forecasts are compared with previous actual figures released by the government.

Forbes Directory.   The Forbes Directory database ranks the 500 largest U.S. corporations according to sales, profits, assets, and market value. It also provides analysis of 46 major industries and ranks them by profitability and growth. The Forbes Directory is compiled from *Forbes'* January Report on American Industry and the May Annual Directory Issue.

Insider Trading Monitor.   The Insider Trading Monitor database provides stock transactions and holdings by insiders of more than 6,500 companies. The database is updated on a daily basis by Invest/Net, Inc. from SEC filings. Information in the database includes insider transactions that go back one year.

INVESTEXT.   The INVESTEXT database gives full texts of company and industry research reports from leading American and Canadian investment banking firms. Database information includes current, forecasted, and historical marketing and financial data. Information is provided for more than 13,000 reports released over the last six months on more than 3,000 companies and 52 industries.

Media General Financial Services. The Media General Financial Services database provides price, volume, and fundamental data on more than 4,300 companies. Information includes reports on revenues, earnings, dividends, price/earnings ratios, and stock market indicators. All information in the database is updated on a weekly basis.

Merrill Lynch Research Service. The Merrill Lynch Research Service contains highlights of reports prepared by the Securities Research Division of Merrill Lynch, Pierce, Fenner, & Smith Incorporated. The database provides a broad range of information that will aid investors in making more informed investment decisions, tracking the market, and obtaining earnings estimates.

Standard & Poor's Online. The Standard & Poor's Online database provides financial profiles on more than 4,600 companies. Major categories include financial overview, projected earnings, dividends, and company operations.

VALUE-ADDED PRODUCTS AND SERVICES

Customer Support

Dow Jones Customer Service Hotline can be reached at (800) 257-5114, or in New Jersey, Alaska, or foreign locations at (609) 452-1511.

The service is available on weekdays from 8 A.M. to 12 midnight (EST) and on Saturdays from 9 A.M. to 6 P.M. (EST).

Database users can visit their local computer store for a free demonstration or call Dow Jones Customer Service Hotline to obtain a demonstration disk.

Documentation

Intro is a free newsletter available to all subscribers. It provides online information on new developments in Dow Jones News/Retrieval, "how-to" guides, new software products, tips on using the database services, and schedules for software and News/ Retrieval seminars.

Dow Jones News/Retrieval User's Guide provides comprehensive details of the Dow Jones News/Retrieval databases and other services. Information includes summaries, descriptions, applications, and examples of the potential uses of the Dow Jones services. The *User's Guide* is available from Dow Jones News/Retrieval for a price of $9.95.

Master Menu is an online listing of the services contained in News/Retrieval. The Master Menu provides access codes for individual databases and a short description of each service.

The free *Dowline* is a magazine published by Dow Jones information services. The magazine, distributed once every two months, describes database uses and updates, software packages and their uses, and other items of interest to database users.

The Wall $treet Week Online provides transcripts from the PBS television show "Wall $treet Week." The four most recent TV shows are available. The database is updated every Thursday at 6:30 A.M., (EST).

The Words of Wall Street is an investment dictionary that contains more than 2,000 definitions, mathematical formulas, and examples used in the securities industry. *The Words of Wall Street* covers formal and informal investment terminology, including jargon identifying new financial techniques and corporate finance terms used by venture capitalists and specialists in mergers and acquisitions.

Symbols is an online listing of the symbols and codes used to access News/Retrieval services.

System Features/Software Packages

Dow Jones provides various investment and communication software products that can be used to access and manipulate data from News/ Retrieval. All Dow Jones Software products are fully supported by thorough documentation, a 60-day warranty, and the toll-free Dow Jones Customer Service hotline.

Market Analyzer is used for technical analysis—charting stock prices to reveal trends in price fluctuations and to compare stock price changes to market changes in general. The price of Market Analyzer is $349.

Market Manager PLUS performs portfolio analysis. Market Manager PLUS simultaneously records and maintains tax information on each security transaction, thus enabling the user to have a more exact evaluation of the portfolio. The Market Manager PLUS is available through News/Retrieval on Apple Macintosh for $199 and on IBM and Apple II for $249.

Investor's Workshop offers a combination portfolio management, charting, and communications service for investors. When used in conjunction with Dow Jones News/Retrieval it can review the value of the current portfolio, discover investment opportunities, and check on tips and hunches. The cost of the Investor's Workshop software is $149.

Spreadsheet Link allows for direct communication between News/Retrieval and Lotus 1-2-3, Multiplan, or VisiCalc spreadsheets. The cost of the software is $249 for IBM and Apple II and $99 for Apple Macintosh (requires Straight Talk).

Straight Talk, especially designed for the Apple Macintosh computer, automatically connects to News/Retrieval and other electronic database services.

Online Communication

MCI Mail transforms a personal computer into a communications device. MCI Mail delivers messages instantaneously or routes it by zip code to the MCI postal center closest to the addressee, then prints it and delivers the message according to user instructions.

MCI Mail allows for sending of printed documents or electronic letters, memos, reports, and other communications. Questions regarding MCI Mail may be directed to MCI Customer Service at (800) 424-6677.

DUFF AND PHELPS, INC.
55 East Monroe Street
Suite 4000
Chicago, IL 60603
Telephone: (312) 263-2610
E-Mail: none
Telex: 25-5165

COMPANY AT-A-GLANCE

Target Market(s):

Commercial banks
Fortune 1000 corporations
Investment banks
Specialized librarians
Thrift institutions

Subject Coverage:

Research reports/
evaluations

DESCRIPTION

Duff and Phelps, Inc. is a privately held company founded in 1932. Headquartered in Chicago, it provides fundamental, objective research on traded securities through its two databases, Duff and Phelps Equity Ideas and Duff and Phelps Fixed Income, and through a range of research and consulting services.

Services available include analyses of publicly traded securities of several hundred large companies, including common and preferred stock, debt issues, and commercial paper. These services are designed for use by securities analysts, equity portfolio managers, investment analysts, fixed-income portfolio managers, and securities traders.

DATABASES

Proprietary

Duff and Phelps Equity Ideas. Duff and Phelps Equity Ideas contains research reports by Duff and Phelps that expedite the decision making processes involving investments for equity analysts and portfolio managers. These reports cover more than 450 companies and 61 industry groups. The database is updated daily with approximately 450 issues at 2 A.M. (EST).

Duff and Phelps Fixed Income. Duff and Phelps Fixed Income database provides information on fixed income ratings for approximately 500 U.S. corporations with significant institutional investment following. The database is available on a time-sharing basis through I.P. Sharp and CompuServe access networks. Data on the 500 corporations are updated on a daily basis.

VALUE-ADDED PRODUCTS AND SERVICES

Customer Support

User support services are available Monday through Friday during regular business hours (EST) by calling (312) 263-2610.

Research Services

Duff and Phelps provides institutional investment research on equity and fixed-income securities. Portfolio consulting and discretionary portfolio management services are also available. Its financial consulting services include securities valuation, acquisition and divestiture consulting, feasibility studies, and rate testimony. Credit ratings are provided for commercial paper and fixed-income securities.

4

DUN'S MARKETING SERVICES
3 Century Drive
Parsippany, NJ 07054
Telephone: (800) 223-0669
  (201) 455-0900
E-Mail: 9103500549
Telex: 4909987001

COMPANY AT-A-GLANCE

Target Market(s):

Commercial banks
Fortune 1000 corporations
Government agencies
Investment banks
Specialized librarians

Subject Coverage:

Company information/
  statistics

DESCRIPTION

Dun & Bradstreet was founded in 1841 as one of the first businesses ever formed solely to provide business information to its customers. Today that business information ranges from commercial credit, to marketing, to television and media research. In 1975 Duns's Marketing Services was established as an operating company of Dun & Bradstreet Corporation to assist customers in identifying and reaching potential customers. Currently they have over 150 consultants nationwide to assist clients in developing effective marketing programs.

DATABASES

Proprietary

Dun's Financial Records.   Dun's Financial Records is produced jointly by Dun & Bradstreet Credit Services and Dun's Marketing Services. The database contains financial information, complete spreadsheet analysis, industry comparisons, company history, and operations information on over 700,000 U.S. business establishments. This data is available through DIALOG File #519.

Dun's Market Identifiers.   Dun's Market Identifiers database is a directory file that is produced by Dun's Marketing Services and Dun & Bradstreet Credit Services. The database contains current address and financial and marketing information on nearly two million U.S. business establishments. The database is available through DIALOG File #516.

International Dun's Market Identifiers.   International Dun's Market Identifiers is produced by Dun & Bradstreet International. The database contains directory listings, sales volume and marketing data, and references to parent companies on over 530,000 leading companies in over 130 countries around the world, including the United States. The database is available through DIALOG File #518.

Million Dollar Directory.   Dun's Million Dollar Directory is a directory file produced by Dun's Marketing Services. The database contains current address and financial and marketing information on the over 110,000 companies listed in the three-volume *Million Dollar Directory* series. The database is available through DIALOG File #517.

VALUE-ADDED PRODUCTS AND SERVICES

Customer Support

Dun's Marketing Services provides subscribers with toll-free user help lines ((800) 223-1026) from 8:30 A.M. to 5:00 P.M. (EST). There is no charge for this service.

Dun's will help formulate searches for customers, but does not search or provide output.

Documentation

Dun's Online User's Guide is available for $50.

Subscribers are provided with *Dun's Guide to Online Codes and Abbreviations* free of charge.

A free newsletter, *Dataline*, is mailed to customers as a training and support device.

Research Services

Besides online retrieval information is also available on a customized basis through Dun's Industrial Marketing Division. The information is available on tape, floppy disk, 3 x 5 prospecting cards, mailing lists and labels, and microfiche. All these options come with varying degrees of company information detail. Normal turn-around time is three to six weeks, depending on the output. Costs vary depending on the output and are charged on a contract fee basis.

Dun & Bradstreet offers a variety of customized services for subscribers. The Customized Information Systems and Services, which deliver in-depth business information, include:

> The Dun's Financial Profile Report is a detailed spreadsheet of a company's financial statements and 14 key financial ratios—including line-by-line comparisons to industry averages—for up to three years. Dun's Financial Profiles are updated on a continual basis. The Dun's Financial Profile Report can be ordered by calling DunsDial at 1-800-DNB-DIAL, and is available by mail, online through DunSprint or DunsPlus terminals, or on magnetic tape.
>
> *The PRO Report* is an in-depth narrative interpretation, based on confidential data supplied by the user, of a company's financial condition. *The PRO Report* can be ordered by calling DunsDial at (800) DNB-DIAL. It is available through mail or via DunSprint terminals. Priority Service is also available.
>
> The Confidential Profile allows users to create a detailed financial profile in the privacy of their office. The user simply enters confidential figures on a terminal, then the Dun & Bradstreet system generates a spreadsheet report that compares the confidential figures to industry norms and key business ratios on a line-by-line basis. The confidential figures never enter the Dun & Bradstreet system. The Confidential Profile is available through mail or online via a DunSprint terminal.

Selective Dissemination of Information (SDI) Services

DunsQuest provides online screening and search services that pinpoint the user's key marketing prospects, as well as merger and acquisition candidates. This highly targeted information is available in five different levels of service. DunsQuest is available through the mail, online via DunSprint terminal, on magnetic tape, or on diskettes.

Document Formatting and Delivery

Information is also available on tape, floppy disk, 3 x 5 prospecting cards, mailing lists and labels, and microfiche. All these options come with varying degrees of company information detail. Normal turn-around time is three to six weeks, depending on the output. Costs vary depending on the output and are charged on a contract fee basis.

4

EVANS ECONOMICS, INC.

1725 Eye Street, NW
Suite 310
Washington DC 20006
Telephone: (202) 467-4900
E-Mail: none
Telex: none

COMPANY AT-A-GLANCE

Target Market(s):

Commercial banks
Credit unions
Fortune 1000 corporations
Government agencies
Investment banks
Specialized librarians
Thrift institutions

Subject Coverage:

Econometric data

DESCRIPTION

Evans Economics provides various online services for the economic and financial communities. In addition to its databases, it also offers the Electronic News Service providing information; analysis; and forecasts on the economy and the stock, bond, and foreign exchange markets.

DATABASES

Proprietary

Evans Economics Full Service Database.   Evans Economics Full Service Database provides both historical and Evans Economics forecasts of key macroeconomic data, and industry and financial indicators for the United States. Coverage includes national income and product accounts, employment, productivity, housing starts, shipments, production, interest rates, money supply, consumer prices, and producer prices.

Evans Economics Macro Core Database.   Evans Economics Macro Core Database provides quarterly historical and forecasted data for the United States. The database contains macroeconomic, industry, and financial time series data. Coverage includes national income and product accounts, employment, productivity, housing starts, shipments, production, interest rates, money supply, consumer prices, and producer prices.

VALUE-ADDED PRODUCTS AND SERVICES

Online Communication

Evans Economics Electronic News Service provides continuous reporting and commentary on the movements of key economic and financial indicators, in-depth news analysis, historical data, and economic forecasts.

4

FINANCIAL POST INFORMATION SERVICE

777 Bay Street
Toronto, Ontario, Canada M5W 1A7
Telephone: (416) 596-5585
E-Mail: none
Telex: 0621954

COMPANY AT-A-GLANCE

Target Market(s):

Commercial banks
Investment banks

Subject Coverage:

Company information/
  statistics
Real-time/Historic market
  quotations

DESCRIPTION

The Financial Post Information Service is a division of the publicly held Maclean Hunter Ltd. Its databases are available on a subscription basis from FRI Information Services, I.P. Sharp Associates, and D.R.I. Canada. Pricing and billing depend on which vendor a customer uses.

DATABASES

Proprietary

Financial Post Bond Database. This provides weekly closing prices and yields on more than 1,500 Canadian bonds.

Financial Post Canadian Corporate Database. This database provides annual coverage on over 400 Canadian publicly owned companies and additional quarterly data on 120 companies.

Financial Post Securities Database. It provides a summary of trading on all the exchanges in Canada, including equity, options, and futures. New York and Amex equity trading is also available.

VALUE-ADDED PRODUCTS AND SERVICES

Document Formatting and Delivery

Data-Speed Bond Pricing Service provides accurate bond price information. Weekly closing prices and yields are supplied on over 1,600 Canadian, provincial, and corporate bonds provided every Friday evening after the market closes. All bonds are priced by professional traders, not model-derived. Month-end prices and yields are supplied on the first business day following the last day of the month.

The Mutual Fund Database is available only on magnetic tape. It provides a cumulative record of mutual fund performance on approximately 250 Canadian funds. Database information includes net asset value per share, total assets and dividends, with history for over ten years. Additional details on fund type, redemption charges, and sales charges are also included. The database is updated each quarter from information solicited from the leading fund managers in Canada.

The Dividend Database is available only on magnetic tape. It provides an accurate and timely record of dividend declarations for all Canadian listed and leading unlisted securities. It contains such pertinent information as amount paid, record, pay, ex-dividend dates, tax status, and indicated annual payment with history since 1980. The data can be sent on a daily basis or accumulated and supplied at the frequency requested.

The Weekly Stock Profile is available only on magnetic tape. It provides a weekly summary of the composite trading for all Canadian listed stocks based on five exchanges: TSE, ME, VSE, ASE, and WSE. It features 53-week high and low, latest indicated annual dividend, earnings, and price/earnings ratio and yield, with history available from the first quarter of 1981. Updates are available on weekly, monthly or quarterly basis.

U.S. Pricing service, which is available only on magnetic tape, provides daily trading summaries for all U.S. equity, bond, futures, and option markets. It furnishes data on dividend declarations and market indexes as well. Updating is available on a daily, weekly, or monthly frequency.

GREGG CORPORATION
100 Fifth Avenue
Waltham, MA 02254
Telephone: (617) 890-7227
E-Mail: none
Telex: none

COMPANY AT-A-GLANCE

Target Market(s):

Commercial banks
Fortune 1000 corporations
Investment banks
Thrift institutions

Subject Coverage:

Real-time/Historic market
quotations

DESCRIPTION

Gregg Corporation is headquartered in Waltham, Massachussetts, with a regional office located in New York City. The company supplies banks, brokerage firms, insurers, capital management firms, investment analysts, and information redistributors with historical securities information and related management systems for data retrieval and analysis. Gregg's products and services are used for investment analysis, portfolio valuation, and securities performance measurement.

DATABASES

Proprietary

Tradeline Securities Database. Tradeline Securities Database provides information on stocks, bonds, options, mutual funds, and indexes, plus data on more than 100,000 securities traded on major exchanges and the over-the-counter market. In addition to current trading statistics, the Tradeline system provides over 12 years of historical information on more than 65,000 securities. It is designed to serve specifically as a complete database system for managing, retrieving, and analyzing both current and historical securities data. It can be used on a time-sharing basis or as an in-house facility.

VALUE-ADDED PRODUCTS AND SERVICES

Customer Support

Two specific customer service groups are organized within the Gregg Corporation. The Securities Information group is available to provide daily data maintenance, applications program and subroutine support, and system training. Users may direct questions to them regarding system function and use. The Technical Support group provides technical assistance to users, as well as customized application development.

Documentation

Several guides are available to Tradeline subscribers. The *Tradeline User's Guide* provides an overview of the database and describes, in tutorial style, how to use the system and other applications programs to access Tradeline data. The *Tradeline Programmer's Guide* gives information on data accessing and programming techniques necessary to create custom application programs. The *Tradeline Administrator's Guide* gives a system introduction and overview, plus a step-by-step description of the updating process.

System Features/Software Packages

The Tradeline library contains more than 35 data retrieval routines that the user can use separately or in conjunction with one another for multiple data access. Types of routines available include CUSIP/ticker, date, issue and item access, keyed-selection, and charting.

Daily updating software is available if the database is being utilized as an in-house facility. At the close of each trading day a tape or transmission of the day's trading activity is supplied directly to a system site by one of the major data vendors. The system administrator simply sets up the information to be read and initiates the updating process. Its capabilities include reading, checking, and filing daily trade information.

Tradeline user application programs provide the user with analyzing, screening, querying, and reporting capabilities. These self-documenting programs are specifically designed for investment professionals. Customized application programs are also available.

The Gregg Corporation also now offers the Tradeline database on floppy diskette. Information on the diskette may be requested by issue and amount of history desired, and time period, time interval (daily, weekly, monthly, quarterly). It can also be requested in adjusted form, adjusted for stock splits and stock dividends or fully adjusted for all cash and stock distributions. It is available in ASCII and EBCDIC formats along with IBM PC formats for Lotus 1-2-3, Symphony, and dBASE II and dBASE III.

THE H.W. WILSON COMPANY

950 University Avenue
New York NY 10452
Telephone: (212) 588-8400
  (800) 462-6060
E-Mail: none
Telex: none

COMPANY AT-A-GLANCE

Target Market(s):

Commercial banks
Credit unions
Fortune 1000 corporations
Government agencies
Investment banks
Law firms
Mortgage banks
Real estate firms
Specialized librarians
Thrift institutions

Subject Coverage:

Company information/
  statistics
Demographic information/
  statistics
Econometric data
Industry information/
  statistics

DESCRIPTION

The H.W. Wilson Company, in business since 1889, was originally founded by Halsey William Wilson on the campus of the University of Minnesota. In its near-century of existence, it has grown to be a significant player in the publication of reference materials. Today the company publishes numerous indexes that provide access to literature in a wide range of disciplines.

In 1981, H.W. Wilson decided to computerize its publishing efforts, leaving behind its well-known method of saving and interfiling lead slugs to produce cumulated volumes. In 1984, the WILSONLINE retrieval system, which provides online access to all 20 of the Wilson indexes, was introduced. Wilson added WILSEARCH, a menu-driven, front-end software package, to its computer services in 1985 to provide direct user access to WILSONLINE.

Subsidiaries of the Wilson Company include Mansell Publishing Ltd. and Wilson-Cambridge, Inc. Mansell, which became a Wilson subsidiary in 1981, publishes a broad range of bibliographies, directories, and other reference works for academic and research libraries worldwide. Wilson-Cambridge was established in 1984. Its principal activities are managing abstracting services designed to complement the Wilson indexes and providing consulting services pertaining to the use of optical disk technology in database publishing.

Wilson has two U.S. sites, one in the Bronx, New York, the other in Cambridge, Massachusetts, plus an overseas office in London. Its services, both online and in print, help countless library users locate information in more than 3,000 periodicals and in hundreds of thousands of books.

DATABASES

Proprietary

Business Periodicals Index. BPI covers June 1982 to the present date. It indexes over 300 international English-language periodicals, including industry-specific trade and research journals. Literature covered spans a broad range of business topics, from management, public relations, and economics to finance and investment, banking, insurance, and accounting, to name a few. The database is updated at least twice weekly. It is available on the WILSONLINE system via Tymnet or Telenet.

VALUE-ADDED PRODUCTS AND SERVICES

Customer Support

Professional searchers thoroughly familiar with WILSONLINE are available to answer users' questions via these toll-free numbers: (800) 622-4002; in New York, (800) 538-3888; in Canada (212) 588-8998 collect. Questions regarding individual accounts will be answered by the Wilson Customer Services Department. For account assistance, call (800) 367-6770; in New York, (800) 462-6060; in Canada (212) 588-8400 collect.

WILSONLINE training programs are offered throughout the United States. These one-day seminars are conducted by training specialists at the user's library or office. The Wilson Company has also established a permanent training site in New York City, where WILSONLINE training seminars and subject seminars are held on a regular basis. Locations and dates of seminars can be obtained by calling (800) 622-4002.

Documentation

A number of publications are provided by Wilson to assist users in logging on to and effectively searching WILSONLINE. These include the *WILSONLINE Tutorial*, a concise booklet designed for use in WILSONLINE training seminars and for searchers who want to learn or review the system on their own, and *WILSONLINE Guide & Documentation*, a comprehensive loose-leaf manual that covers database contents, system features, and searching procedures and techniques in detail.

WILSEARCH Guide also provides database descriptions, as well as explanations of WILSEARCH commands and features. Two quick-reference guides are available for at-a-glance help.

The *WILSEARCH Quick-Reference Card* describes the major decision points in the WILSEARCH process, while the *WILSONLINE Guide* summarizes system commands and features.

Online help is available as well. A "Help" command provides a menu of common problems faced by searchers using WILSONLINE, followed by detailed explanations of their solutions, while the "Explain" command provides detailed explanations for each system command, message, and feature.

System Features/Software Packages

Up to 1,500 citations per search may be printed offline in any available print format, thereby cutting online connect charges. Offline print orders may be requested directly through the system at the end of a search, and will be mailed within 24 hours. Users have the option of sorting their search results up to four different ways, such as alphabetically by periodical title, in descending order of publication, or various other available options.

WILSEARCH, as mentioned earlier, is Wilson's new personal computer software package. This package provides inexpensive, direct customer access to the Wilson databases. Using a menu that prompts for simple user responses, WILSEARCH formulates searches automatically.

I.P. SHARP ASSOCIATES LIMITED

2 First Canadian Place
Suite 1900
Toronto, Ontario, Canada M5X 1E3
Telephone: (416) 364-5361
  (800) 387-1588
Telex: 062259

COMPANY AT-A-GLANCE

Target Market(s):

Commercial banks
Credit unions
Fortune 1000 corporations
Government agencies
Investment banks
Law firms
Mortgage banks
Real estate firms
Specialized librarians
Thrift institutions

Subject Coverage:

Company information/
  statistics
Econometric data
Real-time/Historic market
  quotations
Research reports/
  evaluations

DESCRIPTION

I.P. Sharp Associates, formerly a privately held international software and communications company, was recently acquired by Reuters. Sharp writes and supports software for mainframe and personal computers, as well as for local area networks and their communications network, IPSANET. The company has more than 40 offices throughout Canada, the United States, Europe, the Middle East, Africa, Australia, and Asia.

Sharp provides information geared to the banking and finance industries, the investment and securities industries, information and development centers, semiconductor manufacturing facilities, emergency services organizations, individual investors, and others.

I.P. Sharp's Data Base Services, newly named InfoService, offers a range of information products and services, including data, programming, micro-products, and value-added products and services. Sharp offers users more than 40 database services providing information in the areas of aviation, energy, economics, finance, and news services.

DATABASES

Proprietary

Agricultural Commodities. The Agricultural Commodities database provides short-term trends in prices, volumes, and other indexes for many agricultural products, including grains and oil seeds; cattle and beef products; hogs and pork products; sheep and lamb products; broilers, eggs, fowl, and dairy; and special crops. It also has economic indicators.

Bank of Canada Weekly Financial Statistics. The Bank of Canada Weekly Financial Statistics database provides weekly banking and monetary statistics released by the Bank of Canada. The database contains statistical information on Canada's money supply and data on all banks operating in Canada. Each week the data are reported on Wednesday, released on Thursday afternoon, and updated on Friday morning.

Canadian Bonds. The Canadian Bonds database provides price and yield statistics for approximately 1,200 Canadian bonds. The database's 7,500 time series include information on the following types of bonds: Canadian government bonds, provincial and provincial guaranteed, municipal, corporate, international and noninternational banks, and foreign government bonds traded in the United States. The database is updated by approximately 900 issues each Friday by 11 A.M. (EST). It is available 24 hours a day, seven days a week except during a short maintenance period on Friday and Saturday nights.

Canadian Chartered Banks, Annual Financial Statements. Canadian Chartered Banks, Annual Financial Statements database provides annual financial statements for all chartered banks operating in Canada. Available information includes income statements, balance sheets, statements of shareholders' equity, and statements of accumulated appropriations contingencies. The entire database is updated on a yearly basis, one to three months after the fiscal year-end.

Canadian Chartered Banks, Monthly Statements of Assets and Liabilities.   The Canadian Chartered Banks, Monthly Statements of Assets and Liabilities database contains time series data on 37 assets figures, 45 liabilities figures, and total assets and liabilities figures for all banks operating in Canada. The database also contains totals for the big 5 and big 6 banks, Schedule A and B banks, and domestic and foreign banks. The entire database is updated monthly, approximately three to six weeks after the month-end.

Canadian Chartered Banks, Quarterly Income Statements.   The Canadian Chartered Banks, Quarterly Income Statement database contains quarterly income statements for all chartered banks in Canada. The database contains income statement data for the big 5 and big 6 banks, and Schedule A and B banks. Totals for all banks are provided as aggregates. The entire database is updated quarterly within six to eight weeks after the quarter-end.

Canadian Department of Insurance.   The Canadian Department of Insurance database provides financial information on 600 federally registered insurance or trust companies; fraternal benefit societies; and cooperative credit associations across Canada. The database contains 576 insurance statement forms. The data come from information that each company sends yearly to the Canadian Department of Insurance.

Canadian Options.   The Canadian Options database provides daily trading statistics for more than 2,000 put and call options traded in Toronto, Montreal, and Vancouver as issued by Trans Canadian Options Incorporated. Currently options are provided for stocks, government bonds, indexes, and silver. The database is updated within four hours of the source update, by 11 P.M. (EST) each trading day.

Commodities.   The Commodities database contains prices, volumes, and open interest for all major commodities traded on the London, New York, Chicago, Kansas City, Minneapolis, Winnipeg, and Toronto/Montreal futures markets. The database contains approximately 41,400 time series. Data are updated on a daily basis by 8:30 P.M. (EST).

Commodity Options.   The Commodity Options database provides prices, volumes, and open interest for all major options and commodities futures traded in the United States. The database contains over 11,880 time series pertaining to opening and closing prices, high and low prices, contract volume, and open interest. The database is updated daily by approximately 1,500 items.

Daily Currency Exchange Rates.   The Daily Currency Exchange Rates database provides exchange rates for major world currencies on the Copenhagen, Frankfurt, Helsinki, London, Madrid, Melbourne, New York, Oslo, Paris, Singapore, Toronto, Tokyo, Vienna, and Zurich markets. Rates are reported in terms of the local currency of the reporting country. Forward and spot rates are reported by the London, New York, Copenhagen, Melbourne, and Toronto markets. Updating of the daily data varies with the individual exchange hours, but occurs by the following business day for the exchange.

Federal Reserve Board Weekly Statistics.   The Federal Reserve Board Weekly Statistics database contains weekly American banking and monetary statistics on over 1,200 time series taken from Forms H.3, H.4, H.4.2, and H.6. The database is updated on a weekly basis by approximately 350 issues one day after the data are released.

Money Market Rates.   The Money Market Rates database provides 246 daily and weekly money market rates for Canada, the United States, and many European and Asian countries. The entire database is completely updated every 24 hours.

North American Stock Market.   The North American Stock Market database provides current and historical prices and volumes for securities listed on North American stock exchanges. The database includes data on more than 11,000 common stocks, preferred stocks, warrants, rights, and units. It covers the New York, American, Montreal, Toronto, Alberta, and Vancouver stock exchanges. The database is entirely updated within two hours of the market closings, by 8 P.M. (EST).

Toronto Stock Exchange Intra-Day Information for Stocks and Indices. The Toronto Stock Exchange Intra-day Information for Stocks and Indices database provides 15-minute interval summaries of intraday trading statistics for 61 major and minor indexes, 11 high-technology indexes, and approximately 1,500 stocks listed on the Toronto Stock Exchange. The database contains nine time series and four static facts. Data are added to the database approximately 1 minute after the close of each 15-minute interval from 10:15 A.M. to 4:15 P.M. (EST).

Toronto Stock Exchange Real-Time Information for Stocks and Indices. The Toronto Stock Exchange Real-Time Information for Stocks and Indices database provides real-time information for over 2,000 stocks and indexes on the Toronto Stock Exchange. The database can be used to access data on the most current price, volume, high and low price for the last 15-minute interval, and other daily trading data any time when the Toronto Stock Exchange is open. The database is continuously updated each trading day from 10 A.M. to 4:15 P.M. (EST).

Toronto Stock Exchange 300 Index and Stock Statistics. The Toronto Stock Exchange 300 Index and Stock Statistics database provides trading statistics for the 300 major stocks and 62 major and minor indexes that form the Toronto Stock Exchange 300 Composite Index. The database contains 20 time series and 9 static facts. The entire database is updated each trading day at approximately 11:30 P.M. (EST). Weekly and monthly data are summarized at the end of the period from the daily data file.

United States Bonds. United States Bonds database contains daily trading statistics for more than 4,000 listed bonds, as well as government and agency issues. Data are obtained from the New York and American Bond Exchanges, Federal Farm Credit Banks, Bank for Co-ops, FNMA, GNMA, Student Loan Marketing Association, Federal Home Loan Bank, Federal Land Bank, FIC Bank Debentures, Inter-American Development Bank, Treasury bonds, Treasury notes, Treasury bills, and World Bond Bank. The database is updated with approximately 3,800 issues every day by 6 A.M. (EST).

United States Options. The United States Options database contains daily trading statistics for all put and call options traded on all major exchanges in the United States. The database contains 136,000 time series pertaining to stock options, interest rate options, index options, and foreign currency options. The exchanges covered are updated each trading day by 6 A.M. (EST).

United States Stock Market.   The United States Stock Market database contains current and historical prices and volumes for securities listed on Canadian and U.S. stock exchanges. The data include common and preferred stocks, warrants, rights, and units for issues traded on the New York, American, Montreal, Midwest, Boston, Pacific, Toronto, and Philadelphia exchanges. Data for the over-the-counter bank, insurance and industrial issues on the NASDAQ, mutual funds, and over 200 market indicators are also included. The database is updated daily by 6 A.M. (EST).

Third Party

Disclosure Online.   Disclosure Online database includes current and historical corporate statistics and textual information on approximately 11,000 publicly owned companies that have filings with the U.S. Securities and Exchange Commission (SEC). The database contains 2,000,000 time series. Data are added to the database daily with new releases and updates to earlier information occuring on a weekly basis.

Duff and Phelps Equity Ideas.   Duff and Phelps Equity Ideas contains research reports by Duff and Phelps that expedite the decision making processes involving investments for equity analysts and portfolio managers. These reports cover more than 440 companies and 61 industry groups. The database is updated daily by approximately 440 issues by 2 A.M. (EST).

Duff and Phelps Fixed Income Ratings.   Duff and Phelps Fixed Income Ratings database provides information on fixed-income ratings for approximately 500 U.S. corporations with significant institutional investment following. The data on the 500 corporations are updated on a daily basis.

Financial Post Bonds.   The Financial Post Bonds database contains weekly closing prices and yields for more than 1,500 Canadian bonds. Database coverage includes all publicly issued Canadian, provincial, provincial guaranteed, and corporate bonds, as well as many private placements. The database is updated every Friday night by approximately 1,200 issues.

Financial Post Securities.   The Financial Post Securities database contains trading statistics for securities traded on the New York and American Stock Exchanges and all Canadian exchanges. The database contains 30,000 times series on the daily high, low, and closing prices, plus volume on approximately 3,800 Canadian securities.

Foreign Currency Projections.   Foreign Currency Projections is a foreign currency forecasting service provided by S.J. Rundt and Associates, Incorporated. The service combines fundamental economic assessment with technical analysis and various judgmental factors. The numeric projections, updated monthly, are set in "most likely" ranges for quarter-end spot rates looking one year forward. Textual commentary details what S.J. Rundt and Associates deems to be the most important background trends at the time. The database encompasses the monetary units of 31 countries, but can, on request, be expanded to include currencies not presently in the system. Data updates for all countries in the database occur on a monthly basis at mid-month.

VALUE-ADDED PRODUCTS AND SERVICES

Customer Support

I.P. Sharp's support program includes ongoing training programs and local customer support. User support is provided in North America via a toll-free action line (800) 387-1588 from 8 A.M. to 6 P.M. (EST), Monday through Friday. I.P. Sharp also provides a 24-hour answering service.

Documentation

To facilitate quick and effective searching, InfoService publishes two symbol directories: the *Directory of Data Base Symbols*, and the *Directory of SEDOL Numbers* for the EXSHARE international securities database.

I.P. Sharp Associates' *Financial News* newsletter provides subscribers with information on company services, new product introductions, billing information, and value-added product and services descriptions.

Other user aids include user manuals, reference guides, and complete online documentation and instruction.

System Features/Software Packages

PRICELINK allows for information retrieval and storage for future spreadsheet analysis. PRICELINK allows for spreadsheet analysis on Lotus 1-2-3 and Symphony, and also supports downloading in APL and ASCII formats for custom applications.

SUPERPLOT is a proprietary software package that allows for production of presentation-quality color graphics.

MAGIC is a software package allowing users to customize reports to suit their needs. It is designed to be of use to computer users who have little or no programming experience.

Compu Trac is a third party software package designed for downloading and statistical manipulation of financial data. Compu Trac allows users to track and chart stocks, options, bonds, and commodities.

MICROPOST is a third party access software package designed for downloading and statistical manipulation of financial data.

IPSANET is I.P. Sharp's private international communications network. The IPSANET network provides database access to more than 800 cities and 64 countries worldwide. In addition to offering access to I.P. Sharp's databases, IPSANET also provides custom service and electronic messaging capabilities.

Online Communication

Sharp allows subscribers to send and receive Telex messages electronically through its proprietary MAILBOX communications system, or via custom interface. Members of I.P. Sharp's MAILBOX system can also obtain information or help from I.P. Sharp's staff experts.

Research Services

I.P. Sharp offers consulting services on an individual basis.

INFO GLOBE
444 Front Street West
Toronto, Ontario, Canada M5V 2S9
Telephone: (416) 585-5250
E-Mail: none
Telex: 06-219629

COMPANY AT-A-GLANCE

Target Market(s):

Commercial banks
Fortune 1000 corporations
Government agencies
Investment banks
Law firms
Specialized librarians

Subject Coverage:

Company information/
  statistics
Industry information/
  statistics
Real-time/Historic market
  quotations
News services

DESCRIPTION

Info Globe is an electronic publishing division of *The Globe and Mail*, Canada's national newspaper. The division was formed in 1980. The company is currently headquartered in Toronto, Canada. Regional sales offices are located in Ottawa and Vancouver. Info Globe has a staff of about 25 people.

DATABASES

Proprietary

The Canadian Financial Database. The Canadian Financial Database delivers full-text financial statements from major Canadian publicly held corporations and Crown corporations competing in the private sector. Information is available for 500 Canadian companies, beginning with their 1983 annual reports.

The Globe and Mail Online.   The Globe and Mail Online database contains the full text of virtually all articles that are printed in *The Globe and Mail*, Canada's national newspaper. Articles date back to November 14, 1977 and include the Report on Business, entertainment, news, sports, editorials, letters to the editor, and so on.

INSIGHT.   INSIGHT is a compilation of databases developed by Canadian Systems Group, Canada's largest computer services organization. Databases include Inter-Corporate Ownership, Canadian Federal Corporation and Directors, Corporate Names, Trade Marks, Bankruptcies, and Canadian Trade Index.

Marketscan.   The Marketscan database contains data from six North American stock exchanges—the Toronto, Montreal, Alberta, Vancouver, New York, and American. Data include closing, high, low, bid, and ask prices, as well as volume. The database is updated once each day and maintains information on an individual issue for 250 trading days.

Report on Business Corporate Database.   The Report on Business Corporate Database contains annual financial information on more than 1,700 Canadian publicly held companies. Selected Crown corporations and privately held corporations are also included. Quarterly data are available for more than 350 companies. Historical data are available from as far back as 1974.

VALUE-ADDED PRODUCTS AND SERVICES

Customer Support

Info Globe's customer service staff provides free expert advice on search strategies from 9 A.M. to 5 P.M. (Toronto time).

Info Globe offers workshops across Canada and in the United States. Training fees are $150 per person.

Documentation

The Info Globe News is published every two months. This newsletter provides database update and change information, search terms, price information, and trade show and workshop schedules.

System Features/Software Packages

Software packages are available for some databases. These packages can be run on either Apple or IBM PC.

Research Services

Info Globe's search service will provide custom searches at the user's request. The results are available by the following business day. Fees for this service vary by database.

INFORMATION ACCESS COMPANY

11 Davis Drive
Belmont, CA 94002
Telephone: (415) 591-2333
 (800) 227-8431
E-Mail: none
Telex: 1561004 INFO UT

COMPANY AT-A-GLANCE

Target Market(s):

 Commercial banks
 Credit unions
 Fortune 1000 corporations
 Government agencies
 Investment banks
 Law firms
 Mortgage banks
 Real estate firms
 Specialized librarians
 Thrift institutions

Subject Coverage:

 Company information/
  statistics
 Demographic information/
  statistics
 Econometric data
 Industry information/
  statistics
 News services
 Research reports/
  evaluations

4

DESCRIPTION

Information Access Company (IAC) is a privately held division of the Ziff-Davis Publishing Company. According to IAC, more than five million people use its online and microfilm indexes annually.

Founded and staffed by professional librarians and information specialists, IAC provides online indexing to over three million articles from more than 2,500 magazines, journals, tabloids, and newsletters, as well as 12 major newspapers. Full-text articles from a substantial subset of the indexed journals are available online as well.

To access the IAC databases, users must subscribe to DIALOG, BRS, Mead's NEXIS/LEXIS, Data-Star, or Infomaster. Virtually any communicating terminal, word processor or microcomputer can be used to access these services.

DATABASES

Proprietary

Computer Database.   This database is designed to provide business and computer professionals with answers to questions regarding hardware, software, peripherals, and high-tech fields.

Finsbury Data Services.   IAC is the U.S. representative of Finsbury Data Services, a British company that produces online international business information. Its products include Textline, which contains abstracts of business news from over 120 publications and news monitoring services from around the world; Newsline, which provides daily summaries of international news and comments from over 40 daily and weekly U.K. and European newspapers, and Dataline, which focuses on financial profiles of over 3,000 U.K. and foreign companies, including income statements, finance tables, balance sheets, and accounting ratios.

Industry Data Sources.   This database provides access to sources of marketing, financial, and statistical data on 65 major industries, both national and international.

Legal Resource Index.   LRI covers all major English-language secondary legal literature. Topics covered include corporate law, taxation, labor relations, and copyright, to name just a few.

Magazine ASAP.   This database is the full-text companion to Magazine Index. It includes both the text and indexing to articles in over 60 magazines covered in Magazine Index.

Magazine Index.   Magazine Index contains records of articles appearing in more than 400 widely read magazines from the United States and Canada. Subject coverage includes current affairs, business, education, science, and travel.

Management Contents.   Management Contents covers all aspects of management with current and retrospective abstracting and indexing of over 90 of the top periodicals in the field. Featured topics include accounting and auditing, sales and marketing, operations research, and finance.

National Newspaper Index. NNI is a cover-to-cover index of news from the *New York Times, The Wall Street Journal*, the *Washington Post, Los Angeles Times*, and *Christian Science Monitor*.

NEWSEARCH. NEWSEARCH is the daily updating vehicle for Magazine Index, National Newspaper Index, The Computer Database, Legal Resource Index, Management Contents, and Trade & Industry Index. It contains the most current records from the source publications of each of the databases named until they are added to their respective databases.

Trade & Industry ASAP. This database is the full-text companion to Trade & Industry Index. It includes both the text and indexing to articles in over 80 journals covered in Trade & Industry Index.

Trade & Industry Index. Trade & Industry Index provides indexing for over 300 business periodicals, including trade and general interest business journals, trade magazines, and industry-specific publications. Coverage includes *The Wall Street Journal* and the business section of the *New York Times*.

VALUE-ADDED PRODUCTS AND SERVICES

Customer Support

IAC offers three different seminars to help users become expert searchers in all 10 of its databases. The Basic Course describes indexing and search techniques for Newsearch, National Newspaper Index, Trade & Industry ASAP, and Legal Resource Index (separate courses for DIALOG and BRS searchers.)

The Business Applications Course describes business coverage and search strategy for finding information on companies, products, people, and industries in all IAC files. Management Contents, Industry Data Sources, Newsearch, Trade & Industry Index, and National Newspaper Index are highlighted (separate course for DIALOG and BRS searchers).

The Computer Technology and Information Course describes computer, telecommunications, and electronics coverage; indexing; and DIALOG2 search techniques for finding business and technical information in the Computer Database and other IAC files.

There is a registration fee for each course. The Basic and Business courses are full-day seminars, with online practice time included. The Computer course is a half-day seminar. Each registrant receives a free copy of the *Computer Database Thesaurus & Dictionary*. Information on training or on any of the databases is available via IAC's toll-free number ((800) 227-8431). Search assistance and database information is also available through the various services that provide access to IAC's databases.

Documentation

IAC publishes *Access to Access*, a users' guide to the IAC databases. It details the databases' scope and coverage, as well as editorial policies and search techniques. A computer database thesaurus is included. This publication sells for approximately $100. Other searching aids available for IAC databases include free lists, that provide the user with specifics about database contents, such as journals covered, journal abbreviations used in indexing, and geographic codes. Additionally, *Online News* is a quarterly publication covering recent developments at IAC and in the online industry as a whole.

System Features/Software Packages

IAC's microcomputer software product, SEARCH HELPER, provides easy access to Magazine Index, National Newspaper Index, Trade & Industry Index, Legal Resource Index, NEWSEARCH, and Management Contents databases.

Research Services

IAC's *Ward's Business Directory* is a three-volume set of current data on the largest companies worldwide. Each company record in the directory is updated annually, with demographic and financial data included for nearly 80,000 U.S. private companies. Over 8,000 public companies are profiled so that users can retrieve comprehensive data on major U.S. companies. More than 15,000 international companies are included to keep users abreast of the worldwide scene. Companies are ranked according to sales within industry. The geographic and industry sections provide information for sales territory analysis and for planning marketing strategies. Parent companies' linkages to subsidiaries are also included.

Document Formatting and Delivery

Full text of IAC-indexed articles may be obtained via Infomaster or through offline print orders on any of the vendor services. Alternative forms of output, such as magnetic tape and diskette, are available. Cost depends on the individual vendors.

4

INTERACTIVE DATA CORPORATION

303 Wyman Street
Waltham, MA 02254
Telephone: (617) 895-4300
 (617) 860-8197
E-Mail: none
Telex: none

COMPANY AT-A-GLANCE

Target Market(s):

Commercial banks
Fortune 1000 corporations
Investment banks
Mortgage banks
Specialized librarians
Thrift institutions

Subject Coverage:

Company information/
 statistics
Econometric data
Real-time/Historic market
 quotations

DESCRIPTION

Interactive Data Corporation is a subsidiary of the Chase Manhattan Bank. The company provides current and historical securities-related data for equity research, fixed income management, portfolio management, mutual fund pricing, investment technology, and quantitative analysis.

Interactive Data Corporation has more than 11,000 clients in over 40 countries. The primary users of Interactive Data Corporation's products and services include: investment bankers, stockbrokers, equity research analysts, mutual fund sponsors, economists, fixed-income portfolio managers, equity portfolio managers, pension fund sponsors, financial analysts, quantitative analysts, securities traders, banks, individual investors, merger and acquisition analysts, and hedgers.

Interactive Data Corporation delivers products and services via online connection with the client company's mainframe computer, downloading to personal computers, or on in-house computers. Most data provided by Interactive Data are gathered electronically and checked for accuracy by 80 data professionals.

DATABASES

Proprietary

IDCPRICE. This database provides current and historical securities-related data, as well as information on international securities, options, financial futures, interest rates, institutional bond quotes, mortgage-backed securities, municipal bonds, and commodities.

VALUE-ADDED PRODUCTS AND SERVICES

Customer Support

Subscribers are offered a 24-hour hotline, seven days per week, for questions and problems.

User training services are provided by field consultants at the time of system installation.

Documentation

A user manual is provided at cost.

An online newsletter stating database services, updates, and changes is available.

System Features/Software Packages

Subscribers may store up to 10 portfolios on Interactive Data's computer system at no charge. After the first 10 portfolios, the subscriber is charged a $10 per month storage fee per portfolio. A portfolio consists of a separately identified list of up to 200 securities.

Interactive Data provides IDCPRICE software for screening, analyzing, displaying, and distributing data. This software is generally included in the price of Interactive Data's services.

4

JOURNAL OF ECONOMIC LITERATURE

P.O. Box 7320, Oakland Station
Pittsburgh, PA 15213
Telephone: (412) 621-2291
E-Mail: none
Telex: none

COMPANY AT-A-GLANCE

Target Market(s):

Commercial banks
Fortune 1000 corporations
Government agencies
Investment banks
Specialized librarians
Thrift institutions

Subject Coverage:

Econometric data

DESCRIPTION

The Journal of Economic Literature is a nonprofit organization headquartered in Pittsburgh, Pennsylvania. It is a subsidiary of the American Economic Association.

DATABASES

Proprietary

Economic Literature Index.   The Economic Literature Index database provides bibliographic information from economic articles and books to economists, economic researchers, and reference librarians. The primary sources of data are approximately 285 economic research journals and essays from currently published books on a wide variety of economic subjects. The beginning date for journal articles is 1969. The beginning date for essays is 1979. The database is updated on a quarterly basis with approximately 2,700 new entries.

VALUE-ADDED PRODUCTS AND SERVICES

Customer Support

Training workshops are available through DIALOG, the online vendor of the Economic Literature Index database.

Documentation

A user's manual is available for $5 from DIALOG.

Document Formatting and Delivery

Hardcopy prints are available in the form of *The Journal of Economic Literature*. The publication is produced quarterly and is available through American Economic Association membership or at libraries. Hard copies are also available as the *Index of Economic Articles*, which is published annually and is available at libraries. It can also be purchased from the American Economic Association for $50 per copy. Offline copies are available from DIALOG for 15 cents per full record.

4

KENNY INFORMATION SYSTEMS
55 Broad Street
New York, NY 10004
Telephone: (212) 530-0925
E-Mail: none
Telex: none

COMPANY AT-A-GLANCE

Target Market(s):

Commercial banks
Investment banks

Subject Coverage:

Real-time/Historic market
quotations

DESCRIPTION

Kenny Information Systems (KIS) is the database management and evaluation arm of the Kenny Group. KIS is responsible for compiling accurate descriptive data on 1.5 million outstanding municipal issues and for evaluating them—enabling bondholders to know the characteristics of their bonds and to monitor changes that might impact their value. KIS is also the source of Munibase, Mini-Universe, and a number of notification services.

The company's staff of researchers continually collects and maintains data on individual tax-exempt issues. The database is updated daily to incorporate changes, additions, and deletions.

The primary users of this information include banks, brokerage firms, institutional investors, and law firms.

The total cost of accessing the system is based on a combination of a monthly subscription fee, data usage, and connect time for dial-up service. For direct line, users are charged according to a monthly subscription fee, data usage, a direct line charge, and a one-time installation fee.

DATABASES

Proprietary

Munibase.   This is a complete municipal securities database that furnishes descriptions of over 1.5 million tax-exempt issues. Call/Put bond users may receive daily updates on complete and partial calls, tenders, defaults (municipal and corporate), and putable municipal issues. This database is available through Uninet.

VALUE-ADDED PRODUCTS AND SERVICES

Customer Support

User support is available by calling (212) 530-0900. By calling this number, the user will be routed to the most appropriate Kenny representative for the particular problem at hand. Virtually any problem involving the use of Munibase can be resolved through this service.

System Features/Software Packages

The Evaluation Service employs thorough evaluation methods to arrive at timely, accurate quotes for municipal issues.

The File Maintenance Service enables subscribers to automatically validate CUSIP numbers and call dates/prices, and to update master security records by using complete descriptions drawn from the KIS Munibase service.

The Notification Service provides weekly tape and hardcopy announcements of calls, tenders, and defaults for both corporate and municipal securities, as well as put notifications for municipal issues.

4

**KNIGHT-RIDDER FINANCIAL
INFORMATION**

1 Exchange Plaza
55 Broadway
New York, NY 10006
Telephone: (212) 269-1110
 (800) 433-8430
E-Mail: none
Telex: none

COMPANY AT-A-GLANCE

Target Market(s):

Commercial banks
Credit unions
Fortune 1000 corporations
Investment banks
Mortgage banks
Real estate firms
Specialized librarians
Thrift institutions

Subject Coverage:

Real-time/Historic market
 quotations
News services
Research reports/
 evaluations

DESCRIPTION

Knight-Ridder Financial Information is part of the Knight-Ridder Business Information Services division of Knight-Ridder Newspapers Incorporated, a worldwide enterprise employing more than 22,000 people. Knight-Ridder Business Information Services provides business and financial information to 50,000 subscribers. Other products in the Knight-Ridder news group include: *Knight-Ridder Financial News, Commodity News Services, Unicom News, The Journal of Commerce, Commodity Perspective*, and *Tradecenter.*

The Financial Information division produces MoneyCenter database, an electronic financial information service that provides statistics and quotes; news; and fixed income, futures, equity, commodity, foreign exchange, and money market data to the financial services industry. Knight-Ridder Financial Information's main customers include traders, portfolio managers, investment advisers, investment banks, commercial banks, savings and loans, securities firms, and large corporations.

DATABASES

Proprietary

MoneyCenter. MoneyCenter is a financial services system from Knight-Ridder Business Information Services. The database provides news and statistics; money market prices and rates; quotes on equities, currencies, futures, and option indexes; foreign exchange data; commodities data; data analysis; and data charting services. The database is accessible 24 hours a day, seven days a week via leased lines, microwave communications, or satellite broadcast.

VALUE-ADDED PRODUCTS AND SERVICES

Customer Support

User assistance is available by calling (800) 433-8430.

Documentation

Database documentation includes a user's manual, user quick-reference cards, and online help.

System Features/Software Packages

A news alert feature "beeps" and places a top news story in red. Two top news stories are always displayed as line items at the bottom of the screen and are updated when necessary.

Customized display capabilities include 16 personally designed pages of quotes, "windowing" of data on a single screen, scrolling quotes, split-screen features, double-size characters, and reverse-screen video.

Electronic library services are provided through Vu/Text Information Services (another division of Knight-Ridder Business Information Services).

Research Services

A number of news services provide subscribers with details of credit, commodity, and financial happenings worldwide. These include Knight-Ridder Financial News, which provides in-depth coverage and analysis of the credit markets; Commodity News Services, which provides daily news and futures market information from Commodity News Services, Inc.; Unicom News, which covers financial and commodity information and prices in 31 countries outside the United States; and American Quotation System, which provides news and quotes for the grain industry. In addition, the *Journal of Commerce* provides transportation and trade information. *Commodity Perspective Magazine* is an independent charter of futures.

MCGRAW-HILL, INC.
1221 Avenue of the Americas
New York, NY 10020
Telephone: (212) 512-2000
E-Mail: none
Telex: none

COMPANY AT-A-GLANCE

Target Market(s):

Commercial banks
Fortune 1000 corporations
Government agencies
Investment banks
Specialized librarians

Subject Coverage:

Company information/
  statistics
Industry information/
  statistics
News services

DESCRIPTION

McGraw-Hill, Inc., widely known for its magazines and newsletters, has ventured into all phases of the information industry. Its Book Company offers more than 20,000 books, magazines, newsletters, computer software programs, audiovisuals, and multimedia packages to educate and inform audiences around the world. Its Information Systems Company focuses on two major markets: the construction industry and the fields of computers and communications. The Publications Company produces 60 magazines, newsletters, and news wire services.

DATABASES

Proprietary

McGraw-Hill Business Backgrounder. The McGraw-Hill Business Backgrounder, offered through DIALOG, currently contains 10 McGraw-Hill publications dating back to January 1985. Additional publications are soon coming online. The publications include: *Business Week, Aviation Week & Space Technology, Byte, Coal Age, Electronics, Data Communications, Inside NRC, Chemical Week, Green Markets*, and *Securities Week*. Additional publications will be coming on line.

VALUE-ADDED PRODUCTS AND SERVICES

Customer Support

Customer support is available through DIALOG Information Retrieval Service.

MEAD DATA CENTRAL, INC.
P.O. Box 933
Dayton, OH 45401
Telephone: (800) 227-4908
 (513) 865-6800
E-Mail: none
Telex: none

COMPANY AT-A-GLANCE

Target Market(s):

Commercial banks
Credit unions
Fortune 1000 corporations
Government agencies
Investment banks
Law firms
Mortgage banks
Real estate firms
Specialized librarians
Thrift institutions

Subject Coverage:

Company information/
 statistics
Industry information/
 statistics
News services

DESCRIPTION

Mead Data Central (MDC) is a wholly owned subsidiary of the
Mead Corporation, headquartered in Dayton, Ohio and represented by 21 major sales offices in the United States, Canada,
and England. Mead Data Central's primary database customers are
the accounting, legal, medical, and health-care professions, plus
businesses ranging in type and size. The approximate number of
trained users of Mead Data Central's services was 300,000 in 1985.

MDC runs its own computer facilities in Dayton. Customers can
access its online services through Mead's own custom terminal,
the UBIQ, or through a wide range of personal computers and
terminals. The various services are available 23.75 hours a day,
Monday through Friday, (MDC runs a daily 15-minute system
check at 2 A.M. (EST)); weekend hours exclude 10 P.M. Saturday to
6 A.M. Sunday (EST).

DATABASES

Proprietary

EXCHANGE.   EXCHANGE is an information retrieval service containing company and industry reports written by expert analysts at leading brokerage and investment banking firms. It contains more than 1.7 billion online characters, representing more than 750,000 documents. The information in EXCHANGE is updated on a daily, weekly, monthly, or bimonthly basis, depending on the type of information being updated, frequency of publication, and the agreement with the publisher. Reports are provided in full-text format. Access is available via MDC's own network, Meadnet, or through Telenet, Tymnet, Alaskanet, Datapac, or by calling (800) 543-9470.

NEXIS.   NEXIS contains a vast online library of news, business, financial, and general information. It includes full-text coverage of more than 160 international newspapers, magazines, professional journals, trade journals, newsletters, and wire services. NEXIS has more than 27 billion characters online, representing more than 13 million documents.

It offers the full text of more than 160 information sources, including journals, newsletters, broadcast transcripts, newspapers, and news wires from around the world. Subject coverage includes business, finance, government, trade, technology, health care, and general news and information. Updates are loaded on a daily, weekly, monthly, or bimonthly basis, depending on the type of source, frequency of publication, and the agreement with the publisher. NEXIS may also be accessed through the various telecommunications networks named above, as well as via MDC's toll-free number.

Third Party

NAARS.   The National Automated Accounting Research System (NAARS) is jointly produced by Mead Data Central and the American Institute of Certified Public Accountants (AICPA). NAARS holds more than 1.2 billion online characters, representing more than 48,000 documents. These documents include over 20,000 annual reports; proxy statements; and authoritative pronounce-ments of the AICPA, Securities and Exchange Commission, and the Financial Accounting Standards Board. NAARS is updated on a daily, weekly, monthly, or annual basis depending on the source document, frequency of publication, and agreement with the AICPA. NAARS may be accessed via Meadnet, Telenet, Tym-net, Alaskanet, Datapac, or by calling (800) 543-9470.

VALUE-ADDED PRODUCTS AND SERVICES

Customer Support

All subscribers to MDC's databases are offered training sessions at any of the more than 40 sales and training sites throughout the United States. Local customer service representatives are assigned to subscribers to provide ongoing support. In addition, toll-free telephone assistance is available around-the-clock ((800) 227-4908 or (513) 865-6800 collect).

Documentation

MDC publishes a host of manuals, newsletters, and quick-reference guides that cover searching across the Mead system of databases. These include:

The Guide to NEXIS and Related Services, a twice-yearly publi-cation that covers all the services and libraries offered by MDC (except LEXIS).

The Reference Manual, MDC's database complement, which provides tips on database use and search technique, plus descriptions of databases and other Mead services.

The Thesaurus and Directory, which contains index words that increase search retrieval by finding related terms when included in a search.

Quick reference brochures that list often-used search words from the thesaurus, file selection procedures, system short cuts, printing steps, and other helpful hints.

Customer newsletters that provide search tips, database changes and updates, database contents, and answers to user questions.

System Features/Software Packages

Mead Data Central software Version 1.4 provides the capability to print MAIL-IT and PRINT DOCUMENT requests on the printer attached to the personal computer used to access MDC. This version's session recording feature allows users to save a selected amount of data on diskette.

Selective Dissemination of Information (SDI) Services

ECLIPSE is an electronic clipping service designed for customers who need consistent updating on a particular topic. ECLIPSE automatically repeats a user-specified search on a daily, weekly, or monthly basis. Results are automatically printed, either at the user's site or at MDC's facilities in Dayton, in which case they are then forwarded directly to the subscriber.

Document Formatting and Delivery

In addition to online information services, Mead Data Central also provides hard copy of information retrieved online. These services include printing individual screens, selected documents, or an entire set of documents. Customers may order hard copy simply by pressing a designated key while online. Print orders may be sent to Mead's central computer, in which case they are delivered in two to four days at a cost-per-page plus handling fee, or they may be printed online. Telecommunications and connect-time charges apply to online printing.

MLR PUBLISHING COMPANY
229 South 18th Street
Philadelphia, PA 19103
Telephone: (215) 875-2631
E-Mail: none
Telex: none

COMPANY AT-A-GLANCE

Target Market(s):

Commercial banks
Fortune 1000 corporations
Investment banks
Law firms
Specialized librarians

Subject Coverage:

Company information/
  statistics
Industry information/
  statistics

DESCRIPTION

The MLR Publishing Company, formerly the publication division of The Hay Group, publishes two professional journals, *Mergers & Acquisitions*, a bimonthly that recently celebrated its twentieth anniversary, and *Directors & Boards*, a quarterly in its tenth year of publication.

In terms of online services, MLR produces the M&A Database, a source of data pertinent to analysis of mergers, acquisitions, buyouts, and divestitures.

DATABASES

Proprietary

M&A Database. This database is a comprehensive source of the latest information on mergers, acquisitions, divestitures, leveraged buyouts, tender offers, and partial acquisitions. It contains data on approximately 20,000 transactions valued at $1 million or more involving both public and private companies from 1979 to the present. Continual updates provide new information on pending, completed, and unsuccessful deals. Primary data sources are SEC filings, *The Wall Street Journal*, Dow Jones News Service Wire, and Standard & Poor's *Corporation Records Daily News*. Lag time between source publication and database update is one week.

VALUE-ADDED PRODUCTS AND SERVICES

Research Services

Clients may call the M&A Database Information Center (800-MERGING) to discuss their information requirements. A member of the M&A database staff will search the database and mail the requested documents.

**MONEY MARKET
SERVICES, INC.**

275 Shoreline Drive
Redwood City, CA 94065
Telephone: (800) 227-7304
 (415) 595-0610
E-Mail: none
Telex: none

COMPANY AT-A-GLANCE

Target Market(s):

Commercial banks
Fortune 1000 corporations
Investment banks
Mortgage banks
Thrift institutions

Subject Coverage:

Real-time/Historic market
 quotations

DESCRIPTION

Money Market Services, Inc., is a subsidiary of The Institute of Economic and Monetary Affairs.

DATABASES

Proprietary

MMS Currency Market Analysis. The MMS Currency Market Analysis database was first published in 1982. The database provides fundamental and technical analysis of the factors that affect the international currency exchange and deposit markets. Coverage includes major central bank analysis, currency trends, international economic analysis, and other events that may affect these markets. The database is updated virtually 24 hours a day as reports and analysis information arrives. Several key pages are updated as often as four times an hour.

MMS Fundamental Analysis. The MMS Fundamental Analysis database was first published in 1977. The database provides forecasts and analysis of the supply and demand factors that affect short-term interest rates. Analysis focuses on Fed policy and operations, monetary aggregates, economic conditions, Treasury activity, and other interest-sensitive areas. The service also provides the Weekly Economic Survey, which quantifies the expectations

4

of more than 100 institutional market participants and leading economists for upcoming financial and economic releases, market tone, and other market-sensitive events.

MMS Technical Research.   MMS Technical Research database was first published in 1980. The database provides various technical indicators, which are supported by textual analysis. The data are presented on a daily, hourly, and intrahourly basis. Indicators represent technical conditions of the markets for U.S. government securities, mortgage-backed securities, and metals. Coverage includes spot, futures, and options.

VALUE-ADDED PRODUCTS AND SERVICES

Customer Support

Subscribers are allowed unlimited access to a toll-free analyst hotline.

Documentation

User manuals present page-by-page descriptions of the database, as well as user applications for the database. The manuals are supplied free of charge to subscribers.

FEDWATCH is a weekly newsletter provided by Money Market Services. The newsletter contains current topics of financial interest and periodic in-depth commentary articles. The newsletter is available for $240 per year by mail. *FEDWATCH* is also available online through Compuserve or NewsNet.

MOODY'S INVESTORS SERVICE, INC.

99 Church Street
New York, NY 10007
Telephone: (212) 553-0300
  (800) 342-5647
E-Mail: none
Telex: 421889

COMPANY AT-A-GLANCE

Target Market(s):

Commercial banks
Credit unions
Fortune 1000 corporations
Government agencies
Investment banks
Law firms
Mortgage banks
Specialized librarians
Thrift institutions

Subject Coverage:

Company information/
  statistics
News services

DESCRIPTION

Moody's Investors Service, Inc. is a wholly owned subsidiary of Dun & Bradstreet Corporation. The parent company is comprised of three business segments operating in the United States and abroad. The Business Services segment includes Dun & Bradstreet's Credit Services, which provide commercial credit reporting and collection services. The Plan Services segment provides services related to benefit plans for small businesses. Finally, the Marketing Services segment includes Donnelley Marketing Services and Dun's Marketing Services, which together provide a wide range of commercial and consumer services. Moody's falls into the Plan Services segment along with R.H. Donnelley, Official Airline Guides, and Technical Publishing. Moody's primary business concerns are financial and investment publications, research, and bond rating.

DATABASES

Proprietary

Corporate Profiles.   This database includes concise, descriptive overviews and detailed financial statistics on 3,600 public companies.   Coverage includes all companies listed on the New York and American Stock Exchanges, and 1,300 actively traded over-the-counter companies.

International Corporate News.   This database provides users with current business developments and financial statistics for 4,000 major corporations and institutions in 100 countries.

U.S. Corporate News.   Moody's U.S. Corporate News database contains business and financial news on approximately 14,000 companies. Updated weekly, coverage is drawn from Moody's highly regarded *News Reports.*

VALUE-ADDED PRODUCTS AND SERVICES

Customer Support

Customer support is available through DIALOG and the Infomaster gateway.

Documentation

Fact sheets and chapters that cover searching in Moody's databases are available from DIALOG.

Research Services

Moody's publishes a *Municipal Credit Report (MCR)* for each bond sale of $1 million or more and for every note sale. "Update" *MCRs* are also published providing reviews of outstanding ratings. The *MCR* indicates the key factors examined in coming to the rating decision and explains the rationale for the decision.

MCR Previews offers a condensed version of Moody's *Municipal Credit Reports* arranged for easy access by the following categories: Current Day's Reports; Current Two Weeks' Reports; State;

Purpose/Type; Moody's Rating; Dollar Amount of Issue; and Issuer Name.

Moody's Bond Survey is an authoritative weekly publication that highlights new and prospective fixed income offerings and includes commentaries on economic and market conditions that affect fixed-income instruments.

Moody's Bond Record is a comprehensive, fact-filled monthly guide to over 40,000 fixed-income issues.

Moody's Municipal & Government Manual and News Reports is a two-volume manual, published annually, which provides complete coverage of 14,000 bond-issuing municipalities and government agencies. Semi-weekly *News Reports* keep the manual current.

The *New Issues Calendar* presents a comprehensive listing of upcoming public and negotiated municipal offerings as well as the previous week's sales organized by sale date and by state.

The Rating Monitor service details Moody's municipal rating activity (new issue ratings, upgrades, downgrades, and confirmations) arranged by current day's ratings and by rating activity during the last 45 days organized by state.

4

**MULTINATIONAL COMPUTER
MODELS INC.**

605 Bloomfield Avenue
Montclair, NJ 07042
Telephone: (201) 746-5060
E-Mail: none
Telex: none

COMPANY AT-A-GLANCE

Target Market(s):

Commercial banks
Fortune 1000 corporations
Investment banks

Subject Coverage:

Econometric data
Real-time/Historic market
 quotations
News services

DESCRIPTION

Multinational Computer Models, headquartered in Montclair, New Jersey, has as its goal to provide international financial managers with relevant information and distinctive management systems. The company's services include: international treasury management systems, foreign exchange trading decision systems, and international financial information services.

DATABASES

Proprietary

MATREX. Multinational Computer Models' MATREX database system provides current and historical daily exchange rate data and monthly trade inflation and exchange rate data for 34 countries. The database is updated on a daily basis and contains information dating back to 1971.

VALUE-ADDED PRODUCTS AND SERVICES

Customer Support

Multinational Computer Models provides user support and consulting services for its clients.

Research Services

Custom-designed reporting forms allow the user to instantly establish and coordinate currency exposure reporting consistent with national accounting system standards and the user's own management system approach. Customized reports on up-to-date exchange rates, interest rates, international money market analyses, and worldwide financial information are also available.

System Features/Software Packages

Tradex-2 is a fully integrated foreign exchange trading support system designed to be used by financial institutions and currency traders. Tradex-2 operates on IBM PC-XT, IBM PC-AT, and other compatible computers. The Tradex-2 system is designed to conduct regular, fixing, and hedging currency transactions.

4

**NATIONAL REGISTER
PUBLISHING COMPANY**

3004 Glenview Road
Wilmette, IL 60091
Telephone: (312) 441-2254
E-Mail: none
Telex: none

COMPANY AT-A-GLANCE

Target Market(s):

Commercial banks
Investment banks
Law firms
Specialized librarians

Subject Coverage:

Company information/
statistics

DESCRIPTION

The National Register Publishing Company (NRPC) is recognized as a major provider of business information. Its database is derived from the same information that produces NRPC's *Directory of Corporate Affiliations*, long used as a reference volume in libraries across the United States.

DATABASES

Proprietary

Corporate Affiliations. Corporate Affiliations contains over 42,000 records representing virtually every major corporation in the United States. Included are business profiles and corporate linkage for 550 private and 3,100 public parent companies and 38,800 affiliates.

VALUE-ADDED PRODUCTS AND SERVICES

Customer Support

Customer support is available through DIALOG Information Services, the provider for this database.

Document Formatting and Delivery

Specific data extracted from the Corporate Affiliations database are available in custom reports, magnetic tape, and mailing labels.

4

PREDICASTS INC.

11001 Cedar Avenue
Cleveland, OH 44106
Telephone: (216) 795-3000
  (800) 321-6388
Telex: 985604
E-Mail: none

COMPANY AT-A-GLANCE

Target Market(s):

Commercial banks
Credit unions
Fortune 1000 corporations
Government agencies
Investment banks
Law firms
Mortgage banks
Real estate firms
Specialized librarians
Thrift institutions

Subject Coverage:

Company information/
  statistics
Demographic information/
  statistics
Econometric data
Industry information/
  statistics
News services

DESCRIPTION

Predicasts Inc., part of the Information Technology Group of International Thyssen-Bornemisza, Inc., produces business information and market research in hard copy and electronic form. Its Predicasts Terminal System (PTS) is a system of databases that contain more than 4,000,000 article summaries, forecasts and statistical series prepared from over 2,400 international business, trade, defense, and government periodical publications. PTS offers data on virtually every subject that relates to the world of business and industry, organized in a manner designed to save users the time normally involved in tedious manual research.

Thousands of trade and business journals, business newspapers, annual reports, bank letters, news releases, government publications, and other important information sources—national and international, in 15 languages—are summarized by Predicasts' information professionals, translated when necessary into English, and added to the PTS databases. PTS databases are available through the leading commercial computer host systems and can be accessed with most computer terminals or personal computers. Retrieval methods range from key words and company names to the precise PTS coding systems, including event and country codes and seven-digit product codes based on the U.S. Government's Standard Industrial Classification (SIC) system.

Predicasts' databases can be accessed via DIALOG, BRS, Vu/Text, Data-Star, and Infomaster. Total access charges are based on connect time, offline prints, and online types. The availability of volume discounts depends on the individual vendor.

DATABASES

Proprietary

Annual Reports Abstracts (ARA). ARA contains key information from the annual reports of leading U.S. and selected international companies. Included are 50,000 informative abstracts summarizing historical performance, current activities, strategies, and plans.

Business & Industry News. B&I News contains abstracts from more than 1,200 trade and business journals covering all major industries. The information is available online within 48 hours of its appearance in the publications.

F&S Index. F&S (Funk & Scott) Index provides a broad coverage of online business subjects. In addition to industries and products, F&S is unique in its coverage of international companies, business and financial activities, demographics, government regulation, and economics. In addition to trade and business journals, F&S covers hundreds of additional sources—business and financial newspapers, bank letters, and economic publications not covered in PROMT.

Forecasts. Forecasts is useful for locating projections made by industry and business leaders worldwide. The file contains more than 700,000 abstracts of published forecasts with many new forecasts being added to the database each month. The projections cover all aspects of business including specific products, industries, trends in population and housing, national income, trade, health services, the sciences, and government activities.

Marketing and Advertising Reference Service (MARS). MARS offers access to information on advertising and marketing of consumer products and services. The database provides current information on ad agency accounts and plans, new products and marketing strategies, advertising techniques and campaigns, consumer research, regulation, and more. MARS information is updated weekly.

New Product Announcements (NPA). NPA offers quick access to the full-text announcements of new products and technologies. News releases typically contain the latest new product information and usually include product descriptions, specifications, availability and distribution, applications, market data, and contracts. Updates are added weekly.

PROMT. PROMT (Predicasts' Overview of Markets and Technology) contains company and product information, with more than 800,000 digests from 1,200 domestic and international trade and business journals.

Time Series. The Time Series database contains more than 200,000 historical series covering all aspects of international economic, financial, demographic, and industrial activity with an emphasis on product data. Each series contains an average of 15 years of data in an easy-to-read format, which saves time in data collection and research.

VALUE-ADDED PRODUCTS AND SERVICES

Customer Support

PTS customer assistance is available to users Monday through Friday, 8:30 A.M. to 5:30 P.M. (EST). The availability of online help depends on the individual vendor being used. Infomaster provides 24-hour online search assistance.

Predicasts conducts free PTS training seminars throughout the year in major market areas. The basic PTS Training Seminar is designed for online users unfamiliar with PTS, while the more advanced PTS Update Seminar is for experienced information managers who want to enhance their PTS searching techniques. Also available are seminars prepared and conducted for specific companies and industries.

Documentation

A number of publications are available to users to aid them in searching PTS databases. *PTS Online News*, Predicasts' free bimonthly newsletter, contains information on the time and location of scheduled seminars, the addition of new databases, and the expansion of current products and services. *PTS Source Guide* lists the more than 1,500 trade magazines, business journals, newspapers, and annual publications abstracted in PTS. The *PTS Company Directory* provides a complete alphabetical listing of the more than 100,000 U.S. and international companies included in the PTS databases. Finally, the *PTS User's Manual* is the basic reference aid for all PTS files. It is designed to complement several database-specific user guides also published by Predicasts.

Online Communication

The availability of general interest bulletin boards and electronic mail varies with the vendor being used to access PTS databases.

Document Formatting and Delivery

Predicasts' Article Delivery Service (PADS) offers users a quick and convenient way to order complete articles from most of the PTS Source publications. PADS will process orders received by mail, telephone, telex, or online terminal systems.

QUOTRON SYSTEMS, INC.
5454 Beethoven Street
Los Angeles, CA 90066-0914
Telephone: (213) 827-4600
E-Mail: none
Telex: none

COMPANY AT-A-GLANCE

Target Market(s):

Commercial banks
Investment banks
Thrift institutions

Subject Coverage:

Real-time/Historic market
quotations

DESCRIPTION

Quotron Systems, one of the world's largest suppliers of real-time financial services, provides delivery of information wherever it is needed. In addition to its database of real-time market information, it owns and maintains an international data communications network, develops advanced applications and software productivity tools, and provides customized software solutions.

DATABASES

Proprietary

QUOTDIAL. QUOTDIAL is an online, dial-up market data service covering the stock, bond, option, and commodities markets. The service is available during market hours in real-time or with a 15-minute delay and can also be accessed after market hours.

VALUE-ADDED PRODUCTS AND SERVICES

Customer Support

Quotron provides group classes and individual instruction, accommodating the user's needs in scheduling and course content. Customer training manuals and computer-aided instruction programs are also available from the training department.

SAGE DATA, INC.
104 Carnegie Center
Princeton, NJ 08540
Telephone: (800) 257-9414
  (609) 924-3000
E-Mail: none
Telex: none

COMPANY AT-A-GLANCE

Target Market(s):

Commercial banks
Fortune 1000 corporations
Government agencies
Investment banks
Specialized librarians

Subject Coverage:

Econometric data
Industry information/
  statistics

DESCRIPTION

SAGE DATA offers a wide range of business services to its clients. It provides business planning and analytical support about the client's marketplace, educational programs on computer use, computer applications, and computer time-sharing services on its computer. It is also the North American representative for Electronic Data Systems' World Trade Statistics Database.

DATABASES

Proprietary

Consumer Price Index Database. The Consumer Price Index Database contains more than 9,000 data series on the average change in prices over time as measured by the Consumer Price Index (CPI). The database includes information for two population groups: all urban consumers, and urban wage earners and clerical workers. Much of the data is regional in nature.

Employment and Earnings Database. The Employment and Earnings Database contains more than 3,000 time series on the U.S.

nonagricultural workforce. Information in the database includes wage and salary, employment, average weekly hours, average hourly earnings, and average weekly earnings. The data extend from 1946 to present day and are classified according to Standard Industrial Classification (SIC) codes.

Population Database.   The Population Database contains more than 200 annual time series information of historical, current, and forecasted nature. The database information begins in 1960 and continues through the year 2009. Population data are available by sex, age, and total population.

Producer Price Index Database.   The Producer Price Index Database contains over 7,000 data series on the average changes in prices received in primary markets of the United States by producers of commodities in all stages of processing. Two databases contain the information. The PPI databank consists of reported data, whereas the PPIS databank contains a subset of seasonally adjusted information. The database consists of monthly, quarterly, and annual data dating from 1946 to present day.

TRADSTAT.   SAGE DATA is the North American representative for Electronic Data Systems' World Trade Statistics Database (TRADSTAT). TRADSTAT contains monthly import/export statistics from Europe, Japan, Canada, and the United States. The data are stored by national custom tariffs codes and for each month include the monthly and cumulative year-to-date figures of quantity and value for each country of origin or destination.

U.S. Economic Database.   The U.S. Economic Database contains a variety of information regarding U.S. macroeconomic conditions. Major areas of coverage include national income and product accounts, personal consumption expenditures, retail sales, housing starts, foreign exchange rates, and industrial production. The database contains more than 3,000 time series consisting of monthly, quarterly, and annual data from 1946 to present day. The database is updated on a daily basis with the latest information from government sources.

VALUE-ADDED PRODUCTS AND SERVICES

Customer Support

Users can obtain assistance by calling (800) 257-9414.

Individual training is provided through a series of sessions that are designed to meet the unique needs of the individual user. This one-day training session is available at SAGE DATA's headquarters in Princeton, New Jersey.

SAGE DATA provides seminars on the use of personal computers, analytical problem solving, and information retrieval techniques.

System Features/Software Programs

SAGE DATA provides customized versions of commercially available software. Applications can be constructed for such functions as sales reporting, forecasting, inventory, production control, company profile storage and retrieval, and planning.

Document Formatting and Delivery

SAGE DATA provides information in the following formats: online, diskette, hardcopy printouts, and over the phone.

4

SEC ONLINE, INC.
200 East 23rd Street
New York, NY 10010
Telephone: (212) 686-2650
E-Mail: none
Telex: none

COMPANY AT-A-GLANCE

Target Market(s):

Commercial banks
Fortune 1000 corporations
Investment banks
Law firms
Specialized librarians

Subject Coverage:

Company information/
  statistics

DESCRIPTION

SEC Online markets an online database service providing full-text copies of reports filed by public corporations with the Securities and Exchange Commission to subscriber terminals and personal computers via the Compuserve Communications Network.

DATABASES

Proprietary

SEC Online.   SEC Online is a document-based computer filing system that maintains full-text copies of the original reports filed by public corporations with the Securities and Exchange Commission. These reports are unedited, unabstracted, and unaltered. The database also holds copies of company research reports, company press releases, and other corporate communications. Database access is through subscriber terminals and personal computers via the Compuserve Communications Network.

VALUE-ADDED PRODUCTS AND SERVICES

Document Formatting and Delivery

The SEC Online database allows users to obtain hard copies of the information in the database by:

Printing a copy of the document on the user's printer.

Transferring a copy from SEC Online's database onto the user's floppy diskette.

Ordering a printed copy from the SEC Online in New York, which is then shipped overnight.

System Features/Software Packages

Unlike any other database, SEC Online provides complete documentation of unabstracted, unedited business and financial information contained in periodic reports filed by public corporations with the Securities and Exchange Commission. These documents are keyed at an accuracy rate in excess of 99.9 percent.

4

STANDARD & POOR'S CORPORATION

25 Broadway
New York, NY 10004
Telephone: (212) 208-8735
  (212) 208-8474
  (212) 208-8481
  (212) 208-8622
E-Mail: none
Telex: none

COMPANY AT-A-GLANCE

Target Market(s):

Commercial banks
Fortune 1000 corporations
Government agencies
Investment banks
Law firms
Specialized librarians
Thrift institutions

Subject Coverage:

Company information/
  statistics
Industry information/
  statistics
Real-time/Historic market
  quotations
News services

DESCRIPTION

Standard & Poor's Corporation is a wholly owned subsidiary of McGraw-Hill Incorporated. The company provides various publications, electronic data delivery, information systems, financial services, and economic information services for business and industry. Standard & Poor's divisions include: Standard & Poor's Compustat Services Inc.; Standard & Poor's Securities Inc.; and Standard & Poor's International S. A.

DATABASES

Proprietary

Blue List Bond Ticker. Blue List Bond Ticker online database contains a daily list of approximately 6,000 new offerings and price changes on current corporate and municipal bonds traded on the secondary markets. The database also provides real-time "live" dollar bond quotes and "bids wanted requests" by participating brokers.

COMPUSTAT. The Compustat database contains quarterly and annual financial statement information on publicly traded industrial firms, banks, and utilities. Detailed business segment, SIC code, industry, and company data such as share price, dividends, and earnings are also provided. Standard & Poor's Compustat Services Incorporated is the provider of data for this database.

COMPUSTAT II. The COMPUSTAT II database, from Standard & Poor's Compustat Services Incorporated, provides quarterly and annual financial data on more than 20,000 publicly traded companies. The COMPUSTAT Industrial Research File contains historic annual data for over 2,500 companies that are no longer reporting information due to acquisition, merger, bankruptcy, or change to private ownership.

Corporate Descriptions Online. Corporate Descriptions Online is a full-text database that provides financial and business information for more than 8,200 publicly owned companies. The information contained in the database is obtained from the Standard & Poor's *Corporation Records* business and financial information service. The database is accessible through DIALOG Information Services.

Industrial Financial. Standard & Poor's Industrial Financial database contains income statement and balance sheet data, as well as Standard & Poor's stock price indexes, for more than 100 Standard & Poor's composites.

News Online. Standard & Poor's News Online contains day-by-day business and financial news stories on more than 12,000 publicly owned companies. News Online is available in two related databases: News Online FILE 132 contains business and financial news stories from July 1, 1985 to present day, and News Online FILE 134 contains historical news and financial items from June 15, 1979 through June 30, 1985.

Register-Biographical. The Register-Biographical database is a biographical dictionary of 72,000 key executives and directors of major U.S. and foreign, privately held and publicly held corporations. Database information is obtained from the "Directors and Executives" volume of the *Standard & Poor's Register.*

Register-Corporate. The Register-Corporate database provides business facts on more than 45,000 publicly and privately owned companies. The companies listed in the database must have annual sales over $1 million or more than 50 employees. The database information is derived from the *Standard & Poor's Register* business directory. The database is available through DIALOG Information Services.

VALUE-ADDED PRODUCTS AND SERVICES

Customer Support

Customer support is available by calling the customer service department at (212) 208-8471.

Documentation

The *Blue List Bond Ticker User Guide* provides information on using the Blue List Bond Ticker database. Information includes accessing, printing, and keyboard instructions, as well as information on more specific system capabilities.

Document Formatting and Delivery

Blue List database information is also available in printed form. Blue List information can be ordered by calling (212) 208-8471. Delivery is daily by courier or by mail. Costs vary by order with a $470 annual minimum.

TECHNICAL DATA CORPORATION

330 Congress Street
Boston, MA 02210
Telephone: (617) 482-3341
 (800) 343-7745
E-Mail: none
Telex: none

COMPANY AT-A-GLANCE

Target Market(s):

Commercial banks
Credit unions
Fortune 1000 corporations
Government agencies
Investment banks
Mortgage banks
Real estate firms
Thrift institutions

Subject Coverage:

Econometric data
Real-time/Historic market
 quotations
News services
Newsletters
Research reports/
 evaluations

DESCRIPTION

Technical Data Corporation, a recently acquired company of International Thomson, is headquartered in Boston, Massachusetts. It is a developer and marketer of real-time, online investment analysis and statistical information services, as well as a developer and supplier of computer software for investment professionals.

The company was founded in November 1980 by a group of investment professionals who recognized the need for widespread electronic distribution of fixed-income market analyses. In early 1981, the firm introduced its first service on Telerate Systems' network, providing statistical and technical analysis of the U.S. government bond and financial futures markets. In 1984, Technical Data acquired majority ownership of Software Resources, Inc. and assumed marketing responsibilities for the company's product, PRO/VEST. Its worldwide client base now includes more than 3,000 major corporations, money centers, regional banks, savings and loan companies, insurance firms, mortgage bankers, investment advisers, governments, universities, and broker/dealers.

DATABASES

Proprietary

BondData. Technical Data's BondData is an online technical service for the fixed-income investment industry. The service includes the daily market commentary, "Technically Speaking," a continuously updated treasury yield curve graphic display, technical market indicators, current and historical price spread relationships, cash versus futures arbitrage analysis, and a bond market performance index. The database is accessible via Telerate.

MoneyData. The MoneyData database service advises short-term money market investors about the market direction, trading opportunities, and investment strategies using technical analysis. The service includes the daily commentary, "Money Market Strategies," historical yield spreads on money market instruments, a U.S. Treasury bill yield curve, implied forward rate analysis, arbitrage analysis for money market futures contracts, and technical indicators for, and analysis of, foreign exchange markets. MoneyData is accessible through Telerate.

Third Party

FundamentalData. FundamentalData is a database service provided in conjunction with Data Resources Incorporated (DRI). It offers updated economic and interest rate forecasts from DRI's staff. The database service also presents analysis of domestic and international credit markets, Federal Reserve activity, U.S. Treasury auction statistics, and economic releases. The database is available through Telerate systems.

VALUE-ADDED PRODUCTS AND SERVICES

Customer Support

Technical Data provides customer support services via (800) 343-7745. Its staff also provides direct customer support during installation and implementation of its products. Custom-tailored products and services are available as well.

Documentation

Get Technical is Technical Data's quarterly newsletter. It details upcoming events, lists database additions, provides market viewpoints, and discusses uses of the company's products and services.

System Features/Software Packages

Technical Data's Financial Software Series is a group of microcomputer products designed for management and analysis of equity and fixed income securities. It was designed with investment professionals, and their knowledge of the securities market, in mind. All products in the series operate on IBM or compatible personal computers. They include:

PRO/VEST—a portfolio and reporting system designed for financial institutions, money managers, and individual investors. Features include automatic dividend posting, spreadsheet and word processing interfaces, average cost or tax lot accounting, monthly performance evaluation, and customized report capabilities. The cost of PRO/VEST is $5,500 per year.

Fixed Income Portfolio Manager—an information system for managers of single or multiple fixed-income portfolios. It provides customized reports, summary and distribution statistics, and graphical analysis for investment presentations. The cost of the Fixed Income Portfolio Manager is also $5,500.

The Bond Swap Analyzer—determines the profitability, cash flow benefit, rate of return, and accounting impact of a proposed single or multiple issue bond swap. The program also calculates the break-even spread and break-even reinvestment rate of bonds. The cost is $1,700.

4

TRINET, INC.
9 Campus Drive
Parsippany, NJ 07054
Telephone: (800) 874-6381
  (201) 267-3600
E-Mail: none
Telex: none

COMPANY AT-A-GLANCE

Target Market(s):

Commercial banks
Fortune 1000 corporations
Investment banks
Real estate firms
Specialized librarians

Subject Coverage:

Company information/
  statistics

DESCRIPTION

Trinet Incorporated, a former subsidiary of Control Data Corporation, was sold to Welsh, Carson, Anderson & Stowe, a New York-based venture capital company, in late 1986. It provides information products and services for business-to-business decision making, corporate and strategic planning, competitive analysis, and many other related activities.

Trinet offers a full range of data products and services, including industry-specific databases, business-to-business telemarketing, market reports, consulting, and a fully staffed customer support department. In addition, Trinet maintains its own computer facilities for production of printed products and other related reports and analyses.

DATABASES

Proprietary

Trinet Company Database.   Trinet has divided its databases into two parts: one describing companies, the other establishments. The Company Database is concerned with those legal entities that own and operate one or more establishments. It contains approximately 247,000 records on businesses that employ 20 or more people. Each record provides the company name, full address, telephone number, Metropolitan Statistical Area (MSA) name and code number, public/private ownership, stock symbol (where applicable), number of employees, total sales (with three additional breakdowns), top three lines of business and respective sales figures and foreign ownership (when 10 percent or more).

Trinet Establishment Database.   Trinet defines an establishment as an economic unit producing goods and/or services at a single physical location. Thus, each establishment owned by a company and having more than 20 employees has an individual record in this file. The Trinet Establishment Database contains approximately 430,000 records of information on these establishments. The database contains general information such as the business name, mailing address, telephone number, SIC code(s) and description, number of employees, estimated sales, market share, MSA name and code number, corporate linkage, private/public ownership, foreign ownership (if 10 percent or more), stock symbol (where applicable), and the full address and telephone number of the parent company.

VALUE-ADDED PRODUCTS AND SERVICES

Customer Support

Trinet's customer service department provides search assistance and general information on all facets of the Trinet databases. Trained Trinet representatives can be reached by calling, toll-free (800) TRINET-1, or, in New Jersey, (201) 267-3600. If Trinet representatives are unavailable, callers may opt to leave a recorded message that will be returned at the earliest possible time. Trinet has a nationwide sales force, plus distribution agreements with DIALOG, TRW, Data Resources, Inc. (DRI), and Mead Data Central. Customer service is also available through the vendors.

Documentation

Trinet provides users with search guides for DIALOG, DRI, and Mead. These guides are available to users, free of charge, by telephoning Trinet's customer service department. Additional documentation is published by the individual vendors.

Research Services

Trinet provides individual consulting services on a fee basis. It also maintains an in-house Telemarketing Services department. Services are set to customer-specified requirements. Pricing for telemarketing services is dependent on customer requirements.

Document Formatting and Delivery

In addition to online data retrieval, subscribers can get Trinet database information on diskettes, magnetic tapes, and in hard-copy form. Specialized data formats are also available, including standard and custom reports, mailing lists, telemarketing lists, and sales lead cards. All data received by Trinet are verified with published government statistics and secondary sources to ensure accuracy.

WHARTON ECONOMETRIC FORECASTING ASSOCIATES

3624 Science Center
3rd floor
Philadelphia, PA 19104
Telephone: (800) 523-4520
E-Mail: none
Telex: none

COMPANY AT-A-GLANCE

Target Market(s):

Commercial banks
Credit unions
Fortune 1000 corporations
Government agencies
Investment banks
Specialized librarians
Thrift institutions

Subject Coverage:

Demographic information/
 statistics
Econometric data
Real-time/Historic market
 quotations
News services

DESCRIPTION

Wharton Econometric Forecasting Associates is a worldwide, economic consulting, forecasting, and database provider.

Wharton maintains offices in Chicago, San Francisco, Houston, Washington, D.C., and New York. Internationally, it maintains offices in Paris, Frankfurt, Tokyo, and London.

Wharton's database portfolio is extensive. In addition to the few select databases covered here, Wharton carries a wide spectrum of data covering agriculture, energy, U.S. national and regional statistics, international statistics, industrial data, and a series of databases specializing in Asian and centrally planned economies. Also covered are developing nation, Middle Eastern, and Latin American economies.

Databases comprise only a portion of Wharton's total business. It provides to its clients a "service" consisting of regular economic analysis and reports, individual consulting, and economic forecasting.

DATABASES

Proprietary

CPI. CPI measures the cost of living (consumer price index) for all wage earners and for urban workers for 25 major cities and the U.S. average, covering food, housing, medical care, energy, clothing, transportation, and durable goods. Both seasonally adjusted and unadjusted monthly data are available. The source for the data is the Bureau of Labor Statistics.

CROPMOD. This database has historical data for wheat, soybean meal, corn, soybean oil, and soybeans relating to cash grain prices, supply/demand balance stocks, USDA expectation factors, and prices for competitive and complement goods. The source for the data is *USDA Situation Reports, Agricultural Prices Report, Agricultural Supply and Demand Estimates, Crop Reporting Board Releases,* and *Agricultural Outlook.*

EIAPRICE. This database contains historical data for energy prices by 20 types of fuel and by 6 major end-use sectors. Data are available for the United States and individual states. The source for the data is the Department of Energy's Energy Information Administration.

IMF International Financial Statistics. This database contains data for all information shown in the International Monetary Fund's publication, *International Financial Statistics.* It includes data for about 76 commodities and 137 countries covering exchange rates, international liquidity, monetary series detailing commercial bank positions and money measures, interest rates, prices, production data, international transactions, government financial data, and national accounts statistics.

LTMOD. LTMOD contains historic data variables used in the Wharton long-term economic model. The sources for the data are the department of Commerce, Labor, Transportation, Energy, and the Interior; Internal Revenue Service; Federal Reserve Board; and various published articles. Also available under other LT series databases are the model's forecasts.

News Perspectives. Wharton News Perspectives focuses on recent global economic events. Wharton Econometrics prepares articles by experts in such areas as foreign trade, business indicators, employment, and financial markets. Also included is the Wharton US Services Executive Summary, which covers Wharton's latest economic forecast.

News Releases. This system provides access to U.S. Government press releases as soon as they are available. Included are sources of over 100 government releases on topics covering all segments of the U.S. economy.

PETROL. This database has monthly data for crude oil production, import and export levels of crude and refined products, Big Seven consumption of crude oil, and crude oil prices for 13 OPEC countries. The source for the data is major oil industry publications.

QTRMOD. QTRMOD contains data for all variables needed for short-term macroeconomic analysis of the United States economy including national, demographic, consumer, personal, and financial indicators. The source for the data is Federal Reserve Board, the Departments of Commerce and Labor, and Wharton estimates.

UKFT. UKFT has detailed coverage of international money and gold markets, the London domestic sterling market, and the London and overseas stock exchanges. The source for the data is *The Financial Times*.

WEFA. WEFA includes data on the money supply, money market rates, consumer credit, housing starts and construction, and retail sales. Data sources are the departments of Commerce, Labor, Energy, Transportation, and the Interior; Federal Reserve Board; Internal Revenue Service; various published articles; and trade journals.

WEFAAG. WEFAAG has data for supply, demand, and prices for major agricultural commodities on an annual, quarterly, and monthly basis. The source for the data is the U.S. Department of Agriculture.

WEFAHF. WEFAHF contains selected weekly data on interest rates, reserves at Federal Reserve banks, money stock components, futures and spot price indexes, stock indexes, exchange rates, bank loans, car sales, oil rig counts, business failures, commercial paper outstanding, and other financial and economic indicators. Major data sources are Federal Reserve releases, newspapers, government reports, and trade associations.

WEXBASE. WEXBASE contains data for monthly spot exchange rates, current account, and domestic product deflators. Countries covered include Belgium, Canada, France, Germany, the United Kingdom, Italy, Japan, the Netherlands, Switzerland, and the United States. The forecast extends 60 months into the future. Quarterly average spot exchange rates are available for 55 currencies. The source for the data is the International Monetary Fund's *International Financial Statistics*, and *The Financial Times, The Wall Street Journal*, and Wharton estimates.

WLDREI. This database contains economic indicators for Australia, Belgium, Canada, France, Germany, Italy, Japan, the Netherlands, Sweden, Switzerland, the United Kingdom, and the United States. The sources for the data are *OECD Main Economic Indicators, IMF International Financial Statistics*, national publications, correspondents in Wharton's international network.

VALUE-ADDED PRODUCTS AND SERVICES

Customer Support

Wharton's customer support varies domestically versus internationally. However, on average it is available 18 hours a day.

Documentation

Wharton publishes an extensive array of user documentation and newsletters for its clients.

System Features/Software Packages

AREMOS is a fully integrated micro/mainframe software system that uses a single command language for all tasks: data analysis and retrieval, equation estimation, model building, report writing, and graphics.

AREMOS/PC offers full-screen input for data management and graphics, plus full-screen menus. Communications features link mainframe databanks directly to AREMOS/PC to enhance data transfer. User-friendly menus simplify the downloading process to a few keystrokes. Moving the data into other popular packages such as LOTUS 1-2-3 is a simple operation.

Research Services

A major portion of Wharton's revenues are derived from customized, individual research performed for clients as well as from its standard economic research products.

4

PRODUCT SNAPSHOTS

These Snapshots are the result of information industry research performed during 1986 and 1987. Thousands of labor-hours have gone into this reference work—hours that usually cannot be spent during the course of an individual search. From an initial list of 350 producers detailed questionnaires were sent to over 300 companies. Our information specialists analyzed the producer replies, their marketing literature and technical specifications, and condensed this immense amount of information into Snapshots.

The Methodology, explained earlier in Chapter 3, discusses how the Snapshots are to be used in conjunction with the matrices. Using the Methodology gets you to a decision point faster and maximizes the effects of your results for your company.

The material contained in the Product Snapshots was obtained directly from the producers as well as from reliable industry sources. From time to time, product or company ownership, as well as product descriptions, may change as the industry matures. **Inclusion in this chapter does not constitute an endorsement by either the authors or the publisher**.

PRODUCT SNAPSHOTS INDEX

ABI/INFORM
Data Courier Inc.
620 South Fifth Street
Louisville, KY 40202-2297

PRODUCT AT-A-GLANCE

Subject Coverage:

News services
Local
National
Regional
International

Established in 1971, ABI/INFORM is a business and computer-related database from Data Courier Incorporated. The database contains over 300,000 business articles from over 660 business and management publications worldwide. All foreign publications are translated into English. Articles are formated as 200-word summaries, which are indexed and cross-referenced for easy access. The database is updated by 800 articles on a weekly basis.

The geographic scope of ABI/INFORM is worldwide, with particular emphasis placed on the United States. The ABI/INFORM database abstractors, who are experts in law, employee benefits, business-government relations, data processing, finance, and other business areas, summarize data from research reports, magazines, and trade journals.

The database contains information on the areas of law, computers, telecommunications, taxation, international trade, banking, marketing, human resources, advertising, finance, insurance, real estate, and management. This information is used by security analysts, marketing managers, financial managers, and business executives, as well as universities and government agencies.

Access to the database is through a terminal or computer with a standard modem. Access to ABI/INFORM is available through the following online vendors: BRS, BRS/After Dark, BRS/BrkThru, Data-Star, DIALOG, ESA-Quest, ETSI, ITT Dialcom, Knowledge Index, Mead Data Central, SDC Orbit, and VU/TEXT. Hours of database service and access fees vary depending on the vendor used.

The database supports a restricted vocabulary with indexing terms by abstract, descriptor, title, author, classification code, classification name, CODEN, document type, journal code, journal name, language, ISBN, publication year, and update.

5

User support is available from 9 A.M. to 5 P.M. (EST) on weekdays via toll-free telephone number (800) 626-2823. User inquiries may also be sent by telex 204235 24 hours a day seven days a week.

Value-added products and services include *SEARCH INFORM*, a user's guide containing company and organization names, geographic terms, a guide to searching the database, and a full explanation of ABI/INFORM's editorial policies; document delivery of photocopied articles; a delivery rush service; and custom research services. In addition, subscriptions to two newsletters, database journals, a classified codes list, an ABI brochure, and articles retrieval brochure are offered, all at no charge. User training is also available from ABI/INFORM training specialists.

ACCOUNTANTS

American Institute of Certified Public
 Accountants
1211 Avenue of the Americas
New York, NY 10036-8775

PRODUCT AT-A-GLANCE

Subject Coverage:

 **Industry information/
  statistics**
 Legal actions and issues

The Accountants, bibliographic database provides extensive coverage of English-language literature in accounting and related financial and business-related fields. These fields include cost and managerial accounting, auditing, data processing, financial reporting, financial management, investments and securities, management, taxation, and special businesses and industries.

Source document coverage is primarily journal literature from United States and foreign periodicals, with the remaining 20 percent of the file covering books, pamphlets, government documents, and other forms of nonperiodical literature. Conference proceedings, theses, faculty papers, and documentation of speeches and lectures are also included in the database.

The database contains bibliographic citations covering a period from 1974 to present day. As of February 1986 there were 158,805 records in the database. Quarterly updates of approximately 3,500 records increase the database size by 14,000 records annually.

Access to the database is through public network, either via SDC Orbit or via EasyNet, through an arrangement with SDC Information Services. The SDC Orbit rates are computed on connect time plus charges for offline and online prints. Value-added products and services include the capability of purchasing the *Accountants' Index*, a printed equivalent of the database; guide books; the *Accountants' Index Master List of Subject Headings* on microfiche; *Industry Audit and Accounting Guides* on microfiche; the Orbit User Manual; and the ability to borrow items listed in the Accountants database from the AICPA Library.

5

ACORN

CACI Inc.–Federal
1815 North Fort Meyer Drive
Arlington, VA 22209

PRODUCT AT-A-GLANCE

Subject Coverage:

**Demographic information/
statistics**
*Consumer preference
Income and housing*

CACI's ACORN database, a Classification Of Residential Neighborhoods, was first published in 1978. The goal of the database is to provide socioeconomic, demographic, and housing information that can be used in market research and customer targeting (to determine what financial services are most in demand and by whom) and site selection (to determine the best locations for new offices, branches, and automatic-teller machines).

The demographic information in ACORN is based on data from the 1980 Census of Population and Housing. Updates and forecasts are estimated using CACI's proprietary methodology. The entire database is updated each spring. Data are currently available for 1980, 1985, and 1990.

ACORN demographers have identified 49 socioeconomic characteristics that best describe the lifestyle and behavioral differences among our country's diverse consumer groups. They have applied these criteria to the nearly 260,000 census block groups and enumeration districts that make up the nation's neighborhoods. When each neighborhood is evaluated across the 49 ACORN criteria and then classified according to shared or common socioeconomic characteristics, this results in 44 separate and distinct market segments.

ACORN offers special reports geared directly to the financial and investment services industries. These reports show the potential for and penetration of different financial instruments. These reports can be customized for market areas of any shape or size, located anywhere in the United States. These customized ACORN applications are available on a per request basis.

New data and reports are continually being added to the database. Business data, including payroll data and the number of firms by size, became available in 1986. Information on income by the age of the head of the household, five-year age breakdowns by sex, and a new restaurant report should also be available in 1986. Extensive new financial services information is currently being planned for inclusion in the database.

ACORN is available 24 hours a day, seven days a week. ACORN is a prompt driven system written in FORTRAN. "Help" files are available throughout the program to assist the user with problems.

Access to ACORN is provided by several national time-sharing information networks, including Compuserve, Comshare, and Chase Econometrics. Costs for the database are pay-as-you-go, by the report. Report costs range from $30 to $150, depending on the report and the time-sharing network that is used. Volume discounts and licenses are also available. Any terminal or PC with a standard modem (300 baud or 1200 baud) can be used to access ACORN.

AGRICULTURAL COMMODITIES

I.P. Sharp Associates Limited
Suite 1900 2 First Canadian Place
Toronto, Ontario, Canada M5X 1E3

PRODUCT AT-A-GLANCE

Subject Coverage:

**Real-time/Historic
market quotations**
Spot prices
Futures

The Agricultural Commodities database, produced by I.P. Sharp Associates Limited, provides short-term trends in prices, volumes, and other indexes for many agricultural products, including grains and oil seeds; cattle and beef products; hogs and pork products; sheep and lamb products; broilers, eggs, fowl, and dairy; and special crops.

It also includes economic indicators, and its primary focus is on price/volume information on key U.S. and Canadian cash market commodities.

The raw data are stored as received from Alberta Agriculture, Market Analysis Branch and are updated weekly by Alberta Agriculture. Daily, weekly, monthly, quarterly, and annual statistics are included in this database, with some series going back as far as 1961.

The Agricultural Commodities database is accessible 24 hours a day, seven days a week, except for a brief maintenance shutdown period on Friday and Saturday nights. The database is accessible directly through I.P. Sharp's IPSANET network and also from Datapac, Telenet, Telex, and Tymnet public networks. User access is through a terminal or personal computer with a 300, 1200, or 2400 baud modem; communications software; and a user account number. General purpose software allows for data manipulation, analysis, and downloading to a personal computer.

Users access the database via MAGIC, a database retrieval system for computer users with little programming experience. Other user aids include manuals, reference guides, online documentation, and user instruction. User consulting services are available on an individual basis.

Value-added products and services include individual database search services, user software, data storage capabilities, ongoing user training programs, electronic sending and reception of messages, and custom program applications.

AMERICAN BANKER

American Banker
1 State Street Plaza
New York, NY 10004

PRODUCT AT-A-GLANCE

Subject Coverage:

**Industry information/
  statistics**
Business intelligence
Emerging technologies
*Industry leadership
  changes*
Industry overviews
Legal actions and issues
Market news and forecasts
Product developments

The American Banker database provides subscribers with the full text of the *American Banker*, the daily financial services newspaper. Information contained in the database covers the years 1981 to present day. This information is updated within 24 hours of publication of the newspaper.

The American Banker offers complete coverage of federal and state banking regulations and legislation. All aspects of the domestic banking industry are covered, including commercial banking, trust banking, mortgage lending, and credit card operations.

Also covered by the database are bank earnings reports and mergers and acquisitions in the financial service industry. Other services include the *American Banker*'s authoritative annual ranking of the top 500 banks and the top 500 savings & loan companies, coverage of interest rates, the federal budget situation, and reports on the major economics indicators.

Access to the American Banker database is provided through private network, either via DIALOG or NEXIS (Mead Data Central). The subscriber gains access to the database through any ASCII terminal or via computer with modem. All subscribers are billed on a monthly basis.

The information contained in American Banker is also available in hard copy to yearly subscribers and is delivered daily via courier.

5

AMERICAN BANKER NEWS SERVICE

American Banker
1 State Street Plaza
New York, NY 10004

PRODUCT AT-A-GLANCE

Subject Coverage:

News services
National

The American Banker News Service is a daily online news service for the financial services industry. The news service, available at 6 A.M. (EST) contains key stories from the preceding five days covering the financial services industry. The database provides the complete text of the *American Banker*, a daily newspaper serving the financial services markets. The database's Executive News Summary highlights major stories from the newspaper. Stories of executive personnel changes and a calendar of events are also provided by the database.

Access to the American Banker News Service database is provided through private network, either via BRS or NewsNet. The subscriber gains access to the database through any terminal or computer with a modem. Customers are billed on a monthly basis.

ANNUAL REPORTS ABSTRACT (ARA)

Predicasts Inc.
11001 Cedar Avenue
Cleveland, OH 44106

Predicasts' Annual Reports Abstract (ARA) contains textual abstracts and statistical tables abstracted from the annual reports of public companies. ARA abstracts emphasize the findings, strategies, product discussion, and plans reported in the text sections of annual reports. Also included are five-year statistical summaries of product line sales and profits, capital spending, and other marketing statistics.

Subject coverage includes all relevant discussions pertaining to the corporation's product and industry activities, with an emphasis placed on historical performance; current activities; strategies, sources, and goals; and geographic details by product line (when available).

ARA uses as its principal source the annual report to the stockholders. However, 10-K reports are also used occasionally to supplement the annual report where needed.

The database contains three types of records produced from the textual and statistical sections of the annual report:

Text Abstracts—similar to Predicasts' PROMT database in format. ARA abstracts provide substantive summaries of the text sections of the annual report. Contained are product discussions, technology announcements, facility plans, performance reviews, the chairman's review, acquisitions discussions, and other discussions of the company's performance.

Statistical Tables—contain up to five-year summaries of key statistical indicators of performance. Taken from the financial table series provided, they include sales and profits by production, R&D spending, capital spending, and other market statistics. In most cases geographic detail is also provided.

Corporate Establishment Record—contains directory information such as location, SIC classifications, sales, number of employees, D-U-N-S number, and other similar data.

5

The ARA database is updated monthly. Information within the file covers from 1982 to present.

ARA treats the annual report like any other comprehensive source of product and company information. Predicasts therefore recommends that the file be used with the other PTS files (especially PROMT, F&S Indexes, and MARS). Recommended uses include the following:

Identify product or market information.
Identify companies active in a specific industry or product.
Obtain a comprehensive understanding of a specific company.

The database can be accessed via DIALOG, BRS, VU/TEXT, or Data-Star. Total charges vary according to the vendor being used, but are generally based on a combination of connect time, offline prints, or online type. Users can also download information if desired.

ANNUAL SURVEY OF MANUFACTURES

Chase Econometrics
150 Monument Road
Bala Cynwyd, PA 19004

PRODUCT AT-A-GLANCE

Subject Coverage:

Industry information/ statistics
Industry overviews

Data included in this database are derived from the Census of Manufactures' data and the Annual Survey of Manufactures' data. Data are available out to the four-digit level of the Standard Industrial Classification (SIC) code. The database contains 5,650 time series and company data and is updated on an annual basis.

The database includes 10 categories of data, including total number of employees, total employees' payroll, number of production workers, labor-hours of production workers, wages of production workers, value added by manufacturer, cost of materials, value of shipments, new capital expenditures, and end-of-year inventories.

The Annual Survey of Manufactures database is listed with Chase Econometrics under the database name ASM and disk name USDB. More information on the database service may be obtained by calling (215) 896-4759.

5

BANCALL II
ADP, Inc. Data Services
175 Jackson Plaza
Ann Arbor, MI 48106

PRODUCT AT-A-GLANCE

Subject Coverage:

**Company information/
statistics**
Annual reports
Quarterly reports

Available through ADP Data Services, Bancall II is derived from Federal Reserve Call Reports. The database contains geographic and financial information on FDIC commercial banks, including five years of historical data. Information is updated quarterly.

Bancall II provides users with commercial bank data to be used in market share studies, merger and acquisition prospect screening, correspondent bank surveys, performance analysis, forecasting, and peer group analysis.

Bancall II provides the following:

Historical adjustments—With each update, retroactive adjustments are made to the database reflecting all major changes in bank status due to mergers and acquisitions, name and location changes, and changes in bank regulatory reporting formats. As a result of these adjustments, users can be sure that bank financials from past years are presented in the same format as the most current data.

Holding company information—For each bank, Bancall provides codes and names for both the immediate and the highest parent company in a tiered organization. This allows users to "pyramid" information on all banks in a common holding company relationship. Users may find this capability useful in projecting the consolidated financial results of proposed mergers and acquisitions.

Precalculated ratios—These help Bancall users improve their efficiency in reporting and analyzing banks' core funds, internal capital growth, tax-equivalent interest earned, and other financial information.

Peer group information—With ADP's SCREEN software, Bancall users can create their own peer group classifications based on financial and/or geographical criteria.

Any standard ASCII terminal (and modem) may be used to access ADP databases. If users wish to download and incorporate ADP database information into their LOTUS 1-2-3 files, an IBM PC, XT, or compatible, and ADP's Datapath software are required.

5

BANCORP
ADP, Inc. Data Services
175 Jackson Plaza
Ann Arbor, MI 48106

PRODUCT AT-A-GLANCE

Subject Coverage:

**Company information/
statistics**
Annual reports
Quarterly reports

This database contains company financials, plus subsidiary band and stock market information, on over 2,000 U.S. bank holding companies.

Forming the basis of Bancorp is the data in the Y-9 Supplement, a report filed with the Federal Reserve Board by BHCs annually or semiannually, depending on their size.

For BHCs with assets between $50 million and $100 million, the database provides annual balance sheet and income statement for the parent company. For each BHC with assets greater than $100 million , annual balance sheet and income statement data are featured for both the parent company and the consolidated company, reported separately. Semiannual parent and consolidated data are provided for BHCs with assets of more than $300 million.

To make Bancorp more useful for analysis, ADP takes the Y-9 data and adds:

Information on each bank subsidiary, including total assets, net loans, total equity capital, total deposits, pretax operating income, and net income. The source of this information is the Bancall database.

Weekly and annual prices (high, lows, and closes), as well as volume, dividend, and earnings-per-share figures, for publicly traded BHCs. These data are taken from ADP's securities database and are updated with each Friday closing.

Precalculated ratios that help users determine the extent of BHC "double leverage," report on net charge-offs and loan loss reserves as percentages of average gross loans, etc.

Any standard ASCII terminal (and modem) may be used to access ADP databases. If users wish to download and incorporate ADP database information into LOTUS 1-2-3 files, an IBM PC, XT, or compatible, and ADP's Datapath software are required.

BANK HOLDING COMPANIES
Chase Econometrics
150 Monument Road
Bala Cynwyd, PA 19004

PRODUCT AT-A-GLANCE

Subject Coverage:

**Company information/
statistics**
Annual reports

The Bank Holding Companies database contains balance sheet and income statement data for bank holding companies and their consolidated subsidiaries. The database information is taken from bank holding company filings with the Federal Reserve System. The database information is either semiannual or annual data.

The database provides information on approximately 820 bank holding companies with $50 million or more in consolidated assets. The database covers 108 items from the balance sheet and income statements of the parent bank holding companies, as well as balance sheet and income statement data of consolidated subsidiaries.

Applications are available to screen for bank holding companies, identify bank holding companies by state, make comparisons to user selected groups of bank holding companies, and download data for any bank holding company.

The database is listed with Chase Econometrics under disk name Y9DATA. More information about the database may be obtained by calling (215) 896-4920.

5

BANK OF CANADA WEEKLY FINANCIAL STATISTICS

I.P. Sharp Associates Limited
2 First Canadian Place
Suite 1900
Toronto, Ontario, Canada M5X 1E3

PRODUCT AT-A-GLANCE

Subject Coverage:

Econometric data
Monetary aggregates
National

The Bank of Canada Weekly Financial Statistics database, produced by I.P. Sharp Associates Limited, provides 285 weekly banking and monetary time series statistics released by the Bank of Canada. The database contains statistical information on Canada's money supply as well as data on all banks operating in Canada.

The database time series information includes data on the Bank of Canada's assets and liabilities, the Canadian government's balances and securities outstanding, the Canadian money supply, money market rates, and chartered banks' liquidity, assets, and liability positions. Each week the data are reported on Wednesday, released on Thursday afternoon, and updated on Friday morning.

The Bank of Canada Weekly Financial Statistics database is accessible 24 hours a day, seven days a week, except for a brief maintenance period on Friday and Saturday nights. The database is accessible directly through I.P. Sharp's proprietary IPSANET network and also via Datapac, Telenet, Telex, and Tymnet public access networks. User access is via a terminal or personal computer with a 300, 1200, or 2400 baud modem; communications software; and an account number. Access software is general purpose, allowing for data manipulation, analysis, and downloading to personal computers.

User support is offered via calling toll-free ((800) 387-1588) in North America from 8 A.M. to 6 P.M. (EST) on weekdays. I.P. Sharp Associates also provides subscribers with access to a 24-hour answering service for subscribers to leave messages.

Other user aids include user manuals, reference guides, two printed directories of database symbols, and complete online documentation. User consulting services are available on an individual basis.

Value-added products and services include individual database search services, user software, data storage capabilities, ongoing user training programs, electronic mail transmission, and custom program applications.

BLUE LIST BOND TICKER
Standard & Poor's Corporation
25 Broadway
New York, NY 10004

PRODUCT AT-A-GLANCE

Subject Coverage:

Real-time/Historic market quotations
Bonds, notes, and bills
Municipals

Blue List Bond Ticker online database contains a list of approximately 6,000 daily new offerings and price changes on current corporate and municipal bonds traded on the secondary markets. The database also provides real-time "live" dollar bond quotes and "bids wanted requests" by participating brokers.

The database information includes the state the bond was issued in, the amount, a description of the bond, coupon, maturity, the yield to maturity, the price, and the advertiser of the bond issue. All data are updated on a daily basis with no time lag between the source and the database update.

Features of the Blue List Bond Ticker database are:

Instant access to current municipal and corporate bond offering information.

Offering information sorted by state, maturity range, and/or block size.

Continuous browse capability of market changes throughout the trading day.

Access to new lines and price changes as they are called into the Blue List.

A "Broker Alert" message, flashed on the viewer's screen, identifying hot items out for the bid.

Monitor Active Dollar Bond Markets-Bid and Offering Prices (Available to dealers and dealer banks only).

Direct access to Brokers Bid Wanted (Available to dealers and dealer banks only).

The Bond Ticker database is available 24 hours a day, seven days a week. Customer access is through a hardwire system accessed through the Telerate network. A Blue List terminal or existing Telerate terminal is required to access the database.

The Blue List Bond Ticker is sold via direct sales force to municipal bond dealers, dealer banks, brokers, and institutions.

5

Database information is also provided in hardcopy, printed form. The printed version is delivered daily by courier or mail. Costs vary by city with a $470 minimum annual charge for hard copies.

BNA EXECUTIVE DAY

The Bureau of National Affairs, Inc.
1231 25th Street NW
Room 601 South
Washington, DC 20037

PRODUCT AT-A-GLANCE

Subject Coverage:

News services
National

The BNA Executive Day database is an exclusive electronic news magazine containing information on governmental, economic, and financial developments; tax breaks and liabilities; labor relations; the USDA; nontax monetary issues; health care; management concerns; and women's issues.

The BNA Executive Day database covers topics involving the economy, business, taxes, labor, management, women, and agriculture in the United States. Users can get one week of coverage available online. The database is updated every working day.

Access to the database is via ITT Dialcom, NewsNet, and Human Resource Information Network Executive Telecom Service, Incorporated. These vendors should be contacted directly for information on their user access charges.

5

THE BOND BUYER
American Banker
1 State Street Plaza
New York, NY 10004

PRODUCT AT-A-GLANCE

Subject Coverage:

News services
National
Regional

The Bond Buyer covers municipal bond information from 1981 to present day. It represents the complete text, with the exception of stories credited to other news services, of *The Bond Buyer*, a daily newspaper covering municipal bonds. The Bond Buyer database is updated daily within 24 hours of the publication of the newspaper.

The Bond Buyer contains the most complete record of actual borrowing by municipal authorities available. The database contains detailed articles of federal laws and regulations affecting municipal financing, IRS rulings, Treasury department borrowings, and the general economy. Every aspect of the tax-exempt bond market, including data on planned bond issues and information on the results of bond sales, is covered by the database.

Access to The Bond Buyer is provided through private network, either via DIALOG or NEXIS (Mead Data Central). This access is available through any ASCII terminal or via computer with a modem. All customers are billed on a monthly basis.

The information contained in The Bond Buyer is available in hard copy on a yearly basis. This information is delivered daily via courier.

BONDDATA
Technical Data Corporation
330 Congress Street
Boston, MA 02210

PRODUCT AT-A-GLANCE
Subject Coverage:
Econometric data
Monetary aggregates
Real-time/Historic market quotations
Spot prices
Bonds, notes, and bills
Money rates

Technical Data's BondData database is an online technical service for the fixed-income investment industry. The service includes the daily market commentary, "Technically Speaking," a continuously updated Treasury yield curve graphic display, technical market indicators, current and historical price spread relationships, cash versus futures arbitrage analysis, and a bond market performance index. The database is accessed via Telerate.

Major topics include:

Daily Commentary and Technical Analysis—A detailed, technical evaluation and forecast of the U.S. government bond and financial futures markets. Daily Commentary and Technical Analysis offers a disciplined, technical approach for determining probable, near-term market direction. Daily Commentary and Technical Analysis is updated throughout the trading day.

Yield Curve Analysis—A graphic display of the U.S. Treasury yield curve and its underlying price data, a historical yield curve summary, and projected rate of return analysis. The yield curve graph and data table are updated approximately every seven minutes.

Spread Statistics—Yield spread analysis by maturity displaying current maturity spreads as well as the widest, narrowest, and average spreads for the last 60 trading days. Spread Statistics is updated approximately every seven minutes.

Cash versus Futures Arbitrage—Summary tables showing the relationship between Financial Futures contracts and their deliverable cash instruments. Cash versus Futures Arbitrage is updated four times daily.

5

Performance—Technical Data's Total Return Index showing the realized return from investing in actively traded treasury issues over several holding periods and for differing maturity sectors.

BondData is marketed through on-site visits, telemarketing, direct mailings, and media advertising.

Value-added products and services include financial software, company brochures, a quarterly newsletter, custom services, and toll-free customer support services.

BRANCH DEPOSIT
Chase Econometrics
150 Monument Road
Bala Cynwyd, PA 19004

PRODUCT AT-A-GLANCE

Subject Coverage:

Econometric data
Local

The Branch Deposit database contains deposit information for 85,000 branches of commercial savings banks, mutual savings banks, savings and loan associations, and federal savings banks. Information includes geographic detail at the state, SMSA, county, and zip code levels. Data are obtained from the branch office reports filed with the Federal Deposit Insurance Corporation and the Federal Savings and Loan Insurance Corporation. The database is updated on an annual basis.

The database information covers more than 14,000 commercial banks, 3,500 savings and loans and federal savings banks, and 400 mutual savings banks. Deposit data are available by branch location at the state, SMSA, county, and zip code levels.

User applications are available to determine market shares, obtain detailed deposit breakdown by branch, and determine branch ownership by bank holding company. The Branch Deposit database is listed with Chase Econometrics under the XDMS databases and under disk name BKBRCH. More information on the database service may be obtained by calling (215) 896-4920.

5

BRIDGE INFORMATION SYSTEM
Bridge Data Company
10050 Manchester Road
St. Louis, MO 63122

PRODUCT AT-A-GLANCE

Subject Coverage:

Real-time/Historic market quotations
Futures
Options
Stocks, mutual funds, warrants, and rights
Trading/Brokerage services

The Bridge Information System is available through Bridge Data Company. This database supplies information on over 30,000 listed and OTC stocks, financial futures, commodities, foreign securities, and all listed options to individual investors, stockbrokers, and traders. In addition to specific securities, the Bridge Information System also supplies data on the market as a whole. Much of this information is in real time, but data are also stored for up to 10 years.

Bridge continuously monitors the transactions on the New York and American Stock Exchanges, regional and option exchanges, NASDAQ and commodity exchanges. This price/volume information is available to customers, as are special data that are proprietary to Bridge. The information is presented in a variety of formats including the following:

Displays

Technical—Supplies the basic, real-time price and volume information on every vehicle in the Bridge System

Tabular Trades—Supplies real-time trade-by-trade or quote-by-quote data for every reporting security.

Five-Minute Trade Summary—Based on a security's five-minute trade summary data. This information is available for the current trading day and the five previous trading days.

Other available displays include Available Vehicles; Commodities Technical; Consolidated Quote; Fundamental; Quick Quote; Tabular Historic Data; Trade Spread Matrix; Vehicle Return Distribution; Volume Summary; Index; Indicators and Indexes; Market Ranking; Market Summary; Penetration Recap; and Repeat Ranking.

Charts

Moving Average Chart—Plots a security's moving average.
Relative Strength Chart—Compares the 10-day price performance of one company to another.
Oscillator Chart—charts the ratio between a company's 10-day
and 30-day unweighted moving average using last sale data.

Other available charts include Point and Figure; Price-Earnings;
Probability; Volatility; Liquidity; Volume at a Price; Bridge Technical; Price-Volume; Scattergram; and Weighted Distribution.

The Option System displays designed to help customers invest
in the option market. These displays are divided into three
categories: Option Market Displays, Option Summaries, and
Option strategies. The Option Market Ranking Displays rank
the entire option market according to a specified criterion.
Bridge allows the user to rank a class of options for a selected
stock under the Option Summaries and offers 14 option strategy calculations under the Option Strategy display.

The Portfolio System Bridge provides three types of portfolios
for its customers. All stocks on the Bridge System are in an
Industry Portfolio. There are also Special Ranked Portfolios
each with unique criteria for inclusion. Among the more than
60 ranked portfolios are Relative Strength, Yield, Volatility,
and Average Volume. Upon request, Bridge will establish Customer Portfolios to facilitate management and analysis. The
customer has control over the securities that are listed, the
manner in which the securities are ranked, and other details.

Order Indication System Bridge offers its brokerage customers
the opportunity to enter indications of trading interest directly
into the Bridge Information System. These indications are then
reviewed by the many institutions who use Bridge in their
daily operations. Features of the system are Market Maker;
Order Indication; Order Trades; Orders; and Update entry.

BROKERAGE INFORMATION DATA BASE

Bunker Ramo Corporation
35 Nutmeg Drive
Trumbull, CT 06609

PRODUCT AT-A-GLANCE

Subject Coverage:

**Real-time/Historic
   market quotations**
Bonds, notes, and bills
Futures
Currencies
Money rates
Options
*Stocks, mutual funds,
   warrants, and rights*

Bunker Ramo's Brokerage Information Data Base is comprised of one of the largest inventories of financial market data available to the investment community. This securities database is currently comprised of over 40,000 financial instruments. It contains up-to-the-second trading information on stocks, bonds, options, commodities, futures, and indexes from all U.S. exchanges. The database also covers all Canadian exchanges, as well as several European exchanges. It is continually being updated and expanded, with future expansion to include information on money markets and foreign exchange rates.

Recent additions include London Commodities, London Financial Futures, London metals, INSINET, and INTEX. Coverage available through the database will be detailed further here.

Financial Instruments

Stocks, Warrants, Rights as traded on all U.S. and Canadian exchanges and issues reported by NASDAQ.

Bonds, Notes, Bills as traded at the New York Stock Exchange, American Stock Exchange, and NASDAQ (U.S. Corporate Bonds, Foreign Agency Bonds, U.S. Treasury Notes, Bonds, Investment Growth Receipts, Certificates of Accrual).

Commodities Future Delivery Contracts as traded on all U.S. exchanges as well as Winnipeg and London commodities and international financial futures exchanges (Agricultural Commodities, Precious Metals, Debt Instruments, Stock Indexes, Options on Futures Delivery Contracts, Foreign Currencies).

Options as traded on all U.S. options exchanges and Canadian exchanges (Stock Options, Index Options, Interest Rate Options, Foreign Currency Options).

Gold and Silver Prices reflecting London, Paris, and Zurich fixings and Gold Coin Trades at American Stock Exchange.

Indexes reported by Dow Jones, S&P, exchanges, and NASDAQ.

Exchanges

U.S. Stock Exchanges (American, Boston, Cincinnati, Midwest, New York, NASDAQ, Pacific, Philadelphia).

Bond Exchanges (American, New York, NASDAQ).

U.S. Options Exchanges (American, Chicago Board Options, New York, Pacific, Philadelphia, NASDAQ, Boston).

Commodities Exchanges, U.S. (Chicago Board of Trade; Chicago Mercantile Exchange; Kansas City Board of Trade; Mid-America Commodities Exchange; Minneapolis Grain Exchange; New York Coffee, Sugar, and Cocoa Exchange; New York Commodity Exchange; New York Cotton Exchange; New York Futures Exchange; New York Mercantile Exchange; Philadelphia; American Commodities Exchange).

Commodities Exchanges, Foreign (Winnipeg Grain Exchange, London Commodities, London International Financial Futures, INTEX).

Canadian Stocks and Options Exchanges (Calgary, Montreal, Toronto, Vancouver).

Tickers

U.S. Stocks (Consolidated Tape—Last Sale, Bid/Ask Quotations, NASDAQ—Level-1 Quotes, National Market System Stocks Last Sales).

U.S. Options (OPRA—Options, Last Sales, and Quotes).

Canadian Stocks & Options (Montreal, Toronto, Vancouver/Calgary).

Bonds (NYSE Bond Last Sale, NYSE Bond Quotes, AMEX Bond Quotes, AMEX Bond Last Sale).

Commodities (Commodity Exchange Center—Futures and Options, New York Coffee, Sugar, and Cocoa Exchange—

Options; New York Futures Exchange; AMEX Gold Coin Exchange; London Commodities Exchange; London International Financial Futures Exchange; Chicago Board of Trade; Chicago Mercantile Exchange; Mid-America Commodities Exchange; Kansas City Board of Trade; Minneapolis Grain Exchange; Winnipeg Grain Exchange; INTEX).

BUSINESS & INDUSTRY NEWS
Predicasts Inc.
11001 Cedar Avenue
Cleveland, OH 44106

PRODUCT AT-A-GLANCE

Subject Coverage:

News services
National

Predicast's newest database, Business & Industry News, contains abstracts from over 1,200 trade and business journals covering all major industries. Some of the publications abstracted in this database are the *New York Times, Business Week, Computerworld, MIS Week*, and *Women's Wear Daily*. The information is available online 48 hours after appearing in the publication.

Coverage emphasis is placed on business events especially valuable to users actively involved in the manufacturing, distribution, and marketing of consumer and industrial products and services. This includes corporate affiliations, mergers and acquisitions, new products and services, marketing strategies, management and company plans, market share, research and development activities, new technologies, plant openings and closings, venture agreements, regulations, and business trends.

New records will be added at the rate of 750 records each business day. Each record will average approximately 250 words in length and will contain a bibliographic citation.

B&I News is available through DIALOG.

5

BUSINESS CONDITIONS DIGEST
Chase Econometrics
150 Monument Road
Bala Cynwyd, PA 19004

PRODUCT AT-A-GLANCE

Subject Coverage:

Econometric data
National

The Business Conditions Digest database provides historical coverage of 600 economic time series contained in the *Business Conditions Digest*, including series developed by the Bureau of Economic Analysis. The database's data frequency is monthly, quarterly, and annually. Subscription to the U.S. Macroeconomic database includes access to the Business Conditions Digest database. Data are updated on a monthly basis.

Cyclical indicators include leading indicators, lagging indicators, coincident indicators, diffusion indexes, and other cyclical indicators by economic process. Other economic measures include selected components of the national income and product accounts; measures of wages, prices, productivity, labor force, employment, and unemployment; government activities; U.S. international transactions, international comparisons, and analytical ratios.

The Business Conditions Digest database is listed with Chase Econometrics under the database name BCD and disk name USDB. More information on the database service may be obtained by calling (215) 896-4759.

BUSINESS DATELINE
Data Courier Inc.
620 South Fifth Street
Louisville, KY 40202-2297

```
┌─────────────────────────────────┐
│ PRODUCT AT-A-GLANCE             │
│                                 │
│ Subject Coverage:              │
│   News services                │
│   Regional                     │
│                                 │
└─────────────────────────────────┘
```

Data Courier Incorporated introduced the Business Dateline database in the fall of 1986. The Business Dateline database contains approximately 15,000 full-text articles from more than 100 regional U.S. and Canadian publications. Information in the database dates back to 1985. The database is updated on a monthly basis with each update adding approximately 1,000 records to the database.

The objective of the database is to provide users with information on regional business activities and trends. The database provides information on local companies, products, executives, and regional business activity and trends.

Access to Business Dateline is provided by two public networks—DIALOG and Dow Jones News/Retrieval. Users can access the database via user terminal or a personal computer with a modem. Access fees and hours of access vary depending on the vendor used.

The database supports a restricted vocabulary. Indexing terms include record type, title, classification code, controlled index terms, illustration, publication title, publication city or state, author(s), text, publication country, featured people, publication code, company, volume, issue number, section, dateline, and date of publication.

User support is available from 9 A.M. to 5 P.M. (EST), on weekdays via toll-free number (800) 626-2823. User inquiries may also be sent by telex 204235 24 hours a day, seven days a week.

Value-added products and services include document delivery of photocopied advertisements, document delivery rush service, custom reseaarch services, and free subscriptions to two Data Courier newsletters.

BUSINESS PERIODICALS INDEX
The H.W. Wilson Company
950 University Avenue
New York, NY 10452

PRODUCT AT-A-GLANCE

Subject Coverage:

News services
National
International

The Business Periodicals Index (BPI) is a database of the H.W. Wilson Company. This database provides a complete and accurate indexing of 298 of today's leading business magazines, including *Business Week, Forbes, Institutional Investor, Advertising Age, Inc., Fortune*, and the *Harvard Business Review*, to name a few. Updated twice weekly, the BPI database offers complete retrospective coverage beginning in June 1982 to the present.

To ensure that BPI covers all the most significant business publications, the Wilson Company has devised a selection process based on subscriber vote. The Committee on Wilson Indexes of the American Library Association's Reference and Adult Services Division conducts an in-depth content study of Business Periodicals Index at intervals of about five years. As part of the process, the committee, with the help of consultants in the field, prepares a list of periodicals representative of all subject areas covered by BPI. Subscribers are then asked to vote for the periodicals they want BPI to cover. The most recent study was completed in 1983, resulting in the addition of 80 and the deletion of 36 publications, for a current total of 298 periodicals indexed.

The information contained in the BPI is useful to anyone involved in any aspect of the business world. All items included in the BPI are indexed by professional librarians with expertise in business.

The BPI is available through WILSONLINE, the Wilson Company's online retrieval system. Subscribers to the printed version of the BPI receive a substantial reduction in WILSONLINE hourly connect-time rates.

The Wilson company also offers WILSEARCH personal computer software package that provides inexpensive, direct patron access to BPI and the other WILSONLINE databases. WILSEARCH is a menu-driven system that allows the user to develop a search strategy by choosing menu options and filling out a search screen.

Retrospective volumes of BPI are also available to interested users. Volumes covering the period from July 1969 to the present are available at a service basis rate, and volumes covering January 1958 to June 1969 are available at a flat rate.

A professional searcher thoroughly familiar with WILSONLINE will be available to answer users' questions should help be needed. Users can get assistance by calling toll-free at (800) 622-4002. In New York State, call (800) 538-3888. In Canada, call (212) 588-8998.

Value-added services include free text searching, online the-saurus, online help, online explain messages, offline printing in all standard formats, user guides, tutorials, and training seminars.

**BUSINESS SOFTWARE
DATABASE**

Data Courier Inc.
620 South Fifth Street
Louisville, KY 40202-2297

PRODUCT AT-A-GLANCE

Subject Coverage:

**Research reports/
evaluations**

Products

Established in 1984, Business Software Database is jointly produced by Data Courier Incorporated and Information Sources Incorporated. The database describes computer software packages that have business applications on mini- and micro-computers. It contains approximately 6,600 records of software company and manufacturer literature. Updating of the database occurs on a quarterly basis with approximately 500 records being added with each update.

Descriptions take the form of 100- to 200-word abstracts providing the name, address, and telephone number of the manufacturer; computer language; operating system; and purchase or lease price of the software. In addition, if such information is available, the database also supplies information on the type of hardware on which the software package can run; for whom the software was designed; the date the software package first became available; the number of software installations; descriptors and key words; and other services provided by the manufacturer. Database subject specialties include applications software, system software and utilities, database management programs, word processing, computer graphics, and commercial applications.

The Business Software Database is most often used by data processing professionals, venture capitalists, researchers, analysts, business executives, purchasing managers, and computer hardware and software company executives. The database is used to identify software packages for specific application, produce mailing labels, conduct competitive analysis, track products, and identify potential company acquisitions.

Access to the database is via user terminal or personal computer with a standard (300 baud or 1200 baud) modem. User access is available through the following public networks: BRS, BRS/After Dark, BRS/Brkthru, Data-Star, DIALOG, and ESA-Quest. Hours of database access and database fees vary with the vendor used.

The database supports restricted vocabulary. Indexing terms include abstract, company name, descriptor, title city, documentation available, computer hardware, operating system, program language, services available, state, telephone area code, training available, product type, potential users, year of release, and zip code or postal code.

Database information is also available in a printed form from Information Sources Incorporated and in tape form from Data Courier Incorporated.

User support is available from 9 A.M. to 5 P.M. (EST) Monday through Friday via toll-free telephone number (800) 626-2823 or by telex 204235 24 hours a day, seven days a week.

Value-added products and services include a custom research service, document delivery of photocopied abstacts, a document delivery rush service, subscriptions to two Data Courier newsletters at no charge, and a Business Software Database reference sheet and brochure.

5

CANADIAN BONDS
I.P. Sharp Associates Limited
2 First Canadian Place
Suite 1900
Toronto, Ontario, Canada M5X 1E3

PRODUCT AT-A-GLANCE

Subject Coverage:

**Real-time/Historic
    market quotations**
Bonds, notes, and bills

The Canadian Bonds database, a product of I.P. Sharp Associates Limited, provides price and yield statistics for approximately 1,200 Canadian bonds. The database's 7,500 time series include information on the following types of bonds: Canadian government bonds, provincial and provincial guaranteed, municipal, corporate, international and noninternational banks, and foreign government bonds traded in the United States.

The bond types included in the database are: convertible, extendible, retractable, Euro-Canadian, and Euro-U.S. bonds. There are 21 facts provided for each bond issue including the bid and ask price, maturity date, and coupon rate. There are 6 time series facts and 15 static facts provided for all bonds in the database. The database is updated by approximately 900 issues each Friday by 11 A.M. (EST).

The database's purpose is to provide current bond market data for trading and technical analysis done by securities analysts, portfolio managers, and professional bond traders. Data are obtained from Woody Gundy Limited.

The database is accessible 24 hours a day, seven days a week, except for a brief maintenance shut down period on Friday and Saturday nights. The Canadian Bonds database is accessible directly through I.P. Sharp's IPSANET network and also from Datapac, Telenet, Telex, and Tymnet public database access networks. Access is through a terminal or personal computer with a 300, account number. General purpose software allows for data manipulation, analysis, and downloading to a personal computer.

Users access the database via MAGIC, a database retrieval system for computer users with little programming experience; RETRIEVE, a database access system for users with APL programming language knowledge; or through PRICELINK, an I.P. Sharp software product that allows for statistical data collection and

downloading of data on personal computers. Access fees differ for each product.

Compu Trac, a third party software package designed by I.P. Sharp in close connection with Compu Trac's Technical Analysis Group , can also be used to access the Canadian Bonds database. Compu Trac allows for downloading and statistical manipulation of financial data.

User support is offered via calling toll-free ((800) 387-1588) in North America from 8 A.M. to 6 P.M. (EST) on weekdays. There is also a 24 hour answering service available for subscriber messages.

Other user aids include user manuals, reference guides, a printed directory of database symbols, and complete online documentation. Consulting services are available on an individual basis.

Value-added products and services include individual database search services, electronic sending and reception of messages, user software, data storage capabilities, ongoing user training programs, and custom program applications.

CANADIAN CHARTERED BANKS, ANNUAL FINANCIAL STATEMENTS

I.P. Sharp Associates Limited
Suite 1900 2 First Canadian Place
Toronto, Ontario, Canada M5X 1E3

PRODUCT AT-A-GLANCE

Subject Coverage:

Company information/ statistics
Annual reports
Quarterly reports
Econometric data
Industry specific

Canadian Chartered Banks, Annual Financial Statements database, produced by I.P. Sharp Associates Limited, provides annual financial statements for all chartered banks operating in Canada. Available information includes income statements, balance sheets, statements of shareholders' equity, and statements of accumulated appropriations contingencies. The entire database is updated on a yearly basis, one to three months after the fiscal year-end of October 31.

The database contains historical data dating back to 1972. It provides 100 facts for each of 10 Schedule A banks and 57 Schedule B banks. The sources of this data are the individual banks themselves.

The Canadian Chartered Banks, Annual Financial Statements database is accessible 24 hours a day, seven days a week, except for a brief maintenance period on Friday and Saturday nights. The database is accessible directly through I.P. Sharp's proprietary IPSANET network and also via Datapac, Telenet, Telex, and Tymnet public access networks. Access is through a terminal or personal computer with a 300, 1200, or 2400 baud modem; communications software; and an account number. Access software is general purpose, allowing for data manipulation, analysis, and downloading to personal computers.

User access to the database is through MAGIC, a database access system designed for novice computer programmers, or by RETRIEVE, a database access system for users who are knowledgeable in APL computer language. Access fees differ for each product.

User support is offered via calling toll-free ((800) 387-1588) in North America from 8 A.M. to 6 P.M. (EST) on weekdays. I.P. Sharp Associates also provides subscribers with access to a 24-hour answering service for subscribers to leave messages.

Other user aids include user manuals, reference guides, a printed directory of database symbols, and complete online documentation. Consulting services are available on an individual basis.

Value-added products and services include individual database search services, user software, data storage capabilities, ongoing user training programs, electronic mail, and custom program applications.

5

CANADIAN CHARTERED BANKS, MONTHLY STATEMENTS OF ASSETS AND LIABILITIES

I.P. Sharp Associates Limited
2 First Canadian Place
Suite 1900
Toronto, Ontario, Canada M5X 1E3

PRODUCT AT-A-GLANCE

Subject Coverage:

Company information/ statistics
Monthly reports
Econometric data
Industry specific

The Canadian Chartered Banks, Monthly Statements of Assets and Liabilities database, a product of I.P. Sharp Associates Limited, contains 246 data items in terms of time series data on 37 assets figures, 45 liabilities figures, and total assets and liabilities figures for all banks operating in Canada. The database contains totals for the big 5 and big 6 banks, 10 Schedule A and 57 Schedule B banks, and domestic and foreign banks. The database also contains historical data dating back to November 30, 1981. The entire contents of the database is updated monthly, approximately three to six weeks after the month-end.

The Canadian Chartered Banks, Monthly Statements of Assets and Liabilities database is accessible 24 hours per day, 7 days per week, except during a short maintenance period on Friday and Saturday nights. The database is accessible directly through I.P. Sharp's IPSANET or via four public networks—Datapac, Telenet, Telex, and Tymnet. Access is via user terminal or a personal computer with a 300, 1200, or 2400 baud modem; communications software; and an account number. Access software is general purpose, allowing for data manipulation, analysis, and downloading to a personal computer.

Users access the database through MAGIC, a database access system designed for inexperienced computer programmers; INFO-MAGIC, an interactive information retrieval system from I.P. Sharp Associates; or via RETRIEVE, a database access system for users who are knowledgeable in APL computer language. Access fees differ for each product.

User support is offered via calling toll-free ((800) 387-1588) in North America from 8 A.M. to 6 P.M. (EST) on Monday through Friday. I.P. Sharp Associates also provides subscribers with access to a 24-hour answering service for subscribers to leave messages.

Other user aids include reference guides, user manuals, two printed directories of database symbols, and complete online documentation. Subscriber consulting services are available on an individual basis.

5

CANADIAN CHARTERED BANKS, QUARTERLY INCOME STATEMENTS

I.P. Sharp Associates Limited
2 First Canadian Place
Suite 1900
Toronto, Ontario, Canada M5X 1E3

PRODUCT AT-A-GLANCE

Subject Coverage:

**Company information/
  statistics**
Quarterly reports
Econometric data
Industry specific

The Canadian Chartered Banks, Quarterly Income Statement database, produced by I.P. Sharp Associates Limited, contains quarterly income statements for all chartered banks in Canada. The database contains 37 facts from income statement data for the big 5 and big 6 banks, and Schedule A and B banks. Totals for all banks are provided as aggregates. The database also provides historical data from as far back as January 31, 1981. The information on all banks is updated on a quarterly basis within six to eight weeks of the quarter-end.

The Canadian Chartered Banks, Quarterly Income Statements database is accessible 24 hours per day, seven days a week, with the exception of a short maintenance period on Friday and Saturday nights. The database is accessible directly through I.P. Sharp's IPSANET or via four public networks—Datapac, Telenet, Telex, and Tymnet. Access is via user terminal or a personal computer with a 300, 1200, or 2400 baud modem; communications software; and an account number. Access software is general purpose, allowing for data manipulation, analysis, and downloading to a personal computer.

Database access is through MAGIC, a database access system designed for novice computer programmers; INFOMAGIC, an interactive information retrieval system from I.P. Sharp Associates; or via RETRIEVE, a database access system for users who are knowledgeable in APL computer language. Access fees differ with each product.

User support is offered via calling toll-free ((800) 387-1588) in North America from 8 A.M. to 6 P.M. (EST) on Monday through Friday. I.P. Sharp Associates also provides subscribers with access to a 24-hour answering service for subscribers to leave messages.

Other user aids include user manuals, reference guides, a printed directory of database symbols, and complete online documentation. Consulting services are available on an individual basis.

Value-added products and services include individual data base search services, user software, data storage capabilities, ongoing user training programs, electronic mail, and custom program applications.

5

CANADIAN DEPARTMENT OF INSURANCE

I.P. Sharp Associates Limited
2 First Canadian Place
Suite 1900
Toronto, Ontario, Canada M5X 1E3

PRODUCT AT-A-GLANCE

Subject Coverage:

Company information/ statistics
Annual reports
Econometric data
Industry specific

The Canadian Department of Insurance database, produced by I.P. Sharp Associates Limited, provides a variety of facts on over 500 companies for five years. The goal of this database is to provide a means of comparing various aspects of a company against the industry.

To achieve this goal, the database includes financial information on 600 federally registered insurance or trust companies; fraternal benefit societies; and cooperative credit associations across Canada. The data base contains 576 insurance statement forms.

The data come from information that each company sends yearly to the Canadian Department of Insurance. Some of this information is published in the annual "Blue Book," the report of the Superintendent of Insurance for Canada.

The Canadian Department of Insurance database is accessible 24 hours a day, seven days a week, except for a brief maintenance shut-down period on Friday and Saturday nights. The database is accessible directly through I.P. Sharp's IPSANET network and also from Datapac, Telenet, Telex, and Tymnet public networks. User access is through a terminal or personal computer with a 300, 1200, or 2400 baud modem; communications software; and a user account number.

User aids include manuals, reference guides, complete online documentation, and user instruction. There is a toll-free user support line in North America staffed 8 A.M. to 6 P.M. (EST) with a 24-hour answering service ((800) 387-1588).

THE CANADIAN FINANCIAL DATABASE

Info Globe
444 Front Street West
Toronto, Ontario, Canada M5V 2S9

PRODUCT AT-A-GLANCE

Subject Coverage:

Company information/ statistics
Annual reports

The Canadian Financial Database delivers full-text financial statements from major Canadian publicly held corporations and Crown corporations competing in the private sector. Information is available for 500 Canadian companies, beginning with their 1983 annual reports.

The information in the database includes complete financial statements, auditor's reports, footnotes, a list of officers and directors, and subsidiary data. Information on a company can be used to calculate financial ratios, check dividend and earnings-per-share data, make company and industry comparisons, or conduct in-depth company analysis. General information can be used to study reporting patterns for translation into foreign currency, accounting for inflation, extraordinary items, and discontinued operations.

The information in the database can be accessed on IBM and Amdahl equipment at Canadian Systems Group, the largest time-sharing computer company in Canada. Access is through Datapac, Telenet, and Tymnet public access networks.

5

CANADIAN OPTIONS

I.P. Sharp Associates Limited
2 First Canadian Place
Suite 1900
Toronto, Ontario, Canada M5X 1E3

PRODUCT AT-A-GLANCE

Subject Coverage:

**Real-time/Historic
  market quotations**
Options

The Canadian Options database, produced by I.P. Sharp Associates Limited, provides daily trading statistics for more than 2,000 options traded in Toronto, Montreal, and Vancouver as issued by Trans Canada Options Incorporated. Currently put and call options are provided for stocks, government bonds, indexes, and silver. The database contains time series and static facts for each option, including the open, high, low, and closing prices; volume and value traded; open interest and trading unit; bid and ask prices; and the exercise option price and the price of the underlying security.

In addition to providing daily information on options, the database provides historical data for the previous 200 trading days. All data are obtained from Trans Canada Options Incorporated. The database is updated within four hours of the source update, by 11 P.M. (EST) each trading day.

The Canadian Options database is accessible 24 hours a day, seven days a week, except for a brief maintenance shut-down period on Friday and Saturday nights. The database is accessible directly through I.P. Sharp's IPSANET network and also from Datapac, Telenet, Telex, and Tymnet public networks. User access is through a terminal or personal computer with a 300, 1200, or 2400 baud modem; communications software; and a user account number. General purpose software allows for data manipulation, analysis, and downloading to a personal computer.

Users access the database via MAGIC, a database retrieval system for computer users with little programming experience; RETRIEVE, a database access system for users with APL programming language knowledge; or through PRICELINK, an I.P. Sharp software product that allows for statistical data collection and downloading of data on personal computers.

Compu Trac, a third party software package designed by I.P. Sharp in close connection with Compu Trac's Technical Analysis

Group, can also be used to access the Canadian Options database. Compu Trac allows for downloading of data to personal computers and statistical manipulation of financial data.

User support is offered via calling toll-free ((800) 387-1588) in North America from 8 A.M. to 6 P.M. (EST) Monday through Friday. There is also a 24-hour answering service available for subscriber messages.

Other user aids include two printed directories of database symbols, user manuals, reference guides, and complete online documentation. User consulting services are available on an individual basis.

Value-added products and services include individual database search services, user software, data storage capabilities, ongoing user training programs, electronic sending and reception of messages, and custom program applications.

CISCO
Commodity Information Services
 Company
327 South LaSalle
Suite 800
Chicago, IL 60604

PRODUCT AT-A-GLANCE

Subject Coverage:

**Real-time/Historic
 market quotations**
Spot prices
Bonds, notes, and bills
Futures
Money rates
Options

The CISCO database is a product of the Commodity Information Service Company of Chicago, Illinois. CISCO is composed of a variety of sub-databases associated with futures including standard futures, cash T-bonds, T-bills, GNMAs, and the underlying cash on many futures, options, continuations, interest rates, and indexes. CISCO data take the form of either raw trading statistics (prices, volumes, open interest) or tables of information that are preprocessed to some degree.

CISCO provides database services in the form of current and historical data for stockbrokers, investment analysts, portfolio managers, and personal investors. Other services include custom services, personal computer services, trading data research, electronic mail, and database publications.

The following list is an illustration of the types of data accessible through the CISCO database: (All the information may be downloaded to a PC)

Futures
Cash on the futures
Cash T-bonds, bills, GNMAs
Forwards
Municipal index
Interest rates
Options
Daily settlement
CBOT liquidity data bank
CBOT market profile
Express tables

Live history on the system extends back to 1970 in many cases. For those instruments that began trading since 1970, the live data usually start with inception of trading. In some cases, the data start with the time at which CISCO deemed liquidity adequate for inclusion in the database.

CISCO does not carry some instruments in the database, for instance, stocks, stock options, and forward foreign exchange rates. It does provide, however, a set of update programs for clients to maintain their own databases. Users can build their private data files in a format identical to the standard CISCO format. That personal data may then interact with all CISCO programs and analytical routines.

CISCO pricing schedule is split up into three main classes:

Class 1 is full-access service to CISCO. Database prime time access is from 7 A.M. to 7 P.M. with a reduced rate charged during non-prime time hours from 7 P.M. to 7 A.M..

Class 2 provides data updates only. Monthly charges for data updates are based on the number of contracts performed as well as Telenet charges for the size and location of the city.

Class 3 provides access to CISCO Express electronic mail service.

History data are also available online, on diskette, on printed hard copy, and on magnetic tape. History data charges are on a monthly basis. All CISCO prices are subject to change without notice.

Value-added products and services include custom services; database publications; advisory and consulting services; CISCO library programs; reports; computer software; data storage facilities; research services; electronic mail; and hard copy, diskette, and magnetic tape versions of the history data.

5

CLAREMONT ECONOMICS INSTITUTE

Claremont Economics Institute
Suite 220
250 West First Street
Claremont, CA 91711

PRODUCT AT-A-GLANCE

Subject Coverage:

Econometric data
Industry specific
International
National

The Claremont Economics Institute analyzes current political, economic, and financial conditions, and forecasts future turns and trends in real growth (GNP), inflation, interest rates, and currencies for the United States, Canada, Germany, France, the United Kingdom, Japan, Brazil, Argentina, Chile, and Mexico.

The two most recent issues of the publications of the Claremont Economics Institute can be accessed through the Claremont Economics Institute database. The retrieved information contains both text and data in tabular form. The data are derived from propietary models and are not in predictable form.

Materials can be accessed through the use of almost any personal computer equipped with a standard modem. No special hardware or software is required, unless the user wishes to download text, and in that case, some general-purpose communications software is required.

The database is accessible 24 hours per day, seven days a week. The hours for customer support are from 8:30 A.M. to 6 P.M. (PST) Monday through Friday. Additional user support is available in the form of user manuals, newsletters, training, and online help.

Users must already have a subscription to The Source. Log on fees and time charges are determined by The Source and billed monthly. No additional charges are assessed for searches, and volume discounts are currently not available.

COMMODITIES

I.P. Sharp Associates Limited
Suite 1900 2 First Canadian Place
Toronto, Ontario, Canada M5X 1E3

```
PRODUCT AT-A-GLANCE

Subject Coverage:
   Real-time/Historic
    market quotations
   Futures
```

The Commodities database, produced by I.P. Sharp Associates Limited, gives prices, volumes, and open interest for all major commodities traded on the London, New York, Chicago, Kansas City, Winnipeg, and Toronto/Montreal futures markets. The database contains 41,400 statistical time series on metals and soft commodities. The database is updated daily by 500 data items by 8:30 P.M. (EST).

The database offers information on all current and historical contracts, data error correction within eight hours of the update, static and time series facts, supportive data like continuation/perpetual contracts and cash prices, and screening capabilities.

The primary focus of the database is on commodity data from Europe and North America. Its primary source of data is Wolff Research of the United Kingdom. London historical monthly market data date back to 1960, while London daily data date back to 1973. New York and Chicago market data date back to 1973. Kansas City, Winnipeg, and Minneapolis data date back to March of 1982. Toronto/Montreal data date back to June of 1982.

The database is accessible 24 hours a day, seven days a week, except for a brief maintenance period on Friday and Saturday nights. The Commodities database is accessible directly through I.P. Sharp's IPSANET network and also via Datapac, Telenet, Telex, and Tymnet public networks. Access is through a terminal or personal computer with a 300, 1200, or 2400 baud modem; communications software; and an account number. Access software is general purpose, allowing for data manipulation, analysis, and downloading.

Users access the database via MAGIC, a database retrieval system for computer users with little programming experience; RETRIEVE, a database access system for users with APL programming language knowledge; or through PRICELINK, an I.P. Sharp software product that allows for statistical data collection and

downloading of data on personal computers. Access fees differ for each product.

Compu Trac, a third party software package designed by I.P. Sharp in close connection with Compu Trac's Technical Analysis Group, can also be used to access the Commodities database. Compu Trac is designed for downloading and statistical manipulation of financial data.

User support is offered via calling toll-free ((800) 387-1588) in North America from 8 A.M. to 6 P.M. (EST) Monday through Friday. There is also a 24-hour answering service available for user messages.

Other user aids include user manuals, reference guides, a printed directory of database symbols, and complete online documentation. Consulting services are provided on an individual basis.

Value-added products and services include individual database searches, user software, electronic messaging, data storage capabilities, ongoing training programs, and custom program applications.

COMMODITY OPTIONS
I.P. Sharp Associates Limited
Suite 1900
2 First Canadian Place
Toronto, Ontario, Canada M5X 1E3

The Commodity Options database, produced by I.P. Sharp Associates Limited, provides statistical information in the form of prices, volumes, and open interest for all major options and commodities futures traded in the United States. The database contains over 11,880 time series pertaining to opening and closing prices, high and low prices, contract volume, and open interest. The database is updated daily by approximately 1,500 items within eight hours of the source update.

The database offers current and historical statistics and static and time series facts on all major options and futures traded in the United States, and screening capabilities through RETRIEVE and MAGIC software packages. The primary focus of the database is options and commodity futures traded on U.S. and London exchanges. The information contained in the database dates back to September 1985.

The database is accessible 24 hours per day, seven days a week, with the exception of a short maintenance period on Friday and Saturday nights. Commodity Options database is accessible directly through I.P. Sharp's IPSANET or via four public networks—Datapac, Telenet, Telex, and Tymnet. Access is via user terminal or a personal computer with a 300, 1200, or 2400 baud modem; communications software; and an account number. Access software is general purpose, allowing for data manipulation, analysis, and computer downloading.

User access to the database is through MAGIC, a database access system designed for novice computer programmers; INFO-MAGIC, an interactive information retrieval system from I.P. Sharp Associates; or via RETRIEVE, a database access system for users who are knowledgeable in APL computer language. Access fees differ for each product.

Compu Trac, a third party software package designed by I.P. Sharp in close connection with Compu Trac's Technical Analysis Group, can also be used to access the Commodity Options database. Compu Trac is designed for downloading and statistical manipulation of financial data.

The Commodity Options database is marketed to investment analysts and traders through the company sales force and direct mailings.

User support is offered via calling toll-free ((800) 387-1588) in North America from 8 A.M. to 6 P.M. (EST) on weekdays. There is also a 24-hour answering service available for subscriber messages.

Other user aids include user manuals, reference guides, a printed directory of database symbols, and complete online documentation. Consulting services are available on an individual basis.

Value-added products and services include individual database search services, user software, data storage capabilities, electronic mail services, ongoing user training programs, and custom program applications.

COMPUSTAT
Standard & Poor's Corporation
25 Broadway
New York, NY 10004

Standard & Poor's COMPUSTAT Services is a division of FEICO, the McGraw-Hill Financial and Economic Information Company. The COMPUSTAT database contains quarterly and annual financial statement information on publicly traded industrial firms, banks, and utilities. Detailed business segment, SIC code, industry, and company data such as share price, dividends, and earnings are also provided. Standard & Poor's COMPUSTAT Services Incorporated is the provider of data for the Standard & Poor's COMPUSTAT database.

The contents of the database include:

Industrial companies—Contains data on more than 170 annual and 60 quarterly balance sheet, income statement, and sources. Uses statement items for over 6,000 companies that are traded on the New York and American Stock Exchanges, as well as on the OTC market.

Utilities—Contains information on more than 380 annual and 145 quarterly data items for 185 large utilities and 32 utility subsidiaries.

Banks—Covers more than 230 annual and 140 quarterly statistics on over 135 of the leading U.S. banking institutions by region.

Canadian Companies—Contains more than 175 annual data items on over 320 major Canadian companies.

Business information—Provides unique business segment, geographic segment, and SIC code information on more than 3,000 companies.

Industry composites—Contains aggregate data on 120 industry groups classified by SIC codes for more than 170 annual and 60 quarterly variables.

Price-dividends-earnings—Contains financial and market data on 6,000 companies and 1,200 industry composites and indexes.

User applications include selecting data for spreadsheet reports, analyzing of financial statements of similar firms when investigating acquisition and divestiture candidates, examining balance sheet and income statement data to identify theoretically undervalued or overvalued securities, and projecting lending needs for publicly held companies.

COMPUSTAT II
Standard & Poor's Corporation
25 Broadway
New York, NY 10004

PRODUCT AT-A-GLANCE

Subject Coverage:

**Company information/
statistics**
Annual reports
Quarterly reports

The COMPUSTAT II database provides quarterly and annual financial data on more than 20,000 publicly traded companies. The COMPUSTAT Industrial Research File contains historic annual data for over 2,500 companies that are no longer reporting information due to acquisition, merger, bankruptcy, or change from public to private ownership.

COMPUSTAT II allows users to quickly and easily analyze the financial data of a wide variety of businesses. Special features of the database include:

Quarterly and annual financial data for more than 6,000 American companies whose stock is traded in the United States plus key Canadian firms.

Summary financial data for more than 6,000 corporations by line of business and geographic region.

Financial data and stock information for the 90 largest U.S. telecommunications firms and their subsidiaries.

Financial data and stock information for the 300 largest U.S. utilities and their subsidiaries.

5

COMPUTER DATABASE
Information Access Company
11 Davis Drive
Belmont, CA 94002

PRODUCT AT-A-GLANCE

Subject Coverage:

News services
National
International

The Computer Database is produced by Information Access Company and provides wide-ranging information on computers, telecommunications, and electronics. It is designed to provide business and computer professionals with answers to questions regarding hardware, software, peripherals, and high-tech fields such as robotics, satellite communications, and videotex. It is an overall source of information on any topic concerning computers or the dynamic computer industry.

Cover-to-cover indexing and abstracts to over 600 journals, proceedings, courses, books, newsletters, research reports, and tabloids are provided. Coverage extends from 1983 to the present. Some 3,000 records are added monthly. Available through DIA-LOG and Data-Star.

CONFERENCE BOARD
Chase Econometrics
150 Monument Road
Bala Cynwyd, PA 19004

PRODUCT AT-A-GLANCE

Subject Coverage:

Econometric data
National

The Conference Board database provides coverage of economic data that is monitored by the Conference Board. Database information includes the Conference Board's economic forecasts, as well as consumer and business survey results. The database contains 1,000 time series of data in 10-day, monthly, bimonthly, quarterly, semiannual, and annual form.

Historical data coverage includes diffusion indexes, help-wanted advertising, automotive sales, discretionary spending, utility appropriations, capital appropriations, forecasts of capital appropriations, capital investment and supply conditions, consumer attitudes and buying plans, business executives' expectations, and financial indicators.

Forecast data coverage includes the Conference Board Economic Forecast, Conference Board Economic Forum, Survey of Economic Forecasts, and European Forecasts.

The Conference Board database is listed with Chase Econometrics under the database name CONF and disk name CONFDB. More information on the database service may be obtained by calling (212) 759-0900.

5

THE CONFERENCE BOARD DATA BASE

The Conference Board, Inc.
845 Third Avenue
New York, NY 10022

PRODUCT AT-A-GLANCE

Subject Coverage:

**Demographic information/
statistics**
Consumer preference
Income and housing
Econometric data
Industry specific
Local
Monetary aggregates
National
Regional
Newsletter

The Conference Board Data Base contains 1,013 time series data extending back to 1951. The data are either of monthly, quarterly, semiannual, or annual nature. The database focuses mainly on sectors of the economy, with lesser emphasis on regional and industry data.

The database provides economic projections, capital investment data, consumer data, financial data, attitude surveys, and other macroeconomic data in historical and forecasted time series form. Also included in the database are regular economic forecasts by The Conference Board's chief economist, Albert T. Sommers. Database updates are usually available to online users within 24 hours of their release.

The contents of the database include:

Conference Board Economic Projections—The Conference Board Economic Projections are two-year forecasts of quarterly data of 50 key economic indicators. These projections are updated on a monthly basis.

Survey of Economic Forecasts—The Survey of Economic Forecasts contains two-year forecasts of quarterly data from leading forecasting companies and universities. These forecasts are updated on a monthly basis.

Survey of Capital Appropriations and Expenditures—The Survey of Capital Appropriations and Expenditures contains data on current and future plans for new plant and equipment expenditures. The survey contains quarterly data on the manufacturing and utilities industries. Data in these files extend back to 1953.

Business Executives' Expectations—Business Executives' Expectations contain data on business executives' outlook on the state of the economy and their own industry. The data in these files are in quarterly form dating back to 1976.

Consumer Attitudes and Buying Plans File—The Consumer Attitudes and Buying Plans File contains information on consumer expectations on the economy, employment, and income. It also provides data on consumer plans to make major capital expenditures such as purchases of major appliances, homes, and automobiles. The file also contains regional and demographic data. The Consumer Attitudes and Buying Plans file is updated monthly and contains data dating back to 1967.

Diffusion Indexes—Diffusion Indexes are macroindexes that show the degree of expansion or contraction of the economy. The monthly data in this file date back to 1958.

European Forecasts—European Forecasts contain annual data on macroforecasts of 10 economic indicators for 14 countries.

Financial Indicators—Financial Indicators provide data on sources of internal funds, exchange rate expectations, and expectations of changes in financial indicators. Data in the files are on a semiannual basis dating back to 1976.

The primary goal of The Conference Board Data Base (CBDB) is to provide users with immediate access to timely economic data. The database also allows for data manipulation, statistical analysis, and interface with the user's own company data. Data in the series can be used to follow the economy, either coincidentally or with a lead or lag. Furthermore, the historical time series of the database can be used to track or forecast company sales.

Information in the database is in statistical form, with the exception of two files of text. Contents of the database are produced solely by The Conference Board for CBDB customers and thus are unique. All information contained in CBDB is also available in print form in publications that are only available to Conference Board Associates.

The main clients of the database are economists, marketers, planners, and librarians. The Conference Board promotes its database to these clients via direct mailings, telephone solicitation, conference promotions, company sales force, and advertisements.

The database is accessible 24 hours a day, seven days a week through three time-sharing networks: Data Resources Inc., Chase Econometrics, and Cornell University. Access to CBDB through Cornell University is via public network. Access to CBDB through Chase Econometrics and Data Resources Inc. is through private networks. Data contained in the database are also available on diskette for use on a personal computer.

CBDB is available to subscribers 24 hours a day, seven days a week. Annual subscription fees are payed to The Conference Board. Online charges for the database are payable to the time-sharing vendors. The user should contact the particular vendor to inquire about online charges. The Conference Board will forward subscriber names to each vendor, which will provide users with their own contract and vendor access and fee information.

CONSUMER PRICE INDEX DATABASE

Chase Econometrics
150 Monument Road
Bala Cynwyd, PA 19004

PRODUCT AT-A-GLANCE

Subject Coverage:

Econometric data
National

The Consumer Price Index database provides monthly historical consumer price indexes for the entire United States, 28 urban metropolitan areas, regional areas, and population-size class regions provided by the Bureau of Labor Statistics. The database's 10,000 time series are updated on a monthly basis.

The database provides 900 seasonally adjusted and unadjusted indexes for the total United States; 136 unadjusted indexes available for 28 metropolitan areas; indexes for urban consumers, wage earners, and clerical workers; and indexes by five population-size classes, by census region, and by region cross-classified by population size.

The Consumer Price Index database is listed with Chase Econometrics under the database name CPI and disk name CPIDB. More information on the database service may be obtained by calling (202) 775-0610.

5

**CONSUMER PRICE INDEX
DATABASE**

SAGE DATA, Inc.
104 Carnegie Center
Princeton, NJ 08540

PRODUCT AT-A-GLANCE

Subject Coverage:

Econometric data
National

The Consumer Price Index Database contains more than 9,000 data series on the average change in prices over time in a fixed market basket of goods as measured by the Consumer Price Index (CPI). The SAGE CPI Database contains all data for U.S. city averages for All Urban Consumers.

The database includes information for two population groups: All Urban Consumers, which covers approximately 80 percent of the total noninstitutional civilian population; and Urban Wage Earners and Clerical Workers. Much of the data is regional in nature.

**CONSUMER SPENDING
FORECAST**

Chase Econometrics
150 Monument Road
Bala Cynwyd, PA 19004

PRODUCT AT-A-GLANCE

Subject Coverage:

**Demographic information/
    statistics**
Consumer preference
Income and housing
Econometric data
National

The Consumer Spending Forecast database provides detailed forecasts of U.S. personal consumption expenditures, retail sales, and consumer credit. Selected data from the U.S. Macroeconomic database are also included in the Consumer Spending Forecast database. Short-term forecasts are updated monthly and extend 12 months into the future. Long-term forecasts are updated semiannually and extend 10 years into the future.

The database also contains historical data on consumer spending. Consumption expenditure and price data date back to 1959. Retail sales data begin in 1967.

Short-term and long-term forecasts include implicit price deflators for all consumption expenditure components; retail sales for detailed components of durable and nondurable stores; implicit price deflators for all retail components; and consumption expenditures for detailed components of durables, nondurables, and services categories.

The Consumer Spending Forecast database is listed with Chase Econometrics under the database names SPEND, LTPCE, and LTRET and under disk names CMSDB, and CMSLDB. More information on the database service may be obtained by calling (215) 896-4717.

5

CORPORATE AFFILIATIONS
National Register Publishing
 Company
3004 Glenview Road
Wilmette, IL 60091

PRODUCT AT-A-GLANCE

Subject Coverage:

**Company information/
 statistics**
Company background

Corporate Affiliations contains business profiles and corporate linkage for 42,700 parent companies and affiliates. Included are business profiles and corporate linkage for 550 private and 3100 public parent companies and 38,800 affiliates (divisions, subsidiaries, branches).

Users of Corporate Affiliations can search and extract via company characteristics such as SIC Code, business description, executives, company name, telephone area code, financials, executive functions, ownership, and special features (parent/affiliate, public/private). Corporate Affiliations also features corporate relationship as a searchable characteristic.

Publicly held corporations and their affiliates represented on stock exchanges are included as follows:

New York Stock Exchange (all companies and affiliates, if any)
American Stock Exchange (all companies and affiliates, if any)
OTC Exchange (all companies having affiliates)
Top privately held companies and affiliates (if any)

The database is reloaded quarterly and is available through DIALOG.

CORPORATE DESCRIPTIONS ONLINE
Standard & Poor's Corporation
25 Broadway
New York, NY 10004

PRODUCT AT-A-GLANCE

Subject Coverage:

Company information/ statistics
Annual reports
Company background

Corporate Descriptions Online is a full-text database that provides financial and business information on more than 8,200 publicly owned companies. The database is updated once annually, as soon as the company annual report is published.

Database information consists of:

Company information—Company name, CUSIP number, state or country the company headquarters is located in, stock ticker symbol, primary SIC code and narrative description, and secondary SIC code.

Capitalization summary and corporate background—Company products and services, primary markets, sales and profits breakdowns, subsidiaries and affiliates, property locations, number of employees, incorporation history, capital expenditures, officers and directors, and main office address and telephone number.

Bond descriptions and stock data—Shares authorized and outstanding, principal stockholders, transfer agent and registrar, stock price and dividend, and price and dividend history for up to the last ten years.

Earnings and finances—For up to the previous 10 years.

Annual report data—Three years of consolidated income statement information and two years of balance sheet information.

The database may be searched by company name, free text, business descriptions, primary and secondary SIC codes, and subsidiary names. The information contained in the database can be used in conjunction with other Standard & Poor's database services to obtain personal background information on officers and directors, locate privately held companies that are in the same industry, find more currently updated company information, and more.

The information contained in the database is obtained from

5

Standard & Poor's records business and financial information service. This service contains information from company reports filed with the Securities and Exchange Commission and other regulatory bodies; telephone interviews; annual and interim company reports, press releases; wire services; and newspapers.

The database is accessible through DIALOG. There are no sign-up fees or monthly minimum usage charges. Connect-time fees are $85 per hour. Online and offline prints are available at a cost of $3.50 per full record.

CORPORATE PROFILES

Moody's Investors Service
99 Church Street
New York, NY 10007

PRODUCT AT-A-GLANCE

Subject Coverage:

**Company information/
statistics**
Annual reports
Company background
Forecasts
Lines of business
Market activity
Monthly reports
Officers/Directors
Quarterly reports
SEC filings
Stockholder information
**Research reports/
evaluations**
Company

Corporate Profiles, a publication of Moody's Investors Service, Inc., provides concise, descriptive overviews and detailed financial statistics on 3,600 public companies. Coverage includes all companies listed on the New York and American Stock Exchanges, and 1,300 actively traded OTC companies.

For each company in Corporate Profiles, users will find Moody's profiles of quarterly developments. And for all NYSE and AMEX companies, users will find Moody's exclusive Comments.

Information for each company includes:

Business description—a concise textual background on the company and its products or services
Interim earnings and dividends
Quarterly developments—a summary of the developments of the most recent quarter
Moody's comments—Moody's exclusive analysis of company outlook, available for companies of high investor interest
Five-year records of earnings and balance sheet statistics
Five-year statistical records of book value, p/e ratio, price range, and more
Capitalization

Primary and Secondary SIC Codes, Address, Telephone Number, and so on

In addition, nearly every line item is searchable. Users are provided with a total of 54 searchable fields, such as net income, earnings per share, and others. The companies within the database can also be sorted and ranked using any of the 47 sortable fields. And, with free text search, words in textual situations can be pinpointed for maximum efficiency and control.

Corporate Profiles is available on the DIALOG system 22 hours every weekday. Saturday hours are also available.

In addition, the service forms the basis of information available on Automatic Data Processing (A.D.P.), Bunker Ramo, and E.F. Hutton's Huttonline. The service is also available for internal information systems use by corporate clients and clients in the securities industry.

Charges for accessing the database are based on connect time. Additional charges are assessed for offline prints, types, and displays. There are no initial or annual subscription fees, log on fees, search charges, or storage charges. Users are billed directly from DIALOG, and no discounts are available.

Corporate Profiles can be accessed using almost any brand or model of ASCII-coded personal computer or word processor as long as users have:

Terminal software—asynchronous communications package
Terminal hardware—serial interface and modem
Telephone line

The primary sources for this database include annual and quarterly reports, news releases, proxy statements, regulatory reports, prospectuses, stock exchange bulletins and lists, and leading newspapers and trade journals. The information from these sources dates back five years from the present. The data are updated weekly.

Moody's plans for the future call for continued expansion of its electronic information resource coverage of public companies. As of late 1986, the information contained on over 20,000 corporations, similar to what is available in the Moody's Manuals, was available in machine-readable form.

CPI
Wharton Econometric Forecasting
  Associates
3rd floor, 3624 Science Center
Philadelphia, PA 19104

PRODUCT AT-A-GLANCE

Subject Coverage:

**Demographic information/
  statistics**
Income and housing
Econometric data
National

CPI measures the cost of living (Consumer Price Index) for all wage earners and for urban workers for 25 major cities and the U.S. average, covering food, housing, medical care, energy, clothing, transportation, and durable goods. Both seasonally adjusted and unadjusted monthly data are available. The source for the data is the Bureau of Labor Statistics.

Data are updated monthly and annually and begin in 1914.

5

CROPMOD
Wharton Econometric Forecasting
  Associates
3rd floor, 3624 Science Center
Philadelphia, PA 19104

PRODUCT AT-A-GLANCE

Subject Coverage:

Econometric data
National
**Real-time/Historic
  market quotations**
Spot prices

CROPMOD contains historical data for wheat, soybean meal, corn, soybean oil, and soybeans. These data relate to cash grain & prices, supply/demand balance stocks, USDA expectation factors, and prices for competitive and complement goods. Data sources include *USDA Situation Reports, Agricultural Prices Report, Agricultural Supply and Demand Estimates, Crop Reporting Board Releases,* and *Agricultural Outlook.*

Data are updated monthly and begin in 1950.

DAILY CURRENCY EXCHANGE RATES

I.P. Sharp Associates Limited
2 First Canadian Place
Suite 1900
Toronto, Ontario, Canada M5X 1E3

PRODUCT AT-A-GLANCE

Subject Coverage:

Real-time/Historic market quotations
Currencies

The Daily Currency Exchange Rates database, produced by I.P. Sharp Associates Limited, provides a total of 715 currency exchange rates that are listed on the Copenhagen, Frankfurt, Helsinki, London, Madrid, Melbourne, New York, Oslo, Paris, Singapore, Toronto, Tokyo, Vienna, and Zurich markets. Rates are reported in terms of the local currency of the reporting country. Data for each country are obtained from respected financial institutions, primarily from the Federal Bank.

The database's exchange rate information includes daily spot, buying and selling, and forward rates. Forward and spot rates are reported by the London, New York, Copenhagen, Melbourne, and Toronto markets. Updating of the daily data varies with the individual exchange hours, but occurs by the following business day for each exchange.

The Daily Currency Exchange Rates database is accessible 24 hours a day, seven days a week, except during a brief maintenance shut-down period on Friday and Saturday nights. The database is accessible directly through I.P. Sharp's IPSANET network and also from Datapac, Telenet, Telex, and Tymnet public database access networks. User access is via terminal or personal computer with a 300, 1200, or 2400 baud modem; communications software; and a user account number. General-purpose software allows for data manipulation, analysis, and downloading to a personal computer. Downloading procedures are dependent on the computer hardware used.

The information retrieval systems used to access the database are MAGIC, PRICELINK, and INFOMAGIC. MAGIC is an English-language system that is intended to be used by people who have little or no computer programming experience. PRICELINK is a software package that allows information to be downloaded onto personal computers. INFOMAGIC interactive data retrieval system

5

offers data in preformatted report form. Prices differ for each product.

Compu Trac, a third party software package designed by I.P. Sharp in close connection with Compu Trac's Technical Analysis Group, can also be used to access the Daily Currency Exchange Rates database. CompuTrac is designed for downloading and statistical manipulation of financial data on personal computers.

User support is offered via calling toll-free ((800) 387-1588) in North America from 8 A.M. to 6 P.M. (EST) on weekdays. I.P. Sharp Associates also provides subscribers with access to a 24-hour answering service for subscribers to leave messages.

Other user aids include user manuals, reference guides, a printed directory of database symbols, and complete online documentation. Consulting services are available on an individual basis.

Value-added products and services include individual database search services, user software, data storage capabilities, ongoing user training programs, electronic mail, and custom program applications.

DAILY REPORT FOR EXECUTIVES
The Bureau of National Affairs, Inc.
Room 601 South
1231 25th Street NW
Washington, DC 20037

PRODUCT AT-A-GLANCE

Subject Coverage:

**Industry information/
  statistics**
Legal actions and issues
Market news and forecasts
News services
National

The Daily Report for Executives covers judicial, regulatory, and legislative activity in areas that affect business. These areas include taxation and accounting, securities regulation, export and import regulations, energy development and regulation, product liability, federal grants and contracts, environmental controls, international finance, farm legislation, and the federal budget. The database also includes statistical and economic data such as information on employment, prices, construction, and other economic indicators.

The Daily Report for Executives covers the subjects of taxation, accounting, securities, antitrust, federal contracts, the environment, business and economics, and product liability. The database is updated on a daily basis. Its corresponding printed product is the *Daily Report for Executives.*

Access to the database is via either Mead Data Central; ITT Dialcom; Human Resource Information Network; Executive Telecom System, Incorporated; or NewsNet. User access charges are $68.50 per hour including telecommunications charges for ITT Dialcom; $24 per hour for scan time and $48 per hour for read time at 300 baud on NewsNet; and available on request from Mead Data Central and Executive Telecom System, Incorporated.

The database's time coverages are from January 1982 to present day on Mead Data Central; the latest six months on ITT Dialcom; and from December 1985 to present day on Executive Telecom System, Incorporated.

5

DAILY WASHINGTON ADVANCE

The Bureau of National Affairs, Inc.
Room 601 South
1231 25th Street NW
Washington, DC 20037

PRODUCT AT-A-GLANCE

Subject Coverage:

**Industry information/
  statistics**
*Industry overviews
Legal actions and issues
Market news and forecasts*

The Daily Washington Advance database covers judicial, regulatory, and legislative activity in areas that affect business. These areas include import and export regulations, international finance, energy development and regulation, product liability, federal grants and contracts, farm legislation, environmental controls, and the federal budget. The database also includes economic data on employment, prices, industrial production, construction, and other economic indicators.

The database covers a variety of subjects, including business and economics, securities, antitrust, federal contracts, the environment, and product liability. Its files are updated daily by 7 A.M. (EST) on weekdays. The database files cover the latest six months. Its printed counterpart is the *Daily Report to Executives.* Users may access the database via ITT Dialcom. User access charges are $68.50 per hour including telecommunications charges.

DATATIMES–ASSOCIATED PRESS
DATATEK Corporation
818 NW 63rd
Oklahoma City, OK 73116

PRODUCT AT-A-GLANCE

Subject Coverage:

News services
Local
National
Regional
International

DataTimes–Associated Press is a database of the DATATEK Corporation. This database is available to subscribers from 6 A.M. to 12 A.M. (CST). The database contains national and international stories produced by AP writers in full-text form. The primary goal of the database is to provide access to local, regional, and national information on individuals, companies, trends, and issues.

Every day, the DataTimes database is updated with a total of 400 stories. The lag time between source update and database update is usually 24 hours. Information contained within the database dates back to January 1, 1985.

Users can access this database through Tymnet, Easylink, SAT-PAC (a satellite switching service provided by the Associated Press), and DATATEK's own network (DataTimes). DataTimes is accessible through a local telephone number in most U.S. cities, as well as throughout Canada, Australia, and Europe. Any ASCII terminal or microcomputer equipped with a modem can be used to access the database.

DataTimes charges include all royalties to database suppliers and all telecommunications charges. Connect-time charges are consistent for every database offered. Subscribers can choose one of two rate options. The initial subscription fee includes free training, a user's manual, and quarterly newsletters. Updates to the user's manual are mailed periodically at no additional charge.

There are no log on fees, search charges, or storage charges. Customers are billed monthly and discounts are available for groups.

DataTimes provides numerous customer support services, including comprehensive user guides, free on-site training when possible, or free online time for subscribers not near a local DataTimes office. DataTimes provides quarterly newsletters and

5

updates to subscribers, along with a hotline service available by calling (800) 642-2525.

DataTimes does not provide any capability to manipulate or compute the raw data through value added or decision support software. Neither does the company provide the information in other forms such as hard copy, fiche/film, or tape.

DATATIMES–SOUTHWEST NEWSWIRE

DATATEK Corporation
818 NW 63d
Oklahoma City, OK 73116

DataTimes–Southwest Newswire is a database of the DATATEK Corporation. This database is available to subscribers from 6 A.M. to 12 A.M. (CST). The database provides companies and news sources with historical, full-text, unedited research material. It contains press releases from newspapers, news bureaus, radio and television, financial institutions, companies, public relations groups, and government agencies. The primary goal of the database is to provide access to local, regional, and national information on individuals, companies, trends, and issues.

The database is updated daily with a total of 400 stories. The lag time between source update and database update is usually 24 hours. Information contained within the database dates back to August 1, 1985.

Users can access this database through Tymnet, Easylink, SAT-PAC (a satellite switching service provided by the Associated Press), and DATATEK's own network (DataTimes). DataTimes is accessible through a local telephone number in most U.S. cities, as well as throughout Canada, Australia, and Europe. Any ASCII terminal or microcomputer equipped with a modem can be used to access the database.

The initial subscription fee includes free training, a user's manual, and quarterly newsletters. Updates to the user's manual are mailed periodically at no additional charge. There are no log on fees, search charges, or storage charges. Customers are billed monthly, and discounts are available for groups.

DataTimes provides numerous customer support services, including comprehensive user guides, free on-site training when possible, or free online time for subscribers not near a local DataTimes office. DataTimes provides quarterly newsletters and updates to subscribers, along with a hotline service available by calling (800) 642-2525.

DataTimes does not provide any capability to manipulate or compute the raw data through value added or decision support software. Neither does the company provide the information in other forms such as hard copy, fiche/film, or tape. Planned future enhancements are for an optical disk format in early 1987.

DISCLOSURE ONLINE
Disclosure Inc.
5161 River Road
Bethesda, MD 20816

```
┌─────────────────────────────┐
│ PRODUCT AT-A-GLANCE          │
│                              │
│ Subject Coverage:            │
│   Company information/       │
│     statistics               │
│   Annual reports             │
│   SEC filings                │
│                              │
└─────────────────────────────┘
```

Disclosure Online, produced by Disclosure, Inc., is accessible through 12 different vendors, including DIALOG, BRS, Mead Data Central, Compuserve, and I.P. Sharp, among others. The database contains detailed résumé, financial, and management information for American and foreign public companies. The information is extracted from, or cited to, various documents that the companies file regularly with the Securities and Exchange Commission.

To be included in Disclosure Online, a company must have at least $3 million in assets and have filed a 10-K or 20-F in the past 18 months. A new company must have filed an appropriate Registration Statement. Company records for management investment companies, mutual funds, real estate limited partnerships, and oil- or gas-drilling funds are not included.

Users are provided information from the following reports:

10-K—Official annual business and financial report filed by U.S. public companies 90 days after year-end.

20-F—Official annual business and financial report filed by foreign registrants 90 days after year-end.

10-Q—Income statements filed 45 days after quarter-end.

8-K—Filed as needed, 10 days after unscheduled material events.

Proxy statement—Lists directors' and officers' titles, ages, and remuneration. Summary of ownership by 5 percent owners, financial institution, and insiders. Filed prior to annual meeting.

Annual report to shareholders—The management discussion focusing on the company's basic structure, operational results, and future outlook.

Registration statement—For new registrants only, filed as needed.

5

Résumé information includes, but is not limited to, company name; address; phone number; Fortune, Forbes, CUSIP, and D-U-N-S numbers; SIC codes; auditor stock transfer agent; and legal counsel.

Financial information includes such items as annual balance sheets back to 1977; annual income statements back to 1979; up to three quarters of the most recent quarterly balance sheets and income statements; and so on.

Management information includes such items as annual president's letter and management discussion; a complete list of corporate officers, directors, and subsidiaries; and citations to all exhibits filed with various documents.

Special features include:

The capability to search for New Registrant companies
Supplemental data such as share price information that is updated weekly so that searchers can compute specific values such as shares held by officers and directors

DISCLOSURE/SPECTRUM OWNERSHIP

Disclosure, Inc.
5161 River Road
Bethesda, MD 20816

PRODUCT AT-A-GLANCE
Subject Coverage:
Company information/ statistics
SEC filings
Stockholder information

This product is a joint development effort of Disclosure, Inc. and CDA Technologies, Inc. The database provides detailed and summary stock ownership information for over 5,000 publicly held companies. This information is derived from the following reports filed by the stockholders with the Securities and Exchange Commission on an annual, quarterly, and as-required basis:

13-D and 13-G 5 percent beneficial ownership
14-D1 tender offers
13(f) institutional common stock holdings
13(f) institutional convertible holdings
U.S. investment company holdings
Foreign investment company holdings
Forms 3 and 4 insider ownership

This information is updated daily. Reports can be accessed from any interactive terminal.

All domestic investment companies are required to file shareholder reports with the SEC. Most reports are filed as of each calendar quarter and begin flowing to the SEC shortly after quarter-end. The most recent report date for any or all institutions is provided.

These reports are filed by individual funds, even though such funds may be part of a larger investment management group. Funds that are part of a larger group (filing 13f reports) are flagged.

CDA also obtains the shareholder reports of the 420 largest European funds from 13 countries. Holdings may be sorted by size or alphabetically by fund name. In addition, all of a management company's funds can be identified by entering its symbol.

Voting authority information is subdivided between sole, shared, and none. Investment discretion shared with a nonaffiliate is also noted.

5

Users can also sort institutional owners in zip code sequence. This is highly useful in showing owners in specific metropolitan areas.

Portfolio holdings can be accessed by owner for any of the following:

U.S. investment company
Foreign investment company
13(f) institution's common stock portfolio
13(f) institution's convertible portfolio
5 percent beneficial owner

Such holdings may be sorted by size or alphabetically by name.

Users may obtain unlimited access status for a fixed monthly fee. Unlimited users can subscribe to the complete database as a package or order each section separately. Per report users do not pay fixed monthly fees, but are charged for each report.

DORIS

CACI Inc.–Federal
1815 North Fort Meyer Drive
Arlington, VA 22209

CACI's Demographic Online Retrieval Information System, DORIS, was first published in 1979. The database contains over 16 million data items organized on the basis of market areas. DORIS provides demographic and related information that can be used in market research and customer targeting. This will allow the user to determine what financial services are most in demand and by whom. This also allows the user to make site selections to determine the best locations for new offices, branches, and automatic teller machines. The purpose of DORIS is to allow users to manipulate the data. Users can create their own customized reports, select demographic variables most important to the user's market for downloading, and get lists of areas with user-specified characteristics.

DORIS provides demographic and income profiles and financial services potential for 1980, 1985, and 1990 for areas of any shape and size, anywhere in the United States. Standard geographical units such as Census tracts, zip codes, cities, counties, metropolitan areas, ADI's, and DMA's are available. When the user asks for data that is not predefined, the computer software derives the data based on census-designated block groups.

DORIS's sales potential measuring system spells out consumer income and spending power, and provides updates and forecasts for 16 major retail store types and 3 types of financial institutions. DORIS's products and services aid in site evaluation, market entry planning, promotion planning, unit or outlet analysis, and many other business functions.

DORIS uses the database management system supported by the individual time-sharing network on which it is installed. Data may be scanned, searched, and ranked based on a variety of specifications and logical commands. "Help" files are available to assist the user with problems.

DORIS offers special reports for the financial and investment services industry. These reports show the potential for and penetration of different financial instruments. These reports can be customized for standard market areas anywhere in the United States.

The information contained in DORIS is based on data from the 1980 Census of Population and Housing. Updates and forecasts are estimated by using CACI's proprietary methodology. Site potential information is based on data from the Consumer Expenditure Survey and industry-specific statistics. Data are currently available for the years 1970, 1980, 1985, and 1990.

The entire database is updated annually in the spring. Business data including payroll data and the number of firms by size were available for zip codes and counties in 1986. Information on income by age of the head of the household, five-year age breakdowns by sex, and a new restaurant report were also available in 1986. Extensive new financial services information is currently being planned for inclusion in the database.

DORIS can be accessed 24 hours a day, seven days a week, from any terminal or PC with a standard modem (300 baud or 1200 baud). The service is provided for on several national time-sharing networks, including Compuserve, Comshare, and Chase Econometrics. System support is provided by these networks. Costs for the database are pay-as-you-go, by the data item. Charges per data item depend on the time-sharing network used, but are approximately 50 cents per item. Volume discounts and licenses are available on DORIS.

DOW JONES CURRENT QUOTES

Dow Jones News/Retrieval
P.O. Box 300
Princeton, NJ 08543-0330

PRODUCT AT-A-GLANCE

Subject Coverage:

**Real-time/Historic
market quotations**
*Bonds, notes, and bills
Options
Stocks, mutual funds,
warrants, and rights*

Dow Jones Current Quotes provides current stock quote information on companies listed on the New York, American, Midwest, and Pacific stock exchanges, and NASDAQ over-the-counter market, as well as composite quotes. Stock quotes are available from the floor of the exchanges with a minimum 15-minute delay during market hours. Current quotes are updated on a continuous basis during trading hours.

Current Quotes allows individual or institutional investors to obtain prices on common and preferred stocks, warrants, options, and corporate bonds, as well as the current day's update for U.S. Treasury issues, mutual funds, NASDAQ OTC quotes, foreign bonds, and government securities.

Access to the database is via either a personal computer with a modem or a communicating word processor or a time-share terminal and a News/Retrieval account with a password. Access to the database is through the major public networks of Tymnet, Telenet, and Datapac, and also through DowNet, Dow Jones's own network. The database is available 22 hours a day, seven days a week, from 6 A.M. to 4 A.M. (EST).

5

DOW JONES FUTURES QUOTES
Dow Jones News/Retrieval
P.O. Box 300
Princeton, NJ 08543-0330

PRODUCT AT-A-GLANCE

Subject Coverage:

**Real-time/Historic
market quotations**
Futures

The Dow Jones Futures Quote database provides commodities quotes from the major North American exchanges. Delayed price data (10–30 minutes) are given for more than 80 commodities. Information includes daily open, high, low, last, and settlement prices; lifetime high and low prices; and volume and open interest.

The database is updated continuously throughout the trading day. Access to the Dow Jones Futures Quotes database is via either a personal computer with a modem or a communicating word processor or a time-share terminal and a News/Retrieval account with a password.

Access to the database is through the major public networks of Tymnet, Telenet, and Datapac, and also through DowNet, Dow Jones's own network. The database is available 22 hours a day, seven days a week, from 6 A.M. to 4 A.M. (EST).

DOW JONES HISTORICAL QUOTES

Dow Jones News/Retrieval
P.O. Box 300
Princeton, NJ 08543-0330

PRODUCT AT-A-GLANCE

Subject Coverage:

**Real-time/Historic
market quotations**
*Stocks, mutual funds,
warrants, and rights*

Dow Jones Historical Quotes database provides daily high, low, and closing stock prices, as well as the trading volume for common and preferred stocks, dating back one year. Quotes are available for companies listed on the New York, American, Midwest, and Pacific Stock Exchanges, and NASDAQ over-the-counter–traded companies. Daily historical quotes are accessible by specific date. Composite quotes are available for monthly and quarterly requests. Monthly summaries are available dating back to 1979, while quarterly summaries date back to 1978.

Dow Jones Historical Quotes provides a full year of stock prices for investors who want to review past performance of particular securities. When used in conjunction with Dow Jones Software, Dow Jones Historical Quotes database allows for construction of technical analysis charts that allow comparisons of performance between stocks.

Some Dow Jones Software products provide automatic entry of one year of daily historical quotes for stock and transfer of data for spreadsheet analysis.

Access to Dow Jones Historical Quotes database is via either a personal computer with a modem or a communicating word processor or a time-share terminal and a News/Retrieval account with a password.

5

DOW JONES NEWS

Dow Jones News/Retrieval
P.O. Box 300
Princeton, NJ 08543-0330

PRODUCT AT-A-GLANCE

Subject Coverage:

News services
National
International

The Dow Jones News database provides instant business and financial information. Articles featured are obtained from *The Wall Street Journal, Barron's,* and the Dow Jones News Service (*Broadtape*). The database provides in-depth coverage of companies, industries, the stock market, and the general economy. When news breaks, Dow Jones News makes it available in 90 seconds and is accessible on News/Retrieval. All news stories in the database are from 90 seconds to 90 days old.

The Dow Jones News database is searched by company stock symbol and Dow Jones News category codes. These codes allow the user to focus on categories such as:

Barron's news
Executive changes
Hot business news
Bond market
Commodities
Monetary
Economic indicators
Active stocks
Stock index
Foreign area news
Federal regulatory agencies

User applications of the database information include:

Following company and/or industry developments and research the events that made them happen
Tracking investment and industry trends
Tracking competitors
Follow recent legislation
Scanning industry files and headlines to determine the impact of mergers or acquisitions

Access to the Dow Jones News database is via either a personal computer with a modem or a communicating word processor or a time-share terminal and a News/Retrieval account with a password.

Access to the database is through the major public networks of Tymnet, Telenet, and Datapac, and also through DowNet, Dow Jones's own network. The database is available 22 hours a day, seven days a week, from 6 A.M. to 4 A.M. (EST).

Besides the normal charges to use the News/Retrieval system, the database also carries a surcharge during prime-time hours.

5

DOW JONES TEXT-SEARCH SERVICES

Dow Jones News/Retrieval
P.O. Box 300
Princeton, NJ 08543-0330

PRODUCT AT-A-GLANCE

Subject Coverage:

News services
National

Dow Jones Text-Search Services database provides full text of all stories that appeared or were scheduled to appear in *The Wall Street Journal* from January 1984 to present day. The database also provides selected articles from *Barron's*, Dow Jones News Service (*Broadtape*), and *The Wall Street Journal* from June 1979 to present. Articles contained in the Dow Jones Text-Search Services database are updated on a daily basis.

Dow Jones Text-Search Services is divided into two sections. Section one introduces the user to the fundamental elements of the types of searches that can be performed. Section two offers advanced features that enable the user to refine requests for information.

Access to the Dow Jones Text-Search Services database is via either a personal computer with a modem or a communicating word processor or a time-share terminal and a News/Retrieval account with a password. Access to the database is through the major public networks of Tymnet, Telenet, and Datapac, and also through DowNet, Dow Jones's own network. The database is available 22 hours a day, seven days a week, from 6 A.M. to 4 A.M. (EST).

Besides the normal charges to use the News/Retrieval system, the database also carries a surcharge during prime-time hours and another during nonprime time.

DQI^2

Donnelley Marketing
P.O. Box 10250 1515 Summer Street
Stamford, CT 06904

PRODUCT AT-A-GLANCE
Subject Coverage:
Demographic information/ statistics *Consumer preference* *Income and housing*

The Donnelley Quality Index is a database of Donnelly Marketing Information Services. DQI^2's master file records and redefines demographic data acquired from U.S. Census and proprietary list data. DQI^2 is continually updated with new information.

Database information includes more than 77 million unduplicated household names and addresses-data covering more than 90 percent of all U.S. households. Data can either be selected geographically or based on:

Estimated individual household income
Age, head of household
Five key socioeconomic dimensions—income, education, occupation, ownership, and environment
Length of residence
Year, make, and model of automobile
Interest categories
Marketing targets

Analytic capabilities include:

AID (Automatic Interaction Detector)—to segment data by demographic characteristics.
ClusterPlus—to segment data into 47 common socioeconomic characteristics.
Cross tabulation analysis—to display the relationship between two or more variables.

5

DRI BANK ANALYSIS SYSTEM
Data Resources, Inc.
24 Harwell Avenue
Lexington, MA 02173

PRODUCT AT-A-GLANCE
Subject Coverage:
Company information/ statistics
Annual reports

DRI Bank Analysis System (a product of Data Resources Incorporated) provides income statement and balance sheet data on commercial banks, bank holding companies, and thrift institutions. DRI Bank Analysis System reports range from simple data retrieval of bank reports to complex market share and competitive analysis of domestic and foreign operations. The database also contains deposit information on seven categories of deposits held in bank branches.

Interactive DRI software allows users to screen the database using categories such as location factors, financial criteria, and statistical measures; compare and rank depository institutions on a wide range of user-selected criteria; perform statistical and financial analysis; display results in standard or customized reports in tabular or graphic formats; and download data and reports on personal computers for local analysis, report writing, or to produce graphics.

A breakdown of database contents according to specific institutional types includes:

Commercial Banks—Provides complete FDIC reports on more than 14,000 insured domestic banks and their foreign subsidiaries; data cover reports of bank financial condition, income statements, and supplementary schedules filed by all depository institutions with their regulatory agencies. Quarterly data are available from the fourth quarter of 1974 to present day.

Savings and Loan Associations—Contains semiannual and quarterly reports of financial condition and income statement data on all savings and loan associations insured by the FSLIC. Data are available from the end of 1978 to present day.

Mutual Savings Banks—Gives data on 175 balance sheet and income statement concepts for each of 370 mutual savings banks. Data are available from the fourth quarter of 1978 to present day.

Commercial Bank Holding Companies—Gives data on Y-9 reports of financial condition and income statement data for over 1,600 consolidated banking and parent companies. Annual data are available from 1978 to present day.

Branches—Annual deposit data from 1976 to present day are available for 60,000 commercial bank and thrift institution branches.

Data are derived from three major sources: the Board of Governors of the Federal Reserve System, Federal Deposit Insurance Corporation, and the Federal Home Loan Bank Board.

DRI Bank Analysis System user applications include:

DRIBAS REPORTS, a software system that facilitates financial review, competitive analysis, and acquisition targeting of depository institutions.

Financial and statistical formulations using QUICKSCAN, a screening, ranking, and reporting system on DRI's mainframe computer and PC QUICKSCAN, an integrated software package that allows screening, ranking, and reporting to be done on a personal computer on Lotus 1-2-3.

Targeting geographic markets when combined with regional information and metropolitan area forecasting integrated services and ESTIMARKET market analysis and planning service.

Studying competing banks for merger and acquisition and branch expansion studies when used in tandem with BANK-TRAK REPORTS, a summarization of competitive information for publicly and privately held companies and their subsidiaries.

Accessing the database is either on a time-sharing basis on DRI's mainframe computer or by downloading onto a personal computer using PC GATEWAY, an access package.

5

DRI COMMODITIES
Data Resources, Inc.
24 Harwell Avenue
Lexington, MA 02173

PRODUCT AT-A-GLANCE

Subject Coverage:

**Real-time/Historic
market quotations**
Spot prices
Futures

DRI Commodities (a product of Data Resources Incorporated) contains historical and current data on commodity futures pricing and trading activity, spot prices, and options traded on the U.S., Canadian, and London markets. A breakdown of the database contents includes:

Statistics on opening, high, low, and closing (settlement) prices and futures and options on futures contracts traded on U.S. exchanges and on futures traded on Canadian exchanges.

Information on yields for financial futures listed on the U.S. and Canadian commodity exchanges. High, low, closing bid, offer, and closing average prices for futures listed on the London commodity exchange.

Daily volume and open interest for commodity futures trading on the U.S. and Canadian exchanges.

Total volume and open interest on most U.S. futures contracts.

Spot prices for U.S. commodity futures.

DRI Commodities data are derived from Market Data Systems Incorporated, the *Journal of Commerce*, the U.S. Department of Agriculture, *London Times*, and relevant commodities and options exchanges.

DRICOM user applications include:

Data plotting of past, present, and projected price movements using GRAPHPAK, a software package with graphing capabilities.

Graphing of price spreads and yield spreads to identify outliers by using SPREADER, a securities analysis applications package.

Gauge market psychology and identify opportunities to hedge by assessing price movements and trends in financial futures, options, and all commodities.

Graph displays using FUTURESPLOT, a comprehensive price and volume graphing program from DRI.

Access to the database is either on a time-sharing basis on DRI's mainframe computer or by downloading data onto a personal computer by using PC GATEWAY, a database access package.

5

DRI FINANCIAL AND CREDIT STATISTICS

Data Resources, Inc.
24 Harwell Avenue
Lexington, MA 02173

PRODUCT AT-A-GLANCE

Subject Coverage:

**Company information/
  statistics**
Annual reports
Quarterly reports
**Real-time/Historic
  market quotations**
Futures
Currencies
Money rates

DRI Financial and Credit Statistics (a product of Data Resources Incorporated) contains financial data such as money market rates, foreign exchange rates, commercial banking assets and liabilities, thrift institution activity, cash options, financial futures, and stock indexes. The database covers both the domestic and foreign marketplace on a daily, weekday, weekly, and monthly basis.

A breakdown of database contents according to financial area includes:

Domestic Instruments—Contains information on financial instruments such as commercial paper, primary certificates of deposit, secondary certificates of deposit, bankers' acceptances, federal funds, repurchase agreements, Treasury bills, secondary discount notes, project and municipal notes, quoted broker loan rates, and bank prime lending rates.

U.S. Government Securities—Data on Treasury notes, Treasury bonds, federal agency coupons, and secondary market Treasury bills.

Financial Futures—Gives prices on foreign currency, Treasury bills, Treasury bonds, Treasury notes, bank certificates of deposit, and stock index futures.

U.S. Banking—Tells about supply factors in the domestic capital markets, Federal Reserve bank reserves and credits, U.S. Treasury holdings, thrift institution activity, and weekly financial condition of large commercial banks.

DRIFACS data are derived from the Bank of America, Barclay's Bank International, Board of Governors of the Federal Reserve System, Chicago Board of Options Exchange, Federal Home Loan Bank Board, Moody's Investor Service Incorporated, U.S. Department of Treasury, and Telerate Systems Incorporated.

DRI Financial and Credit Statistics user applications include:

Access to historical and current price, yields, and yield spreads on fixed-income securities and foreign exchange rates.

Comparison pricing of securities offered for acquisitions with that of U.S. bond and money market instruments.

Trend and pro forma analysis on financial instruments.

Analysis and plotting of yield curves for domestic and international money market instruments by using YIELDCURVES, a historical yield curve applications package.

Development of trading and hedging strategies through use of CONTRACT RESEARCH, a DRI project research service.

Monitor mortgage markets, and foreign and domestic money markets.

Plot data using GRAPHIC and GRAPHPAK, two DRI software packages that have graphing capabilities.

Graph or tabulate historical yield spreads by using SPREADER, a securities analysis applications package.

Examine rates of return resulting from various spreads between futures contracts by using with FUTURESMONITORS, a series of DRI analytical programs on futures.

Graph displays using FUTURESPLOT, a comprehensive price and volume information graphing program from DRI.

Accessing the database is either on a time-sharing basis on DRI's mainframe computer or by downloading onto a personal computer using PC GATEWAY, a database access package.

5

DRI SECURITIES
Data Resources, Inc.
24 Harwell Avenue
Lexington, MA 02173

PRODUCT AT-A-GLANCE

Subject Coverage:

**Real-time/Historic
market quotations**
Bonds, notes, and bills
Options
*Stocks, mutual funds,
warrants, and rights*

DRI Securities (a product of Data Resources Incorporated) contains daily price, volume, and basic information for more than 45,000 securities including debt, equity, government agency issues, and options traded on the New York, American, regional, and Canadian stock exchanges as well as the OTC market. In addition, DRISEC contains information on over 200 industry and market indexes. Also included are price histories for all NYSE and AMEX stocks dating back to 1968 and OTC stocks and mutual funds dating back to 1972.

Database contents according to financial instruments include:

Equity Issues—Gives the daily high, low, and closing prices and trading volume, indicated annual dividend, earnings-per-share data, Standard & Poor's quality rating, dividend yield, and ex-dividend data.

Options—Information on the underlying stock price, the option expiration date, open interest, underlying CUSIP number, and underlying shares of stock.

Corporate and Government Bonds—Merrill Lynch data on bond prices and yields, bid and ask prices, coupon rate, maturity date, interest payments, frequency of interest payments, number of bonds outstanding, and yield to maturity.

Convertible Securities—Contains data on conversion ratio, call price and date, underlying stock price, and underlying CUSIP number.

Other Information—Ticker symbol, CUSIP number, exchange code, and the SIC code are available for all issues.

DRI Securities data are derived from Merrill Lynch historical prices and yields, and Telstat Systems Incorporated.

DRI Securities user applications include:

Preparation of charts and graphs for presentation using GRAPH-PAK and GRAPHICS, two software packages with graphing capabilities.

Gather fundamental stock data such as company name, dividend, and price information by using EXAMINE, an applications package providing historical data on over 45,000 companies.

Tabulate stock price histories using STOCKPRICE, a tabulator of stock price history including high, low, and closing prices in addition to trading volume and dollar volume on all issues traded on all major exchanges and the OTC market.

Make graphical comparisons of performance of an issue by using INDEXPLOT, an applications package allowing for price performance graphing for any issue on all exchanges and over 200 market and industry indexes.

Screen, sort, rank, and make reports on issues by using KEYISSUES, an applications package providing analysis of stock, bond, and option information on over 45,000 issues.

Screen and rank issues based on user-specified criteria by using QUICKSCAN (mainframe) or PC QUICKSCAN (personal computer), two screening, sorting, ranking, and reporting systems.

Monitor and review daily stock and bond price movements for over 60,000 issues.

Determine appropriate price for divested businesses based on the market performance of similar companies.

Analyze the relationships between price changes of equities and the volume of shares traded by using PRICEVOLUME, a stock price and volume analysis applications package from DRI.

Graph historical and current price and volume for all common and preferred stocks from the New York and American stock exchanges plus the OTC market by using in conjunction with STOCKPLOT, a graphical display package from DRI.

Access to the database is available either on a time-sharing basis on DRI's mainframe computer or by downloading data onto a personal computer by using PC GATEWAY, a database access package.

5

DUFF AND PHELPS EQUITY IDEAS

Duff and Phelps, Inc.
55 East Monroe Street
Suite 4000
Chicago, IL 60603

PRODUCT AT-A-GLANCE

Subject Coverage:

Research reports/ evaluations
Company

Duff and Phelps Equity Ideas contains research reports by Duff and Phelps that aid in the decision-making processes involving investments for securities analysts and portfolio managers. These reports cover more than 450 companies and 61 industry groups. The database is updated immediately on a daily basis by approximately 450 issues by 2 A.M. (EST). The primary sources of database information are from Duff and Phelps research analysts.

More than 40 variables can be manipulated to allow the analyst to screen data against user-selected criteria. Variables include a variety of statistics common to equity analysis, as well as company and industry rankings, and company earnings and dividend growth rates over two- and five-year spans.

The services provided by the database include:

Duff and Phelps Equity research services.

Projected and historical operating and pricing information provided in summary form, accompanied by a Duff and Phelps investment opinion.

Company and industry buy/sell recommendations.

Screening of companies against up to 48 user-selected investment criteria.

Daily updates of company earnings and dividends changes, as well as Duff and Phelps analysts' five-year earnings and dividends forecasts.

The Duff and Phelps database is marketed to securities analysts, portfolio managers, and securities traders via sales force and direct mailings. Subscription to the Duff and Phelps Equity database is a two-step process. First, a customer contracts with a time-sharing vendor offering the database service. Second, a subscription fee is paid to Duff and Phelps. This subscription fee varies depending on whether or not other Duff and Phelps services are being used. The subscription fee may be paid in cash or through a commission arrangement with Sanford C. Bernstein & Company, a New York brokerage firm.

5

DUFF AND PHELPS
FIXED INCOME

Duff and Phelps, Inc.
Suite 4000 55 East Monroe Street
Chicago, IL 60603

PRODUCT AT-A-GLANCE

Subject Coverage:

**Research reports/
evaluations**
Fixed income

Duff and Phelps Fixed Income database provides statistical and textual information on fixed-income ratings for approximately 500 U.S. corporations that have a large institutional investment following. The service is tailored to the busy fixed-income portfolio manager, analyst, or trader who needs to be assured of the rapid availability of the latest thinking of Duff and Phelps' analysts and Credit Rating Committee.

The database offers:

Coverage of preferred and preference issues and all types of long-term debt (bonds, debentures, convertibles, etc).

Comparisons of the Duff and Phelps ratings on the fixed-income securities of several hundred companies to the ratings of two other major rating agencies.

Daily updates of the data.

All companies are referred to throughout the database by their name and ticker symbol. The information contained in the database is presented in four main categories:

New financings—A calendar of new fixed-income financings that have recently been announced or are still pending.

Watch list—Fixed-income issues that are currently on the Duff and Phelps', watch list where a ratings change is being considered.

Ratings changes—Upgrades or downgrades of fixed-income issues' ratings made by Duff and Phelps within the past three months.

Individual company analysis—Key statistics and commentary supporting the ratings, and also the major risks associated with the companies that are rated by Duff and Phelps.

Subscription to the Duff and Phelps Fixed Income database is a two-step process. First, a customer contracts with a time-sharing vendor offering the database service. Current Duff and Phelps Fixed Income database vendors include I.P. Sharp and Compuserve.

Second, a subscription fee is paid to Duff and Phelps. This subscription fee varies depending on whether or not other Duff and Phelps services are being used. The subscription fee may be paid in cash or through a commission arrangement with Sanford C. Bernstein & Company, a New York brokerage firm.

The database is marketed primarily to investment analysts, fixed-income portfolio managers, and bond traders via sales force or direct mailings.

5

DUN'S FINANCIAL RECORDS
Dun's Marketing Services
3 Century Drive
Parsippany, NJ 07054

PRODUCT AT-A-GLANCE

Subject Coverage:

**Company information/
 statistics**
Annual reports
Company background
Lines of business
Quarterly reports

D&B-Dun's Financial Records (DFR), produced jointly by Dun & Bradstreet Credit Services and Dun's Marketing Services, contains financial information, complete spreadsheet analysis, industry comparisons, company history, and operations information on over 700,000 U.S. business establishments. DFR includes up to three years of financial statements and key ratios on each company. Of the companies featured in this database, 98 percent are private. The information featured consists of all live data—no model statements are used.

The public and private U.S. companies covered in this database represent commercial as well as industrial establishments from all product areas. DFR includes companies for which Dun & Bradstreet has detailed financial information.

The DFR file is generated from Dun & Bradstreet's data on more than six million U.S. businesses. This data is collected and maintained by a staff of nearly 2,000 business analysts through in-person interviews and supplemented by large volume mailings and phone interviews.

Typically, a credit report is requested, which initiates the process of information gathering. Business analysts may obtain information from a company's financial department, accounting or law firm, or the principals themselves. Analysts may make use of annual reports and 10-K's. Information is keyed into the central computer on a daily basis. Once a month Dun's Marketing is supplied new tapes. DFR on DIALOG is reloaded quarterly. As a result, the time lag between reloads is at least 4 months and some records may be as old as 18 months.

The database is available 24 hours a day Monday through Friday, from noon until 8 P.M. on Saturday, and from 5 P.M. to midnight on Sunday (EST). Users can access the database through DIALOG by using either a terminal or personal computer with a modem. Access may also be attained using Menlo's In-Search or Pro-Search, as well as DIALOGLINK. Information is accessed through a variety of datalines including Dialnet, Tymnet, and Telenet.

Charges for access to its databases are based on connect time, with volume/usage discounts available through DIALOG. Customer support is available in the form of user manuals, newsletters, and online instruction.

5

DUN'S MARKET IDENTIFIERS
Dun's Marketing Services
3 Century Drive
Parsippany, NJ 07054

PRODUCT AT-A-GLANCE

Subject Coverage:

**Company information/
statistics**
Annual reports
Company background
Lines of business
Quarterly reports

Dun's Market Identifiers (DMI), a directory file produced by Dun's Marketing Services and Dun & Bradstreet Credit Services, contains current address and financial and marketing information on nearly two million U.S. business establishments. The database was first published in 1982.

The DMI database covers both public and private U.S. companies that have 10 or more employees, $1 million or more in sales, or are a member of a company that meets any one of the two previous criteria. In addition, the file contains records for all companies in the corporate family, even though these companies may have fewer than 10 employees. Over 700,000 records contain additional detailed financial information, corresponding to records in D&B-Dun's Financial Records. The database covers all types of commercial and industrial establishments as well as all product areas. The DIALOG DMI file was created from Dun & Bradstreet records updated within the last 18 months.

Information is gathered by approximately 2,000 field business analysts. Typically, a credit report is requested, which initiates the process of information gathering. The business analyst makes a personal visit to the firm. Information may be obtained from its financial department, its accounting or law firm, or the principals themselves. They may make use of annual reports and 10-K's. Information is keyed into the company's central computer center on a daily basis. Once a month, Dun's Marketing is supplied new tapes. DMI on DIALOG is reloaded quarterly. As a result, the time lag between reloads is at least four months and in some cases up to 18 months. However, all records are no older than 18 months.

Larger, more actively pursued corporations may be updated several times a year. The average reload remains fairly constant at two million company records, 700,000 of those having financial spreadsheets and history/operations information available on them.

The focus of DMI is marketing/financial and all functions leading from those points including sales, competitive analysis, mergers and acquisitions, new product development, and financial analysis.

Linkage of the corporate structure to the database is facilitated through the use of the D-U-N-S number, a "social security" number for businesses. Every corporate profile lists not only a unique number for that establishment, but an ultimate family number, and a parent D-U-N-S number. The hierarchy of any corporation can be established through manipulation of that ultimate corporate number.

The database is available 24 hours a day Monday through Friday, from noon until 8 P.M. on Saturday, and from 5 P.M. to midnight on Sunday (EST). Users can access the database through DIALOG by using either a terminal or personal computer with a modem. Access may also be attained using Menlo's In-Search or Pro-Search, as well as DialogLink. Information is accessed through a variety of datalines including Dialnet, Tymnet, and Telenet.

Charges for access to its databases are based on connect time, with volume/usage discounts available through DIALOG. Customer support is available in the form of user manuals, newsletters, and online instruction.

5

ECONOMIC LITERATURE INDEX

Journal of Economic Literature
P.O. Box 7320, Oakland
 Station
Pittsburgh, PA 15213

PRODUCT AT-A-GLANCE

Subject Coverage:

Econometric data
Industry specific
Monetary aggregates
International
National

The Economic Literature Index database provides bibliographic information on economic articles and essays in books. Subject coverage includes economic theory, economic history, econometrics, managerial economics, industrial relations, monetary theory, financial institutions, demography, international economics, regional and urban economics, agricultural and natural resources economics, labor economics, and welfare programs. Articles are indexed by subject areas.

The database contains approximately 117,000 records from approximately 285 economic research journals and essays from currently published books on a wide variety of economic subjects. The beginning date for journal articles is 1969. The beginning date for essays is 1979. The database is updated on a quarterly basis with approximately 2,700 new entries. There is approximately a six-month lag between source update and database update.

Articles are indexed by subjects and may carry as many as seven subject descriptor codes. In addition, articles may carry up to five searchable geographic descriptors. Approximately 25 percent of the articles indexed since 1984 include abstracts as part of the full record. Free text searching of abstracts may be used in conjunction with subject descriptors, titles, words, and dates.

Users of the database information include economists, economic researchers, and reference librarians. The database information may also be of relevance to researchers in the fields of business, law, politics, demography, history, sociology, and public administration.

The database is available through DIALOG during regular DIALOG hours. Customers may contact DIALOG through their marketing department by calling (800) 227-1927 or in California at (800) 982-5838.

EIAPRICE

Wharton Econometric Forecasting
  Associates
3rd floor, 3624 Science Center
Philadelphia, PA 19104

```
┌─────────────────────────────────┐
│ PRODUCT AT-A-GLANCE             │
│                                 │
│ Subject Coverage:               │
│                                 │
│   Econometric data              │
│   Industry specific             │
│   National                      │
└─────────────────────────────────┘
```

EIAPRICE contains historical data for energy prices by 20 types of fuel and by 6 major end-use sectors. Data are available for United States and the entire states. The source for the data is the Department of Energy's Energy Information Administration.

  Data are updated annually and begin in 1970.

ELECTRONIC COMPANY FILING INDEX

Disclosure, Inc.
5161 River Road
Bethesda, MD 20816

PRODUCT AT-A-GLANCE

Subject Coverage:

Company information/ statistics
SEC filings

The Electronic Company Filing Index is available from Disclosure, Inc. With this index and a personal computer, users can discover which SEC documents have just been filed by any of more than 30,000 registrants within 24 hours. Plus, for the 10,000 public companies whose securities are traded on the American Stock Exchange, New York Stock Exchange, NASDAQ, or over-the-counter, the index also generates an up-to-the-minute corporate profile.

Within 24 hours of the document's arrival at Disclosure, users can ascertain which companies have filed which reports, plus other crucial data. Users have unlimited access to early-warning information on more than 30,000 registrants.

In addition to alerting users to the reports that arrived yesterday, the Electronic Company Filing Index provides unlimited access to the same data on filings back to 1966.

The index also allows users to access, view, and print out Disclosure Corporate Profiles on more than 10,000 companies. These profiles include over 256 key financial and management variables and, in seconds, users can pinpoint top-level information on everything from a company's outstanding shares to its net sales to officers' salaries.

Among the SEC Filings included in the database are: Annual Report to Shareholders; 10-K; 8-K; Proxy Statement; Registration Statement; Prospectus; and Listing Application.

The Electronic Company Filing Index is updated daily and is available Monday through Friday between 8 A.M. and 8 P.M. (EST). Required equipment includes an IBM PC, XT, or AT microcomputer with at least 256K memory, and a 1200 baud Hayes-compatible modem.

EMPLOYMENT AND EARNINGS DATABASE

SAGE DATA, Inc.
104 Carnegie Center
Princeton, NJ 08540

PRODUCT AT-A-GLANCE

Subject Coverage:

  Econometric data
  National

The Employment and Earnings Database contains more than 3,000 time series on the U.S. nonagricultural workforce. Information in the database includes wage and salary, employment, average weekly hours, average hourly earnings, and average weekly earnings. The data extend from 1946 to present day and are categorized according to Standard Industrial Classification (SIC) codes.

5

EVANS ECONOMICS FULL SERVICE DATABASE

Evans Economics, Inc.
1725 Eye Street, NW
Suite 310
Washington, DC 20006

PRODUCT AT-A-GLANCE

Subject Coverage:

Econometric data
Monetary aggregates
National

Evans Economics Full Service Database provides both historical and Evans Economics forecasts of key macroeconomic data, and industry and financial indicators for the United States. Coverage includes national income and product accounts, employment, productivity, housing starts, shipments, production, interest rates, money supply, consumer prices, and producer prices.

The database contains both monthly and quarterly data from 1950 to present day. Quarterly forecasts extend from 10 to 12 quarters out. Information for the database is obtained from the Commerce Department, Labor Department, Bureau of Economic Analysis, Federal Reserve, and Federal Home Loan Bank Board.

Hardware required to access the database includes an IBM XT or AT with 512k of internal memory or an IBM-compatible with Delta-DSS and LOTUS 1-2-3. Cost of the database is $5,000 per year for monthly updates via diskettes or $7,000 per year for bimonthly updates.

EVANS ECONOMICS MACRO CORE DATABASE

Evans Economics, Inc.
1725 Eye Street, NW
Suite 310
Washington, DC 20006

PRODUCT AT-A-GLANCE

Subject Coverage:

Econometric data
Monetary aggregates
National

Evans Economics Macro Core Database provides quarterly historical and forecasted data for the United States. The database contains macroeconomic, industry, and financial time series data. Coverage includes national income and product accounts, employment, productivity, housing starts, shipments, production, interest rates, money supply, consumer prices, and producer prices.

The database contains quarterly data from 1950 to present day. Quarterly forecasts, including short-term forecasts, extend 10 quarters out. Information for the database is obtained from the Commerce Department, Labor Department, Bureau of Economic Analysis, Federal Reserve, and Federal Home Loan Bank Board.

Hardware required to access the database includes an IBM XT or AT with 512k of internal memory or an IBM-compatible with Delta-DSS, LOTUS 1-2-3, and Multiplan.

5

EXCHANGE
Mead Data Central, Inc.
P.O. Box 933
Dayton, OH 45401

PRODUCT AT-A-GLANCE

Subject Coverage:

**Company information/
  statistics**
Annual reports
Quarterly reports
SEC filings
**Research reports/
  evaluations**
Company
Industry

EXCHANGE is an online database of financial and business information containing company and industry reports written by analysts of leading brokerage, investment banking, and research firms. EXCHANGE contains more than 750,000 documents on subjects covering company and industry research reports, and various corporate filings with the Securities and Exchange Commission. The information contained in the database is updated on a daily, weekly, bimonthly, or monthly basis, depending on the type of information being updated, the frequency of publication, and the agreement made with the publisher.

The primary goal of EXCHANGE is to provide current, accurate, useful information to subscribers in an easy-to-use manner that meets the user's needs. EXCHANGE includes information consensus earnings projections, the full text of SEC 10-Q and 10-K filings, abstracts of other SEC filings by State News Services, Disclosure II, Abecor country reports, and economic reports and forecasts from Evans Electronic News Service.

The geographic scope of EXCHANGE is international. Current users of the database include a wide variety of business users, accounting firms, the news media, the legal industry, and others.

EXCHANGE provides information in full-text form and abstracts, covering various corporate filings with the Securities and Exchange Commission. The full-text information can be viewed in several formats, including cite, KWIC (Key Work in Context—window text of 15 words), and VAR KWIC (variable KWIC—window text from 1–999 words).

Subscribers access the EXCHANGE database through Mead-net, Telenet, Tymnet, Alaskanet, Datapack, or via an 800 number. Customer access can be through Mead Data Central's custom UBIQ terminal, a video terminal, or a personal computer; a printer; Mead Data Central's software (for use with personal computers); and a 1200 baud modem. EXCHANGE database services are available 23 hours and 45 minutes per day Monday through Friday—15 minutes of downtime is required to check the system. On weekends, the system is not available from 10 P.M. Saturday to 6 P.M. Sunday.

The monthly subscription fee for using EXCHANGE is $50–$125, depending on the type of subscription. Connect time and telecommunications charges are $30 to $35 per hour, depending on the telecommunications network used. If Meadnet or Telenet is used, the charges are $30 per hour; if WATS is used, then the charge is $35 per hour. Search charges are $9 to $18 per search, with a 30 percent discount offered for off-peak hour searching between 7:30 P.M. and 7:30 A.M. Volume discounts are also available.

Value-added products and services include a reference manual, user training, online help instruction, the *Reference Manual*, the Quick-Reference Guide brochure, customer newsletters, applications brochures, a customer service department to handle inquiries, printed hard copies of online data, and software packages that allow the users to print documents and save data on a diskette.

5

F&S INDEX

Predicasts Inc.
11001 Cedar Avenue
Cleveland, OH 44106

PRODUCT AT-A-GLANCE

Subject Coverage:

News services
National
International

Predicasts' Funk & Scott (F&S) Index is a comprehensive list of business information sources covering all aspects of industry, the economy, government, and society. The F&S Index includes one- or two-line summaries of the essential facts of an article.

F&S Index provides comprehensive coverage of products, industries, and companies from the trade literature. In addition, the F&S Index also contains similar information from 1,200 business newspapers and other business publications. The database is also unique in its coverage of international business and financial activities, demographics, federal governments, economics, and other business environments affecting industries.

F&S Index contains a total of three million one- and two-line informative summaries of articles from U.S. and international sources. The 2,400 international sources used include trade journals, business magazines, research studies, government and agency reports, business newspapers, news releases, and bank and brokerage house reports.

This database can also be used as a complement to Predicasts' PROMT file. While the F&S Index file contains at least one citation for each comparable PROMT abstract, the file also contains numerous unique citations about companies and industries. This results from the additional sources covered by the F&S Index file.

The F&S Index file also offers comprehensive coverage of information about population and households, labor and employment, economics, general business, finance, and other topics.

Government and regulatory information is also provided by this database. Included are discussions on government spending, legislation, and other government activities. The discussions cover both domestic and international items of interest.

While the concise summaries provide an overview of the topic and offer direct responses to many factual questions, they also guide the searcher to more in-depth journal articles.

The database can be accessed via DIALOG, BRS, VU/TEXT, or Data-Star. Total charges vary according to the vendor being used, but are generally based on a combination of connect time, offline prints, or online type. Users can also download information if desired.

5

FASTOCK II

ADP, Inc. Data Services
175 Jackson Plaza
Ann Arbor, MI 48106

PRODUCT AT-A-GLANCE

Subject Coverage:

**Real-time/Historic
market quotations**
Bonds, notes, and bills
Options
*Stocks, mutual funds,
 warrants, and rights*
Municipals

ADP Data Services' Fastock II database is a comprehensive online source of historical securities information, providing daily history since 1971 on 100,000 issues. The core of this database is produced by Gregg Corporation under the name Tradeline Securities database, and ADP includes data from Muller Data Corporation and Merrill-Lynch.

Within the database are daily prices and trading volumes, dividends and interest payment data, and descriptive data items for the following securities:

Common stocks
Mutual funds
Preferred stocks
Money market funds
Warrants and rights
Options
Convertible bonds
Convertible preferreds
Municipal bonds
U.S. government or agency debt issues and unit trusts
Corporate debt issues

Also contained in the database are daily and weekly updates on almost 250 market indicators. Information may be retrieved in graphic, tabular, and textual form. Fastock II may be used for applications ranging from market and security analysis to pension and mutual fund performance measurement to formulating security pricing strategies.

Fastock II comes equipped with an applications library, developed in response to the brokerage community and designed to meet users' most frequent analysis and reporting needs:

StPlot—A set of six preformatted graphs that use Fastock II data to display price, volume, and index information for individual stocks or groups of stocks. Included is a price/volume plot in the standard *New York Times* format.

Index—Enables the user to create an index of the price of one stock against that of another.

Display—Provides flexible reporting formats for user-created stock indexes.

Volume–Helps users perform volume turnover for any two issues over a specified interval.

VolPlot—Lets users graph volume turnover for specific pairs of issues.

Periodically throughout the year, ADP provides Fastock II users with an updated securities directory. This directory serves as a reference for quickly and easily identifying tickers, CUSIPs, exchanges, descriptive information, and beginning and ending dates for all securities in the database. Users pay only a small fee for each updated directory.

5

FDIC
Chase Econometrics
150 Monument Road
Bala Cynwyd, PA 19004

PRODUCT AT-A-GLANCE

Subject Coverage:

**Company information/
  statistics**
Annual reports
Quarterly reports
Econometric data
Local
National

The FDIC database contains balance sheet and income statement information for commercial banks. Data are derived from the Reports of Condition and Income filed by banks with the Federal Reserve Board, Federal Deposit Insurance Corporation, and the Comptroller of the Currency. The database is updated twice quarterly using preliminary and final data releases.

The database covers more than 14,000 U.S. commercial banks with both foreign and domestic operations. Information includes total loans outstanding by type and maturity; borrowings and securities held by type and maturity; total deposits by type, size, and maturity; past due, nonaccrual, and renegotiated loans by type; total income and total expenses by type; and charge-offs and recoveries on loans by type.

Database applications include screening banks on user-specified criteria, retrieval of selected items for an individual bank or group of banks, and production of preformatted reports. The FDIC database is listed with Chase Econometrics under the XDMS databases and under disk names FDICDB1, FDICDB2, and FDICDB3. More information on the database service may be obtained by calling (215) 896-4920.

FEDERAL RESERVE BOARD WEEKLY STATISTICS

I.P. Sharp Associates Limited
2 First Canadian Place
Suite 1900
Toronto, Ontario, Canada M5X 1E3

PRODUCT AT-A-GLANCE

Subject Coverage:

Econometric data
Industry specific
Monetary aggregates

The Federal Reserve Board Weekly Statistics database, produced by I.P. Sharp Associates Limited, contains weekly American banking and monetary statistics on over 1,200 time series taken from Forms H-3, H-4, H-4.2, and H-6. The database is updated on a weekly basis by approximately 350 issues one day after the data are released. Database information is obtained from the Board of Governors of the Federal Reserve System and the Federal Reserve Banks in New York and Chicago. The database contains historical information dating back to October of 1980.

The database is accessible 24 hours a day, seven days a week, except during a brief maintenance shut-down period on Friday and Saturday nights. The Federal Reserve Board Weekly Statistics database is accessible directly through I.P. Sharp's IPSANET network and also from Datapac, Telenet, Telex, and Tymnet networks. User access is via a terminal or personal computer with a 300, 1200, or 2400 baud modem; communications software; and a user account number. General-purpose software allows for data manipulation, analysis, and downloading to a personal computer. Downloading procedures are dependent on the computer hardware used.

The information retrieval systems used to access the database are MAGIC and INFOMAGIC. MAGIC is an English-language system that is intended to be used by people who have little or no computer programming experience. INFOMAGIC database access system offers data in preformatted report form. Access fees differ for each product.

User support is offered via calling toll-free ((800) 387-1588) in North America from 8 A.M. to 6 P.M. (EST) on weekdays. I.P. Sharp Associates also provides subscribers with access to a 24-hour answering service for subscribers to leave messages.

Other user aids include user manuals, reference guides, a printed directory of database symbols, and complete online documentation. Consulting services are available on an individual basis.

Value-added products and services include individual database search services, user software, data storage capabilities, ongoing user training programs, electronic mail, and custom program applications.

FINANCIAL

Chase Econometrics
150 Monument Road
Bala Cynwyd, PA 19004

PRODUCT AT-A-GLANCE

Subject Coverage:

Econometric data
Industry specific
National

The Financial database provides historical key financial indicators for the U.S. market from the Federal Reserve Board and other relevant sources. The database contains 3,500 series of weekly, monthly, quarterly, and annual data. Most database data are updated as soon as they are released.

The database provides monthly projections for loans and deposits at commercial banks and monetary reserve aggregates. Data coverage includes Treasury debt operations; stock activity; consumer credit; mortgages; commercial paper; corporate and municipal bonds; and interest rates in the money, credit, and debt markets.

The Financial database is listed with Chase Econometrics under the database name FIN and disk name FINDB. More information on the database service may be obtained by calling (215) 896-4755.

5

FINANCIAL FORECAST
Chase Econometrics
150 Monument Road
Bala Cynwyd, PA 19004

PRODUCT AT-A-GLANCE

Subject Coverage:

Econometric data
National

The Financial Forecast database provides forecasts of key financial market indicators for the U.S. economy. The database also includes historical data beginning in 1950. Forecasts are updated on a monthly basis and extend at least 24 months into the future.

Each financial forecast will include a standard forecast and three alternative forecasts: higher interest rates, lower interest rates, and a topical alternative. Data coverage includes interest rates in the money, credit, and debt markets; loans and deposits at commercial banks; monetary and reserve aggregates; Treasury debt operations; consumer credit; commercial paper; corporate and municipal bonds; mortgage debt holdings of various financial institutions; and savings and loan activity.

The Financial Forecast database is listed with Chase Econometrics under the database names IRB, IRBL, IRBH, and IRBA and under the disk name MONEYDB. More information on the database service may be obtained by calling (215) 896-4708.

FINANCIAL POST BOND DATABASE

Financial Post Information Service
777 Bay Street
Toronto, Ontario, Canada M5W 1A7

PRODUCT AT-A-GLANCE

Subject Coverage:

Real-time/Historic market quotations
Bonds, notes, and bills

The Financial Post Bond Database contains weekly closing prices and yields for approximately 1,550 Canadian bonds. The database also provides descriptive facts such as coupon and bond features. Historical bond information is available from as far back as March 9, 1984. Database coverage includes all publicly issued Canadian, provincial, provincial guaranteed, and corporate bonds, as well as many private placements. The database is updated every Friday night by approximately 1,200 issues.

5

FINANCIAL POST CANADIAN CORPORATE DATA

Financial Post Information Service
777 Bay Street
Toronto, Ontario, Canada M5W 1A7

PRODUCT AT-A-GLANCE

Subject Coverage:

Company information/ statistics
Annual reports
Quarterly reports

The Financial Post Canadian Corporate Data database contains 100,000 time series financial data covering 500 companies listed on the Toronto Stock Exchange 300 composite index, as well as stocks with high growth and investor interest.

The first data set provides annual balance sheet and income statement information for approximately 530 public Canadian corporations. Data on each company are provided in approximately 180 time series, of which 50 are financial ratios, and 30 are adjustments for stock splits. There are also nine static facts provided for each company.

The second data set contains quarterly information on revenues, taxes, and dividends for approximately 140 companies. The data are comprised of 20 time series and 9 static facts for each company.

The quarterly and annual data include, in addition to active company information, data on defunct companies and predecessors of the active companies. The database is updated shortly after the quarterly and annual data are released.

The primary focus of the database is to provide data for fundamental analysis for securities analysts and portfolio managers. The annual data date back to 1959 and the quarterly data to 1958.

FINANCIAL POST SECURITIES

Financial Post Information Service
777 Bay Street
Toronto, Ontario, Canada M5W 1A7

PRODUCT AT-A-GLANCE

Subject Coverage:

Real-time/Historic market quotations
Options
Stocks, mutual funds, warrants, and rights

The Financial Post Securities database contains trading statistics for securities traded on the New York Stock Exchange (NYSE) and the American Stock Exchange (AMEX), as well as all Canadian exchanges. The database contains 30,000 times series that are updated daily within six hours of the source update.

The Financial Post Securities database gives data on the daily high, low, and closing stock prices, plus daily volume statistics on approximately 3,800 Canadian securities listed on the Montreal, Toronto, Calgary, and Vancouver exchanges.

Securities data for the New York and American stock exchanges consist of daily closing prices for approximately 3,000 securities listed on the New York Stock Exchange, and approximately 1,700 securities listed on the American Stock Exchange.

The database also contains weekly price and volume data for Canadian securities, and weekly and monthly closing prices for NYSE and AMEX securities.

FINIS

Bank Marketing Association
309 West Washington
Chicago, IL 60606

PRODUCT AT-A-GLANCE

Subject Coverage:

News services
National
International

FINIS (Financial Industry Information Service) is the database of the Bank Marketing Association. This database is available to subscribers 24 hours a day, seven days a week.

FINIS contains over 35,000 abstracts and bibliographic citations on the financial services industry, with special emphasis on marketing. Each month 1,000 articles from 200 monitored newspapers, periodicals, and newsletters are added to the database. This updating occurs on a bimonthly basis with a time lag of four to six weeks between the source update and the database update.

The geographic scope of FINIS is international, with emphasis placed on the U.S. domestic scene. All items included in FINIS are selected by BMA's information specialists and focus on practical information required by the financial services industry.

The information contained in FINIS is mainly used by financial service practitioners, special librarians, and marketing professionals. This information can either appear on a CRT screen or be printed on paper, depending on the computer hardware that is used.

FINIS is available through DIALOG and Mead Data Central (through a Reference service file). Access to FINIS via DIALOG is through a "dumb" terminal or a microcomputer with a modem. Access via Mead Data Central is through a UBIQ terminal or microcomputer with a modem and Mead Data Central's software. Customers can access FINIS via long distance, an 800 number, Tymnet, Telenet, Dailnet, or Meadnet.

User support is offered via calling toll-free (800) 433-9013. By calling this number, subscribers can get search strategy assistance or order full-text articles.

Other user aids include the *Thesaurus of Financial Services and Marketing Terms*, which details the vocabulary necessary to access FINIS; the *FINIS Users Manual*, which is an instructional guide to searching FINIS; and the *FINIS Newsletter*.

Value-added services include price quotes, research services, user training, online ordering, electronic mail, magazines, specialized newsletters, a yearly convention, seminars, workshops, audio cassettes, professional schooling, and a rush service available on research services and document delivery.

The Bank Marketing Association is currently developing database records for monographs in BMA's Information Center to be included in FINIS by 1987.

FINSBURY DATA SERVICES
Information Access Company
11 Davis Drive
Belmont, CA 94002

PRODUCT AT-A-GLANCE

Subject Coverage:

**Company information/
  statistics**
Annual reports
News services
Local
National
Regional
International

Information Access Company is the U.S. representative of Finsbury Data Services, a British company that produces online international business information. Its products include:

Textline, which contains abstracts of business news from over 120 publications and news monitoring services from around the world. It provides immediate access to information on industries, companies, markets, and products, including current economic data, trends and forecasts. Also included are summaries of parliamentary and political events and coverage of legislation and public affairs affecting commerce.

Newsline, which provides daily summaries of international news and comments from over 40 daily and weekly U.K. and European newspapers. Newsline contains daily updates of political, financial, and business information including facts on companies, industries, economics, and the EEC.

Dataline, which focuses on financial profiles of over 3,000 U.K. and foreign companies, including income statements, finance tables, balance sheets, and accounting ratios. This database provides essential information for investment analysts, corporate financial planners, bankers, and credit analysts.

Finsbury's online retrieval service allows searching by company name, industry, geographic area, or topic. In addition to free text searching, an extensive range of index terms provide even greater search precision. Search terms may be entered one at a time, or by using Boolean operators for multiple term searches. The service will display headlines alone or with abstracts for instant facts, figures, and comment. Complete documentation and simple-to-use software make it easy to find the facts needed.

FLOW OF FUNDS
Chase Econometrics
150 Monument Road
Bala Cynwyd, PA 19004

PRODUCT AT-A-GLANCE

Subject Coverage:

Econometric data
National

The Flow of Funds database provides 3,500 quarterly series, historical flow of funds data, and Federal Reserve Board accounting system data. The historical data date back to 1952. The database provides information on the effects the nonfinancial economy has on the financial markets, while simultaneously identifying the influence that the financial sector has on demand for goods and services, sources and amounts of savings and investment, and income structures. The database is updated each quarter, approximately six weeks after the end of the quarter.

Transaction accounts are grouped by monetary reserves, deposit claims on financial institutions, insurance and pension reserves, credit market instruments, and other financial claims. Accounts are measured as unadjusted flows, seasonally adjusted flows, and/or outstanding levels.

The Flow of Funds database is listed with Chase Econometrics under the database name FLOW and disk name FLOWDB. More information on the database service may be obtained by calling (215) 896-4755.

FORECASTS

Predicasts Inc.
11001 Cedar Avenue
Cleveland, OH 44106

> **PRODUCT AT-A-GLANCE**
>
> **Subject Coverage:**
>
> **Econometric data**
> *Industry specific*
> *Local*
> *Monetary aggregates*
> *International*
> *National*

Forecasts is produced by Predicasts and contains more than 700,000 statistical abstracts of published forecasts from the international trade and business literature, reports, and statistical services. These abstracts contain short- and long-range annual forecasts and cover all business, economic, industry, and product areas. The Forecasts files provide a consensus of forecasts from publishers and industry experts, economists and research firms alike. Authors of the projections are also provided, if available. Multiple forecasts on a topic allow the user to compare the projections of experts.

This database includes detailed and general projections concerning specific products, aggregate industries, leading indicators, government expenditures, disposable income, national income, and all other subjects. Transactions specific to these subjects might include market data such as sales, production, consumption, prices, and trade.

General topic areas for which most specific forecasts appear include population and labor; national income; finance; trade; soft goods (all specific products); and hard goods (all specific products); and more.

Sources are textual as well as statistical, ranging from the trade and business literature to specific forecasting services such as trade journals, business newspapers and bank letters. Information in the database dates from 1972 to the present. Each month some 5,000 new records are added to the file.

Some recommended uses for the database include the following:

Forecasts should be used along with any other Predicasts Terminal System (PTS) file when evaluating products, markets, economic conditions, or any other business subject.

To identify forecasts made by individuals or firms that a user considers to be reliable sources.

To identify current market size. Most forecasts contain the most current year as a base point.

The database can be accessed via DIALOG, BRS, VU/TEXT, or Data-Star. Total charges vary according to the vendor being used, but are generally based on a combination of connect time, offline prints, or online type. Users can also download information if desired.

FOREIGN EXCHANGE
Chase Econometrics
150 Monument Road
Bala Cynwyd, PA 19004

PRODUCT AT-A-GLANCE

Subject Coverage:

**Real-time/Historic
    market quotations**
Currencies

The Foreign Exchange database contains historical data for foreign exchange rates vis-à-vis the U.S. dollar for 200 countries. The database contains 1,300 series of weekly and monthly data. The database is updated on a weekly basis.

Historical data for the monthly series are obtained from the IMF International Financial Statistics. Weekly data are collected from the *London Financial Times*. All exchange rates are expressed in units of foreign currency per dollar and vice versa. Monthly data are available for both end of period and period average exchange rates. Weekly data are Wednesday quotes.

The Foreign Exchange database is listed with Chase Econometrics under the database name FOREX and disk name FOREXDB. More information on the database service may be obtained by calling (215) 896-4795.

FOREIGN EXCHANGE FORECAST

Chase Econometrics
150 Monument Road
Bala Cynwyd, PA 19004

PRODUCT AT-A-GLANCE

Subject Coverage:

**Real-time/Historic
market quotations**
Currencies
Money rates

The Foreign Exchange Forecast database provides foreign exchange and interest rate forecasts for more than 30 currencies. The database also includes macroeconomic forecasts for industrialized countries and provides historical data beginning from 1960. Monthly and quarterly forecasts are updated on the first business day of every month.

Data coverage includes exchange rates, interest rates, and forward currency quotations. Supplemental coverage for developed countries includes Gross Domestic Product, consumer prices, monetary aggregates, and trade flow data.

The Foreign Exchange Forecast database is listed with Chase Econometrics under the database name FEX and under the disk name FEXRATE. More information on the database service may be obtained by calling (215) 896-4792.

FSLIC
Chase Econometrics
150 Monument Road
Bala Cynwyd, PA 19004

```
PRODUCT AT-A-GLANCE

Subject Coverage:

  Company information/
    statistics
  Annual reports
  Quarterly reports
  Econometric data
  National
```

The FSLIC database contains balance sheet and income statement information from quarterly financial reports filed by savings and loan associations and federal savings banks with the Federal Savings and Loan Insurance Corporation and the Federal Home Loan Bank Board. The database is updated on a quarterly basis.

The database provides information on more than 3,500 U.S. savings and loans and federal savings banks. Information includes mortgage holdings by type and property size, nonmortgage loans by type, savings activity and deposits by type, and total income and expenses by type.

Database applications include screening banks on user-specified criteria, retrieval of selected items for an individual bank or group of banks, and production of preformatted reports. The FSLIC database is listed with Chase Econometrics under disk name FSLICDB. More information on the database service may be obtained by calling (215) 896-4920.

5

FUNDAMENTALDATA

Technical Data Corporation
330 Congress Street
Boston, MA 02210

PRODUCT AT-A-GLANCE

Subject Coverage:

Econometric data
Industry specific
Monetary aggregates
National
News services
National
International
Newsletter

FundamentalData is a database service provided by Technical Data Corporation in conjunction with Data Resources Incorporated (DRI). The database offers updated economic and interest rate forecasts from DRI's economic staff. The database service also provides analysis of domestic and international credit markets, Federal Reserve activity, U.S. Treasury auction statistics, and economic releases. The database is available through Telerate systems. Major topics include:

Fundamentally Speaking—A concise daily commentary on the fundamental economic forces affecting the market. There is also a discussion on the Federal Reserve activity and international monetary markets. The commentary is authored by DRI's chief financial economist, David Wyss.

Rolling News Pages—Up-to-the-minute analysis of major economic news releases.

Economic Calendar—A list of scheduled releases and DRI forecasts for major economic indicators and statistics.

Weekly Commentary—An intermediate-term overview and analysis of the economy and the international credit and currency markets, and their influence on the domestic credit market.

Treasury Auction Analysis—A comprehensive analysis of recent Treasury Bill and Treasury Bond sales, as well as historical statistical comparisons with these sales.

Bank Reserve Statistics—A graphical presentation of the five-day moving average of Federal Funds. The statistics are presented in graphical form for the recent values of free reserves and borrowed reserves.

Zero Coupon Yields—A table presenting the current yield to maturity for Treasury securities and zero coupon bond yields.

FundamentalData is marketed through on-site visits, telemarketing, direct mailings, and media advertising.

Value-added products and services include financial software, company brochures, a quarterly newsletter, custom services, and toll-free customer support services.

FUTURES PRICE QUOTATION SERVICE

Bridge Data Company
10050 Manchester Road
St. Louis, MO 63122

PRODUCT AT-A-GLANCE

Subject Coverage:

Real-time/Historic market quotations
Futures
Options
News services
National

The Futures Price Quotation Service, a product of Bridge Market Data, Inc., provides futures prices from the following commodity exchanges:

American Gold Coin Exchange
London Metal Exchange
Chicago Board of Trade
MidAmerica Commodity Exchange
Commodity Exchange Center
Minneapolis Grain Exchange
International Futures Exchange
New York Futures Exchange
London Commodity Exchange
Philadelphia Board of Trade
Winnipeg Commodity Exchange

Features of this database include:

30 user programmable pages of quotations. The user can select the format for displaying the data, the commodity, and the delivery months on which to receive the continuous price quotes.

Inquiry pages displaying prices, net change, and volume and open interest of the nearby delivery months and each succeeding delivery month for a given commodity.

Graphics, including 10 pages of bar charts for plotting futures contracts.

24 lines of scrolling news provided by Commodity News Service.

Continuous access to the Futures Price database is provided by dedicated telephone lines and/or satellite connection to Bridge Market Data's central processing system in St. Louis. Clients can also access this database with their own personal computer and communications software. All communications arrangements are handled by Bridge and are included in the monthly service charge if the client is located in one of its 900 network cities.

The Futures Price database is updated continuously over high-speed direct communications links to the above commodity exchanges.

5

THE GLOBE AND MAIL ONLINE
Info Globe
444 Front Street West
Toronto, Ontario, Canada M5V 2S9

PRODUCT AT-A-GLANCE

Subject Coverage:

News services
Local
National
Regional
International

The Globe and Mail Online database contains the full text of virtually all articles that are printed in *The Globe and Mail*, Canada's national newspaper. Articles date back to November 14, 1977 and include the Report on Business, news, sports, *Globe* magazines, editorials, letters to the editor, and entertainment.

The database is updated every morning at about 6 A.M. with that day's newspaper. *The Globe and Mail* is published Monday through Saturday. All information found in *The Globe*, including stories from the early edition and the national edition, is fully indexed and stored on the Info Globe database. Database information can be used to monitor the progress of mergers and acquisitions, check on current news topics, and verify most recent trade and industry statistics.

The information in the database can be accessed on IBM and Amdahl equipment at Canadian Systems Group, the largest time-sharing computer company in Canada. Access is through Datapac, Telenet, and Tymnet public access networks.

HISTORICAL DOW JONES AVERAGES

Dow Jones News/Retrieval
P.O. Box 300
Princeton, NJ 08543-0330

PRODUCT AT-A-GLANCE

Subject Coverage:

Real-time/Historic market quotations
Stocks, mutual funds, warrants, and rights

Historical Dow Jones Averages database provides daily summaries of the transportation, industrial, utility, and 65 stock composite indexes. The Dow Jones industrial stock average, comprised of 30 industrial stocks, is commonly used as an indicator of changes in the general level of stock prices. The Historical Dow Jones Averages database contains the high, low, and closing price on the Dow Indexes, as well as volume information for a full trading year. A database user may request a specific average, or all of the averages for a 12-day trading period. The database may be used to compare the performance of an individual stock portfolio with that of the market.

Access to the Historical Dow Jones Averages database is via either a personal computer with a modem or a communicating word processor or a time-share terminal and a News/Retrieval account with a password. Access to the database is through the major public networks of Tymnet, Telenet, and Datapac, and also through DowNet, Dow Jones's own network. The database is available 22 hours a day, seven days a week, from 6 A.M. to 4 A.M. (EST).

5

IDCPRICE
Interactive Data Corporation
303 Wyman Street
Waltham, MA 02254

PRODUCT AT-A-GLANCE

Subject Coverage:

**Company information/
 statistics**
Annual reports
Econometric data
National
**Real-time/Historic
 market quotations**
Spot prices
Bonds, notes and bills
Futures
Currencies
Money rates
Options
*Stocks, mutual funds,
 warrants, and rights*
Municipals

IDCPRICE provides current and historical securities-related data to more than 11,000 clients in more than 40 countries. The primary users of the IDCPRICE database service include investment bankers, stockbrokers, equity research analysts, mutual fund sponsors, economists, fixed-income portfolio managers, equity portfolio managers, pension fund sponsors, financial analysts, quantitative analysts, securities traders, banks, individual investors, merger and acquisition analysts, and hedgers.

The IDCPRICE database provides:

Current high, low, and closing prices, and volume data on more than 43,000 major market stocks. In addition, historical stock data are available from as far back as 1968.

Current high, low, and closing prices plus volume data and open interest, the next evening, for stock and index options. Historical options data are available since 1973.

Current and historical opening, high, low, and settle prices for specific commodities contracts, as well as cash, volume, and

open interest, the following evening, on more than 100 underlying commodities.

Call features and sinking fund provisions for U.S. corporate and
government bond issues, and conversion terms for convertible
bonds and preferred stock also.

Annual and quarterly earnings estimates for more than 2,000
companies.

Descriptive information on more than 1.7 million municipal
issues.

Financial statement data via COMPUSTAT or Value Line.

Historical and forecasted economic information.

Capitalizations changes, dividends, earnings per share, and
number of shares outstanding data.

Money market rates.

Currency exchange rates.

Market indexes data since 1973.

Market indicator data since 1981.

IDCPRICE is menu-driven. Users can store and retrieve data in
programs and graphics packages for charting and data analysis.
The database is updated daily. Current data are available by the
early evening of every trading day. Historical data are available
online, with no advance telephoning required.

Database information is obtained through direct contact with
securities dealers, publications, and daily computer-to-computer
data transmission. Sources also include the Associated Press,
EXTEL Computing Limited, Reuters Limited, Standard & Poor's
Corporation, Arnold Bernhardt & Company, the Federal Reserve
System, and many others.

The database is accessible through the following public communications networks: IDCNET, Tymnet, Telenet, and Datapac.
The database hours of service are from 5 A.M. Sunday to 8 P.M.
Saturday. Prime time hours are from 9 A.M. to 6 P.M. every trading
day.

In addition to its database services, Interactive Data also provides software for screening, analyzing, displaying, and distributing data. Interactive Data Corporation delivers products and
services via online connection with the company's mainframe
computer, downloading to personal computers, or on in-house
computers.

User support services include a 24-hour user's hotline, a user manual, and user training services via filed consultants. Value-added products and services include an online newsletter, software programs, and portfolio storage facilities.

IMF INTERNATIONAL FINANCIAL STATISTICS

Wharton Econometric Forecasting
 Associates
3rd floor, 3624 Science Center
Philadelphia, PA 19104

<table>
<tr><td>PRODUCT AT-A-GLANCE</td></tr>
<tr><td>Subject Coverage:</td></tr>
<tr><td>Econometric data
International</td></tr>
</table>

IMF International Financial Statistics carries data for all information shown in the International Monetary Fund's publication, *International Financial Statistics*. Data for about 76 commodities and 137 countries cover exchange rates, international liquidity, monetary series detailing commercial bank positions and money measures, interest rates, prices, production data, international transactions, government financial data, and national accounts statistics. The source for the data is IMF's *International Financial Statistics*.

Data are updated monthly, quarterly, and annually and begin in 1948.

5

INDUSTRIAL FINANCIAL
Standard & Poor's Corporation
25 Broadway
New York, NY 10004

PRODUCT AT-A-GLANCE

Subject Coverage:

Company information/ statistics
Annual reports
Company background
Industry information/ statistics
Industry overviews
Real-time/Historic market quotations
Stocks, mutual funds, warrants, and rights

The Standard & Poor's Industrial Financial database contains income statement and balance sheet data, as well as Standard & Poor's stock price indexes, for more than 100 Standard & Poor's composites.

The contents of the database include:

Disaggregation of manufacturing, transportation, financial, and utilities sectors.

Company-specific information such as book value, depreciation, earnings per share, dividends per share, operating profits, sales, income taxes, and working capital employed.

High, low, and average price indexes.

User applications of the database information include:

Graphing of historical price movements of individual stocks and stock indexes.

Compare individual companies' operating and stock performance to industry benchmarks.

Report on comparative financial data for stock valuation purposes.

Obtain industry benchmarks for evaluating financial performance of acquisition and divestiture candidates.

Monitor current and historical financials of all Standard & Poor's industry groups.

INDUSTRY DATA SOURCES
Information Access Company
11 Davis Drive
Belmont, CA 94002

PRODUCT AT-A-GLANCE

Subject Coverage:

News services
National
International

Produced by Information Access Company, Industry Data Sources provides access to sources of marketing, financial, and statistical data on 65 major industries, both American and foreign. Sources include market research reports, investment research studies, conference papers, numeric databases, special issues of trade journals, directories, statistical reports, industry statistics, and more.

Records are composed of bibliographic citation and abstract. Citations include publisher address, author, title, journal or publication name, date and issue information, subject headings, standard industrial classification codes, and language in which the original document was written. Display formats vary by information provider.

Industry Data Sources is designed for researchers who need a comprehensive, varied reference database for marketing or financial information on an industry, an industry sector, or a specific product. Typical users include information specialists, corporate librarians, consultants, financial planners, corporate planners, and economists.

Coverage extends from 1979 to the present. Some 2,200 records are added each month. Available through DIALOG, BRS, Mead Data Central, and Data-Star.

5

INDUSTRY 480
Chase Econometrics
150 Monument Road
Bala Cynwyd, PA 19004

```
PRODUCT AT-A-GLANCE

Subject Coverage:
  Econometric data
  Industry specific
```

Industry 480 database provides complete long-term forecasts for 480 U.S. industries. The Industry 480 forecasting system combines a large-scale input/output model with econometric techniques to capture both demand activity and industry financial performance simultaneously.

Information includes industry output, prices, sales to 55 categories of investment and 30 types of construction, sales to intermediate markets and to all other industries, sales to the Defense Department and 3 other government sectors, imports and exports, sales to final demand, and SIC-based production prices. In addition, profit and loss statement forecasts are provided for 50 manufacturing and service industries.

Quarterly forecast and analysis reports cover the outlook for all 480 industries covered by the database. These forecasts are based on Chase Econometrics macroeconomic projections spanning 10 years. The database subscriber can choose two economic scenarios most appropriate for his/her use.

Industry 480 database offers software for creating custom tabular reports. Full-forecast databases for all scenarios can be accessed online to allow for preparation of these customized reports. Analysis can be performed either online through Chase Econometrics's planned language, XSIM, or on the user's IBM PC XT using Chase Econometrics's planning environment PC PLANR. Customized scenarios can be developed by using the Industry 480 system independently or in conjunction with Chase Econometrics's macroeconomic model.

Clients of the Industry 480 database have unlimited telephone access to the service staff in Chase Econometrics's world headquarters in Philadelphia. Management presentations on industry outlooks and the impact on an organization are also available. Local support for performing analysis is available through Chase Econometrics's worldwide office network.

The database can be accessed on a time-sharing basis on Chase Econometrics' mainframe computer or by downloading data to a personal computer.

INSIDER TRADING DATA BASE

ADP, Inc. Data Services
175 Jackson Plaza
Ann Arbor, MI 48106

PRODUCT AT-A-GLANCE

Subject Coverage:

　**Company information/
　　statistics**
　Insider trading

ADP Data Services' Insider Trading Data Base is an online source of corporate insider trading information, containing the latest data on securities trades made by officers, directors, or owners of 10 percent or more of a publicly held company's stock, as filed with the SEC.

The database came online in 1986 and provides users with an extensive, easily accessed record of insider trading to be used in conjunction with the company's library of databases.

Special features include the following:

Insider trading information that is updated daily
Ownership percentages
Price and volume stock market data from before, on, and after the date of the transaction
Preformatted reports
The capability to be used in concert with ADP's library of text and numeric financial databases

Any standard ASCII terminal (and modem) may be used to access the data. If users wish to download and incorporate ADP database information into Lotus 1-2-3 files, an IBM PC, XT, or compatible and ADP's Datapath software are required.

Trading information comes from The Invest/Net Group, as gathered from the SEC. It dates back to 1982 and is updated daily with approximately 300 entries. The updating process occurs in a matter of hours.

Insider Trading's supplemental stock market information is taken from ADP's Fastock II database. The stock market information also dates back to 1982 and is updated daily according to that day's insider transactions, in the same time frame.

Information is retrieved on a variety of bases (company, date, transaction, market activity, etc.) and is therefore in a variety of textual and numeric forms.

INSIGHT

Info Globe
444 Front Street West
Toronto, Ontario, Canada M5V 2S9

INSIGHT is a compilation of databases developed by Canadian Systems Group, Canada's largest computer services organization. Databases include Inter-Corporate Ownership, Canadian Federal Corporation and Directors, Corporate Names, Trade Marks, Bankruptcies, and Canadian Trade Index.

Inter-Corporate Ownership provides information on the structure and interrelationship of Canadian corporate society. Information can be used to determine who holds what companies and where they are held. Company lists can be obtained by industry group (SIC code).

Canadian Federal Corporation and Directors monitors more than 140,000 federally incorporated corporations. The information can be used to determine who owns what and how much; what the revenues, assets, and earnings are; who the directors are and where they live; as well as identification of corporations that operate in a specific geographic region.

Corporate Names contains summary information on more than two million private and public, federal and provincial corporations and business names. Information can be used to check company registration information and compare newly planned corporate names to existing registered names.

Trade Marks allows for searching of more than 200,000 registered and pending marks based on the files of the Trade Mark Branch of Consumer and Corporate Affairs in Canada. Information can be used to screen names of planned companies, products, or services and to identify wordmarks, designs, registration, and first-used dates for registration or pending trademarks.

Bankruptcies provides summary information on all open files of Canadian corporate and personal bankruptcy records, and those files that have been closed in the past two years.

Canadian Trade Index provides product, location, and executive information for more than 13,000 Canadian manufacturers.

The information in the database can be accessed on IBM and Amdahl equipment at Canadian Systems Group, the largest time-sharing computer company in Canada. Access is through Datapac, Telenet, and Tymnet public access networks.

INTERNATIONAL CORPORATE NEWS

Moody's Investors Service
99 Church Street
New York, NY 10007

PRODUCT AT-A-GLANCE

Subject Coverage:

News services
National
International

International Corporate News, produced Moody's Investors Service, Inc., provides current business developments and financial statistics for 5,000 major corporations and institutions in 100 countries. This information is updated weekly and contains both textual and tabular data.

This database can be searched by using any of over 130 event codes, such as merger and acquisition developments, management changes, new products and contracts, joint venture and financing plans, annual and interim reports, bankruptcy proceedings, balance sheet items, and more. These event codes are used to classify news items and enable users to search not only by company, but across companies for specific events or activities.

The database can be accessed via the DIALOG service through Telenet, Tymnet, Uninet, or Dialnet, the proprietary DIALOG network. Access is available 22 hours every weekday. Saturday hours are also available.

Charges for accessing the database are based on connect time. Additional charges are assessed for offline prints, types, and displays. There are no initial or annual subscription fees, log on fees, search charges, or storage charges. Users are billed directly from DIALOG and no discounts are available.

International Corporate News can be accessed using almost any brand or model of ASCII-coded personal computer or word processor as long as users have:

Terminal Software—asynchronous communications package
Terminal Hardware—serial interface and modem
Telephone line

The primary sources for this database include annual and quarterly reports, news releases, proxy statements, regulatory reports, prospectuses, stock exchange bulletins and lists, leading periodicals, and news wire services.

International Corporate News is also available in hard copy via *Moody's News Reports* on a subscription basis and in tape format with the cost and turn-around time dependent on the specific request.

Users may call the company toll free for assistance with various questions at (800) 342-5647. This number is staffed Monday through Friday, 9 A.M. through 5 P.M. (EST).

In addition, product brochures and mini-search guides are available as a quick and easy reference tool to supplement the standard "blue sheets" and "chapters" provided by DIALOG. Moody's literature is free of charge.

Moody's plans for the future call for continued expansion of its electronic information resource coverage of public companies. As of late 1986, the information contained on over 20,000 corporations, similar to what is available in the Moody's Manuals, are available in machine-readable form.

INTERNATIONAL DUN'S MARKET IDENTIFIERS

Dun's Marketing Services
3 Century Drive
Parsippany, NJ 07054

PRODUCT AT-A-GLANCE

Subject Coverage:

Company information/ statistics
Annual reports
Company background
Forecasts
Lines of business
Quarterly reports

The International Dun's Market Identifiers (IDMI) database contains directory listings, sales volume and marketing data, and references to parent companies on over 530,000 leading companies in over 130 countries around the world, including the United States. Annual sales volume is supplied in both local currency and U.S. dollars. Produced by Dun & Bradstreet International, the database corresponds in part to the *Principal International Businesses Directory* available in hard copy.

Dun & Bradstreet has selected the businesses contained in this file on the basis of their size (as determined by annual sales volume), national prominence, and international interest, that is their actual or potential trading position with businesses located outside their own country. Communist-bloc countries are not included in the file. Firms chosen are both commercial and industrial establishments from all lines of business. These establishments may be either publicly held, government-controlled, or privately owned.

The International Dun's Market Identifiers file has been developed from interviews conducted by Dun & Bradstreet International business analysts located throughout the world.

The database was first made available in 1982 under the name of Principal International Businesses. The name was changed to IDMI in 1985. Today, the database's total size consists of 530,000 company profiles, which focus on marketing, sales, corporate intelligence, and competitive analysis.

Information is reloaded quarterly with a lag time between source update and database update of at least four months and

5

as long as 18 months. The information provided is both textual and numeric.

The database is available 24 hours a day Monday through Friday, from noon until 8 P.M. on Saturday, and from 5 P.M. to midnight on Sunday (EST). Users can access the database through DIALOG by using either a terminal or personal computer with a modem. Access may also be attained using Menlo's In-Search or Pro-Search, as well as DialogLink. Information is accessed through a variety of datalines including Dialnet, Tymnet, and Telenet.

Charges for access to its databases are based on connect time, with volume/usage discounts available through DIALOG. Customer support is available in the form of user manuals, newsletters, and online instruction.

INVESTEXT
Business Research Corporation
12 Farnsworth Street
Boston, MA 02210

PRODUCT AT-A-GLANCE

Subject Coverage:

**Research reports/
evaluations**
Company
Industry

INVESTEXT is a full-text database of company and industry research reports produced by leading domestic investment banking firms (Wall Street and regional firms) as well as financial research organizations in the major industrial countries worldwide.

INVESTEXT coverage includes 7,000 U.S. companies, 1,500 publicly held foreign companies, and over 50 industry groups. INVESTEXT reports are written by professional analysts who specialize in researching one or more industries and individual companies within those industries. The reports provide not only historical analyses, but also short-term and long-term forecasts of sales, earnings, R&D expenditures, market share, and so on. All textual and tabular data contained in the reports are included in the database.

Depending on their information needs, clients can access INVESTEXT in three versions: menu-driven, query-driven, and electronic newletter format.

Business Research Corporation recommends using Investext for such typical applications as:

Performing competitive analysis
Conducting market research
Analyzing potential merger/acquisition candidates
Researching industry trends
Obtaining product information
Analyzing a company's lines of business
Locating financial information, both current and historical, on
   competitors
Supporting business/corporate planning decisions
Supplying background information for sales planning

5

Information within the database dates from 1982 to present. The information is updated weekly. The database's full size was over 35,000 reports (ca. 160,000 pages) as of January 1986.

No specific hardware is required to use INVESTEXT. Any computer terminal supported by a 300 or 1200 baud modem can be used to access the database. The 72-character format readily fits most terminals and personal computers by IBM, DEC, and Apple.

LEGAL RESOURCE INDEX

Information Access Company
11 Davis Drive
Belmont, CA 94002

PRODUCT AT-A-GLANCE

Subject Coverage:

 **Industry information/
 statistics**
 Legal actions and issues

Produced by Information Access Company, Legal Resource Index covers all major English language secondary legal literature. Legal researchers and other information specialists will find a wealth of information on corporate law, real property law, the legal profession, taxation, environment, labor relations, civil rights, copyright and legal perspectives on many other topics.

The database provides cover-to-cover indexing of articles from over 730 law reviews, bar association journals, and subject specific law journals. Articles of national interest from seven legal newspapers are also indexed.

Coverage extends from January 1980 to the present. Some 3,500 records are added each month. Daily updates are included in NEWSEARCH. The database is available through DIALOG.

5

LONG-TERM INTERINDUSTRY FORECAST

Chase Econometrics
150 Monument Road
Bala Cynwyd, PA 19004

PRODUCT AT-A-GLANCE

Subject Coverage:

Econometric data
Industry specific
National

The Long-Term Interindustry Forecast database provides detailed forecasts for more than 400 industries. The 8,500 series of forecasts include industry production, sales to major markets, investment, employment, value added, profits, and other income. Forecasts are updated semiannually and extend 10 years into the future. Historical data begin in 1959.

Data coverage includes 480 categories of industrial output, prices, and final and intermediate demands; 55 categories of investment, employment, and productivity; and 50 categories of labor compensation, profits, net interest, and value added.

The Long-Term Interindustry Forecast database is listed with Chase Econometrics under the database names LTIND and LTIND2 and under the disk name LTINDDB. More information on the database service may be obtained by calling (215) 896-4850.

LTMOD

Wharton Econometric Forecasting
 Associates
3rd floor, 3624 Science Center
Philadelphia, PA 19104

PRODUCT AT-A-GLANCE

Subject Coverage:

Econometric data
National

LTMOD contains historic data variables used in the Wharton long-term economic model. The sources for the data are the departments of Commerce, Labor, Transportation, Energy, and the Interior; Internal Revenue Service; Federal Reserve Board; and various published articles. Also available under other long-term series data bases are the model's forecasts.

Data are updated annually and date back to 1929.

5

M&A DATABASE

MLR Publishing Company
229 South 18th Street
Philadelphia, PA 19103

PRODUCT AT-A-GLANCE

Subject Coverage:

**Company information/
statistics**
Lines of business
Market activity
**Industry information/
statistics**
Business intelligence

The M&A Database is a product of MLR Publishing Company. This database is a comprehensive source of the latest information on mergers, acquisitions, divestitures, leveraged buyouts, tender offers, and partial acquisitions. The database contains information on transactions valued at $1 million or more involving both public and private companies from 1979 to the present. Continual updates provide new information on pending, completed, and unsuccessful deals.

Information for the M&A Database is gathered from a wide variety of sources including:

Wall Street Journal
Dow Jones News Service Wire
SEC filings
Standard & Poor's Corporation Records Daily News
New York Stock Exchange listing applications
Phone calls to companies

The database first came into existence in 1984 and currently contains 20,000 records. Each record represents a transaction involving a merger, acquisition, or acquisition of interest. These records may be used to evaluate companies, identify potential buyers and sellers, monitor the competition, compute premiums paid, and structure transactions.

Transaction information includes total price paid, price paid per share, p/e ratios, premiums over market price, premiums over book value, and effective date. More specific company information includes names, locations, description of products and services, SIC codes, sales, assets, net income, earnings per share, shares outstanding, and market prices. Pending, unsuccessful, and completed transactions since 1979 are also included.

Access to the database is available through ADP Data Services' proprietary network 24 hours a day.

MLR Publishing Company also publishes a bimonthly journal, *Mergers & Acquisitions*, which contains some of the information within this database. This publication is available with an annual subscription.

MCGRAW-HILL BUSINESS BACKGROUNDER

McGraw-Hill, Inc.
1221 Avenue of the Americas
New York, NY 10020

PRODUCT AT-A-GLANCE

Subject Coverage:

News services
National

Subscribers are able to access the full text of 10 of McGraw-Hill's magazines and newsletters. Publications covered in this file include *Business Week, Aviation Week & Space Technology, Byte, Coal Age, Electronics, Data Communications, Inside NRC, Chemical Week, Green Markets*, and *Securities Week*.

The Business Backgrounder provides coverage of not only business issues, new products, international business, and government regulation, but also key scientific and technological developments.

Key features of the Business Backgrounder include:

No charge for online types or displays.
Full-text search capability through buzzwords, acronyms, or jargon.
Background on people, companies, and products.

MACROECONOMIC

Data Resources, Inc.
24 Harwell Avenue
Lexington, MA 02173

PRODUCT AT-A-GLANCE

Subject Coverage:

Econometric data
Industry specific
Local
Monetary aggregates
National
Regional

The MACROECONOMIC database (a product of Data Resources Incorporated) contains data on financial, economic, and demographic activity for the United States.

Database contents include:

U.S. Central—Information on national income and product accounts; retail and wholesale trade; manufacturers' shipments; inventories and orders; labor force data such as employment, hours, and earnings; housing starts and completions; and industry, financial, and consumer credit data.

U.S. Prices—Provides consumer, producer, and industry-sector price indexes compiled by the Bureau of Labor Statistics; a "market basket" of 265 consumer items; sample prices of 2,800 commodities; and output prices by SIC and commodities classifications.

Flow of Funds—Provides Federal Reserve Board accounting statistics on financial activities with 5,800 series disaggregated by institutional group and type of transaction.

News Services—Provides text and selected tables from regularly scheduled and intermittent news releases on key U.S. economic indicators issued by federal agencies and private sources.

The major sources of information for the database are the Board of Governors of the Federal Reserve System, Federal Home Loan Bank Board, an all major U.S. government departments and agencies.

MACROECONOMIC database's user applications include:

5

Development of monetary movement forecasts using historical data and the ECONOMIC MONITORING SERVICE, an applications package providing user access to economic news releases and newsletters.

Monitoring and analysis of economic trends by using the MACROECONOMIC database in conjunction with MACRO-ECONOMIC SERVICES, an integrated services system that provides monitoring, forecasting, and analysis of U.S. economic performance.

Use Telerate or the DRI system to receive government news releases.

Preparation of charts and graphs for presentation and reports using GRAPHICS, a software package with graphing capabilities.

Access detailed data to supplement and support forecasts from the PC MACRO MODEL, containing over 1,000 equation models on the economy, and the KEYRATES interest rate model.

Use the weekly "Money and Credit Memo" to time new product introductions, monitor short- and intermediate-term interest rates, and alert trading and sales to the current interest rate movements.

Access to the database is either on a time-sharing basis with DRI's mainframe computer or by downloading data onto a personal computer by using PC GATEWAY, a database access package.

MAGAZINE ASAP
Information Access Company
11 Davis Drive
Belmont, CA 94002

PRODUCT AT-A-GLANCE

Subject Coverage:

News services
National

Produced by Information Access Company, Magazine ASAP provides full text plus indexing to articles from over 60 magazines covered in Magazine Index. The database also provides flexible searching capability—choose free text or controlled vocabulary, or any combination of words from the text or index terms. For instance, the database can be searched for quotations, figures, or any mention of a person's or company's name.

Subject areas include current affairs, computer science, music, arts and entertainment, consumer affairs, education, lifestyles, science and technology, and business and economics.

Coverage begins with January 1983 issues, with some 2,500 records added on a monthly basis. Magazine ASAP is available through DIALOG, Mead Data Central, and BRS.

5

MAGAZINE INDEX
Information Access Company
11 Davis Drive
Belmont, CA 94002

PRODUCT AT-A-GLANCE

Subject Coverage:

News services
National

Produced by Information Access Company, Magazine Index covers current affairs, business, education, consumer information, home and leisure activities, performing arts, science, and travel. It also includes information on government relations, journalism, public relations, market research, food and nutrition, and social sciences.

Virtually cover-to-cover indexing of more than 400 widely read magazines from the United States and Canada, with coverage extending from 1959 to the present, is included. Updates are done on a monthly basis when some 10,000 records are added to the database. The full text of selected articles may be displayed online or printed offline. It is available through DIALOG.

MANAGEMENT CONTENTS
Information Access Company
11 Davis Drive
Belmont, CA 94002

The Management Contents database is produced by Information Access Company. It provides comprehensive coverage on all aspects of management, business, and industry. Current and retrospective information on technological trends, applied business techniques, trade and industry news, as well as scholarly and theoretical analysis are covered in the file. Information on companies, products, and people is also prominently featured.

The database provides access to over 700 U.S. and international English language journals and magazines as well as proceedings, books, courses, tabloids, newsletters, and research reports. Every article from these publications, except book reviews and letters to the editor, is condensed into 50–300 word abstracts by industry-specific specialists for inclusion in the file. In addition, summaries of major research studies and other publications of the Employee Benefit Research Institute are indexed.

This database was created to aid individuals in research, business, consulting organizations, law firms, educational institutions, labor relations, market research, or business law. *The Management Contents Database and Dictionary*, a controlled list of keywords selected to reflect the subject matter covered in current business literature, is the authority list used for indexing. The file is updated daily on NEWSEARCH. *Business Periodicals and Abstracts* is the printed version of the database. All records include informative abstracts.

Recommended uses for the Management Contents database include:

Locating information on companies, addresses, and prominent people.
Tracking trade and industry news and technological trends.
Finding background information for strategic and long-range planning for new ventures, new products, or markets.

Monitoring regulatory and legal trends affecting specific industries, general business practices, commerce, and taxation.

Monitoring theoretical and scholarly developments in management, finance, logistics, economics, marketing, operations, human resources, and so on.

Finding financial data on a company's profits, losses, sales, and so on.

Locating references to articles containing charts, graphs, photographs, diagrams, and other visuals.

Immediately retrieving company information by ticker symbol or D-U-N-S number.

MARKETING AND ADVERTISING REFERENCE SERVICE (MARS)

Predicasts Inc.
11001 Cedar Avenue
Cleveland, OH 44106

PRODUCT AT-A-GLANCE

Subject Coverage:

Demographic information/ statistics
Consumer preference
Income and housing
Industry information/ statistics
Business intelligence
Emerging technologies
Market news and forecasts
Product developments

Predicasts' Marketing and Advertising Reference Service provides fast access to detailed information on the advertising and marketing of consumer goods and services—from foods, beverages, personal care products, and health care services to fast food retailing, apparel, consumer electronics, and financial services. The database combines thorough coverage of advertising agencies, consumer-related companies, and the media with highly specific indexing and superior retrieval capabilities. MARS was designed to bring together in a single source the diverse information vital to anyone active in consumer advertising, marketing, and public relations.

Each week approximately 800 new abstracts are added to the MARS database within weeks of their publication. Over 40,000 abstracts are added every year, assuring users the current reliable advertising information they need.

MARS covers over 75 key source publications. Informative sources range from trade publications covering consumer markets to advertising research and method journals, pertinent newsletters, and the advertising sections and columns from major newspapers.

The proprietary indexing systems used in other Predicasts databases are all available in MARS. Hierarchical coding offers an extremely powerful retrieval capability, allowing users to perform broad or very specific searches. Users can search by product, by type of information, or by geographic location.

5

In addition to Predicasts' standard indexing system, MARS offers a number of unique retrieval capabilities developed expressly for this database with members of the advertising industry. Chief among them is the ability to search by the slogan or spokesperson used in any given ad campaign.

MARKETSCAN
Info Globe
444 Front Street West
Toronto, Canada, Ontario M5V 2S9

The Marketscan database contains data from six North American stock exchanges–the Toronto, Montreal, Alberta, Vancouver, New York, and American. Data include closing, high, low, bid, and ask prices, as well as volume. The database is updated once each day and maintains information on an individual issue for 250 trading days.

Historical data are available in weekly summary form for as far back as 200 weeks. Canadian mutual fund information is available from January of 1986. Searching can be done by company, day, period, or exchange. Portfolio manipulation software is available for Apple and IBM PC microcomputers for direct use with Marketscan data.

The information in the database can be accessed on IBM and Amdahl equipment at Canadian Systems Group, the largest time-sharing computer company in Canada. Access is through Datapac, Telenet, and Tymnet public access networks.

MARSTAT
Commodity Systems Inc.
200 W. Palmetto Park Road
Suite 200
Boca Raton, FL 33432

```
PRODUCT AT-A-GLANCE

Subject Coverage:

  Real-time/Historic
    market quotations
  Futures
  Options
  Stocks, mutual funds,
    warrants, and rights
```

The Market Statistics Database (MARSTAT), a product of Commodity Systems Inc., holds a multitude of financial data products that support the interests of commodity traders, stock traders, and economic and financial analysts. This extensive collection of market and economic indicator data can benefit the user by supporting both historical and ongoing daily updates for analysis purposes.

The MARSTAT user can choose among 200 commodities from over 35 worldwide exchanges, over 750 securities listed on the New York Stock Exchange, and data on other financial indicators including the Dow Jones Industrial Average, the Dow Jones Transportation Average, the Dow Jones Utility Average, the NYSE Up Volume, Down Volume, Advance and Decline, plus the widely followed market indexes.

When signing up for access to the MARSTAT database, customers may specify their portfolio. In doing so, they give the commodity number, symbol, candidate delivery months desired, date of delivery month to roll forward, and the number of contracts to receive each day. Or they may bypass the detailed portfolio and subscribe to the generic portfolio. This subscription offers customers their choice from 29 generally used commodities. The order is set up on a roll-forward basis so that as the expiring contract approaches the first day of the delivery month (or the last trading day), the customer receives the next nearest contract in its place.

Access to the MARSTAT database is available via Tymnet or Telenet. Users can also dial long distance directly into the database. The CSI computer center in Florida is available for access 24 hours a day, seven days a week with random occasional 30-minute periods of required downtime for file maintenance. File maintenance will consume 90 minutes per week.

Charges for accessing the system are based on a combination of an initial log on fee and the actual volume of information accessed. Users are not charged for connect time. Volume discounts are available. Billing is done on a monthly basis.

Value-added products and services include a variety of software, a monthly newsletter, a user's manual, and dial-in customer assistance available from 7 A.M. to 12 A.M. (EST) Monday through Friday.

MATREX
Multinational Computer Models, Inc.
605 Bloomfield Avenue
Montclair, NJ 07042

PRODUCT AT-A-GLANCE

Subject Coverage:

Econometric data
International
Real-time/Historic
  market quotations
Spot prices
Currencies
News services
International

MATREX is a fully integrated microcomputer-based system that interacts with specialized proprietary databases on a mainframe computer. The MATREX database system provides current and historical daily exchange rate data and monthly trade inflation and exchange rate data for 34 countries. The database is updated on a daily basis and contains information dating back to 1971.

MATREX consists of five modules:

1. The FX Exposure Management System is designed for reporting, compiling, and managing foreign exchange exposure. The system allows the user to develop rational strategies or to reduce or eliminate currency risk.
2. The Optimum Hedging Module provides a systematic approach to allow users to take advantage of natural currency hedges. The system identifies the currency exposures that tend to offset each other or increase the risk due to the correlation between them.
3. The Contract Tracking & Accounting System is a fully integrated system that allows the handling of all aspects of tracking and accounting for the company's spot and forward currency contracts. The information can be readily downloaded onto a personal computer to monitor the performance of each contract.
4. The Information and Analytical Systems provides the user with current and historic databases that are updated daily. The user can create subdatabases within a personal computer for analysis and graphics. The databases included are:

WORLD—WORLD database gives full-text economic, financial, and political information on more than 125 countries. Information contained in the database is obtained from wire services and more than 60 publications. Information is updated on a daily basis.

ENFORM—ENFORM gives current and historical international economic and financial information for more than 75 countries. ENFORM contains analysis and modeling tools including statistical analysis and graphics capabilities. Information is updated daily.

International Money Market Data—This provides spot and forward exchange rates for 37 countries, local interest rates for major countries, Eurocurrency interest rates, and gold and silver prices.

5. Forecasting Systems. There are three primary forecasting systems:

Technical Momentum Model—30/90 Days FX Positioning Strategy. The systems are designed to assist both currency traders and foreign exchange exposure managers of multinational corporations. The recommendations provided by the systems are updated simultaneously with the daily updates for the currency databases.

Macroeconomic Forecasts—The system will provide information and data for one-year forecasts, one to five-year economic forecasts, and currency forecasts.

Currency Forecasts—Provides 1-, 3-, 6-, and 12-month forecasts for selected currencies. The forecasts are updated each month for 30 major countries.

The MATREX database system is available through Multinational Computer Models Incorporated. It can be accessed from 9 A.M. to 5:30 P.M. via IBM PC XT or compatible computers.

The WORLD database, which is part of MATREX, is available through Mead Data Central via user terminal connected to the time-sharing service.

METALS WEEK

Chase Econometrics
150 Monument Road
Bala Cynwyd, PA 19004

PRODUCT AT-A-GLANCE

Subject Coverage:

Real-time/Historic market quotations
Spot prices
Currencies

The Metals Week database provides historical data for all metal prices quoted by *Metals Week,* as well as four currency exchange rates. The database's 500 series are daily, weekly, monthly, and annual in nature. Metals Week is updated on a weekly basis.

Prices for approximately 60 metals include daily prices, weekly and monthly averages of daily prices, weekly prices, monthly averages of weekly prices, and yearly averages of monthly averages. Foreign currency exchange rates include the British pound sterling, German deutsche mark, Japanese yen, and the Malaysian dollar.

The Metals Week database is listed with Chase Econometrics under the database name NEWDB and disk name METALDB. More information on the database service may be obtained by calling (215) 896-4764.

MILLION DOLLAR DIRECTORY
Dun's Marketing Services
3 Century Drive
Parsippany, NJ 07054

PRODUCT AT-A-GLANCE

Subject Coverage:

**Company information/
statistics**
Annual reports
Company background
Forecasts
Lines of business
Quarterly reports

The D&B-Million Dollar Directory, a directory file produced by Dun's Marketing Services, contains current address and financial and marketing information on the over 110,000 companies listed in the three-volume Million Dollar Directory series. These establishments may be either headquarters or single-location establishments with a net worth of $500,000 or more. The establishments included account for over $1 trillion in sales.

This database was first published in 1982 and covers both public and private U.S. companies that have a net worth of $500,000 or more. The database covers all types of commercial and industrial companies as well as all product areas. The total size of the database includes 160,000 corporate profiles of headquarters and single locations.

Information for the database is gathered annually by questionnaires sent to companies in the Dun & Bradstreet database that have a net worth of $500,000 or more.

The database is available 24 hours a day Monday through Friday, from noon until 8 P.M. on Saturday, and from 5 P.M. to midnight on Sunday (EST). Users can access the database through DIALOG by using either a terminal or personal computer with a modem. Access may also be attained using Menlo's In-Search or Pro-Search, as well as DIALOGLINK. Information is accessed through a variety of datalines including Dialnet, Tymnet, and Telenet.

Charges for access to its databases are based on connect time, with volume/usage discounts available through DIALOG. Customer support is available in the form of user manuals, newsletters, and online instruction.

5

MMS CURRENCY MARKET ANALYSIS

Money Market Services, Inc.
275 Shoreline Drive
Redwood City, CA 94065

PRODUCT AT-A-GLANCE

Subject Coverage:

Real-time/Historic market quotations
Currencies

The MMS Currency Market Analysis database was first published in 1982. The database provides fundamental and technical analysis of the factors that affect the international currency exchange and deposit markets. Coverage includes major central bank analysis, currency trends, international economic analysis, and other events that may affect these markets.

All forecasts and analyses are originally generated from company analysts located in financial centers around the world. The database is updated virtually 24 hours a day as reports and analysis information arrive. Daily, hourly, and intrahourly updates provide 20–40 minute updates on the "Constant Comments" page. Other updates occur as often as four times an hour.

The primary goal of the MMS Currency Market Analysis database is to provide timely fundamental and technical analysis for participants in the international currency and deposit market. Its client base is comprised of institutional investors, traders, portfolio managers, cash managers, treasurers, and pension fund managers.

The database is available through Telerate. Subscription to Telerate is on a monthly basis, as is the subscription for Money Market Services. There are no log-on or connect time fees. Discounts are available for multiple-year and/or multiple-screen contracts.

All hardware required to access the database is included with the subscription agreement. User access is available 24 hours a day online through the provided hardware. The service spans 45 pages on the Telerate system and is retrievable simply by calling up the page numbers.

MMS FUNDAMENTAL ANALYSIS
Money Market Services, Inc.
275 Shoreline Drive
Redwood City, CA 94065

```
PRODUCT AT-A-GLANCE

Subject Coverage:
  Real-time/Historic
    market quotations
  Money rates
```

The MMS Fundamental Analysis database provides forecasts and analysis of the supply and demand factors that affect short-term interest rates. Analysis focuses on U.S. federal policy and operations, monetary aggregates, economic conditions, Treasury activity, and other interest-sensitive areas. The service also provides the Weekly Economic Survey, which quantifies the expectations of more than 100 institutional market participants and leading economists for upcoming financial and economic releases, market tone, and other market-sensitive events.

All forecasts and analyses are originally generated from company analysts located in financial centers around the world. The database is updated virtually 24 hours a day as reports and analysis information arrive. Daily, hourly, and intrahourly updates provide 20–40 minute updates on the "Constant Comments" page. Other updates occur as often as four times an hour.

The primary goal of the MMS Fundamental Analysis database is to provide timely fundamental analysis for participants in the U.S. government securities market and other interest-sensitive securities markets. Its client base encompasses institutional investors, traders, portfolio managers, cash managers, treasurers, and pension fund managers.

The database is available through Telerate. Subscription to Telerate is on a monthly basis, as is that for Money Market Services. There are no log-on or connect time fees. Discounts are available for multiple-year and/or multiple-screen contracts.

All hardware required to access the database is included with the subscription agreement. User access is available 24 hours a day online through the provided hardware. The service spans 25 pages on the Telerate system and is retrievable simply by calling up the page numbers.

5

MMS TECHNICAL RESEARCH

Money Market Services, Inc.
275 Shoreline Drive
Redwood City, CA 94065

PRODUCT AT-A-GLANCE

Subject Coverage:

**Real-time/Historic
market quotations**
Spot prices
Bonds, notes, and bills
Futures
Mortgage backed securities
Options

The MMS Technical Research database was first published in 1980. The database provides various technical indicators, which are supported by textual analysis. The data are presented on a daily, hourly, and intrahourly basis. Indicators represent technical conditions of the markets for U.S. government securities, mortgage-backed securities, and metals. Coverage includes cash, futures, and options. The database is updated near and during market hours.

Technical indicators presented include moving averages, yield spread and basis data, point and figure charts, support and resistance levels, oscillators, relative strength indicators, option spreads, implicit forward rates, rate of return data, and hedge ratios. All data are current and are generated from real-time quotes and observations from company analysts on the exchange floors.

The primary goal of the MMS Technical Research database is to provide timely technical analysis for participants in the U.S. government securities market, mortgage-backed securities market, and the precious metals market. Its client base is comprised of institutional investors, traders, portfolio managers, cash managers, treasurers, and pension fund managers.

The database is available through Telerate. Subscription to Telerate is on a monthly basis, as are the subscription fees for Money Market Services. There are no log-on or connect time fees. Discounts are available for multiple-year and/or multiple-screen contracts.

All hardware required to access the database is included with the subscription agreement. User access is available 24 hours a day online through the provided hardware. The service spans 35 pages on the Telerate system and is retrievable simply by calling up the page numbers.

MONEYCENTER
Knight-Ridder Financial Information
1 Exchange Plaza, 55 Broadway
New York, NY 10006

PRODUCT AT-A-GLANCE

Subject Coverage:

**Real-time/Historic
  market quotations**
Spot prices
Bonds, notes, and bills
Futures
Currencies
Money rates
Options
*Stocks, mutual funds,
  warrants, and rights*
News services
National
Regional
International
**Research reports/
  evaluations**
Industry
Fixed income

MoneyCenter is a financial services database of Knight-Ridder Financial Information, a subsidiary of Knight-Ridder Newspaper Services, Incorporated. The database contains 10,000 pages of data providing news and statistics; money market prices and rates; quotes on equities, currencies, futures, and option indexes; foreign exchange data; commodities data; data analysis; and data charting services. Data are both real-time and historical in content.

The primary goal of the database is to provide portfolio managers, traders, and securities dealers with real-time prices and quotes on money markets, Treasury securities, and government agency issues along with up-to-the-minute news and statistics, analysis, and charting services. Database information is obtained from Knight-Ridder News, Associated Press, United Press International, Agence France Presse, Deutsche Press, OPEC news, various security exchanges, and contributor banks and dealers.

MoneyCenter offers the following:

News Service—Provides U.S. and international financial and economic news coverage; credit market commentary; corporate news; and news coverage on foreign exchange, money markets,

Euro-markets, equities, banking, and more. Up to 1,000 news stories may be stored through the MoneyCenter News Service.

Charts—Provides bar, continuous, departure, spread, oscillating, tick, and moving average charts. The service allows for open interest, volume, movable trend lines, time and sales, relative strength, and user-defined chartable quotes, and intraday or interday charting.

Futures Service—Provides futures and options quotes from all exchanges. Futures and options quote coverage includes financial, currencies, metals, energy, agriculture, and indexes.

Equities Service—Provides equity quotes and indexes from the New York and American Stock Exchanges and the NASDAQ OTC market.

Private Commentary Service—Provides third party fundamental and technical analysis, research, and commentary.

The database is accessible 24 hours a day, seven days a week via leased lines, satellite broadcast, or microwave communications. Access hardware required includes an IBM XT or AT&T computer, a 4,800 baud modem, and a printer.

MoneyCenter is marketed to traders, portfolio managers, investment advisers, investment banks, commercial banks, savings and loans, securities firms, and large corporations through direct sales force, direct mailings, and telemarketing.

MONEYDATA
Technical Data Corporation
330 Congress Street
Boston, MA 02210

The MoneyData database service, produced by Technical Data Corporation, advises short-term money market investors about the market direction, trading opportunities, and investment strategies using technical analysis. The service includes the daily commentary, "Money Market Strategies," historical yield spreads on money market instruments, a U.S. Treasury Bill yield curve, implied forward rate analysis, arbitrage analysis for money market futures contracts, and technical indicators and technical analysis of foreign exchange markets. The database is accessed through Telerate.

Major topics include:

Money Market Strategy—A daily commentary of technical and trading insights into money market investment opportunities.

Yield Curve Analysis—A graphic display of the U.S. Treasury bill yield curve, forward rate calculations for Treasury bills, domestic certificates of deposit, banker's acceptances, term repos, Euro-CDs, and time deposits. Yield curve analysis is updated throughout the trading day.

Historical Spreads—A comparison of historical and current quality and maturity spread relationships among money market issues.

Financial Futures Arbitrage Analysis—This series provides a matrix of implied repo rates over a range of prices and yield IMM Bill, CD, and Euro contracts. Current maturity and quality spread relationships are compared to historical levels. Financial Futures Arbitrage Analysis is updated throughout the trading day.

5

Foreign Exchange—Provides moving averages, covered interest arbitrage, interest rate differentials, momentum, and Euro Time Deposit forward rate analysis for five major currencies.

MoneyData is marketed through on-site visits, telemarketing, direct mailings, and media advertising.

Value-added products and services include financial software, company brochures, a quarterly newsletter, custom services, and toll-free customer support services.

MONEY MARKET PRICE QUOTATION SERVICE

Bridge Data Company
10050 Manchester Road
St. Louis, MO 63122

PRODUCT AT-A-GLANCE

Subject Coverage:

Real-time/Historic market quotations
Bonds, notes, and bills
Money rates
News services
National

Developed by the Bridge Data Company, the Money Market Price Quotation Service provides streamlined information on what rates are available for the major money market instruments.

This service provides:

Pages on domestic and international money markets.
Prices with equivalent yield presentations.
Yield curve graphs to show comparison of one instrument with another.

The Money Market Price Quotation Service provides continuous updating on these domestic and international instruments:

U.S. Treasury Bills
U.S. Treasury Bonds
U.S. Government Agencies
Federal Funds–Overnight and Term
U.S. Treasury Repurchase Agreements
London Interbank Offered Rates
Commercial Paper
Banker's Acceptances
Bank CDs
Spot Foreign Exchange
Yankee BAs
Overnight EuroDollars
EuroFederal Funds
EuroDollar CDs
EuroDollar Deposits
EuroCanada Deposits
EuroMark Deposits
EuroSterling Deposits

5

EuroSwiss Deposits
EuroYen Deposits
Historical Federal Funds Rates

MarketWire, a financial and economic newswire furnished by Market News Service, Inc. of Belmont, California, is being added to the Money Market Price Quotation Service. MarketWire will be a continuously scrolling news wire, available for approximately 12 hours each day. This information may be viewed on a video display screen or on hard copy from an attached printer. The news wire service tracks the major financial, economic, and monetary indicators regularly compiled and released by the federal government and monitors and interprets daily Federal Reserve activity in the securities markets.

MONEY MARKET RATES

I.P. Sharp Associates Limited
2 First Canadian Place
Suite 1900
Toronto, Ontario, Canada M5X 1E3

PRODUCT AT-A-GLANCE

Subject Coverage:

**Real-time/Historic
market quotations**
Money rates

The Money Market Rates database, produced by I.P. Sharp Associates Limited, provides 246 daily and weekly money market rates for 13 countries including Canada, the United States, and many European and Asian countries. The entire database of over 500 time series items is completely updated within 24 hours of the information source update by 9 A.M. local time the following day.

The database focuses primarily on primary market rates of interest for money market instruments (short-term rates), mainly for North American markets. The main goal of the database is to provide investment and securities analysts with a general trend of short-term, fixed-income securities.

The database contains U.S. interest rate data for prime lending rates, dollar swaps, Treasury bills, certificates of deposit, banker's acceptances, commercial paper, conventional first mortgages, broker loans (margin rates), discount rates, special drawing rights, finance company paper, and trust company paper.

Money Market Rates also provides data on Euro-currency interest rates and interbank currency rates (rates on international financial transactions) reported in London, Copenhagen, and Singapore. Interest rates are also given for various currencies including the U.S. dollar, British pound, Swiss franc, Dutch guilder, Italian lira, Danish krone, French franc, West German mark, Belgian convertible franc, Canadian dollar, Japanese yen, and the Asian dollar.

The database contains information obtained from *The Financial Times* of London starting January 2, 1979; *The Globe and Mail* from Toronto from as far back as March 31, 1980; *The Wall Street Journal* dating back to January 2, 1981; *Bond and Money Market Letter* from McLeod Young Weir starting November 6, 1980; and from *The Business Times* from Singapore.

The database is accessible 24 hours a day, seven days a week, except for a brief maintenance shut-down period on Friday and Saturday nights. Money Market Rates database is accessible di-

5

rectly through I.P. Sharp's IPSANET network and also from Datapac, Telenet, Telex, and Tymnet networks. User access is via a terminal or personal computer with a 300, 1200, or 2400 baud modem; communications software; and a user account number. General-purpose software allows for data manipulation, analysis, and downloading to a personal computer. Downloading procedures are dependent on the computer hardware used.

Users access the database via MAGIC, a database retrieval system for computer users with little programming experience, or through PRICELINK, an I.P. Sharp software product that allows for statistical data collection and downloading of data on personal computers.

Compu Trac, a third party software package, can also be used to access the Money Market Rates database. Compu Trac is designed for downloading and statistical manipulation of financial data on personal computers.

User support is offered via calling toll-free ((800) 387-1588) in North America from 8 A.M. to 6 P.M. (EST) on weekdays. I.P. Sharp Associates also provides subscribers with access to a 24-hour answering service for subscribers to leave messages.

Other user aids include a printed directory of database symbols, user manuals, database reference guides, and complete online documentation. Subscriber consulting services are available on an individual basis.

Value-added products and services include individual database search services, electronic message transmission, user software, data storage capabilities, ongoing user training programs, and custom program applications.

MUNIBASE
Kenny Information Systems
55 Broad Street
New York, NY 10004

PRODUCT AT-A-GLANCE

Subject Coverage:

**Real-time/Historic
market quotations**
Municipals
**Research reports/
evaluations**
Capital markets

Munibase is a product of Kenny Information Systems. It is a complete municipal securities database that furnishes comprehensive descriptions of over 1.5 million tax-exempt issues. Updating occurs on a daily basis with information available the next morning.

The sources of the Munibase information are primarily bond certificates and indentures. However, in the interim the company will take verbal verification of issues from the underwriter.

The information contained in Munibase is mainly used by broker/dealers, broker operations and reorganization departments, municipal finance and syndication departments, bank dealers, bank investment and trust departments, insurance companies, and depositories.

This information is compiled by the company's research department. The research department is broken down into two areas: New Issues and Prerefunded (called-in-prior-to-maturity).

Munibase is available through UNINET. However, users need only call Kenny Information Systems to set up service. Kenny will provide users with the necessary information to access the system.

Hardware required to access the system can consist of virtually any terminal with dial-up capabilities (300 or 1200 baud). Charges for accessing the system are based on a monthly subscription fee, connect time, and data usage.

User support is available via calling (212) 530-0900. By calling this number, the user will be routed to the most appropriate Kenny representative for the particular problem at hand. Virtually any problem involving the use of Munibase can be resolved through this service.

5

Other user aids include *Munibase User's Guide,* a bimonthly newsletter, and KIS-K-Sheets.

Value-added services include training seminars, Evaluation Service, File Maintenance Service, Notification Service, Index Service, KIS Prefunded Bond Service, and KIS Dollar Bond Evaluation.

NAARS

American Institute of Certified Public
 Accountants
1211 Avenue of the Americas
New York, NY 10036-8775

PRODUCT AT-A-GLANCE

Subject Coverage:

**Company information/
 statistics**
Annual reports
**Industry information/
 statistics**
Legal actions and issues

The National Automated Accounting Research Service, NAARS,
is an online database of the American Institute of Certified Public Accountants (AICPA) and Mead Data Central. The NAARS
database contains more than 48,000 documents, including 20,000
annual reports; proxy information; and authoritative pronounce-
ments of the AICPA, Securities and Exchange Commission, and
the Accounting Standards Board. Information in the database is
updated on a daily, weekly, monthly, or annual basis, depending
on the type of information being updated, frequency of publication, and the agreement made with the AICPA. Since most information in NAARS consists of annual reports, updating occurs primarily on a yearly basis.

The primary goal of NAARS is to provide current, accurate,
useful information to subscribers in an easy-to-use manner that
meets the user's needs. NAARS enables business firms, the legal
profession, and accounting firms to search, retrieve, disseminate,
and explain financial information and accounting trend practices.
NAARS employs a full-text approach for each document retrieved.

NAARS subscribers receive a NAARS terminal, a NAARS
printer, and complete training in the methods of formulating
search strategies and operation procedures. Associate subscribers
can research their own problems on the AICPA terminal rather
than having a terminal in their office. Full training is also provided
for associate subscribers. Access to NAARS is also available on an
individual inquiry basis to those who are not full subscribers or
don't have an AICPA terminal. Inquiries are channeled through
the NAARS department, where trained AICPA reseachers determine the best search strategy and then provide a hard copy of the
information desired.

5

Subscribers access the database through Meadnet, Telenet, Tymnet, Alaskanet, Datapack, or an 800 number. Customer access is either through Mead Data Central's UBIQ terminal, a video terminal, or a personal computer with a 1200 baud modem. The NAARS database is available 23 hours and 45 minutes a day on weekdays. Access is not available from 10 P.M. Saturday to 6 A.M. Sunday (EST).

Value-added products and services include a reference manual, complete user training, online help instruction, the Quick-Reference brochure, access to a customer service department, the *Reference Manual*, hard copy printing services, applications brochures, customer newsletters, and software packages that allow the user to print documents and save data on diskettes.

NATIONAL NEWSPAPER INDEX
Information Access Company
11 Davis Drive
Belmont, CA 94002

PRODUCT AT-A-GLANCE

Subject Coverage:

News services
Local
National
Regional

National Newspaper Index is produced by Information Access Company and is billed as a one-stop source for news from five of the most important nationally distributed newspapers. It is a source of business information (contracts, mergers, products, companies) and information on current affairs, people, social conditions, scientific developments, and consumer issues.

The database includes virtually cover-to-cover indexing of the *New York Times, The Wall Street Journal*, and the *Christian Science Monitor*, with coverage beginning January 1979.

Coverage of national and international news as reported by the staff writers for the *Washington Post* and the *Los Angeles Times* is included, with coverage beginning October 1982.

Some 14,000 records are added each month. Daily updates are included in NEWSEARCH, another IAC database. IAC databases are available through DIALOG.

5

**NEW PRODUCT
ANNOUNCEMENTS (NPA)**

Predicasts Inc.
11001 Cedar Avenue
Cleveland, OH 44106

PRODUCT AT-A-GLANCE

Subject Coverage:

**Industry information/
statistics**
Market news and forecasts
Product developments

Predicasts' New Product Announcements contains the full text of news releases detailing the introduction of all types of new products and services issued directly by the companies and their authorized marketing representatives. NPA news releases typically contain detailed discussions of trade names, model numbers, prices, availability, performance specifications, applications, and markets. The full-text records range in length from one to five pages. In addition, each release includes the name, address, and telephone number of a company contact for convenience in obtaining additional information or for ordering purposes.

NPA provides users with the same information offered to the press within days of its availability. Information within the database dates from 1985 to the present. Weekly updates add some 600 new releases to the database.

NPA releases are received from over 15,000 companies—large and small; public and private, manufacturers, distributors, and service companies. All newsworthy announcements received are included in their entirety.

NPA includes all products and services, with special emphasis placed on high-technology and emerging industries. Users are thus provided with information that may otherwise be hard to find but is important in dynamic, fast-changing industries.

Searching the NPA database is made easier through the use of Predicasts' proprietary indexing schemes. This hierarchical coding permits quick and precise retrieval of the exact information users need. The coding system is the same as that used throughout the Predicast Terminal System (PTS) databases. PTS codes are continually expanded to accommodate the introduction of new products, services, and technology to the marketplace. The system's versatility allows the user to perform broad or very specific searches with NPA. Users can search by product, company, or geographic location.

In addition to standard PTS coding, NPA offers a number of unique retrieval capabilities developed expressly for this database. Users can search according to product tradename, dateline, special feature, or use.

The database can be accessed via DIALOG, BRS, VU/TEXT, or Data-Star. Total charges vary according to the vendor being used, but are generally based on a combination of connect time, offline prints, or online type.

5

NEWSEARCH

Information Access Company
11 Davis Drive
Belmont, CA 94002

PRODUCT AT-A-GLANCE

Subject Coverage:

News services
Local
National
Regional

Produced by Information Access Company, NEWSEARCH is a daily index to periodicals and news releases covering a wide range of subjects and issues. Over 1,900 sources are used in covering news, business, lifestyles, current affairs, law, and a myriad of additional topics. NEWSEARCH is ideal for regular monitoring of specific issues, people, and companies. IAC recommends using this database for the latest information on a topic, then using the same search strategy on its other databases for in-depth information.

NEWSEARCH contains the daily indexing for Magazine Index, National Newspaper Index, Trade & Industry Index, and Legal Resource Index. Some 1,600 new records are added daily.

Included are daily additions of news releases from PR Newswire (representing 7,500 corporations and other news sources), all available in full text.

Indexing to the *New York Times, The Wall Street Journal*, and the *Christian Science Monitor* are available the morning after publication date. This database is available through DIALOG.

NEWS ONLINE
Standard & Poor's Corporation
25 Broadway
New York, NY 10004

> **PRODUCT AT-A-GLANCE**
>
> **Subject Coverage:**
>
> **News services**
> *National*

Standard & Poor's News Online contains day-by-day business and financial news stories on more than 12,000 publicly owned companies. News Online is available in two related databases. News Online, FILE 132, contains business and financial news stories from July 1, 1985 to present day. News Online–Historical FILE 134 contains historical news and financial items from June 15, 1979 through June 30, 1985 on more than 500,000 stories on companies covered by the database.

News Online FILE 132 is updated with 300–400 news stories and financial items each day. News Online–Historical FILE 134 is no longer being updated.

Both files contain both textual information and tabular financial data. News stories can be retrieved in any format.

Textual information is provided on more than 12,000 companies and their subsidiaries. This information includes news on merger and acquisition activity, leveraged buyouts, going private negotiations, new product announcements, officer and director changes, new issues of securities, labor negotiations, litigation, and more.

Tabular financial data include consolidated income accounts and balance sheets from annual reports, interim earnings information, pro forma statements, and the company's current financial position.

The News Online databases can be searched by company name, title of record, publication date, or free text. Additionally, the News Online FILE 132 database can also be searched by ticker symbol, SIC code that best describes the parent company's line of business, the year of publication, and any of 28 event names or event codes provided by News Online.

The News Online database can be used in conjunction with other Standard & Poor's databases to obtain a complete business and financial profile of the company, to get a full executive roster of the company, to find personal information on executives and

5

directors, to find out if an executive has recently moved to or from a company, and more.

News Online database information is obtained from reports filed with the SEC and other regulatory bodies, telephone interviews, annual and interim company reports, press releases, wire services, and newspaper stories. All stories are written and edited by Standard & Poor's professional staff.

News Online database is available through DIALOG as FILE 132 or FILE 134. There are no sign-up fee or monthly minimum usage charges required. Online prints are available at no charge.

NEWS PERSPECTIVES
Wharton Econometric Forecasting
 Associates
3rd floor, 3624 Science Center
Philadelphia, PA 19104

PRODUCT AT-A-GLANCE

Subject Coverage:

News services
National
International

Wharton News Perspectives focuses on recent global economic events. Wharton Econometrics prepares articles by experts in such areas as foreign trade, business indicators, employment, and financial markets. Also included is the Wharton US Services Executive Summary, which covers Wharton's latest economic forecast as well as recent economic events.

The Wharton News Perspectives is revised weekly.

5

NEWS RELEASE SYSTEM
Wharton Econometric Forecasting
 Associates
3rd floor, 3624 Science Center
Philadelphia, PA 19104

PRODUCT AT-A-GLANCE

Subject Coverage:

News services
National

The News Release System provides access to U.S. government press releases as soon as they are available. Included are sources of over 100 government releases on topics covering all segments of the U.S. economy.

Topics include assets and liabilities in financial institutions, consumer credit, capital market prices, employment, foreign exchange, mortgage activity, money stocks, and other macroeconomic information.

Updates occur based on release of information.

NEXIS
Mead Data Central, Inc.
P.O. Box 933
Dayton, OH 45401

PRODUCT AT-A-GLANCE

Subject Coverage:

News services
Local
National
Regional
International

The NEXIS database is the world's largest online, full-text instant information service. NEXIS is a research and information retrieval database containing news, business, financial, and general information. It includes full-text information from more than 160 international newspapers, magazines, professional journals, trade journals, newsletters, and wire services. The Reference Service, which can be accessed through NEXIS, provides bibliographic references on a range of information sources plus such databases as ABI/INFORM and Management Contents.

NEXIS contains information from over 13 million documents on subjects covering business, finance, government, trade and technology, and general news and information. The database is updated on a daily, weekly, monthly, or bimonthly basis, depending on the type of information being updated, the frequency of publication, and the agreement made with the publisher.

The NEXIS library is comprised of over 160 files from the United States and overseas. Users may search a wide variety of files or file combinations in the NEXIS library. Each of the individual files may be searched separately or all at one time.

NEXIS contains the full text of *The New York Times*. Its sources include the full text of all Time-Life publications. Leading publications include *Fortune, The Harvard Business Review, The Economist*, and *Financial Times*.

The primary goal of NEXIS is to provide subscribers with easy-to-use, current, accurate information suiting the user's needs. This information is geared to the legal industry, accounting firms, the news media, a wide range of business users, health care industry, medical professionals and others.

Subscribers access NEXIS through Meadnet, Telenet, Tymnet, Alaskanet, Datapac, or an 800 number. Customer access can be through Mead Data Central's custom UBIQ terminal, a video terminal, or on a personal computer with a 1200 baud modem. NEXIS services are available 23 hours and 45 minutes every weekday. On weekends, the system is unavailable from 10 P.M. Saturday to 6 A.M. Sunday

NEXIS is sold through sales force, telemarketing, direct mailings, and other marketing means.

The monthly subscription fee for NEXIS depends on the type of subscription, connect-time and network charges. Search charges range from $7 to $23 per search, with a 30 percent discount offered for off-peak hour searching between 7:30 P.M. and 7:30 A.M.. Volume discounts are also available.

Value-added products and services include training sessions, *The Guide to NEXIS and Related Services*, the *Reference Manual*, the Quick-Reference brochure, applications brochures, a customer service department, newsletters, online help services, printed hard copies of online data, and software that provides the user with the capability to print documents and save data on a diskette.

NORTH AMERICAN STOCK MARKET

I.P. Sharp Associates Limited
2 First Canadian Place
Suite 1900
Toronto, Ontario, Canada M5X 1E3

PRODUCT AT-A-GLANCE

Subject Coverage:

Real-time/Historic market quotations
Stocks, mutual funds, warrants, and rights

The North American Stock Market database provides current and historical prices and volumes for securities listed on North American stock exchanges. The database includes data on more than 11,000 common stocks, preferred stocks, warrants, rights, and units. The database contains over 85,000 time series statistics covering the New York, American, Montreal, Toronto, Alberta, and Vancouver stock exchanges. The database is entirely updated within two hours of the market closings, by 8 P.M. (EST).

The data contained in the North American Stock Market database includes bid and ask, high and low, and open and closing prices, as well as the dollar volume and actual volume traded. Historical information provided by the database is from June 22, 1979 for the Toronto Stock Exchange and from May 22, 1981 from all other exchanges followed.

The database is accessible 24 hours a day, seven days a week, except during a brief maintenance period on Friday and Saturday nights. The North American Stock Market database is accessible directly through I.P. Sharp's proprietary IPSANET network and also via Datapac, Telenet, Telex, and Tymnet public networks. Access is through a terminal or personal computer with a 300, 1200, or 2400 baud modem; communications software; and an account number. Access software is general purpose, allowing for data manipulation, analysis, and downloading.

User access to the database is through MAGIC, a database access system designed for novice computer programmers; INFO-MAGIC, an interactive information retrieval system from I.P. Sharp Associates; RETRIEVE, a database access system for users who are knowledgeable in APL computer language; or by PRICELINK, an I.P. Sharp software package that allows information downloading to personal computers. Access fees differ for each product.

5

Compu Trac, a third party software package designed by I.P. Sharp in close connection with Compu Trac's Technical Analysis Group, can also be used to access the North American Stock Market database. Compu Trac is designed for downloading and statistical manipulation of financial data on personal computers.

User support is offered via calling toll-free ((800) 387-1588) in North America from 8 A.M. to 6 P.M. (EST) on weekdays. I.P. Sharp Associates also provides subscribers with access to a 24-hour answering service for subscribers to leave messages.

Other user aids include user manuals, reference guides, a printed directory of database symbols, and complete online documentation. Consulting services are available on an individual basis.

Value-added products and services include individual database search services, user software, data storage capabilities, ongoing user training programs, an electronic message service, and custom program applications.

PC BRIDGE

Bridge Data Company
10050 Manchester Road
St. Louis, MO 63122

PRODUCT AT-A-GLANCE

Subject Coverage:

**Real-time/Historic
   market quotations**
Futures
Options
*Stocks, mutual funds,
   warrants, and rights*

PC Bridge, a joint development by Bridge Data Company and PC Quote, Inc., is billed as a "trader's toolbox." It has been designed to include the complete range of information that a trading operation needs. Included are real-time last sale and quote, technical and fundamental data, charts, news, market indexes, and more.

Designed for a multiterminal installation, PC Bridge has combined leased data circuits, satellite broadcast, and advanced communications software to provide real-time last sales and quotes with instant updates.

Some of these trader's tools include:

The 100-UP page—A display of up to 100 symbols that can be monitored on one page. These 100 symbols can be chosen from over 35,000 of listed and OTC stocks, options, and commodities. Ten 100-UP pages are available.

Intraday, real-time and historic price-volume charts—Includes relative strength, moving averages, and on-balance studies.

Time and trades and quotes—Includes information for the last five days plus the current day.

Quote composite—By exchange for every symbol.

Intraday, real-time market summaries.

Intraday, real-time technical summaries.

Fundamental information—Five-year capsules of earning and dividends.

Under Level II service within PC Bridge, the customer may access some of the Bridge Information displays such as trading strategy, options strategy, and advanced charting.

Level III service provides complete Bridge Information System and complete PC Quote service including PC Plot and Tickmaker.

5

PETROL
Wharton Econometric Forecasting
 Associates
3rd floor, 3624 Science Center
Philadelphia, PA 19104

PRODUCT AT-A-GLANCE

Subject Coverage:

Econometric data
Industry specific
International
National

PETROL contains monthly data for crude oil production, import and export levels of crude and refined products, Big Seven consumption of crude oil, and crude oil prices for 13 OPEC countries. The source for the data is major oil industry publications.

PETROL also provides Crude oil prices for each OECD country's volume and dollar value of crude oil imports.

Data are updated annually and monthly and begin in 1900.

POPULATION DATABASE
SAGE DATA, Inc.
104 Carnegie Center
Princeton, NJ 08540

PRODUCT AT-A-GLANCE

Subject Coverage:

Econometric data
National

The Population Database contains more than 200 annual time series information of historical, current, and forecasted nature. The database information begins in 1960 and continues through the year 2009. Population data are available by sex, age, and total population.

PRODUCER PRICE INDEX DATABASE

SAGE DATA, Inc.
104 Carnegie Center
Princeton, NJ 08540

PRODUCT AT-A-GLANCE

Subject Coverage:

Econometric data
National

The Producer Price Index Database contains over 7,000 data series on the average changes in prices received in primary markets of the United States by producers of commodities in all stages of processing. Two databases contain the information. The PPI databank consists of reported data, whereas the PPIS databank contains a subset of seasonally adjusted information. The database consists of monthly, quarterly, and annual data.

These data were previously represented by the Wholesale Price Index. The name Producer Price Index was chosen to better reflect the data coverage. Producer Price Indexes are compiled primarily from transaction price data from producing companies. Some prices are obtained from trade publications. List prices are used if transaction prices are unavailable. The Indexes are weighted averages of commodity prices with weights being assigned by importance of the commodity. The database information is available from 1946 to present and is arranged by Standard Industrial Classification (SIC) code.

PRODUCER PRICE INDEX
BY COMMODITY

Chase Econometrics
150 Monument Road
Bala Cynwyd, PA 19004

PRODUCT AT-A-GLANCE

Subject Coverage:

Econometric data
National

The Producer Index by Commodity database provides monthly historical producer price indexes for nearly 3,700 listed commodities by commodity and by stage of processing. Database information is obtained from the Bureau of Labor Statistics. The database is updated monthly.

Commodity price indexes include farm products, processed foods, textile products and apparel; fuels, related products and power; rubber and plastics products; pulp, paper, and allied products; machinery and equipment; nonmetalic mineral products; hides, skins, leather, and related products; chemicals and allied products; lumber and wood products; metals and metal products; furniture and household durables; transportation equipment; and miscellaneous products.

Also available are durability of product indexes, stage of processing indexes, and selected seasonally adjusted data. The Producer Price Index by Commodity database is listed with Chase Econometrics under the database name WPI and disk name WPIDB. More information on the database service may be obtained by calling (202) 775-0610.

5

PROMT

Predicasts Inc.
11001 Cedar Avenue
Cleveland, OH 44106

PRODUCT AT-A-GLANCE

Subject Coverage:

News services
National

Predicasts' Overview of Markets and Technology (PROMT) is a broad-spectrum source of business information that covers all manufacturing and service industry areas. It contains over 800,000 article abstracts from more than 1,200 business and trade press sources published around the world. Updated each week with 2,500 additional entries, PROMT is equally effective for either current awareness or retrospective searching. The information provided by PROMT dates back to 1972.

PROMT abstracts all significant articles on all areas of business and industry from over 700 industry-specific trade publications, over 200 business-oriented newspapers and newsletters, studies published by a number of marketing research organizations, and corporate news releases.

PROMT also provides users with access to the important information published abroad. Nearly 50,000 abstracts drawn from over 200 periodicals published outside the United States are included in PROMT every year.

In addition to providing the user with substance, the PROMT records also provide the important bibliographic information, including full article title and complete bibliographic citation. There are two basic types of PROMT records, depending on the magnitude of hard data contained in the article:

Text Abstracts—These abstracts contain discussions about products, technologies, markets, and companies often containing quantitative data. Each abstract varies in length (up to a maximum of 500 words) but averages 150–200 words.

Statistical Abstracts—These are created when an article contains numerous quantitative (historical or forecast) data. A typical table provides market share by company, consumption of materials by type, forecasts of a product by market, or other quantitative comparisons.

PROMT abstracts are indexed by product, type of information, geographically, and by company. The indexing systems are continually updated and expanded to accommodate the advent of new products and technologies and changes in corporate and country identities as they occur.

The database can be accessed via DIALOG, BRS, VU/TEXT, or Data-Star. Total charges vary according to the vendor being used, but are generally based on a combination of connect time, offline prints, or online type. Users can also download information if desired.

5

QTRMOD

Wharton Econometric Forecasting
 Associates
3rd floor, 3624 Science Center
Philadelphia, PA 19104

```
PRODUCT AT-A-GLANCE

Subject Coverage:

  Econometric data
  National
```

QTRMOD contains data for all variables needed for short-term macroeconomic analysis of the U.S. economy including national, demographic, consumer, personal, and financial indicators. The source for the data is Federal Reserve Board, the Departments of Commerce and Labor, and Wharton estimates.

Data are updated quarterly and begin in 1946.

QUOTDIAL
Quotron Systems, Inc.
5454 Beethoven Street
Los Angeles, CA 90066-0914

With QUOTDIAL, the individual investor can access the Quotron financial database of current market data on stocks, bonds, options, and commodities.

The QUOTDIAL service covers all securities markets, including major domestic and foreign exchanges. QUOTDIAL also delivers price information, such as dividends, earnings, and annual highs and lows. The database service features a selection of investor support services, including intraday graphs of trading activity, options class display, and a monitor service that provides automatic last sale updates for as many as 40 securities.

Users can access QUOTDIAL during or after market hours with the option of real-time delivery or 15-minutes-delay delivery. QUOTDIAL is reached by calling the nearest Tymnet access location.

5

REAL-TIME QUOTES
Dow Jones News/Retrieval
P.O. Box 300
Princeton, NJ 08543-0330

PRODUCT AT-A-GLANCE

Subject Coverage:

**Real-time/Historic
 market quotations**
Options
Stocks, mutual funds,
warrants, and rights

The Real-Time Quotes database provides no-delay price quote information for stocks that are traded on the New York, American, Pacific, and Midwest stock exchanges. The database service features a news alert that identifies companies on which current-day news has run on the Dow Jones News Service.

Access to the Real-Time Quotes database is via either a personal computer with a modem or a communicating word processor or a time-share terminal and a News/Retrieval account with a password. Access to the database is through the major public networks of Tymnet, Telenet, and Datapac and also through DowNet, Dow Jones's own network. The database is available 22 hours a day, seven days a week, from 6 A.M. to 4 A.M. (EST).

Besides the normal fees for using the Dow Jones News/Retrieval Service, Real-Time Quotes requires a monthly exchange fee. This fee applies to nonprofessionals only.

REGIONAL AND COUNTY DATABASE

Data Resources, Inc.
24 Harwell Avenue
Lexington, MA 02173

PRODUCT AT-A-GLANCE

Subject Coverage:

Econometric data
Local
Regional

The REGIONAL and COUNTY Database (products of Data Resources Incorporated) monitors demographic and economic activity in U.S. census regions, Federal Reserve districts, states, metropolitan areas, and counties.

Database contents broken down by geographic area include:

U.S. County—Contains over 280,000 annual time series covering employment by industry, personal income and its components, and population on the basis of age and sex for each of the 3,033 counties in the United States.

U.S. Regional—Provides information pertaining to economic, financial, and demographic activity by state, SMSA, U.S. census region, and Federal Reserve district levels. Contains more than 44,500 series detail on historical and cross-sectional regional performance.

1980 U.S. Census—Contains detailed population, housing, and income statistics on each of the census regions, SMSAs, states, and 3,033 counties in the United States. U.S. Census Summary Tape Files One and Three are available.

County Business Patterns—Contains county employment, payroll, and number of firms at the two-, three-, and four-digit SIC levels. Available data are on an annualized basis from the years 1975, 1979, 1981, and 1982.

The major sources of data contained in the database are the U.S. Department of Commerce, Bureau of Economic Analysis, Bureau of the Census, National Planning Data Corporation, Federal Home Loan Bank Board, and other major U.S. departments and agencies.

REGIONAL and COUNTY database user applications include:

Analysis and targeting of geographic areas for merger and acquisition activity when used in conjunction with REGIONAL INFORMATION SERVICES, a DRI integrated service that provides forecasts, analysis, and commentary on economic and

5

demographic activity for 9 U.S. census regions, all states, metropolitan areas, and counties in the United States.

Support municipal financing decisions through use of state, SMSA, and county data and the METROPOLITAN AREA FORECASTING SERVICE, an integrated service that provides forecasts and statistical analysis of economic and demographic activity for 306 SMSAs in the United States.

Location of profitable areas for bank branch expansion when used with DRI BANK ANALYSIS SYSTEM REPORTS, a bank report retrieval system.

Access detailed data supporting analyses and forecasts on a personal computer by using with the REGIONAL MONITOR, an applications package allowing data access on a personal computer.

Evaluate the growth potential of targeted geographic markets when used with ESTIMARKET, a market analysis and planning service.

Identify lending opportunities at the state and regional level.

Identify profitable states, counties, and regions for marketing campaigns.

Understand the current economic mix and growth potential of any U.S. region or county for marketing and investment purposes.

Forecast real estate supply, demand, and vacancy rates by city and by type of commercial or residential structure.

Compare key financial, economic, demographic, and industrial indicators across regions, states, and counties to evaluate a corporate client's key regional markets.

Compare raw material, labor costs, and product availability across all regions, states, and counties in the United States.

Compare municipal securities issued by states, cities, and counties by comparing different economies and their growth prospects.

Access to the databases is on a time-sharing basis on DRI's mainframe computer or by downloading data onto a personal computer by using PC GATEWAY, a database access package.

REGIONAL FINANCIAL FORECAST

Chase Econometrics
150 Monument Road
Bala Cynwyd, PA 19004

The Regional Financial Forecast database provides detailed forecasts of financial activity for all 50 states, the District of Columbia, and 263 Standard Metropolitan Statistical Areas. The short-term forecast is updated quarterly and extends 10 quarters into the future. The long-term forecast is updated semiannually and extends 10 years into the future. The majority of the historical data dates back to 1979.

The database provides institutional detail for commercial banks, mutual savings banks, savings and loans, and federal savings banks. Data coverage for states includes deposits; mortgage activity; commercial and industrial loans; and consumer credit for auto loans, revolving credit, mobile home loans, and other consumer loans. Data coverage for Standard Metropolitan Statistical Areas includes deposits, mortgage activity, auto loans, revolving credit, and other consumer loans.

The Regional Financial Forecast database is listed with Chase Econometrics under the database names RFINFOR and SFINFOR and under the disk name RFINDDB. More information on the database service may be obtained by calling (215) 896-4920.

5

REGIONAL INDUSTRY FORECAST

Chase Econometrics
150 Monument Road
Bala Cynwyd, PA 19004

PRODUCT AT-A-GLANCE

Subject Coverage:

Econometric data
Industry specific
Regional

The Regional Industry Forecast database provides detailed industrial employment forecasts for all 50 states and the District of Columbia by two- and three-digit SIC codes. The short-term forecast is updated quarterly and extends 12 quarters into the future. The long-term forecast is updated semiannually and extends 10 years into the future. Historical data begin in 1967.

Algorithms allow the user to generate an industrial forecast for counties, SMSAs, or any combination of counties. Data coverage includes 50 manufacturing industries and 50 nonmanufacturing industries.

The Regional Industry Forecast database is listed with Chase Econometrics under the database names RINHIST, RINFOR, and RINFORLT and under the disk name RINPLAN. More information on the database service may be obtained by calling (215) 896-4715.

REGIONAL MACRO FORECAST

Chase Econometrics
150 Monument Road
Bala Cynwyd, PA 19004

PRODUCT AT-A-GLANCE

Subject Coverage:

Econometric data
Regional

The Regional Macro Forecast database provides detailed macroeconomic forecasts for all 50 states, the District of Columbia, and 276 Standard Metropolitan Statistical Areas. The short-term forecast is updated quarterly and extends 10 quarters into the future. The long-term forecast is updated semiannually and extends 10 years into the future. The majority of the historical data dates back to 1960.

Data coverage includes employment and unemployment, income by source, housing starts, manufacturing shipments, retail sales, new car registrations, manufacturing employment, relative costs, and population and demographics.

The Regional Macro Forecast database is listed with Chase Econometrics under the database names RFOR, RFOR1, RFORLT, RFOR1LT, SMFOR, SMFORLT, ASMFOR, and ASMFORLT and under the disk names RFORDB and SMFORDB. More information on the database service may be obtained by calling (215) 896-4865.

REGISTER-BIOGRAPHICAL
Standard & Poor's Corporation
25 Broadway
New York, NY 10004

PRODUCT AT-A-GLANCE

Subject Coverage:

Company information/ statistics
Officers/Directors

The Register-Biographical database is a biographical dictionary of 72,000 key executives and directors of major U.S. and foreign, privately held and publicly held corporations. The database is updated at least once a year, and often on a semiannual basis when new information is received.

The information contained in the database includes:

Business information—Full name of the executive or director, reported title, position and department, name and address of the principal business, secondary business affiliations and positions, and fraternal and professional association memberships.

Personal information—Home address, date and place of birth, graduate and undergraduate alma maters, and the date of graduation.

The Register-Biographical database is searched by executive name; company name; fraternal organization; position with the company; company department; or by business or residence city, state, or zip code.

Register-Biographical database information can be used in conjunction with other Standard & Poor's databases in order to discover what products and services a company provides, get full descriptions of parent and subsidiary companies, find recent management changes involving executives, find background information and interlocking affiliations on company executives, and more.

The database information is provided by questionnaires that are completed by company executives, telephone interviews, company press releases, the "Directors and Executives" volume of the *Standard & Poor's Register*, and other Standard & Poor's publications.

The database is accessed through DIALOG Information Services. There are no sign-up fees or monthly minimum usage charges. Online and offline prints are available for a charge per full record.

REGISTER-CORPORATE

Standard & Poor's Corporation
25 Broadway
New York, NY 10004

PRODUCT AT-A-GLANCE

Subject Coverage:

**Company information/
  statistics**
*Company background
Lines of business
Officers/Directors*

The Register-Corporate database provides business facts on over 45,000 publicly traded and privately owned companies. The companies listed in the database have either annual sales over $1 million or more than 50 employees.

The company information contained in the database includes company name, address, and telephone number; a narrative description of the company products and services; the company's principal markets; the number of employees; sales volume; its primary bank, accounting, and law firms; the stock exchange it is listed on; whether it is publicly or privately held; and other company information.

Executive information includes a complete roster of company officers and directors, including an "as reported" title; officer or director department or position; and whether a director is an inside or an outside director.

The Register-Corporate database may be searched by business description, primary or secondary SIC codes, sales volume, number of employees, market territory, bank names, accounting firm name, law firm name, or an executive's position and/or company name.

The database information may be used in conjunction with other Standard & Poor's databases to get descriptions of publicly held companies and their subsidiaries, discover business affiliations of corporate executives, attain up-to-date company news, and more.

The database is updated at least once a year, but often updating is on a quarterly basis, when new information is attained. The information provided by the database is obtained from annual questionnaires that are completed by each listed company, telephone interviews conducted by the database staff, company press releases, and other Standard & Poor's publications.

The database is available through DIALOG Information Services. There are no sign-up fee or monthly minimum usage for the database service. Connect-time charges are $84 per hour. Online and offline prints are available for $1.50 for a full record.

5

**REPORT ON BUSINESS
CORPORATE DATABASE**

Info Globe
444 Front Street West
Toronto, Ontario, Canada M5V 2S9

PRODUCT AT-A-GLANCE

Subject Coverage:

**Company information/
statistics**
Annual reports
Quarterly reports

The Report on Business Corporate Database contains annual financial information on more than 1,700 Canadian publicly held companies. Selected Crown corporations and privately held corporations are also included. The database's time series data are available either online or on magnetic tape. Quarterly data are available for more than 350 companies. Historical data are available from as far back as 1974.

Database information is used by bankers, real estate companies, brokers, financial analysts, and individual investors. The information in the database can be accessed on IBM and Amdahl equipment at Canadian Systems Group, the largest time-sharing computer company in Canada. Access is through Datapac, Telenet, and Tymnet public access networks.

SAVINGS AND LOAN
ADP, Inc. Data Services
175 Jackson Plaza
Ann Arbor, MI 48106

PRODUCT AT-A-GLANCE

Subject Coverage:

**Company information/
statistics**
Annual reports
Quarterly reports

Produced by ADP Data Services, the Savings and Loan database contains over five years of financial data, including balance sheets and income statements, on over 4,000 FSLIC-insured Savings and Loans, about 75 percent of which are currently active. More than 200 data items, updated quarterly since the beginning of 1984, are provided for each Savings and Loan. Pre-1984 financials are semiannual.

Aggregate information on thrift institutions is contained in ADP's U.S. ECON. Major data groupings, updated monthly for the Savings and Loan database, include:

Consolidated assets and liabilities for FSLIC-insured institutions. Source: Federal Home Loan Bank Board.

Consolidated assets and liabilities for all operating savings and loan associations. Source: Federal Home Loan Bank Board.

Consolidated assets and liabilities for mutual savings banks. Source: The National Association of Mutual Savings Banks.

Aggregate investments of U.S. life insurance companies. Source: American Council of Life Insurance.

Consolidated credit union assets, loans, and savings outstanding. Source: National Credit Union Association.

Trends in mutual fund activity. Source: Investment Company Institute.

Any standard ASCII terminal (and modem) may be used to access ADP databases. If the user wishes to download and incorporate ADP database information into LOTUS 1-2-3 files, an IBM PC, XT, or compatible, and ADP's Datapath software are required.

5

SEC ONLINE

SEC Online, Inc.
200 East 23rd Street
New York, NY 10010

SEC Online is a document-based computer filing system that maintains full-text copies of the original reports filed by public corporations with the Securities and Exchange Commission. These reports, which are unedited, unabstracted, and unaltered, are keyed at an accuracy rate in excess of 99.9 percent.

SEC reports include:

10-K Reports—The official annual business and financial report filed by most public companies.

10-Q Reports—Quarterly financial reports that provide an updated picture of the company's ongoing financial position.

8-K Reports—The report of unscheduled material events or corporate changes considered important to shareholders or to the SEC.

Annual Reports—Management's annual report to shareholders regarding corporate business and reports of past performance.

Registration Statements—These are of two principal types: "offering" registrations that refer to securities before they are offered to investors, and "trading" registrations that are filed to permit trading among investors on an exchange or the OTC market.

Prospectus—This document must be available to investors before new securities are issued by a company.

20-F Reports—The official annual business and financial report filed by non-U.S. registrants.

Acquisition Reports—These reports contain summaries of ownership, primarily from 13-Ds and 13-Gs.

Company Research File—This file contains research material, company abstracts, and other detailed corporate information filed with the SEC Online at the company's discretion.

> Publicity File—This file contains copies of company press releases and other communication not filed with the SEC.

Information in the database can be used to research new investment opportunities, monitor investment performance, make comparisons of corporate and industry performance, compare auditing procedures and tax treatments, assist in market planning, obtain credit information, and prospect for potential customers, as well as being a general research tool.

Primarily users of the database are brokerage firms, commercial banks, accounting firms, consulting firms, law libraries, insurance companies, colleges and universities, and public corporations.

The SEC Online electronic database is marketed by Disclosure Incorporated and Business Research Corporation. It is available on the following networks: DIALOG, SIBRC, Dow Jones, The Source, NewsNet, BRS, Mitsui, Data-Star, First Call, ADP Network Services, ADP/MIF, Compuserve Business Information Services, Compuserve Executive Business Information Services, Control Data, I.P. Sharp & Associates, Isys Corporation, Mead Data Central, Quotron Systems, Savant Investors Services, VU/TEXT, and Warner Computer Systems.

The database is accessible 23 hours a day, seven days a week. Database access is through subscriber terminals and personal computers via the Compuserve Communications Network.

5

SECURITIES REGULATION AND LAW REPORT

The Bureau of National Affairs, Inc.
Room 601 South
1231 25th Street NW
Washington, DC 20037

PRODUCT AT-A-GLANCE

Subject Coverage:

Industry information/ statistics
Legal actions and issues

The Securities Regulation and Law Report contains information on securities and commodity activity at the state and federal levels. It includes developments in Congress, the Administration, the Securities and Exchange Commission, the Commodities Futures Trading Commission, the Financial Accounting Standards Board, the North American Securities Administration Association, and professional associations.

The database is accessible via Mead Data Central and West Publishing Company. The information in the database covers from January 1982 to present day. The database files are updated on a weekly basis. Its printed counterpart is the *Securities Regulation and Law Report*.

SMSA MACRO
Chase Econometrics
150 Monument Road
Bala Cynwyd, PA 19004

```
PRODUCT AT-A-GLANCE

Subject Coverage:
    Econometric data
    Regional
```

The SMSA Macro database provides historical macroeconomic information for more than 350 Standard Metropolitan Statistical Areas (SMSA's) and Standard Consolidated Statistical Areas (SCSA's). The database contains 39,000 monthly, quarterly, and annual series. Selected categories are available for both unadjusted and seasonally adjusted data. Database information is updated according to the frequency of the source update.

Data coverage includes personal income, population, employment, unemployment, housing permits, mortgage interest rates, and retail sales. The SMSA Macro database is listed with Chase Econometrics under the database name SMMAC and disk name RMACDB. More information on the database service may be obtained by calling (215) 896-4911.

5

STATE AND SMSA FINANCIAL
Chase Econometrics
150 Monument Road
Bala Cynwyd, PA 19004

PRODUCT AT-A-GLANCE

Subject Coverage:

   Econometric data
   Regional

The State and SMSA Financial database contains statistics from the FDIC and FSLIC income and condition reports covering four major types of financial institutions: commercial banks, mutual savings banks, savings and loan associations, and federal savings banks. Data are available for all 50 states, the District of Columbia, and more than 300 Standard Metropolitan Statistical Areas. The 13,600 series in the database are updated on both a quarterly and annual basis.

   Data coverage includes operating income and expenses, net income, loans outstanding, deposits, IRA and Keogh plan accounts, assets and liabilities, mortgage and savings activity, employees, and number of branches.

   The State and SMSA Financial database is listed with Chase Econometrics under the database name REGFIN and disk name REGFINDB. More information on the database service may be obtained by calling (215) 896-4911.

STATE MACRO
Chase Econometrics
150 Monument Road
Bala Cynwyd, PA 19004

PRODUCT AT-A-GLANCE

Subject Coverage:

   Econometric data
   Regional

The State Macro database provides historical macroeconomic detail for 50 states, nine census divisions, the total United States, and the District of Columbia, and selected detail for Puerto Rico, the Virgin Islands, BEA regions, and census regions. Selected data are available in both unadjusted and seasonally adjusted form. The database's 47,000 series are monthly, quarterly, and annual in nature. The database is updated according to the frequency of the source update.

Data coverage includes personal income; employment, hours, and earnings; housing permits, valuations, and starts; unemployment; manufacturing activity; financial activity; population, births, deaths, migration, and immigration; number of households; retail sales; taxes, revenues, and expenditures; farm cash receipts; defense spending; and motor vehicle registrations.

The State Macro database is listed with Chase Econometrics under the database name RMAC and disk name RMACDB. More information on the database service may be obtained by calling (215) 896-4911.

5

SUPERSITE
CACI Inc.–Federal
1815 North Fort Meyer Drive
Arlington, VA 22209

PRODUCT AT-A-GLANCE

Subject Coverage:

**Demographic information/
statistics**
*Consumer preference
Income and housing*

The SUPERSITE database, CACI's proprietary geodemographic information retrieval system, was first published in 1973. The goal of the database is to provide users with demographic and related information that can be used in market research and customer targeting. These data can be used to determine what financial services are most in demand and by whom they are demanded. The database also provides data useful in site selection so users can determine the best locations for new offices, branches, and automatic teller machines.

SUPERSITE data are produced for areas of any geographic size or shape, anywhere in the United States. Standard geographical units such as census tracts, zip codes, cities, counties, metropolitan areas, DMAs, and ADIs are available. When the user asks for areas that are not predefined, the software derives the data based on census-designated block groups.

SUPERSITE offers special reports for the financial and investment services industry. These reports show the user the potential for and penetration of different financial instruments. The reports can be customized for market areas of any size or shape, anywhere in the United States. Customized SUPERSITE applications are available on a per request basis.

The demographic information on SUPERSITE is based on data from the 1980 Census of Population and Housing. Updates and forecasts are estimated using CACI's proprietary methodology. Site potential information is based on data from the Consumer Expenditure Survey and industry-specific statistics.

Data are currently available for 1970, 1980, 1985, and 1990. The entire database is updated annually in the spring. New data and reports are continually being added. Business data , including payroll data and the number of firms by size, were available for zip codes and counties in 1986. Income by age of the head of the household, five-year age breakdowns by sex, and a new restaurant report were also available in 1986. Futhermore, extensive new financial service information is currently being planned.

SUPERSITE provides user friendly, interactive prompting and is thoroughly documented through its online "Help" facility. Its menu selection capability is designed to be used without special technical training or assistance.

The database can be accessed 24 hours a day, seven days a week, via any terminal or PC with a standard modem (300 baud or 1200 baud). User access is provided by several national time-sharing networks including Compuserve, Comshare, and Chase Econometrics. System support is provided by these time-sharing companies and their representatives. User costs are pay-as-you-go, by the report. Charges for reports range from $30 to $150, depending on the report and the time-sharing network used.

5

TIME SERIES
Predicasts Inc.
11001 Cedar Avenue
Cleveland, OH 44106

PRODUCT AT-A-GLANCE

Subject Coverage:

**Demographic information/
 statistics**
Consumer preference
Income and housing
Econometric data
Industry specific
Monetary aggregates
International
National

Predicasts' Time Series database provides over 170,000 historical statistical series covering all aspects of worldwide economics, demographics, industry, finance, and other business activities. The data are extracted, series-by-series, from a wide range of statistical sources with particular emphasis on specific products. The breadth of coverage enables the user to identify data on most subjects that may have a direct or indirect impact on a company's products.

Each series contains an average of 15 years worth of data in an easy-to-read format, which saves time in data collection and research. While the database contains series on most detailed business subjects, for illustration it can be classified into the following major categories: Population and Labor; National Income; Finance; Trade; Soft Goods (all specific products); Hard Goods (all specific products); Health; Sciences; Business Trends; and others.

The depth of coverage enables the user to retrieve several series on a specific product (e.g., as production, capacity, imports, end uses), or information on business indicators impacting a company's products (e.g., as GNP, population, capital spending, housing starts, and more).

Updated quarterly, the series are extracted from hundreds of statistical sources, including U.S. and international government publications; U.S., Common Market, and other worldwide trade and research organizations; as well as banks and other financial institutions.

The database can be accessed via DIALOG, BRS, VU/TEXT, or Data-Star. Total charges vary according to the vendor being used, but are generally based on a combination of connect time, offline prints, or online type. Users can also download information if desired.

TORONTO STOCK EXCHANGE INTRA-DAY INFORMATION FOR STOCKS AND INDICES

I.P. Sharp Associates Limited
2 First Canadian Place
Suite 1900
Toronto, Ontario, Canada M5X 1E3

PRODUCT AT-A-GLANCE

Subject Coverage:

Real-time/Historic market quotations
Stocks, mutual funds, warrants, and rights

The Toronto Stock Exchange Intra-day Information for Stocks and Indices database, produced by I.P. Sharp Associates Limited, provides 15-minute interval summaries of intraday trading statistics for 61 major and minor indexes, 11 high-technology indexes, and approximately 1,500 stocks listed on the Toronto Stock Exchange. Database facts include 15-minutes high, low, close, volume, bid, ask, trade time, cumulative daily volume, stock symbol, stock description, stock number, and industry classification.

The database contains nine time series and four static facts, as well as historical data for the 10 most recent trading days. Data are added to the database approximately 1 minute after the close of each 15-minute interval from 10:15 A.M. to 4:15 P.M. (EST).

The database is accessible 24 hours a day, seven days a week, except for during a brief period on Friday and Saturday nights for maintenance. The Toronto Stock Exchange Intra-Day Information for Stocks and Indices database is accessible directly, through I.P. Sharp's IPSANET network and also via Datapac, Telenet, Telex, and Tymnet public database access networks. User access is through a terminal or personal computer with a 300, 1200, or 2400 baud modem; communications software; and an account number. Access software is general purpose, allowing for data manipulation, analysis, and downloading to a personal computer.

Users access the database via MAGIC, a database retrieval system for computer users with little programming experience, or via RETRIEVE, a database access system designed for users with APL programming language knowledge. Access fees differ for each product.

User support is offered via calling toll-free ((800) 387-1588) in North America from 8 A.M. to 6 P.M. (EST) on weekdays. I.P. Sharp Associates also provides subscribers with access to a 24-hour answering service for subscribers to leave messages.

Other user aids include reference guides, complete online documentation, user manuals, reference guides, and two printed directories of database symbols. Consulting services are available on an individual basis.

Value-added products and services include individual database search services, data storage capabilities, ongoing user training programs, user software, and an electronic message service.

5

TORONTO STOCK EXCHANGE REAL-TIME INFORMATION FOR STOCKS AND INDICES

I.P. Sharp Associates Limited
2 First Canadian Place
Suite 1900
Toronto, Ontario, Canada M5X 1E3

PRODUCT AT-A-GLANCE

Subject Coverage:

Real-time/Historic market quotations
Stocks, mutual funds, warrants, and rights

The Toronto Stock Exchange Real-Time Information for Stocks and Indices database, produced by I.P. Sharp Associates Limited, provides real-time information for over 2,000 stocks and indexes on the Toronto Stock Exchange. The database can be used to access data on the most current price, volume, and high and low price for the last 15-minute interval, and other daily trading data any time when the Toronto Stock Exchange is open. The database is continuously updated each trading day from 10 A.M. to 4:15 P.M. (EST).

The database focuses on providing analysts and traders with the most current trading data from stocks listed on the Toronto Stock Exchange. The database facts include the latest trade time-stamp, date, bid quote, and ask quote; the 15-minute closing, high and low prices, as well as the volume; and the cumulative daily volume. Data are derived from the Toronto Stock Exchange High-Speed Vendor Feed.

The Toronto Stock Exchange Real-Time Information for Stocks and Indices database is accessible 24 hours a day, seven days a week, except for a brief maintenance shut-down period on Friday and Saturday nights. The database is accessible directly through I.P. Sharp's IPSANET network and also from Datapac, Telenet, Telex, and Tymnet public database access networks.

User access is via a terminal or personal computer with a 300, 1200, or 2400 baud modem; communications software; and a user account number. General-purpose software allows for data manipulation, analysis, and downloading to a personal computer. Downloading procedures are dependent on the computer hardware used.

Access to the database is via MAGIC, a language system with which users with little computer knowledge can access a variety of public or private databases. User support is provided via calling toll-free ((800) 387-1588) in North America from 8 A.M. to 6 P.M. (EST) on weekdays. I.P. Sharp Associates also provides subscribers with access to a 24-hour answering service for subscribers to leave messages.

Other user aids include user manuals, reference guides, two printed directories of database symbols, and complete online documentation. User consulting services are available on an individual basis.

Value-added products and services include individual database search services, user software, data storage capabilities, ongoing user training programs, electronic mail transmission, and custom program applications.

TORONTO STOCK EXCHANGE 300 INDEX AND STOCK STATISTICS

I.P. Sharp Associates Limited
Suite 1900 2 First Canadian Place
Toronto, Ontario, Canada M5X 1E3

PRODUCT AT-A-GLANCE

Subject Coverage:

Real-time/Historic market quotations
Stocks, mutual funds, warrants, and rights

The Toronto Stock Exchange 300 Index and Stock Statistics database, produced by I.P. Sharp Associates Limited, provides trading statistics for the 300 major stocks and 62 major and minor indexes that form the Toronto Stock Exchange 300 Composite Index. The database contains 20 time series data and 9 static facts, including daily high, low, and closing prices; earnings per share; dividends per share; quoted market value; volume and total value traded; earnings adjusted to index; price-earnings ratio; relative weight on the composite index; adjusted shares; dividends adjusted to the index; aggregate earnings pool; dividend yield; and aggregate dividend payout. The database also contains total return index values for all 62 indexes.

The entire database is updated each trading day at approximately 11:30 P.M. (EST). Weekly and monthly data are summarized at the end of the period from the daily data file. Daily information dates back to January 1976. Weekly information dates back to January 1971. Monthly database information starts from January 1956 for both stocks and indexes. Information on indexes starts from January 1976 and on stocks from March 1978.

The Toronto Stock Exchange 300 Index and Stock Statistics database is accessible 24 hours a day, seven days a week, except for a brief maintenance period on Friday and Saturday nights. The database is accessible directly through I.P. Sharp's proprietary IPSANET network and also via Datapac, Telenet, Telex, and Tymnet public access networks. Users access the database through a terminal or personal computer with a 300, 1200, or 2400 baud modem; communications software; and an account number. Access software is general purpose, allowing for data manipulation, analysis and downloading to a personal computer.

User access to the database is through MAGIC, a database access system designed for novice computer programmers; INFO-

MAGIC, an interactive information retrieval system from I.P. Sharp Associates; RETRIEVE, a database access system for users who are knowledgeable in APL computer language; or by PRICELINK, an I.P. Sharp software package that allows information downloading to personal computers. Access fees differ for each product.

Compu Trac, a third party software package from I.P. Sharp and Compu Trac's Technical Analysis Group, can also be used to access the Toronto Stock Exchange 300 Index and Stock Statistics database. Compu Trac is designed for downloading and statistical manipulation of financial data on personal computers.

User support is offered via calling toll-free ((800) 387-1588) in North America from 8 A.M. to 6 P.M. (EST) on weekdays. I.P. Sharp Associates also provides subscribers with access to a 24-hour answering service for subscribers to leave messages.

Other user aids include two printed directories of database symbols, user manuals, reference guides, and complete online documentation. Consulting services are available on an individual basis.

Value-added products and services include an electronic message service, individual database search services, user software, data storage capabilities, ongoing user training programs, and custom program applications.

5

TRADE & INDUSTRY ASAP
Information Access Company
11 Davis Drive
Belmont, CA 94002

PRODUCT AT-A-GLANCE

Subject Coverage:

News services
National

Produced by Information Access Company, Trade & Industry ASAP includes full text plus indexing to articles from over 80 journals covered in Trade & Industry Index. Flexible searching capability allows the user to choose free text or controlled vocabulary, or any combination of words from the text or index terms.

Subject areas include advertising and marketing, industrial engineering, insurance, retail trade, banking, arts and interior design, aerospace and aviation, business and economics, transportation, and oil and gas.

This product offers full text plus indexing of news releases from PR Newswire, representing over 7,500 corporations, government agencies, and other organizations. It includes quarterly earnings reports, new product announcements, mergers, personnel changes, government activities, and other news.

Coverage begins with January 1983 issues. Some 14,000 records are added each month. It is available through DIALOG, Mead Data Central and BRS.

TRADE & INDUSTRY INDEX
Information Access Company
11 Davis Drive
Belmont, CA 94002

PRODUCT AT-A-GLANCE

Subject Coverage:

News services
National

Produced by Information Access Company, the Trade & Industry Index is an excellent source of information concerning business and technological development for all major industries. The database provides information on new products, company mergers, personnel, management, technological innovations, the regulatory environment, industry trends, forecasts, and statistics.

Three major sources of information are included:

Over 300 trade and general business periodicals.

Cover-to-cover indexing of articles from *The Wall Street Journal* and the business section of the *New York Times*, as well as business-related articles from over 1,100 other magazines, journals, and newspapers.

News releases from PR Newswire, representing over 7,500 companies, government agencies, public relations firms, and other news sources.

Coverage extends from January 1981 to the present. Some 20,000 records are added each month. Daily updates are included in NEWSEARCH. Full text of PR Newswire releases and selected journals may be displayed online or printed offline. It is available through DIALOG.

5

TRADELINE SECURITIES DATABASE

Gregg Corporation
100 Fifth Avenue
Waltham, MA 02254

PRODUCT AT-A-GLANCE

Subject Coverage:

Real-time/Historic market quotations
Bonds, notes, and bills
Options
Stocks, mutual funds, warrants, and rights

Gregg Corporation's Tradeline Securities Database system provides for the management, retrieval, and analysis of current trading statistics, as well as historical securities information. The database provides information on more than 100,000 securities from all major U.S. and Canadian exchanges and the OTC market.

The information contained in the database covers:

Stocks—Historical and current high, low, and closing prices, as well as the trading volume on more than 10,000 equities.

Mutual funds—Current and historical prices on more than 1,000 separate mutual fund issues.

Bonds—High, low, and closing prices, as well as volume traded on over 4,000 corporate bonds and 500 convertible bonds.

Options—Information on more than 16,000 current and recently expired put and call options.

Indexes—Values for more than 225 market and industry group indexes.

Historical coverage of the previous 12½ years of pricing and dividend information is available. Price and volume data include high, low, close, and volume. Dividend and interest information includes record, ex-dividend, payment dates, and the amount and type of distribution on each transaction. Descriptive historical information such as CUSIP number, earnings, and the Beta coefficient is also provided.

The database services brokerage firms, investment analysts, banks, insurers, information redistributors, and capital management firms. These users can use the database to search for and track the history of specific issues, evaluate portfolios, and analyze pricing trends.

The Tradeline database is accessible on a time-sharing basis on the company's mainframe computer or by downloading data to a personal computer. Data are also furnished to nonsystem users on floppy diskette or magnetic tape.

For over 10 years the Tradeline system has been available through major information redistributors. The time-sharing companies and information services offering Tradeline, and their respective market labels, include:

ADP, Inc. Data Services—Fastock II
Citicorp Information Services—Citiquote
Compuserve, Inc.—Value
Data Resources, Inc.—DRI-SEC
McDonnell Douglas Applied Communications Systems Co.—
 Tymquote
National Computer Network, Inc.—Tradeline
National Data Corporation—Rapidquote II

TRADSTAT
SAGE DATA, Inc.
104 Carnegie Center
Princeton, NJ 08540

```
PRODUCT AT-A-GLANCE

Subject Coverage:

   Industry information/
      statistics
   Market news and forecasts
```

SAGE DATA is the North American representitive for Electronic Data Systems' World Trade Statistics Database (TRADSTAT). TRADSTAT contains monthly import/export statistics from Europe, Japan, Canada, and the United States. The data are stored by national custom tariffs codes and for each month include the monthly and cumulative year-to-date figures of quantity and value for each country of origin or destination.

Data are extracted in a variety of formats. To produce a report a user selects the appropriate report type, desired countries of observation, and relevant product codes. The user then has the option of displaying the information in the reporting countries' currency and quantity classification, or entering a predefined conversion factor.

The import/export data derived from TRADSTAT can be used make decisions regarding pricing, new market entrance, and trend and new development reaction. TRADSTAT can be accessed through any national telecommunications network that is linked to the United Kingdom through British Telecom's I.P.S.S. connection. A booklet describing TRADSTAT is available from SAGE DATA upon request.

TRINET COMPANY DATABASE
Trinet, Inc.
9 Campus Drive
Parsippany, NJ 07054

PRODUCT AT-A-GLANCE

Subject Coverage:

**Company information/
 statistics**
*Company background
Lines of business
Market activity
Officers/Directors*

Trinet, Inc. defines a company as a legal entity that owns and operates one or more establishments. Trinet Company Database, therefore, contains approximately 247,000 records on publicly owned, as well as privately held, companies that employ 20 or more people. Each record provides the company name, full address, telephone number, Metropolitan Statistical Area name and code number, public/private ownership, stock symbol (where applicable), number of employees, total sales (with three additional breakdowns), top three lines of business and respective sales figures, and foreign ownership (when 10 percent or more).

A typical search of Trinet Company Database could result in Line-of-Business Reports, which produce the following data allowing a client to analyze strengths and weaknesses of its competitors: Analyzation of a company's structure and detailing of each—industry in which it has operations (by four-digit SIC Code).

> Listing of the top 50 SIC Codes in which the company conducts business.
> Ranking of each four-digit SIC Code by its importance (sales dollars generated).
> Lists for each SIC Code of annual sales generated, percentage of total sales, cumulative share of market held per SIC Code, number of establishments operated, total of manufacturing sales, and total of nonmanufacturing sales.

The primary sources of the database include direct telephone contact; data "exchange" contracts; state directories; trade associations; annual reports and other company filings; and business magazines, periodicals, and clipping services. The database is updated on a daily basis, with complete database reloads sent to subscribers on a quarterly basis.

Trinet Company Database is accessible through DIALOG's Files 531 and 532, Data Resources Incorporated's EstiMarket, Control Data's Business Information Services' X/Market, and Mead Data Central's NEXIS. Further information on the database access services may be obtained by dialing (800) TRINET-1, or in New Jersey (201) 267-3600. User access is via a terminal with a modem and a telephone. The database is accessible through all online vendors approximately 20 hours per day, seven days a week.

Trinet Company Database can also be provided on diskette, which comes ready to use with LOTUS 1-2-3 and dBase software programs.

User support is available through Trinet's Customer Service department. Trained Trinet representatives can be reached by calling toll-free (800) TRINET-1, or in New Jersey (201) 267-3600. If Trinet representatives are unavailable, subscribers can leave a recorded message.

TRINET ESTABLISHMENT
DATABASE

Trinet, Inc.
9 Campus Drive
Parsippany, NJ 07054

Trinet, Inc. defines an establishment as an economic unit producing goods and/or services at a single physical location. Therefore, each discrete physical activity (SIC Code) has an individual record in this file. The Trinet Establishment Database contains approximately 430,000 records of information on publicly owned, as well as privately held, businesses that have 20 or more employees.

The database contains general information such as the business name, mailing address, telephone number, SIC code and description, number of employees, estimated sales, market share, Metropolitan Statistical Area name and code number, corporate linkage, private/public ownership, foreign ownership (if 10 percent or more), stock symbol (where applicable), and the full address and telephone number of the parent company.

A Share-of-Market Report can be generated from this database identifying competitors and a company's position in the industry relative to that of its competitors. This report may also include:

Analysis of the competitive position and market concentrations of companies within any four-digit Standard Industrial Classification Code.

Listing of the top 50 companies, ranked by order of their importance within the designated industry.

Details of each company's annual sales in the designated SIC Code, share of market they hold, and number of establishments they operate in the designated SIC Code.

The primary sources of the database include direct telephone contact; state directories; trade associations; annual reports and other company filings; data "exchange" contracts; and business magazines, periodicals, and clipping services. The database is updated on a daily basis, with complete database reloads sent to subscribers on a quarterly basis.

5

Trinet Establishment Database is accessible through four database access networks—DIALOG, Data Resources Incorporated, Control Data's Business Information Services, and Mead Data Central's NEXIS. Further information on the database access services may be obtained by dialing (800) TRINET-1, or in New Jersey (201) 267-3600. User access is via a terminal with a modem and a telephone. The database is accessible through all online vendors approximately 20 hours per day, seven days a week.

Access is through Data Resources's EstiMarket Service. Charges vary according to the structure of the data received.

Record charges vary according to the reporting structure used. To utilize Data Resources forecasting capabilities in conjunction with Trinet data, a subscription fee of $14,500 per year is charged.

UKFT

Wharton Econometric Forecasting
  Associates
3rd floor, 3624 Science Center
Philadelphia, PA 19104

PRODUCT AT-A-GLANCE

Subject Coverage:

**Real-time/Historic
  market quotations**
*Spot prices
Currencies
Money rates
Stocks, mutual funds,
  warrants, and rights*

UKFT contains detailed coverage of international money and gold markets, the London domestic sterling market, and the London and overseas stock exchanges. The source for the data is the *Financial Times*.

Currency series include spot and forward exchange rates against the dollar and pound, closing Eurocurrency rates for major currencies and different maturities, London money rates, and gold prices. Stock indexes include Financial Times (FT) actuaries for all share and subindexes; FT 30-share; gold; government securities; fixed-interest stock indexes; and major indexes for Europe, North America, the Far East, and Australia.

Data are updated daily and monthly and run until 1986.

5

U.S. CORPORATE NEWS
Moody's Investors Service
99 Church Street
New York, NY 10007

PRODUCT AT-A-GLANCE

Subject Coverage:

News services
National

U.S. Corporate News, produced by Moody's Investors Service, Inc., contains business and financial news on approximately 14,000 companies. First published in 1984, the database is updated weekly with coverage drawn from *Moody's News Reports*. These are the same reports that update Moody's manuals on industrial, financial, utility, and transportation developments, and include data in both textual and tabular formats.

U.S. Corporate News can be used in conjunction with Moody's Corporate Profiles database or by itself. Users can search this database using any of over 100 searchable fields, from SIC Codes to specific event codes such as merger development or stock interest change. These event codes are used to classify news items and let users search not only by company but also across companies for specific events or activities.

This database is particularly useful for users who need current information on financing activity; mergers and acquisitions; management changes; or the most current financial statistics, earnings reports, or changes in bond ratings.

This database is available on the DIALOG system 22 hours every weekday and is accessible during both the workday and evening hours. Saturday hours are also available.

In addition, the service forms the basis of information available on Automatic Data Processing (ADP), Bunker Ramo, and E.F. Hutton's Huttonline. The service is also available for internal information systems use by corporate clients and clients in the securities industry.

Charges for accessing the database are based on connect time. Additional charges are assessed for offline prints, types, and displays. There are no initial or annual subscription fees, log on fees, search charges, or storage charges. Users are billed directly from DIALOG, and no discounts are available.

U.S. Corporate News can be accessed using almost any brand

or model of ASCII-coded personal computer or word processor as long as users have:

Terminal software—asynchronous communications package
Terminal hardware—serial interface and modem
Telephone line

The primary sources for this database include annual and quarterly reports, news releases, proxy statements, regulatory reports, prospectuses, stock exchange bulletins and lists, leading periodicals, and news wire services.

U.S. Corporate News is also available in hard copy via *Moody's News Reports* on a subscription basis and in tape format with the cost and turn-around time dependent on the specific request.

Users may call the company toll-free for assistance with various questions at the following number: (800) 342-5647. This number is staffed Monday through Friday, 9 A.M. to 5 P.M. (EST).

In addition, product brochures and mini-search guides are available as a quick and easy reference tool to supplement the standard "blue sheets" and "chapters" provided by DIALOG. Moody's literature is free of charge.

Moody's plans for the future call for continued expansion of its electronic information resource coverage of public companies. As of late 1986, the information contained on over 20,000 corporations, similar to what is available in the *Moody's Manuals*, was available in machine-readable form.

5

U.S. COST PLANNING FORECAST
Chase Econometrics
150 Monument Road
Bala Cynwyd, PA 19004

PRODUCT AT-A-GLANCE

Subject Coverage:

Econometric data
National

The U.S. Cost Planning Forecasts database provides forecasts of growth rates for more than 300 industrial commodities and wage rates for more than 30 industries. Price forecasts cover all sectors of the U.S. economy. The short-term forecast is updated monthly and extends eight quarters into the future. The long-term forecast is updated quarterly and extends 10 years into the future. Historical data date back as far as 1947.

Data coverage includes aggregate price indexes, commodity price indexes, industrial price indexes, energy price indexes, wage indexes, and construction cost indexes. Special routines include building a weighted index for specific items, development of custom cost indexes, conversion of price series into indexes, production of cost planning graphs and reports, and rebasing a price index to a different base period.

The U.S. Cost Planning Forecast database is listed with Chase Econometrics under the database names IP, IP1, IP2, IPLC, and IPLD and under the disk name IPDB. More information on the database service may be obtained by calling (215) 896-4762.

U.S. ECON
ADP, Inc. Data Services
175 Jackson Plaza
Ann Arbor, MI 48106

To keep the user up-to-date on the overall direction of the banking industry, ADP Data Services has consolidated balance sheet information for banks designated by the Federal Reserve Board as "weekly reporting member banks." These are the larger U.S. banks in key urban areas.

The consolidated summary call reports are updated weekly, compiled by the Federal Reserve Board, and made available to U.S. Econ users within hours of their release. Four reports are offered:

H.4.2C for banks with assets more than $1 billion.
H.4.2 for banks with assets greater than $750 million.
H.4.2A featuring separate consolidations for each Federal Reserve Board District. Contains also a consolidated Call Report for Money Center Banks.
H.4.2D consolidating U.S. branches and agencies of foreign banks.

U.S. Econ includes prime rates, rates on Treasury bills, certificates of deposits, corporate bonds, and all significant financial instruments. It is updated on a daily basis and provides daily rates for the past four years, weekly rates since 1970, and monthly rates since 1946.

5

U.S. ECONOMIC DATABASE
SAGE DATA, Inc.
104 Carnegie Center
Princeton, NJ 08540

PRODUCT AT-A-GLANCE

Subject Coverage:

  Econometric data
  National

The U.S. Economic Database contains a variety of information regarding U.S. macroeconomic conditions. Major areas of coverage include national income and product accounts, personal consumption expenditures, retail sales, housing starts, foreign exchange rates, and industrial production. The database contains more than 3,000 time series consisting of monthly, quarterly, and annual data from 1946 to present day. The database is updated on a daily basis with the latest information from various government indexes, databases, and publications.

The database information is compiled from the *Business Conditions Digest*, *Consumer Price Index*, *Industrial Production Index*, industrial employment, money stock measures, national income and product accounts, personal consumption expenditures, *Producer Price Index*, retail sales, and the *Survey of Current Business*. Forecasts of selected series are available through Probe Economics, Incorporated.

U.S. MACROECONOMIC

Chase Econometrics
150 Monument Road
Bala Cynwyd, PA 19004

U.S. Macroeconomic database provides 13,200 time series of short-term and long-term analysis and forecasts of the U.S. economy. Data are expressed both in current and constant dollars. The database provides detailed forecasts on over 700 national income and product accounts, price, financial, and industry variables. The majority of data is updated within hours of its release.

Specific sector analysis includes the areas of consumer demand, population, military expenditures, financial statistics, retail and wholesale sales and inventories, employment, wages, labor, housing, industrial production, foreign trade, the public sector, the monetary sector, energy, commodity prices, corporate profits, and agriculture. Data are provided on a weekly, monthly, quarterly, semiannual, and annual basis.

Industry data coverage includes gross product originating and factor shares, Annual Survey of Manufactures, shipments and price deflators, investment anticipations, employment and earnings, industrial production index, producer price index, stock price index, manufacturers' shipments, manufacturers' inventory and orders, and automobile and truck data.

The U.S. Macroeconomic database is listed with Chase Econometrics under the database name US and disk name USDB. More information on the database service may be obtained by calling (215) 896-4759.

5

U.S. MACROECONOMIC FORECAST

Chase Econometrics
150 Monument Road
Bala Cynwyd, PA 19004

PRODUCT AT-A-GLANCE

Subject Coverage:

Econometric data
National

The U.S. Macroeconomic Forecast database provides detailed forecasts for the U.S. economy. Special emphasis is placed on national expenditures, income, and production. The short-term forecast is updated within five days of release of the most recent National Income and Product Accounts data.   This short-term forecast extends 9 to 13 quarters into the future. The long-term forecast is updated monthly and extends 10 years into the future. Historical data date back to 1954.

At least three alternative scenarios are available for each forecast: short-term high, low, and topical, and long-term high, low, and cycles. Data categories include: major economic, product, and income indicators; components of consumer and producer prices; personal and national income; federal, state, and local government receipts and expenditures; monetary data; investment and consumption data; export and import data; energy consumption; and industrial production indexes.

The U.S. Macroeconomic Forecast database is listed with Chase Econometrics under the database names MSTS and MSLT and under the disk name MACSIM. More information on the database service may be obtained by calling (215) 896-4705.

UNITED STATES BONDS

I.P. Sharp Associates Limited
2 First Canadian Place
Suite 1900
Toronto, Ontario, Canada M5X 1E3

PRODUCT AT-A-GLANCE

Subject Coverage:

**Real-time/Historic
market quotations**
Bonds, notes, and bills

The United States Bonds database, produced by I.P. Sharp Associates Limited, provides daily trading statistics for more than 4,000 listed bonds, as well as government and agency issues. Data are obtained from the New York and American Bond exchanges, Federal Farm Credit Banks, Bank of Co-ops, FNMA, GNMA, Student Loan Marketing Association, Federal Home Loan Bank, Federal Land Bank, Inter-American Development Bank, and The World Bank. Data also include statistics on FIC Bank Debentures and Treasury bonds, notes, and bills. Every evening the database is updated by 6 P.M. (EST) by approximately 3,800 issues.

Daily trading statistics include the high, low, and closing prices of the bonds, as well as the volume and yield to maturity. Several descriptive facts such as the bond coupon rate and maturity date are also available.

The primary focus of the database is current analysis and historical study of the bond markets of North America. Daily information on government and agency issues is available from July 1, 1983 and from March 1, 1984 for listed bonds.

The database is accessible 24 hours a day, seven days a week, except for a brief maintenance shut-down period on Friday and Saturday nights. The United States Bonds database is accessible directly through I.P. Sharp's IPSANET network and also from Datapac, Telenet, Telex, and Tymnet public networks. Access is through a terminal or personal computer with a 300, 1200, or 2400 baud modem; communications software; and a user account number. General-purpose software allows for data manipulation, analysis, and downloading to a personal computer.

Users access the database via MAGIC, a database retrieval system for computer users with little programming experience; RETRIEVE, a database access system for users with APL programming language knowledge; or through PRICELINK, an I.P. Sharp software product that allows for statistical data collection and

downloading of data on personal computers. Access fees differ for each product.

Compu Trac, a third party software package designed by I.P. Sharp in close connection with Compu Trac, can also be used to access the United States Bonds database. Compu Trac allows for downloading and statistical manipulation of financial data.

User support is offered via calling toll-free ((800) 387-1588) in North America from 8 A.M. to 6 P.M. (EST) on weekdays. There is also a 24-hour answering service available for subscriber messages.

Other user aids include user manuals, reference guides, a printed directory of database symbols, and complete online documentation. Consulting services are available on an individual basis.

Value-added products and services include individual database search services, electronic sending and reception of messages, user software, data storage capabilities, ongoing user training programs, and custom program applications.

UNITED STATES OPTIONS
I.P. Sharp Associates Limited
2 First Canadian Place
Suite 1900
Toronto, Ontario, Canada M5X 1E3

PRODUCT AT-A-GLANCE

Subject Coverage:

**Real-time/Historic
market quotations**
Options

The United States Options database, produced by I.P. Sharp Associates Limited, contains daily trading statistics for all put and call options traded on all major options exchanges in the United States. The primary purpose of the database is to provide options pricing data to securities analysts and options traders. The database contains 136,000 time series pertaining to 14,000 stock options, interest rate options, index options, and foreign currency options. The major exchanges covered by the database include the New York Stock Exchange, American Stock Exchange, Pacific Stock Exchange, Philadelphia Exchange, and the Chicago Board of Options Exchange. The database is updated each trading day within 12 hours of the source update (by 6 A.M. (ET).

The database is accessible 24 hours a day, seven days a week, except for a brief maintenance period on Friday and Saturday nights. The United States Options database is accessible directly through I.P. Sharp's proprietary IPSANET network and also via Datapac, Telenet, Telex, and Tymnet public networks. Access is through a terminal or personal computer with a 300, 1200, or 2400 baud modem; communications software; and an account number. Access software is general-purpose, allowing for data manipulation, analysis, and downloading.

User access to the database is through MAGIC, a database access system designed for novice computer programmers; RETRIEVE, a database access system for users who are knowledgeable in APL computer language; or by PRICELINK, an I.P. Sharp software package that allows information downloading to personal computers. Prices differ for each product.

Compu Trac, a third party software package, can also be used to access the United States Options database. Compu Trac is designed for downloading and statistical manipulation of financial data on personal computers.

5

United States Options database is marketed to investment and portfolio analysts and options traders through a company sales force and via direct mailings.

User support is offered via calling toll-free ((800) 387-1588) in North America from 8 A.M. to 6 P.M. (EST) on weekdays. I.P. Sharp Associates also provides subscribers with access to a 24-hour answering service for subscribers to leave messages.

Other user aids include a printed directory of database symbols, user manuals, database reference guides, and complete online documentation. Subscriber consulting services are available on an individual basis.

Value-added products and services include individual database search services, user software, data storage capabilities, electronic mail services via Telex, ongoing user training programs, and custom program applications.

UNITED STATES STOCK MARKET
I.P. Sharp Associates Limited
2 First Canadian Place
Suite 1900
Toronto, Ontario, Canada M5X 1E3

The United States Stock Market database, produced by I.P. Sharp Associates Limited, contains current and historical prices and volumes for securities listed on Canadian and U.S. stock exchanges. The database provides trading statistics in the form of time series and static data for more than 15,000 common and preferred stocks, warrants, rights, and units for issues traded on the New York, American, Montreal, Midwest, Boston, Pacific, Toronto, and Philadelphia exchanges. Also included are data on the OTC bank, insurance and industrial issues on the NASDAQ, mutual funds, and over 200 market indicators. The database is updated by 6 A.M. (EST) daily within 12 hours of the source update.

United States Stock Market provides current, as well as historical, data on time series facts that include the high and low, bid and ask prices; closing price; volume traded; number of shares outstanding (in 1000's); and earnings and dividends per share. Static facts provided include stock symbols, stock descriptions, SIC codes, CUSIP number, stock split and symbol change data, stock history, and rankings.

The database is accessible 24 hours a day, seven days a week, except for a brief maintenance period on Friday and Saturday nights. The United States Stock Market database is accessible directly through I.P. Sharp's proprietary IPSANET network and also via Datapac, Telenet, Telex, and Tymnet public networks. Access is through a terminal or personal computer with a 300, 1200, or 2400 baud modem; communications software; and an account number. Access software is general purpose, allowing for data manipulation, analysis, and downloading.

User access to the database is through MAGIC, a database access system designed for novice computer programmers; INFO-MAGIC, an interactive information retrieval system from I.P. Sharp Associates; RETRIEVE, a database access system for users who are knowledgeable in APL computer language; or by PRICELINK, an I.P. Sharp software package that allows information downloading to personal computers. Access fees differ with each product.

Compu Trac, a third party software package, can also be used to access the United States Stock Market database. Compu Trac is designed for downloading and statistical manipulation of financial data on personal computers.

United States Stock Market database is marketed to securities analysts, portfolio managers, and options traders through a company sales force and via direct mailings.

User support is offered via calling toll-free ((800) 387-1588) in North America from 8 A.M. to 6 P.M. (EST) on weekdays. I.P. Sharp Associates also provides subscribers with access to a 24-hour answering service for subscribers to leave messages.

Other user aids include a printed directory of database symbols, user manuals, database reference guides, and complete online documentation. Subscriber consulting services are available on an individual basis.

Value-added products and services include electronic message transmission, individual database search services, user software, data storage capabilities, ongoing user training programs, and custom program applications.

THE WALL STREET JOURNAL HIGHLIGHTS ONLINE

Dow Jones News/Retrieval
P.O. Box 300
Princeton, NJ 08543-0330

PRODUCT AT-A-GLANCE

Subject Coverage:

News services
National
Regional
International

The Wall Street Journal Highlights Online database gives headlines and summaries of major news stories in *The Wall Street Journal.* Headlines and summaries include front-page news, front- and back-page features, market pages, editorial columns, and commentaries. If more information is desired after reading the summary, Dow Jones News database or Dow Jones Text-Search Service database can be searched.

Access to The Wall Street Journal Highlights Online database is via either a personal computer with a modem, a communicating word processor or a time-share terminal. The user must have a News/Retrieval password. Access to the database is through the major public networks—Tymnet, Telenet, Datapac, and DowNet (Dow Jones's own network). The database is available 22 hours a day, seven days a week, from 6 A.M. to 4 A.M. (EST).

5

WASHINGTON FINANCIAL REPORTS

The Bureau of National Affairs, Inc.
Room 601 South
1231 25th Street NW
Washington, DC 20037

PRODUCT AT-A-GLANCE

Subject Coverage:

Industry information/ statistics
Industry overviews
Legal actions and issues

Washington Financial Reports contains information on and analysis of federal financial institutions, regulatory policy, litigation, banking legislation, and investment. The database includes official reports of agency rulings and speeches by industry and government leaders.

The database covers developments affecting banks, savings and loan associations, and credit unions. Specific topics include deposit insurance reform, adjustable rate mortgages, international banking, credit union practices, bank mergers and acquisitions, bank holding companies, and agency regulations.

Agencies reported on include the Federal Reserve Board, the Federal Deposit Insurance Corporation, the Comptroller of the Currency, the Federal Home Loan Bank Board, the National Credit Union Administration, and the Federal Savings and Loan Corporation.

The database is accessible via NEXIS of Mead Data Central and via Executive Telecom Systems, Incorporated. It covers the time from January 1982 to present day on NEXIS and from March 1985 to present day on Executive Telecom Systems, Incorporated. The database files are updated on a weekly basis. The database's corresponding printed product is the *Washington Financial Reports.*

THE WEEKLY ECONOMIC UPDATE
Dow Jones News/Retrieval
P.O. Box 300
Princeton, NJ 08543-0330

```
PRODUCT AT-A-GLANCE

Subject Coverage:
  News services
  National
```

This database provides a brief roundup of critical economic news and statistics. It's compiled by the News/Retrieval editorial staff from *The Wall Street Journal*, the Dow Jones News Service, and *Barron's*.

It includes:

Executive summary of the week's economic news.
Day-by-day summary of the past week's events.
Recently released economic indicators (inflation rate, unemployment).
Analysis of the week's economic topics.
Schedule of when the new economic indicators will be released in the near future.

Access to The Weekly Economic Update database is via either a personal computer with a modem or a communicating word processor or a time-share terminal and a News/Retrieval account with a password. Access to the database is through the major public networks of Tymnet, Telenet, and Datapac and also through DowNet, Dow Jones' own network. The database is available 22 hours a day, seven days a week, from 6 A.M. to 4 A.M. (EST).

5

WEFA

Wharton Econometric Forecasting
 Associates
3rd floor, 3624 Science Center
Philadelphia, PA 19104

PRODUCT AT-A-GLANCE

Subject Coverage:

Econometric data
Monetary aggregates
National

WEFA includes data on the money supply, money market rates, consumer credit, housing starts and construction, and retail sales. Data sources are the departments of Commerce, Labor, Energy, Transportation, and the Interior; Federal Reserve Board; Internal Revenue Service; and various published articles and trade journals.

Varying series are updated monthly, quarterly, or annually. The data begin in 1900.

WEFAAG
Wharton Econometric Forecasting
 Associates
3rd floor, 3624 Science Center
Philadelphia, PA 19104

PRODUCT AT-A-GLANCE

Subject Coverage:

> **Econometric data**
> *National*
> *Regional*

WEFAAG has data for supply, demand, and prices for major agricultural commodities on an annual, quarterly, and monthly basis. The source for the data is the U.S. Department of Agriculture.

Commodities carried include rice, wheat, corn, chicken, beef, pork, dairy products, and cotton.

The data are updated annually, quarterly, or monthly and begin in 1910.

WEFAHF
Wharton Econometric Forecasting
  Associates
3rd floor, 3624 Science Center
Philadelphia, PA 19104

PRODUCT AT-A-GLANCE

Subject Coverage:

Econometric data
Monetary aggregates
National
Regional

WEFAHF contains selected weekly data on interest rates, reserves at Federal Reserve banks, money stock components, futures and spot price indexes, stock indexes, exchange rates, bank loans, car sales, oil rig counts, business failures, commercial paper outstanding, and so on. Major data sources are Federal Reserve releases, newspapers, government reports, and trade associations.

Data are updated weekly and begin in 1959.

WEXBASE
Wharton Econometric Forecasting
 Associates
3rd floor, 3624 Science Center
Philadelphia, PA 19104

PRODUCT AT-A-GLANCE

Subject Coverage:

Econometric data
International
**Real-time/Historic
 market quotations**
Spot prices

WEXBASE contains data for monthly spot exchange rates, current account, and domestic product deflators. Countries covered include Belgium, Canada, France, Germany, the United Kingdom, Italy, Japan, the Netherlands, Switzerland, and the United States. The forecast extends 60 months into the future. Quarterly average spot exchange rates are available for 55 currencies. The source for the data is the International Monetary Fund's *International Financial Statistics*, the *Financial Times, The Wall Street Journal*, and Wharton estimates.

Data are updated monthly, quarterly, and annually and begin in 1956.

5

WLDREI

Wharton Econometric Forecasting
 Associates
3rd floor, 3624 Science Center
Philadelphia, PA 19104

PRODUCT AT-A-GLANCE

Subject Coverage:

Econometric data
International

WLDREI provides recent economic indicators for Australia, Belgium, Canada, France, Germany, Italy, Japan, the Netherlands, Sweden, Switzerland, the United Kingdom, and the United States. The sources for the data are *OECD Main Economic Indicators,* IMF *International Financial Statistics*, national publications, and correspondents in Wharton's international network.

Data are updated monthly and begin in 1960.

CHAPTER FIVE

Enabling Resources: Telecommunications and Complementary Application Software

The online products and services we have discussed thus far represent only one component of the information equation. In order to calculate an optimal solution, a portfolio of enabling resources has to be constructed. This portfolio takes the form of communications software (and required hardware), which provides the electronic link to the online product or service, and complementary application software, which provides the capability to manipulate the raw data for analysis and decision making.

To access any of the online database services that we've discussed, you will first need a way to communicate with them to make inquiries, review results, or download specific information. The telephone network becomes your electronic window to the world of online information only after you have the right hardware and software environment.

Application software makes its contribution only after information has been downloaded. When the software is used to analyze the information, the equation is completed. In Chapter 3, we used a spreadsheet package to analyze numeric data and a word processor to format and complete the report. However, in many instances, more sophisticated technical or fundamental analysis capability or portfolio management software may be required before the information retrieved from an online source has any value.

This chapter helps you understand the differences between a

"dumb" terminal and a microcomputer, lists several of the communications alternatives available to you, and provides a working vocabulary and a features and functions checklist to help you obtain the right combination of hardware and software. Appendix C is another quick index of popular communications software products.

In the case of complementary software, we've surveyed the marketplace for software that can be used with many of the products and services contained in the matrices. Based on your specific requirements, the software packages profiled at the end of the chapter can be used as a starting point for the acquisition of your own portfolio of analytical tools.

TELECOMMUNICATIONS — THE ELECTRONIC LINK BETWEEN YOU AND YOUR INFORMATION

In the 1970s, telecommunications access to online databases was limited to the use of a "dumb" terminal and a modem. The hardware only had the capability to provide a keyboard to input requests and a printer or video screen to receive the output. The database host ccmputer ran all the programs to construct your inquiry and configure the data in the right format so that you could view or print the results. The capability to bring raw data or summarized information back from the database computer, or download, for further analysis or manipulation was nonexistent. Now, new microcomputer technology has made it possible to access online databases quickly and economically. The introduction of the microcomputer has changed the entire approach to online access.

Instead of having to rely on the database computer to provide everything for you, you can do it yourself with the processing power and capability of your microcomputer. With the right combination of hardware and software, you can construct your inquiry, submit it to the host, and then review the results on the video screen or printer, or bring data back from the host computer and store them on hard or floppy disks for further analysis.

In general, there are three communications alternatives you have to understand before you spend money on microcomputer hardware and software. The various databases can be accessed using specialized vendor-provided software, generalized communications software, or a gateway. Keep in mind, however, that neither vendor-provided nor general communications software makes the connection with the telephone company. This function is performed by a piece of hardware called a modem. Not only must your software be compatible with your micro and the database, it must also be compatible with the modem. As with the hundred or so varieties of microcomputers and terminals available on the market today, you can find communications packages and modems ranging in price from $50 to $600 or more depending on their capabilities.

Many of the large information providers, such as The Source and DIALOG, market specialized communications software in addition to providing databases and other information services. These packages provide all of the software you need to communicate with the database computer. All you have to do is correctly connect your modem and load the software. In addition, they often provide automated routines that will dial the number you want and provide your log-on, password, and account information to the service. Although this may sound great at first, this alternative offers you the least flexibility. Because the software has been specifically written to interface with a provider's computer, it probably won't work with other database products or services. Thus, you may find that you will be using a different package for each provider to set up your computer hardware, construct inquiries, and make the telephone connection to the database.

The second alternative, general purpose communications software, provides you the most technical flexibility. Most of the packages on the market today allow you to emulate several terminals and operate either in command or menu mode. Most novice users begin by using the menu mode. Menus have been developed that ask for specific information needed by the software program to dial and connect with a service or database. General purpose packages also provide the correct emulation software to make hardware electronically behave like the type of terminal that is accepted by the particular database computer being accessed.

Command mode allows you to interact with the modem using commands similar to those provided with your operating system. For example, these commands allow you to change the modem settings, dial the telephone number, or end the call and disconnect. Unless you are a frequent user, another set of commands to remember may be more of a distraction than a help. We've found that the menu approach usually provides everything you need to communicate with your service.

Several of the integrated packages on the market today, like Symphony, Framework2, and JAZZ, offer communications packages in addition to spreadsheets, word processing, databases, and graphics. The features of these packages may be just what you need, but make sure the communications function is compatible with the databases you use. Just because JAZZ can be used to access Mead Data Central's LEXIS and NEXIS databases, it doesn't necessarily mean you can also use it for databases offered by THE Source.

The third alternative, gateways, provides the greatest flexibility for both novice and experienced users. Not only does this software provide the technical interface, it also takes much of the confusion out of using online databases—especially when you are using more than one. Gateways act as a "one-stop shop" for information. Once you learn how to use the package, it will modify your inquiry into the format required by the service you are using. Obviously, learning only one set of rules is better than having to learn several.

Gateway products may be marketed as either a remote or a local package. The local version consists of the software that modifies your inquiries locally on your own computer and makes it possible for you to experiment without running up a big telephone bill. In this mode, the only time you dial out to get access to the databases is after you have structured your query and are ready to go. The remote version runs only on the gateway computer. You can use a dumb terminal, a microcomputer equipped with communications software, and a modem, or even a communicating word processor, to use this version of a gateway. With any configuration, though, you must access the gateway by using the telephone system, which begins to build up the charges right away. In either instance, local or remote, the services provided by the gateway are usually the same.

There are several features and functions that you should consider as you evaluate these alternatives. As you found in the preceding chapters, a new vocabulary must be learned in order to understand the differences between products and how they can be used to your benefit. Once you understand the differences, you will be able to create and use a checklist to determine the right approach to take based on the information needs of your business.

A COMMUNICATIONS FEATURES AND FUNCTIONS PRIMER

To get you started, we've provided a list of important features, functions, and concepts that should be understood before you select the hardware and software products that allow you to access your databases. This list is not all-inclusive, but does address most of the common features and functions accommodated by the major providers. Be sure to examine the technical literature provided by your proposed database vendors before you buy.

Auto-dial

The auto-dial feature provides the capability of placing a telephone call. A telephone number can be entered from the keyboard, dialed from a directory, or used as part of an automated logon command sequence. While some packages allow you to create a directory with several different telephone numbers, others limit you to entering the number manually from the keyboard each time you use the software. In the case of specialized packages, the only number you may be able to use is that of the provider.

Auto-search or SDI (Selective Dissemination of Information)

Some specialized packages will automatically submit a search, set your computer up to receive the information, and then print or store it. Using macros, complex searches can be developed, stored, and then used repeatedly. This feature is usually provided with the specialized packages and can often be developed with the more sophisticated general purpose software. The searches can also be performed automatically by the provider so that the information is ready when you sign on. If your business requires that you ask for specific information concerning a business or industry on a repetitive basis, the SDI/auto-search feature is a must.

Break Keys

When was the last time you made a mistake? A better question may be: Once you realize a mistake, do you have the capability to correct it? You will want the ability to transmit a break key to tell the database computer to stop what it is doing. Read your documentation carefully, because using the break key may save you a lot of money.

Documentation

We can't overemphasize the value of good documentation. Even though many of the software vendors provide a telephone number for questions, we've found that the best resource is the documentation provided with the software. Make sure that it is readable, easy to use, and most of all, comprehensive. (Several important topics are included in the checklist.) If you can't use the documentation easily, you won't be able to use the software either. Most important, before you buy, find someone else that invested time and money in the package and ask them what they think of it.

Downloading

There are several methods of downloading information from a service (bringing the results of an inquiry "down" from the database computer to your microcomputer), but the best one is the ability to receive and store data directly on a disk or diskette. Some of the packages we've seen only allow you to store the information in RAM (random access memory), which is the memory in your microcomputer. You may find that the quantity retrieved during a search will be greater than you thought, especially if you're just getting started and haven't got your search strategies tuned just right. The end result is that some, or even possibly all, of the information will be lost. Worse yet, from a cost standpoint, is downloading the data directly to a printer. The communications connection is much faster than the printer and must wait for the printer before the next batch of information is transmitted. When you're paying for total time, a slow printer can really build up the charges.

Error Checking

Error checking means that certain rules are followed by both your computer and the host. When information is transmitted, your terminal has to check it and tell the sender whether or not it has been received correctly. If something happened during transmission and the information is not good, it will be sent again. There are many vendor-specific error-checking programs available, so make sure that you have one that is supported by the database computer. Even though you may use your software for textual data, where the meaning is not lost if one letter is incorrect, you may often work with numbers, where it may cost you a lot of money if a transmission mistake goes undetected. Without getting technical about how error-checking works, suffice it to say that it is an essential function to look for in communications software. It may save you a lot of problems and a lot of money.

Help

Most of the packages we've examined have some form of online help. When you type HELP or strike a specified key, the program will respond with a definition of what you can do or will provide a "Help" menu. This feature is valuable to both the novice and the expert user as it may eliminate lengthy searching through documentation.

Macros

Macros are a series of commands that can be stored and then used again and again. For example, the commands for auto–log on set the computer and modem up to communicate, dial the correct number for the services that you want, log on to the service, and provide the necessary identification, password, and account information. Other macros can be established to automatically store retrieved information on disk, to print unattended, or to log off a service at the end of a session.

Protocols

Protocols are the rules that must be observed while communicating with another computer. They establish what the data will look like when your computer receives or sends them. For example, protocols, or rules, will be established for the size of a "word" (7 or 8 bits), speed of transmission (300, 1200, or 2400 bits per second), parity checking (for the detection of errors), start/stop conventions, and if carriage returns or line feeds are used for textual data. Many of the general purpose communications packages provide the capability to make technical changes so that your particular configuration can talk to many different computers using different rules.

Accuracy and throughput are important factors when looking at protocols. There are no industry error-correcting standards yet, so many vendors have developed their own protocols. A problem, though, is that both computers must be able to understand what the other is sending it. If you get a package with a proprietary protocol, you may find that you will have no one to talk to. For the near term, you should probably stay with a vendor that supports XMODEM or X.PC, or for the UNIX operating system environment, the Columbia–University produced KERMIT.

Status Lines and Screens

Status lines usually appear at the bottom of the screen. They are designed to keep you informed of what is going on when you are communicating with the database computer. You will usually find such information as printer status, disk status, and elapsed time.

Status screens, on the other hand, indicate the technical settings you have made to your computer. The status screen is the first place you would look if you were having trouble connecting to a provider.

You don't have to be a technical wizard to use your communications package. Generally, the most you have to be able to do is to read the requirements specified by the service and then use the status screen to change the options displayed until your computer conforms to the technical communication rules imposed by the service. You really don't need to know the engineering behind such terms as "baud," "parity," or "comm port," or the difference between stop/start bits and data bits. Any package should allow you the opportunity to change one or more of these parameters, but usually you will find this flexibility only in the generalized packages.

Printer Control

At times it may be convenient to use the printer to capture small amounts of information. In the event you find that you want to do this, your communications package should be able to control the printer and turn it off or on during a session.

Tutorials

The easiest way to learn a new task is by doing it. Take the time to look over the materials offered with a package. A tutorial will take you through many of the features and functions of a package at your own pace. When you have mastered the basics, use the manual to learn more sophisticated procedures.

Uploading

Uploading an inquiry is particularly important when you are paying for connect time or communications charges. Rather than connecting to your service and composing an inquiry online, you would construct your inquiry offline and then transmit it "up" to the computer on which the database resides. The only difference you should expect in the service you receive will be in your monthly bill.

WHO PAYS FOR THE TELEPHONE CALL?
"1-800" AND PUBLIC NETWORK ALTERNATIVES

Even after you have made all your decisions regarding hardware and software, you still have to decide how you will place the telephone call to your vendor. If your database provider doesn't give you an "800" number, you'll probably have to pay for the call by dialing direct or by using one of the privately owned networks that buy telecommunications transmission time and circuits from AT&T in bulk and then resell it to individuals or companies. These carriers make their money by buying at wholesale and selling at a price below AT&T. Any discussion about database communications is incomplete without a brief overview.

The oldest and best known time-sharing or value-added networks (VAN) are Tymnet, Telenet, and Uninet. These service providers have been relatively unchallenged in the market place for the last 15 years because of the size and growth of the market. In 1986, Telenet bought Uninet and announced a new service called PC Pursuit. TELENET is now a subsidiary of US Sprint. There are other regionally based companies, but you should check their geographical coverage before you pass up the services provided by the nationals.

In many cases, these network vendors have a local telephone

number in major metropolitan areas for gaining access to the network. They all operate at least 20 hours a day and provide discounts for off-hour use. However, you may not be billed directly for the time spent on the system. It has been the industry practice for the database provider to pay the telecommunications bills and then bill the user.

Depending on the provider that you want to access, detailed sign-on instructions may differ. For the most part, however, these companies provide a good way to access your data at a low cost per minute when compared to normal long distance rates.

New Ways to Communicate

Emerging technologies are playing an increasingly important role in this industry. As the breakup of AT&T continues, new companies enter the communications field with satellites, FM sideband, and pocket radio communications products. These technologies are designed to bypass either the local telephone company or the long distance telephone network, or both. All of the new entries have the potential of saving a lot of money when compared to long distance dial or leased line charges.

We have looked at several of these companies and have found them to be both technically feasible and cost effective. Many of the large database providers have indicated that they will support your use of these technologies. In many cases, however, it requires orders involving multiple sites before the economics make these alternatives cost effective.

When it appears that these new communications technologies are the way to go, implementation becomes a minor issue: The communications vendors provide all necessary hardware, software, and installation support. All you usually have to do is hook up your terminals or micros and get to work.

What's Important and What's Not

Compatibility is the key to success. The communications software and modem that you acquire must work together with the entire configuration as a team, whether you already have a system or you're just putting one together. This team includes hardware components such as random access memory (RAM), disk drives, and input/output ports. The communications system software must be able to execute under the supervision of the operating system software. If all of the pieces don't work together properly, you won't be getting the return on the investment you expected.

Even though there are hundreds of products and combinations of products available on the market today, there are only a few technical features and functions that you must consider before you make the acquisition. If you take the time to make a few comparisons, you'll find the combination that will provide the simplicity, versatility, and power that you need for the right price.

FEATURES AND FUNCTIONS CHECKLIST

Operating Systems

Pay attention to the release levels required. For IBM and compatibles, look for systems that require release 3.0 or higher. You may have some trouble finding software that has been written for IBM's new OS-2. Most vendors, however, are working to create packages that take advantage of this new operating system.

Hardware Requirements

Examine the memory requirements and disk drives required disk, one or two floppies, or both). These requirements are important to consider before downloading search results.

Error-Correcting Protocols Used

Avoid custom designed protocols compatible only with certain database products. Look for standard protocols supported such as XMODEM.

Modems Supported

Make sure that modems sold by several different vendors are supported with such features as variable speeds (300, 1200, or 2400 bps), auto-dial, and unattended mode.

Software Features

On-Screen Help
Menu- or Command-Driven
Macro Capability
User-Definable Function Keys
Automatic Hang-up

Documentation

Ensure that the documentation provided is complete and up-to-date. Submit it to a 30-minute test. If you can't navigate through the software with the help of the manual with minimum effort, beware!

COMPLEMENTARY APPLICATION SOFTWARE

Online information products and services are only one piece of the information equation. To effectively analyze data and turn them into decision information requires complementary application software working in concert with your online sources.

Word Processing

This software may be as simple as a word processing package, which helps prepare textual files such as abstracts or investment reports into well formatted, concise, executive presentations. There are hundreds of word processing packages on the market today. Each package may have different "bells and whistles," but all are capable of manipulating text and formatting it for presentation. Some of the more popular packages are WordStar Professional, WordPerfect, and Displaywrite 4 for the IBM PC (and compatibles) world and Word Version, WordPerfect, and Apple Writer II for the Apple and Apple Macintosh world.

Spreadsheet

Spreadsheets are software packages that can save you a lot of manual effort with a pencil and calculator. These packages provide the capability to analyze numeric information. Their features and functions have been significantly enhanced since their introduction in the form of VisiCalc, SuperCalc, and Lotus 1-2-3. Although one or another package may have a unique capability that sets it apart in the market, all of them provide the basic capabilities necessary to eliminate some drudgery from your life.

More Technically Elegant Packages

Be it a technical analysis package to chart futures prices, a fundamental analysis system to sensitize earnings, or a portfolio management system to track trade performance, application software to accomplish these functions is available in the market today. The bulk of this type of application software focuses on the capital markets: stocks, bonds, futures, and the like. These systems are used in banks as well as in brokerage houses, portfolio management firms, and investment banks. A common element of all the packages is that they magnify the value of the information you retrieve from an online source.

Software Futures

On the horizon is a new genre of software that will retrieve information from multiple services and then analyze and format that information for you. These so-called expert systems are presently being developed for financial planning, interest rate forecasting, and demographic analysis. These application packages should be commercially available early in 1988 and run on a variety of microcomputer hardware.

We recommend that whenever you need specialized software to help you accomplish your tasks, you first call the marketing or customer service department of the provider or producer of your online database. They should have an up-to-date list of all software that will work with their system. As a user of online information, you should carefully monitor the trade press of your industry and the major PC publications for breakthroughs in this area.

SOFTWARE PROFILES

The material contained in the Software Profiles was obtained directly from both the companies and reliable industry sources.

From time to time, product or company ownership, as well as product descriptions, may change. **Inclusion in this chapter does not constitute an endorsement by either the authors or the publisher.**

SOFTWARE PROFILES INDEX

Software:	Analytical Broker

Company:	Analytical Traders Group P.O. Box 5132 Columbus, GA 31906
Phone:	(404) 327-5511 (404) 645-2100
E-Mail:	None
Telex:	None
Features:	An extensive collection of timing indicators for hedging or speculation, using technical analysis. Contains nine technical analysis systems with reports and graphs for traders or brokers. Allows simulation of past data for profitability on different systems. Provides auto-process mode and auto-daily reports.
Providers:	Nite-Line and Securities Data Access
Target Market:	Brokers, hedgers, commodities traders, stock traders
Distribution:	Direct marketing
Hardware:	IBM PC or compatible, 256K, two drives
Price:	$395 to $695 20 percent volume discount

Software:	CNS Analyst

Company:	Commodity News Services, Inc. 2100 W. 89th Street Leawood, KS 66206
Phone:	(913) 642-7373 (800) 255-6490
E-Mail:	None
Telex:	None
Features:	Provides intraday and historical charting, quotes, and cash price information. Allows algebraic equations to be programmed by the user. Uses windows to display multiple screens. All information is from Knight-Ridder. The system is command-driven.
Providers:	Commodity News Service
Target Market:	Brokers and private traders
Distribution:	Telemarketing
Hardware:	IBM PC, 256K RAM
Price:	Starts at $650 a month plus exchange fees. Leasing programs are available.

Software:	DAIS-GRAPH

Company:	Drexel Burnham Lambert, Inc. / DAIS GROUP 60 Broad Street, 28th Floor New York, NY 10004
Phone:	(212) 480-6281
E-Mail:	None
Telex:	None
Features:	DAIS-GRAPH provides online color graphics capabilities to investment managers with IBM or IBM-compatible personal computers.

Graphics applications include:

> **Price and Volume**—A chart covering three years of history and displaying closing price, daily volume, 50-day average price, and S&P 500.
>
> **Market Flow**—A graphical presentation of cumulative, block, and nonblock money flow patterns along with price and volume since fourth quarter 1983.
>
> **Relative Valuation**—A chart of historical relative valuation measures (price, EPS, P/E, P/B, and ROE) covering either a five- or ten-year period.
>
> **Equity Risk Premium**—A chart displaying the S&P 500, long-term bond rate, and Equity Risk Premium.

Providers:	Drexel Burnham Lambert equity valuation databases, COMPUSTAT, Value Line, I/B/E/S, and Zacks consensus earnings databases
Target Market:	Professional investors
Distribution:	Direct
Hardware:	IBM PC, XT, AT, or any fully IBM-compatible microcomputer (requires IBM graphics board), DOS 2.0 and up, 256K, two disk drives
Price:	Varies based on client relationship

Software:	DAIS-LINK

Company:	Drexel Burnham Lambert, Inc./DAIS GROUP 60 Broad Street, 28th floor New York, NY 10004
Phone:	(212) 480-6281
E-Mail:	None
Telex:	None
Features:	Accesses Drexel equity investment information from Lotus 1-2-3 or Symphony, and enabling users to automatically retrieve data from more than 25 fundamental, techncial, and exception databases containing over five million pieces of equity information (e.g., daily pricing, relative valuation measures, earning estimates, COMPUSTAT, Value Line, and much more). User's spreadsheets are automatically updated with a single keystroke.
Providers:	Drexel Burnham Lambert equity valuation databases, COMPU-STAT, Value Line, I/B/E/S, and Zacks consensus earnings databases
Target Market:	Professional investors
Distribution:	Direct
Hardware:	IBM PC, XT, and AT, or any fully IBM-compatible microcomputer, DOS 2.0 and up, 256K, two disk drives
Price:	Varies based on client relationship

Software:	DAIS-SCREEN

Company:	Drexel Burnham Lambert, Inc./DAIS GROUP 60 Broad Street, 28th floor New York, NY 10004
Phone:	(212) 480-6281
E-Mail:	None
Telex:	None
Features:	An interactive screening and reporting system that selects stocks based on specified financial criteria. Users may screen against any existing data item on the DAIS SYSTEM (e.g., daily pricing, relative valuation measures, earnings estimates, COMPUSTAT, Value Line, and much more) or derive their own analytic ratios and formulas. Once a group of stocks is selected, users can either examine the results online or save the results in a file for further analysis.
Providers:	Drexel Burnham Lambert equity valuation databases, COMPUSTAT, Value Line, I/B/E/S, and Zacks consensus earnings databases
Target Market:	Professional investors
Distribution:	Direct
Hardware:	IBM PC, XT, and AT, or any fully IBM-compatible microcomputer, DOS 2.0 and up, 256K, two disk drives
Price:	Varies based on client relationship

Software:	THE DATA CONNECTION

Company:	QFS, Inc. P.O. Box 565 Ardsley, NY 10502
Phone:	(914) 591-6990
E-Mail:	Compuserve 76706, 440
Telex:	None
Features:	Updates automatically from Compuserve without requiring user knowledge of commands.
Providers:	Compuserve Information Service
Target Market:	Private investors and professional brokers, market analysts
Distribution:	Referral
Hardware:	IBM PC, XT, AT or compatibles with 128K memory, Hayes (300, 1200, or 2400 baud) modem
Price:	$99.95

Software:	DSG/INSIGHT

Company: Decision Support Group, Inc.
P.O. Box 82
Chester, NJ 07930

Phone: (201) 879-5211

E-Mail: None

Telex: None

Features: Integrates the primary technical analysis functions of time series processing, modeling, graphics, trading system development and evaluation, automation, and communications.

Provides the ability to establish buy, sell and/or short positions, run decision models and then conduct professional evaluations of these models using past history and considering both stop-loss and commission parameters established by the user.

Providers: Hale Systems Dial/Data Merlin Database

Target Market: Professional traders, serious private investors

Distribution: Direct marketing

Hardware: IBM PC, XT or 100 percent compatibles, 320K, two disk drives, either a dual floppy or a floppy-hard disk system, composite video, RGB color, IBM color graphics board

Epson or compatible (e.g., KX-P1091.)

DC Hayes Smartmodem, AT&T 4000

Price: DSC/INSIGHT Software package is $495. Purchase of five or more is 40 percent off. Demo Diskette is $35 with credit toward purchase of full system

Software:	EASY

Company:	Zacks Investment Research, Inc. 2 North Riverside Plaza Chicago, IL 60606
Phone:	(312) 559-9405
E-Mail:	None
Telex:	None
Features:	Complete system for equity research and equity portfolio management
Providers:	Zacks, Value Line, Media General, COMPUSTAT
Target Market:	Professional equity management firms
Distribution:	Direct sales force
Hardware:	XT/512K optical disk, included with product
Price:	Leased at $6000 per year

| **Software:** | THE EQUALIZER |

Company:	Charles Schwab & Company, Inc. Investor Information Services 101 Montgomery Street—Dept. S San Francisco, CA 94104
Phone:	(800) 334-4455
E-Mail:	None
Telex:	None
Features:	Provides access to real-time and 15-minute delayed quotes and news. Trades can be executed online with Schwab. Includes a portfolio management system that is updated online. THE EQUALIZER is menu-driven.
Providers:	Dow Jones News/Retrieval; Standard and Poor's Marketscope and COMPUSTAT; Warner; and Lynch, Jones, & Ryan
Target Market:	Individual investors
Distribution:	Direct sales and marketing
Hardware:	IBM PC, XT, or compatible, 128K RAM Apple IIe, IIc, 128K RAM Modem required Graphics monitor and printer recommended
Price:	$99

Software:	FINPAK

Company:	Warner Computer Systems, Inc. One University Plaza Hackensack, NJ 07601
Phone:	(201) 489-1580 (212) 661-2860 (800) 626-4634
E-Mail:	None
Telex:	None
Features:	Screens a universe of over 6,000 companies from COMPUSTAT's annual and quarterly databases, which provide balance sheet, income statements, and other financial data. **Exchange Master**, Warner's proprietary database providing stock market trading data on all public companies is also available. **Institutional Broker Estimate Systems** (I/B/E/S), which monitors weekly forecasts for over 3,000 companies from 2,000 plus security analysts, provides additional important data. First-time screening package for **Disclosure II**, a database that provides fundamental financial and textual information on all publicly traded companies. Can be downloaded into Lotus 1-2-3 or Symphony.
Providers:	Warner Computer Systems, Inc
Target Market:	Investors
Distribution:	Sales force and direct marketing
Hardware:	IBM family of PCs with 256K memory
Price:	Varies based on usage
Other:	Also offers database retrieval and spreadsheet download.

Software:	THE FUNDAMENTAL INVESTOR

Company: Savant Corporation
P.O. Box 440278
Houston, TX 77244

Phone: (713) 556-8363 (in Texas)
(800) 231-9900

E-Mail: None

Telex: None

Features: Contains fundamental analysis, communications, and fundamental database programs. The fundamental database allows storage of over 35 parameters on 2,000 securities per floppy disk, or up to 400 items on fewer securities.

Data can be entered and edited manually or automatically by modem. The analysis program allows screening of all securities in the database on up to 100 user-defined criteria per screen; sorting of stocks on a single parameter (before or after screening); calculation of financial ratios from basic financial information (using spreadsheet-like functions); and sorting of stocks on the weighted average of a group of parameters. Data can be downloaded from online databases, and almost any commercial database can be accessed manually with the terminal program included with the package.

Providers: Warner Computer Systems; Disclosure, Inc.; Ford Investor Services; Hale Systems Merlin; Dow Jones News/Retrieval databases

Target Market: Brokers, institutions, and private investors

Distribution: Direct marketing

Hardware: IBM PC, XT, AT, or compatible with 320K or more RAM, DOS 2.0 or later operating system, two disk drives or fixed disk (fixed disk strongly recommended)

Hayes, Novation, or Racal Vadik (300, 1200, or 2400 baud) modems

Price: $395

Software:	FutureSource

Company:	Commodity Communications Corporation 420 Eisenhower Lane North Lombard, IL 60148
Phone:	(800) 621-2628
E-Mail:	None
Telex:	None
Features:	Real-time quotes direct from exchanges of choice with over a dozen different studies and technical analysis
Providers:	Product interfaces with an in-house database
Target Market:	Brokers, hedgers, and speculators
Distribution:	Telemarketing and field sales force
Hardware:	IBM PC or compatible, 256K, two disk drives
Price:	Based on usage

Software:	High Tech
Company:	Microvest P.O. Box 272 Macomb, IL 61455
Phone:	(309) 837-4512
E-Mail:	None
Telex:	None
Features:	Tracks market indicators using technical analysis. Utilizes up to 33 different indicators; has auto-run feature and split screens; uses both command set and menus.
Providers:	Uses Commodity Systems, Inc. and Nite-Line databases, or any service that offers CSI compatible format
Target Market:	Professional traders, bankers, brokers, and farmers
Distribution:	Sold via a sales force, direct marketing, and retail sales
Hardware:	IBM PC or compatible, 256K RAM, color graphics card, Epson or IBM Compatible printer
Price:	$495 $35 for running demo plus manual $10 for demo disk

Software:	Marketactics Intraday Demand Graphs

Company:	RAC Information Systems, Inc. 11 Middle Neck Road Great Neck, NY 11021
Phone:	(516) 829-9500
E-Mail:	None
Telex:	None
Features:	A system designed to improve traders' and portfolio managers' market transaction timing with proprietary graphs based on David Bostian's "Intraday Demand Analysis" model. Plots, displays, and prints a chart that shows, for each stock or index that the subscriber maintains on his/her PC, one year of daily prices and the proprietary Intraday Demand line.
Providers:	Marketactics RAC's Database
Target Market:	Professional investors
Distribution:	Direct
Hardware:	IBM PC or compatible, 256KB memory, one floppy drive, Epson-type dot matrix printer, 300 or 1200 baud modem (e.g., Hayes)
Price:	Monthly billing is $500 for a total annual cost of $6,000 Quarterly billing is $1450 for a total annual cost of $5,800 Semiannual billing is $2,800 for a total annual cost of $5,600 Annual billing is $5,400

Software:	MetaStock

Company:	Computer Asset Management P.O. Box 26743 Salt Lake City, UT 84126
Phone:	(801) 964-0391 (800) 882-3040
E-Mail:	None
Telex:	None
Features:	The program features a multiwindow environment that allows charts to be displayed on the screen in multiple movable windows. This allows the user to display up to 36 charts on the screen at one time. Windows are also used to display "Help" windows and to provided a smooth menu-driven interface during graphic charting. The program also features many studies, user formulas, manual or modem updating, extensive trend lines, and much more.
Providers:	Commodity System, Inc.; Compuserve; Hale Systems, Inc.; Interactive Data Corp.; I.P. Sharp Associates; National Computer Network; Warner Computer, Inc
Target Market:	Investment professionals and individual investors
Distribution:	Direct advertising, word-of-mouth, and a limited dealer network
Hardware:	IBM PC, XT, AT, or true compatible, 256K (suggest 640K), two disk drives, a color graphics card, and IBM DOS 2.0 or greater Hayes 1200 or 1200B modem (or true compatible) Epson/IBM compatible printer.
Price:	$195 Volume discounts can be arranged but are not published.

Software:	OptionVue Plus

Company:	Star Value Software 12218 Scribe Drive Austin, TX 78759
Phone:	(512) 837-5498
E-Mail:	None
Telex:	None
Features:	Strategy maintenance and analysis system for options. Pricing models are employed for projecting profit/loss scenarios and identifying strategies for the reduction of risk and enhancement of returns. Applies to stock, index, and gold options. Also handles convertible securities and warrants.
Providers:	Dow Jones News/Retrieval databases
Target Market:	Private investors, brokers, professional money managers
Distribution:	Direct mail
Hardware:	IBM PC/XT/AT or close compatible with 192K of memory, PC-DOS or MS-DOS. Works with any type of monitor. Printer recommended but not required
Price:	$695 No volume discounts.

Software:	PC/Compudown
Company:	RAC Information Systems, Inc. 11 Middle Neck Road Great Neck, NY 11021
Phone:	(516) 829-9500
E-Mail:	None
Telex:	None
Features:	Service provides access to COMPUSTAT data. Users may search, select, and download data to a Lotus 1-2-3 spreadsheet. Data may be manipulated and formulas applied to produce customer reports and analysis. Users must be authorized COMPUSTAT users. Customized templates are available.
Providers:	Standard & Poor's COMPUSTAT data
Target Market:	Professional investors
Distribution:	Direct
Hardware:	IBM PC
Price:	Fixed price per month depending on usage level

Software:	QUICKTRIEVE

Company:	Commodity Systems, Inc. 200 W. Palmetto Park Road Boca Raton, FL 33432
Phone:	(305) 392-8663 (800) 327-0175
E-Mail:	None
Telex:	522107
Features:	Creates price, moving average, RSI, volume and open interest, trend line, and various other charts.
Providers:	Commodity Services Inc. MARSTAT database
Target Market:	Futures industry
Distribution:	Direct marketing
Hardware:	IBM PC, AT, or compatibles, 256K RAM. Apple II+, IIe, IIc, and Franklin. Commodore 64
Price:	$95

Software:	SOAP (Stock Option Analysis Program)

Company: H&H Scientific, Inc.
13507 Pendleton Street
Fort Washington, MD 20744

Phone: (301) 292-2958

E-Mail: None

Telex: None

Features: The expected profit/loss on transactions involving up to three (Apple version) or five (IBM version) different options can be calculated and graphed for any time until the options expire. SOAP is suited for doing "what if" calculations for complicated stock option positions.

Providers: Dow Jones and Warner

**Target
Market:** Individual or professional options traders

Distribution: Direct marketing and from selected software dealers

Hardware: Apple: Requires Apple II/+/e/c, DOS 3.3, at least one disk drive, and for Apple II AUTOSTART ROM, ROM Applesoft and 48K RAM. Communications supported for Hayes Micromodem II/e and Apple Super Serial Card. High-Resolution graphics can be printed using Grappler (or equivalent) printer interface or saved on disk

IBM: Requires IBM PC/XT/Jr., PC DOS 0.9 (or higher), 128K Ram, and at least one disk drive. IBM monochrome board supports alphanumeric graphics; colorgraphics board displays bit mapped graphics.

Price: Apple: $250
IBM: $350

Software:	SOS (Stock Option Scanner)

Company:	H&H Scientific, Inc. 13507 Pendleton Street Fort Washington, MD 20744
Phone:	(301) 292-2958
E-Mail:	None
Telex:	None
Features:	Scans up to 3,000 stock options (downloaded from Dow Jones or Warner or entered manually) and rank orders the top 50 and bottom 50 options (or option positions) according to the statistically expected rate of return. Horizontal spreads, vertical spreads, straddles, and neutral hedges can be ranked. Although SOS can be used alone, it serves as a prefilter for identifying favorable option positions for more detailed analysis using SOAP.
Providers:	Dow Jones and Warner
Target Market:	Individual or professional options traders
Distribution:	Direct marketing and from selected software dealers
Hardware:	Apple: Requires Apple II/+ /e/c, DOS 3.3, at least one disk drive, and for Apple II AUTOSTART ROM, ROM Applesoft and 48K RAM. Communications supported for Hayes Micromodem II/e and Apple Super Serial Card IBM: Requires IBM PC/XT/Jr., PC DOS 2.0 (or higher), 128K RAM, and at least one disk drive
Price:	Apple: $350 IBM: $400

Software:	Stock Market Securities Program

Company: COMPU-CAST CORPORATION
1015 Gayley Avenue, #506
Los Angeles, CA 90024

Phone: (213) 476-4682

E-Mail: None

Telex: None

Features: Looks for accumulation or distribution in a security regardless of its direction. The program shows buying in a security that is going down, thereby alerting to a possible bottom or turnaround point. It also shows selling in a rising security, thereby alerting the user to move up stops, close, or sell if the price objective has been reached

Providers: Dow Jones News/Retrieval and Compuserve databases

Target Market: Individual investors, brokerage firms, and individual brokers

Distribution: Direct mail

Hardware: MS-DOS 2.0 or higher, IBM products, AT&T computers, Radio Shack 1000 or 1200, NEC, Compaq, etc. that use MS-DOS. 128K, one disk drive, modem, and printer are required to fully use the program.

Price: There are two versions: copy and noncopy.
(Both versions allow back-ups.)

The copy version retails for $325.

The noncopy version retails for $275.

Wholesale prices:	10 or less	11 or more
Copy	$165	$150
Noncopy	$140	$125

Software:	TELESCAN ANALYZER

Company: Telescan, Inc.
11011 Richmond Avenue
Suite 600
Houston, TX 77042

Phone: (713) 952-1060

E-Mail: None

Telex: None

Features: Telescan provides instant graphs on historical stock information to depict stock trends.

Providers: Telescan database

Target Market: Individual and professional investors (brokers, analysts, financial planners)

Distribution: Direct mail, advertising, and sales force

Hardware: IBM PC, XT, AT, Jr., 100 percent compatibles, double-sided disk drive, IBM color graphics adapter board, or Hercules monochrome graphics board

1200 Hayes Smartmodem or compatible modem

Price: Initial or annual subscription fees:
$49.95 for the Telescan Software

Log-on Fees to Telescan database:
50 cents per minute prime time (7 A.M. to 6 P.M.)
25 cents per minute non–prime time (6 P.M. to 7 A.M., weekends, and holidays)

Software:	VALUE/SCREEN PLUS

Company:	Value Line, Inc. 711 Third Avenue New York, NY 10017
Phone:	(212) 687-3965
E-Mail:	None
Telex:	None
Features:	Rapid screening for investment candidates through a 1,600 stock database. Also, individual stock reports and portfolio management.
Providers:	In-house database
Target Market:	Private and institutional investors
Distribution:	Direct mail and media
Hardware:	IBM 256K, two floppy drives or one floppy and hard disk parallel printer
Price:	Annual subscriptions: $348 with monthly data updates $211 with quarterly data updates

Software:	VESTOR

Company:	Investment Technologies, Inc. Metropark/510 Thronall Street Edison, NJ 08837-2212
Phone:	(201) 494-1200 (800) 524-0831
E-Mail:	None
Telex:	None
Features:	VESTOR is an online service of over 30 programs that allows an investor to evaluate over 4,500 stocks, options, commodities, and indexes. It also offers historical information, screens using up to 13 criteria, charts, and even offers stock recommendations. Uses any personal computer that has modem capability.
Providers:	In-house service
Target Market:	Individual, corporate, or institutional investors
Distribution:	Direct sales and reseller channels
Hardware:	Any computer terminal or personal computer with a modem
Price:	Promotional price is $495, which includes sign-on fees and 12 months of usage

Retail discount is:

Quantity	Discount
1 to 5	40 percent
6	45 percent
24	50 percent
48	60 percent

Quick Index to Providers

ADP Comtrend

1345 Washington Boulevard
Stamford, CT 06902
(800) 243-2556

ADP Data Services

175 Jackson Plaza
Ann Arbor, MI 48106
(313) 769-6800

**ADP Financial Information
Services**

East Park Drive
Mount Laurel, NJ 08054
(609) 235-7300

Bank Administration Institute

60 Gould Center
Rolling Meadows, IL 60008
(312) 364-8800

The Bond Buyer

One State Street Plaza
New York, NY 10040
(212) 943-4830
(800) 223-3009

Bridge Market Data, Inc.

10050 Manchester Road
St. Louis, MO 63122
(314) 821-5660
(800) 325-3282

BRS Information Technologies

1200 Route 7
Latham, NY 12110
(518) 783-1161
(800) 833-4707

Bunker Ramo Corporation

35 Nutmeg Drive
Trumbull, CT 06609
(203) 386-2700
(203) 386-2000
(609) 235-7300

Chase Econometrics

150 Monument Road
Bala Cynwyd, PA 19004
(215) 667-6000

**CISInetwork Corporation,
Uni-Coll Division**

3401 Science Center
Philadelphia, PA 19104
(215) 387-3890

CitiShare

Sort 1157
850 Third Avenue
New York, NY 10043
(212) 572-9623

Compuserve Business Information Service

5000 Arlington Center Boulevard
P.O. Box 20212
Columbus, OH 43220
(614) 457-8600
(800) 848-8990

Compuserve Information Service

5000 Arlington Center Boulevard
P.O. Box 20212
Columbus, OH 43220
(614) 457-8600
(800) 848-8990

Control Data Corporation/ Business Information Services

500 West Putnam Avenue
P.O. Box 7100
Greenwich, CT 06836
(203) 622-2000

Data Resources, Inc

Seventeenth Floor
25 Broadway
New York, NY 10002
(212) 208-1200

Data-Star

D-S Marketing Ltd.
Plaza Suite
114 Jermyn Street
London, England SW1Y 6HJ
44 (1) 930-5503

DIALOG Information Services, Inc.

3460 Hillview Avenue
Palo Alto, CA 94304
(415) 858-3785
(800) 334-2564

Dispatched Analytical Data Corporation

104 Carnegie Center
Princeton, NJ 08540
(609) 987-0050

Dow Jones News/Retrieval

P.O. Box 300
Princeton, NJ 08540
(609) 452-1511
(800) 257-5114

Dun & Bradstreet, Inc.

99 Church
New York, NY 10007
(212) 285-7669

General Electric Information Services Company

401 North Washington Street
Rockville, MD 20850
(301) 294-5405
(800) 638-9636

General Videotex Corporation/DELPHI

3 Blackstone Street
Cambridge, MA 02139
(617) 491-3393
(800) 544-4005

GTE Telenet Financial Information Network

12490 Sunrise Valley Drive
Reston, VA 22096
(703) 442-2500
(800) 368-4215

Hale Systems, Inc.

1044 Northern Boulevard
Roslyn, NY 11576
(516) 484-4545
(800) 645-3120

InnerLine, Inc.
95 West Algonquin Road
Arlington Heights, IL 60005
(312) 364-8800
(800) 323-1321

Interactive Data Corporation
150 Monument Road
Bala Cynwyd, PA 19004
(617) 895-4300
(617) 860-8197

I.P. Sharp Associates, Ltd.
2 First Canadian Place
Suite 1900, Exchange Tower
Toronto, Ontario, Canada M5X
  1E3
(416) 364-5361

ITT Dialcom
1109 Spring Street
Suite 410
Silver Spring, MD 20910
(301) 588-1572
(800) 435-7342

Mead Data Central
9393 Springboro Pike
P.O. Box 933
Dayton, OH 45401
(513) 865-6800
(800) 227-4908

NewsNet, Inc.
945 Haverford Road
Bryn Mawr, PA 19010
(215) 527-8030
(800) 345-1301

Pergamon Orbit InfoLine, Inc.
8000 Westpark Drive
McLean, VA 22101
(703) 442-0900
(800) 336-7575

Quotron Systems, Inc.
5454 Beethoven Street
P.O. Box 66914
Los Angeles, CA 90066-0914
(213) 827-4600

Reuters, Ltd.
2 Wall Street
New York, NY 10005
(212) 603-3300

Securities Data Company, Inc.
62 William Street
6th Floor
New York, NY 10005
(212) 668-0940

Shaw Data Services
122 East 42d Street
New York, NY 10168
(212) 682-8877

Source Telecomputing Corp.
1616 Anderson Road
McLean, VA 22102
(703) 734-7500
(800) 336-3366

Telerate Systems, Inc.
1 World Trade Center
104th Floor
New York, NY 10048
(212) 938-5200

Tymshare, Inc.
20705 Valley Green Drive
Cupertino, CA 95014
(408) 446-6000
(800) 538-9350

VU/TEXT Information Services, Inc.
1211 Chestnut Street
Philadelphia, PA 19107
(215) 665-3300
(800) 258-8080

6

Warner Computer Systems, Inc.

245 East 40th Street
New York, NY 10016
(212) 697-0110

Zacks Investment Research, Inc.

2 North Riverside Drive
Room 1900
Chicago, IL 60606
(312) 559-9405

Quick Index to Gateways

BRS Information Technologies
1200 Route 7
Latham, NY 12110
(518) 783-1161
(800) 833-4707

Compuserve Information Service
5000 Arlington Center Boulevard
Columbus, OH 43220
(614) 457-8600
(800) 848-8990

Data-Tek Publishing Company
P.O. Box 8265
North Haledon, NJ 07538
(201) 427-0330

DIALOG Information Services, Inc.
3460 Hillview Avenue
Palo Alto, CA 94304
(415) 858-3785
(800) 334-2564

EasyNet
Telebase Systems, Inc.
763 West Lancaster Avenue
Bryn Mawr, PA 19010
(215) 664-6972

IBM Information Network
3101 West Buffalo Avenue
Tampa, FL 33607
(813) 872-3632

InFact
Western Union Telegraph
  Company
One Lake Street
Upper Saddle River, NJ 07458
(201) 825-5000

Info Master
Western Union Telegraph
  Company
9229 LBJ Freeway, Suite 234
Dallas, TX 75243
(800) 247-1373

ITT Dialcom
1109 Spring Street
Suite 410
Silver Spring, MD 20910
(301) 588-1572
(800) 435-7342

KEYCOM Electronic Publishing
945 Plum Grove Road
Schaumburg, IL 60195
(312) 310-3200

**Mead Data Central,
LEXIS Service**

Mead Data Central
P.O. Box 933
Dayton, OH 45401
(513) 865-6800
(800) 227-4908

**Mead Data Central,
NEXIS Service**

Mead Data Central
P.O. Box 933
Dayton, OH 45401
(513) 865-6800
(800) 227-4908

NewsNet, Inc.

945 Haverford Road
Bryn Mawr, PA 19010
(215) 527-8030
(800) 345-1301

**OCLC Online Computer Library
Center, Inc.**

6565 Frantz Road
Dublin, OH 43017
(614) 764-6000

Pergamon Orbit InfoLine, Inc.

8000 Westpark Drive
McLean, VA 22101
(703) 442-0900
(800) 336-7575

PRONTO Link Corporation

300 Jerico Quadrangle
3rd Floor
Jerico, NY 11753
(516) 937-7280

West Publishing Company

50 West Kellogg Boulevard
P.O. Box 43526
St. Paul, MN 55164
(612) 228-2433
(800) 328-0109

Quick Index
to Communications Software

APPLE SERIES (AND COMPATIBLES)

ASCII PRO/ASCII EXPRESS PRO
United Software Industries
8399 Topanga Canyon Boulevard
Canoga Park, CA 91304
(818) 887-5800

Converse
Professional Software Products
216 Haddon Avenue
Sentry Plaza Office Building,
Suite 503
Westmont, NJ 08108
(609) 854-5234

1stPort
Template Systems, Inc.
7 Industrial Park Road
Medway, MA 02053
(617) 533-2203
(800) 522-2286

Jazz
Lotus Development Corporation
55 Cambridge Parkway
Cambridge, MA 02142
(617) 577-8500

Lync
Norton-Lambert Corporation
P.O. Box 4085
Santa Barbara, CA 90403
(805) 687-8896

MicroPhone
Software Ventures Corporation
2907 Claremont Avenue
Suite 220
Berkeley, CA 94705
(415) 644-3232

Microsoft Works
Microsoft Corporation
16011 Northeast 36th Way
P.O. Box 97017
Redmond, WA 98073
(206) 882-8080
(800) 426-9400

NEXIS
Mead Data Central, Inc.
P.O. Box 933
Dayton, OH 45401
(513) 865-6800
(800) 227-4908

Terminus
Quark
2525 West Evans
Suite 220
Denver, CO 80219
(303) 934-2211

Transend 2
Transend Corporation
884 Portola Road
Portola Valley, CA 94025
(415) 851-3402

IBM PC SERIES (AND COMPATIBLES)

ASCOM
Dynamic Microprocessor
Associates
545 Fifth Avenue
Suite 1103
New York, NY 10017
(212) 687-7115

BIT Com
Bit Software, Inc.
1048 Nicklaus Avenue
Milpitas, CA 95035
(408) 262-1054

BLAST
Blast/Communications
Research Group
5615 Corporate Boulevard
3rd Floor
Baton Rouge, LA 70808
(504) 923-0888
(800) 24-BLAST

Commstar VI
Sourceview Software International
835 Castro Street
Martinez, CA 94553
(415) 680-0202
(800) 443-0100

Communicator/Text Editor
Electronic Data Systems
 Corporation (EDS)
Technical Products Division
1780 Jay El Drive
Richardson, TX 75081
(214) 699-8400

Crosstalk XVI
Microstuf, Inc.
1000 Holcomb Woods Parkway
Roswell, GA 30076
(404) 998-3998

DATATALKER X.25
Winterhalter, Inc.
P.O. Box 2180
3796 Plaza Drive, #1
Ann Arbor, MI 48106
(313) 662-2002
(800) 321-7785

DIALOGLINK
DIALOG Information Services,
 Inc.
3460 Hillview Avenue
Palo Alto, CA 94304
(415) 858-2700
(800) 3-DIALOG

Framework II

Ashton-Tate
20101 Hamilton Avenue
Torrance, CA 90502
(213) 329-8000

I*S Talk

Batteries Included
30 Mural Street
Richmond Hill, Ontario, Canada
CD L4B 1B5
(416) 881-9941

MOVE-IT

Woolf Software Systems, Inc.
6754 Eton Avenue
Canoga Park, CA 91303
(818) 703-8112

NEXIS

Mead Data Central, Inc.
P.O. Box 933
Dayton, OH 45401
(513) 865-6800
(800) 227-4908

PAB-COM Communications Program

Dynacomp, Inc.
P.O. Box 18129
Rochester, NY 14618
(716) 671-6167

pcExpress

Information Resources, Inc.
200 Fifth Avenue
Waltham, MA 02254
(617) 890-1100

PC/InterComm

Mark of the Unicorn, Inc.
222 Third Street
Cambridge, MA 02142
(617) 576-2760

PFS:ACCESS

Software Publishing Corporation
1901 Landings Drive
Mountain View, CA 94043
(415) 962-8910

Polywindows Talk

Polytron Corporation
1815 NW 169th Place, #2110
Beaverton, OR 97006
(503) 645-1150
(800) 547-4000

Pro-Search

Personal Bibliographic
  Software, Inc.
P.O. Box 4250
Ann Arbor, MI 48106
(313) 996-1580

ReadiTerm

ReadiWare Systems, Inc.
P.O. Box 515
Portage, MI 49081
(616) 327-9172

Relay Silver

VM Personal Computing
41 Kenosia Avenue
Danbury, CT 06810
(203) 798-3800

Signal

Lotus Development Corp.
55 Cambridge Parkway
Cambridge, MA 02142
(617) 577-8500

Smartcom II

Hayes Microcomputer
Products, Inc.
P.O. Box 105203
Atlanta, GA 30348
(404) 449-8791

6

SmarTerm

Persoft, Inc.
465 Science Drive
Madison, WI 53711
(608) 273-6000

Symphony

Lotus Development Corp.
55 Cambridge Parkway
Cambridge, MA 02142
(617) 577-8500

V TERM

Techland Systems, Inc.
25 Waterside Plaza
New York, NY 10010
(212) 684-7788

Index

Index